Lecture Notes in Computer Science 4849

Commenced Publication in 1973
Founding and Former Series Editors:
Gerhard Goos, Juris Hartmanis, and Jan van Leeuwen

T0223141

Marco Winckler   Hilary Johnson
Philippe Palanque (Eds.)

Task Models and Diagrams for User Interface Design

6th International Workshop, TAMODIA 2007
Toulouse, France, November 7-9, 2007
Proceedings

 Springer

Volume Editors

Marco Winckler
Philippe Palanque
Université Paul Sabatier (Toulouse 3)
Toulouse, France
E-mail: {winckler,palanque}@irit.fr

Hilary Johnson
University of Bath, UK
E-mail: H.Johnson@bath.ac.uk

Library of Congress Control Number: 2007940837

CR Subject Classification (1998): H.5.2, H.5, D.2, D.3, F.3, I.6, K.6

LNCS Sublibrary: SL 2 – Programming and Software Engineering

ISSN   0302-9743
ISBN   3-540-77221-9 Springer Berlin Heidelberg New York
ISBN   978-3-540-77221-7 Springer Berlin Heidelberg New York

Springer is a part of Springer Science+Business Media

springer.com

© Springer-Verlag Berlin Heidelberg 2007

Typesetting: Camera-ready by author, data conversion by Scientific Publishing Services, Chennai, India
Printed on acid-free paper   SPIN: 12201389   06/3180   5 4 3 2 1 0

Preface

Task analysis and modelling have existed for many years, initially for training purposes but latterly for providing a principled approach to improving the usability of existing and proposed interactive systems. There have been many successes along with critical appraisal of the utility of task analysis. The community remains strong, active and enthusiastic. Over the years we have developed a plethora of theoretical approaches, models and techniques. These differ in terms of what is modelled, the nature of the representations and notations used, their scalability, the ease with which they can be applied with good effect, and the ease with which they can direct the design of systems to support task execution.

Task models and associated diagrams that represent task knowledge and behavior are in demand now as much as they ever were. Good design is fundamental, appreciated by users, sells and improves the quality of our daily lives, and good system design means supporting users and their interaction with technology. Technology is changing – we now have mobile and pervasive systems – and yet we still need to analyze the goals and tasks undertaken using these systems. The nature of the tasks might be different (shorter in duration, overlapping, needing to be performed more quickly, be routed in communication and entertainment), but it is still important to understand, model and support user goals.

The proceedings give a flavor of the issues facing task modelling at this moment in time. A primary aim of Tamodia as a conference series is to educate, to promote and exchange existing ideas and problem solutions, and to generate new ideas and associated research programmes. As in previous years the scope of the papers is broad. This year we were very privileged that the invited talk on 'Modelling Activity Switching' was given by Stephen Payne, from Manchester Business School. Other highlights of the conference included sessions on Workflow-Based Systems; Task Patterns; Task Models for Non-standard Applications; Model-Driven Engineering; Task-Based Evaluation and Testing; and Extending Task Models.

A rigorous refereeing process was applied to the papers, and the standard of the accepted papers is high and represents a good cross-section of academic research and to a lesser extent industrial research. We are grateful to the authors for submitting their papers to Tamodia and to the many people who took part in refereeing including the Programme Committee members. These contributions have made the conference series a success.

The proceedings is a valuable information resource for both researchers and industry members alike, who are interested in applying task analysis and modelling techniques to an ever-widening range of domains and problems. The reported research is diverse and gives some indication of the new directions in which task analysis theories, methods, techniques and tools are progressing.

Additionally, there are several new challenging opportunities for the use of task modelling in the future, and we are sure that the Tamodia conference series will be at the forefront in promoting research in these new areas.

November 2007   Hilary Johnson
                                                                Marco Winckler

TAMODIA 2007 Technical Committee

General Chair

Philippe Palanque, University Paul Sabatier (Toulouse 3), France

Program Chairs

Hilary Johnson - University of Bath, UK
Marco Winckler - University Paul Sabatier (Toulouse 3), France

Program Committee

Sandrine Balbo, University of Melbourne, Australia
Eric Barboni, University Paul Sabatier (Toulouse 3), France
Rémi Bastide, University Toulouse 1, France
Birgit Bomsdorf, University of Hagen, Germany
Gaëlle Calvary, University of Grenoble I, France
Gilbert Cockton, University of Sunderland, UK
Karin Coninx, Hasselt University, Belgium
Maria-Francesca Costabile, Universita di Bari, Italy
Anke Dittmar, University of Rostock, Germany
Alan Dix, Lancaster University, UK
Peter Forbrig, University of Rostock, Germany
Elizabeth Furtado, UNIFOR, Brazil
Nick Graham, Queen University, Canada
Hilary Johnson, University of Bath, UK
John Karat, IBM T.J. Watson Research Center, USA
María-Dolores Lozano, Universidad de Castilla-La Mancha, Spain
Kris Luyten, Hasselt University, Belgium
Mieke Massink, CNR-ISTI, Italy
David Navarre, University Toulouse 1, France
Jeffrey Nichols, Carnegie Mellon University, USA
Philippe Palanque, University Paul Sabatier (Toulouse 3), France
Thomas Pederson, University of Umeå, Sweden
Fabio Paternò, ISTI-CNR, Italy
Costin Pribeanu, ICI Bucuresti, Romania
Matthias Rauterberg, Eindhoven University of Technology, The Netherlands
Carmen Santoro, ISTI-CNR, Italy
Corina Sas, Lancaster University, UK
Dominique Scapin, INRIA, France
Kevin Schneider, University of Saskatchewan, Canada

Marcin Sikorski, Gdansk University of Technology, Poland
Pavel Slavík, Czech Technical University in Prague, Czech Republic
Christian Stary, University of Linz, Austria
Jean Vanderdonckt, Université catholique de Louvain, Belgium
Gerrit Van der Veer, Vrije University, The Netherlands
Peter Wild, University of Cambridge, UK
Marco Winckler, University Paul Sabatier (Toulouse 3), France

Local Organization Chair

Florence Pontico

Local Organization Committee

Eric Barboni
Syrine Charfi
Guillaume Gauffre
Jean-François Ladry
David Navarre
Joseph Xiong

Sponsors and Supporters

ACM SIGCHI - Special Interest Group in Computer-Human Interaction
http://www.acm.org/sigchi/

AFIHM: Association Francophone d'Interaction Homme-Machine
http://www.afihm.org/

In cooperation with IFIP WG 13.2 and 13.5
http://www.ifip-hci.org/

Organization

Logiciels Interactifs et Interaction Homme-Système
http://liihs.irit.fr/

Institut of Research in Informatics of Toulouse
http://www.irit.fr/

University Paul Sabatier (Toulouse 3)
http://www.ups-tlse.fr/

Table of Contents

Task-Based Evaluation and Testing

Task Patterns

Workflow Based Systems

Part 4: Short Papers

Modelling Activity Switching

Stephen Payne

School of Informatics, University of Manchester
PO Box 88, Sackville Street
Manchester M60 1QD, UK
stephen.payne@manchester.ac.uk

Abstract. How do people decide what to do when? Why is it that people often given up one task to begin another, only later to resume the first? In this talk I will briefly review some experiments on how people allocate their time adaptively across multiple texts and multiple tasks. I will then focus on how strategies for adaptive time allocation can be modelled. The model I develop derives from heuristic accounts of animal foraging behaviour. In the course of the talk I will review recent arguments by Roberts and Pashler to suggest that the standard criterion of fitting models to experimental data is too lax, even though the model I am considering has only two free parameters and even though it's output is being fitted simultaneously to several quantitative dependent variables. Focussing instead on whether the model can predict the data leads to a more complicated but more interesting model. This model suggests that people orient to their activities in terms of either goal accomplishment or currency accumulation, and may switch between these orientations. To understand human activities and in particular the decisions that people make to continue or switch activities, we need to understand not only goal-subgoal hierarchies but also moment-by-moment gain curves.

Brief Biography. Stephen Payne is Professor of Interactive Systems Design in Manchester Business School. Previously he has been a lecturer in psychology and computing at the University of Lancaster, a research scientist in IBM T.J. Watson Research Centre, User Interface Institute, and a Professor of Psychology at Cardiff University (1991-2005). Stephen has consulted for several commercial organizations, including Xerox PARC. He has served on the editorial board of 4 major HCI journals (currently on the boards of Behaviour and Information Technology and Human-Computer Interaction). He is papers co-chair for the ACM CHI conference in 2007. Between 2000 and 2006 he was a member of the management committee for the Joint Research Councils' PACCIT (People at the Centre of Communications and Information Technologies) programme. Stephen continues to be on the EPSRC computing college and to serve occasionally as a chair and committee member for EPSRC panels. He is also a member of BPS, EPS and ACM. Stephen Payne is interested in many aspects of the psychology of human-computer interaction, and more generally in the psychology of learning and performance. One major strand of work has been on users' mental models. He is currently interested in user interactions with on-line information, multi-tasking, and social effects of communications technologies.

M. Winckler, H. Johnson, and P. Palanque (Eds.): TAMODIA 2007, LNCS 4849, p. 1, 2007.
© Springer-Verlag Berlin Heidelberg 2007

Agile Development of Workflow Applications with Interpreted Task Models

Markus Stolze[1], Philippe Riand[2], Mark Wallace[3], and Terry Heath[1]

[1] IBM Watson Research Center, Yorktown Heights, NY 10598,
mgstolze@us.ibm.com
[2] IBM WPLC, Westford TP, Westford, MA 01886-3141
[3] IBM WPLC, Dublin 15, Ireland

Abstract. We demonstrate that the development of interactive workflow applications can be made easier by providing developers with custom user interface components that interpret a workflow task model. This enables occasional developers to create workflow applications by adapting template data objects, template user interface pages, and a template workflow task definition. The resulting interactive workflow system is open to agile adaptation by experienced developers. This is an improvement over existing workflow systems which use workflow task models to create workflow application user interfaces that are difficult to extend.

1 Introduction

Workflow applications are used in enterprise settings to increase visibility, efficiency and compliance of important business processes. They help to realize efficiency potentials through the elimination of transport and wait times between process activities and provide a detailed level of control over the assignment of work to process participants [9]. Examples of such processes are the tracking of candidates, tracking of benefit changes, order tracking, prospect follow-up and generation and review of quotes and proposals. In these examples, important enterprise data (employee, customer, and contract) are worked on by multiple people in predefined roles and steps. The Workflow Management Coalition (WFMC) defines workflow as the automation of a business process during which documents, information, or tasks are passed from one participant to another for action, according to a set of procedural rules [8]. These rules (i.e. workflow task models) define the organizational units, roles, and activities as well as data, events, and tools that comprise the workflow [7]. Interactive workflow applications coordinate the tasks of human actors. Data is frequently represented as forms that are passed from one participant to another.

Development of interactive workflow applications usually follows one of two approaches. The first approach uses a workflow system that provides a high-level workflow modeling language. Here, system development involves mainly the description of the desired workflows in the provided modeling language. Using techniques from model-driven development, the workflow model is then used to generate the application code of the running system. Examples of commercial systems supporting such an approach are FileNet (www.filenet.com), VDoc (www.vdocprocess.com) and

M. Winckler, H. Johnson, and P. Palanque (Eds.): TAMODIA 2007, LNCS 4849, pp. 2–14, 2007.
© Springer-Verlag Berlin Heidelberg 2007

Teamworks (www.lombardisoftware.com). The advantage of such a model-driven approach is that a running workflow system can be produced very rapidly. Model creation and maintenance can be done by people that have a good understanding of the business requirements. The disadvantage is that the workflow specification determines not only the system architecture and behavior, but also the layout and content of the user interface. This is problematic if there are specific user needs that have not been anticipated in the design of the workflow modeling language and the associated customization points of the system. In this case it can be very cumbersome to adapt the generated system to match the specific user requirements. This makes these tools not well suited for the development of workflow applications that need to be adapted to specific user requirements in an agile way.

The alternative approach is to develop the workflow application as a custom web-application. This means that the system needs to be created by software engineers who program the system behavior and manually create the web user interfaces. With this approach it is possible to accommodate a wide range of user requirements during the system development and over the lifetime of the system. The disadvantage is that the development cycle is much longer and that the people that have the detailed business knowledge are less directly involved in the system development.

In this paper we present an approach for the development of interactive workflow applications that supports rapid creation of an initial workflow system by "occasional" developers and also supports flexible adaptation of the user interface for agile development and maintenance of the system. This paper focuses on the technical implementation of the system.

2   Workflow Task Model Interpretation with Declarative User Interface Components

The approach presented here leverages the capability of Lotus Component Designer 6.0 (LCD) (www.ibm.com/software/lotus/products/componentdesigner/) to create template applications and custom UI components. LCD is an IDE (integrated development environment) for creating web applications. Systems developed with LCD are deployed to a web application server with integrated support for data management. LCD uses XML documents for data storage. Developers define their data as XML documents. These XML documents are then persisted by the runtime infrastructure. LCD also includes a graphical user interface builder and a declarative user interface specification language. One of the special features of LCD is that it supports the definition of "custom user interface components" (CUICs). These are user-definable user-interface components that specify the layout and other properties for one or more constituting UI components. For example, a developer might define a "PageHeader" UI component for an application that provides the template for laying out the top part of a page. The PageHeader component could define placement of icons, background color and text elements. Custom components can define parameters. These are used for adapting the appearance or behavior of a component instance. For example, the PageHeader component could support the display of bread-crumb links. In this case, each instance of the PageHeader CUIC in a page needs to be parameterized with a list of link names and URLs to determine the text and target pages of the bread-crumb links. CUICs can also access global web-application data from the application database and the file system to determine their appearance and behavior. Once defined, CUICs appear in the palette of GUI components in the visual UI builder that is part of LCD. From the palette, the CUICs can be dragged-and-dropped onto pages just like any other (standard) UI component.

CUICs can be stored together with template pages in template applications. These template applications are later loaded and adapted for rapid application development. The ease of development makes LCD particular useful for the development of situational applications by occasional developers who focus on solving business problems.

We used these features of LCD to create a specialized template application for the development of interactive workflow applications. The template includes template data, a template XML task definition, and template pages and CUICs. The template pages reference the data and task definition. Occasional developers create a workflow application by (1) adapting the template data objects, (2) adapting the template user interface pages, and (3) adapting the template workflow task definition that defines the layout and behavior of the workflow-specific user interface components.

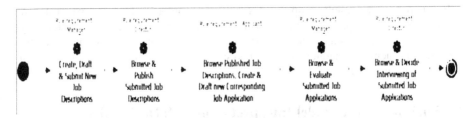

Fig. 1. High Level Overview of the Hiring Process. The diagram show the creation and processing of a single Job Description and a single associated Job Application by the different roles involved in the process.

Below we will discuss the adaptation of template pages and the workflow task definition for a concrete example application that supports a hiring process. The application supports the publication of job descriptions and the collection and evaluation of job applications that are send in response to the published job descriptions. Figure 1 provides a high-level view of the process. It describes the processing of a single job description and a single associated job application by the different roles involved in the process. The roles defined in this application are:

- Applicants: Applicants can browse all published job descriptions. They can read the public information of the job descriptions, but they cannot see, for example, the responsible manager or director. Applicants can add and draft a job application as a response to a job description. They can browse and edit the job applications that they created. They can also submit their job application. Applicants cannot edit the main part of a submitted job application. After submission they can only add individually logged "notes" to a job application.
- Managers: Managers can add and draft job descriptions. They can submit job descriptions for publication. Managers can browse their own job descriptions and

all job applications that have been submitted in response to the job applications that they published. Managers can edit comments of a job application. These comments are visible to directors, but not to applicants.

- Directors: Directors can browse all job descriptions submitted for publication. They can decide to either return them for additional drafting, or publish the job description. Directors can also browse all job applications in their area and decide the invitation of an applicant for an interview.

In this example we see that different roles have different rights to browse, read, edit, and add forms-data in the different situations. For example, applicants can only edit the main part of a job application before it is submitted. Thus, the page presenting data of a submitted job application to an applicant should not provide the information in editable fields. Similarly, the button that lets applicants submit their application should not be displayed any more for a job application that has been submitted already.

Figure 2 shows the example of a "Welcome" page of the hiring portal application. The page is created from the unmodified template page by interpreting the application-specific workflow task model (Figure 3). The workflow task model specifies explicitly the BREAD (Browse, Read, Edit, Add, Delete) operation for each role, the available data-objects to that role and the states in which this operation is available (canBrowse, canRead, etc). Furthermore, it defines with the "canSubmit" clauses which role can initiate a state transition on which object in which state.

The template Welcome page assembles two workflow specific CUICs. Figure 4 provides the detailed XML definition of the Welcome page and Figure 5 the definition of the swfRoleLinks component. Currently there is no visual editor for the XML task definition, so occasional developers will need to edit the XML task definition. Instead, changes to pages can be performed in the graphical page editor. Thus, occasional developers do not need to edit directly the page code provided in Figure 4 and Figure 5.

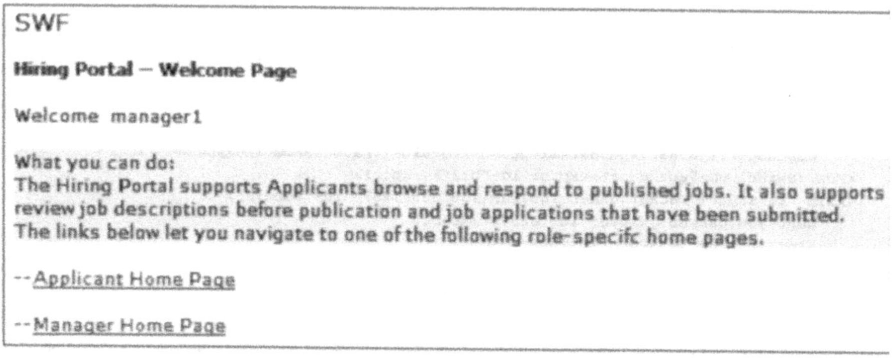

SWF

Hiring Portal – Welcome Page

Welcome manager1

What you can do:
The Hiring Portal supports Applicants browse and respond to published jobs. It also supports review job descriptions before publication and job applications that have been submitted. The links below let you navigate to one of the following role-specific home pages.

-- Applicant Home Page

-- Manager Home Page

Fig. 2. Manager Welcome Page: On her Welcome Page "managers1" see a general description of the application and the tasks associated with the different roles. As manager1 is in the group of managers she is provided with links to the Applicant Home Page (available to every user) and a link to the Manager Home Page (available only to members of the group "managers").

```
<accessModel appName="Hiring Portal" welcomePage="WelcomePage.xsp">
    <task>
            The Hiring Portal supports Applicants browse and respond to published jobs. It also supports Managers to publ
    </task>
    <role name="applicant" printName="Applicant" group="*" homePage="ApplicantHomePage.xsp">
            [...]
    </role>
    <role name="manager" printName="Manager" group="managers" homePage="ManagerHomePage.xsp">
        <task>
            Managers can create new job descriptions. They can browse all job applications that have been submitt
        </task>
        <artefact name="JobApp" printName="Job Application" detailPage="ManagerJobAppPage.xsp">
            [...]
        </artefact>
        <artefact name="JobDesc" printName="Job Description" detailPage="ManagerJobDescPage.xsp">
            <task>
                Managers can edit a Job Description with status DRAFTING. Managers can submit a Job Descripti
            </task>
            <canBrowse requireUserInViewColumn="ManagerId" />
            <canCreate initialState="DRAFTING" recordUserIn="headerSection/managerId" />
            <canWrite state="DRAFTING" path="headerSection/directorId" />
            <canWrite state="DRAFTING" path="managerSection/*" />
            <canSubmit state="DRAFTING" nextState="PUBLISHING" preCondition="true" postExecuteAction="" />
            <canSubmit state="PUBLISHING" nextState="DRAFTING" preCondition="true" postExecuteAction="" />
        </artefact>
    </role>
    <role name="director" printName="Director" group="directors" homePage="DirectorHomePage.xsp">
        <task>
            Directors can review and publish job descriptions, they can also review job applications and invite a
        </task>
        <artefact name="JobApp" printName="Job Application" detailPage="DirectorJobAppPage.xsp">
            [...]
        </artefact>
        <artefact name="JobDesc" printName="Job Description" detailPage="DirectorJobDescPage.xsp">
            <task>
                Directors can review and publish job descriptions.
            </task>
            <canBrowse requireUserInViewColumn="DirectorId" />
            <canWrite state="PUBLISHING" path="directorSection/readyForPublication" initVal="YES" />
            <canSubmit state="PUBLISHING"
                preCondition="document.getStringValue('directorSection/readyForPublication')=='YES'"
                nextState="PUBLISHED"
                postExecuteAction=" " />
            <canSubmit state="PUBLISHING"
                preCondition="document.getStringValue('directorSection/readyForPublication')=='NO'"
                nextState="DRAFTING"
                postExecuteAction=" " />
        </artefact>
    </role>
</accessModel>
```

Fig. 3. Workflow task model (extract) for the Hiring Portal workflow application

```
<xp:view xmlns:xp="http://www.ibm.com/xsp/core" xmlns:swf="component/swfTemplate">
[...]
    <xp:this.data>
        <xp:xmlData var="swfXml" src="/swf.xml"> <xp:this.rowExpressions></xp:this.rowExpr
    </xp:this.data>

    <swf:swfWelcomePageHeader id="swfWelcomeHeader1"
        appName="${javascript:swfXml.getStringValue('/accessModel/@appName')}" >
    </swf:swfWelcomePageHeader><xp:br id="br2"></xp:br>
    <xp:panel style="background-color:rgb(255,255,128)" id="panel1">
        What you can do: <xp:br id="br5"></xp:br>
        <xp:text id="taskDescriptionFromXML">
            <xp:this.value>
                <![CDATA[${javascript:swfXml.getStringValue('/accessModel/task')}]]>
            </xp:this.value>
        </xp:text> <xp:br id="br1"></xp:br>
        The links below let you navigate to one of the following role-specifc home pages.
    </xp:panel>
    <swf:swfRoleHomePageLinks id="swfRoleLinks1"></swf:swfRoleHomePageLinks>
</xp:view>
```

Fig. 4. Welcome Page XML: The Welcome page assembles two CUICs, the swfWelcomePage-Header and the swfRoleHomePageLinks. The top-level task description text is directly retrieved from the workflow definition.

```
<xp:view xmlns:xp="http://www.ibm.com/xsp/core">
    <xp:repeat id="repeat1" value="#{xpath:swfXml:/accessModel/role}" var="role">
        <xp:panel id="panel1">
            <xp:this.rendered>
                <![CDATA[#{javascript:isCurrentUserInGroup(role.getStringValue('@group'));}]]>
            </xp:this.rendered><xp:br id="br6"></xp:br>
            --
            <xp:link id="swfRoleHomePageLink"
                text="#{javascript:role.getStringValue('@printName')+' Home Page'}"
                value="#{javascript:role.getStringValue('@homePage')}">
            </xp:link>
        </xp:panel>
    </xp:repeat>
</xp:view>
```

Fig. 5. swfRoleHomePageLinks Custom UI Control XML. The UI control lays out the block of links to the role-specific home pages. It retrieves the list of defined roles from the workflow task model. For each role it creates a panel with a link UI component that has as text the printName of the role (plus appended "Home Page") and as target page the homePage attribute specified in the workflow task definition. The JavaScript function isCurrentUserInGroup is called to determine whether the link should be made available to the user.

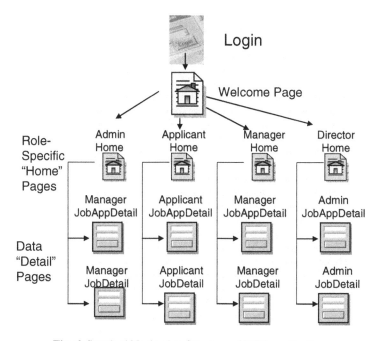

Fig. 6. Standard Navigation Structure of IBPA applications

Basic interactive workflow applications follow a standard navigation pattern with a single "Welcome" page as the entry point for logged-in users (Figure 6). The Welcome page lists the available "Home" pages for the current user. Home pages let users browse the data-objects available for the user in the selected role. Users can select data-objects for reading or editing, or they can add a new data object or delete an existing object. Thus, the IPPA pages are supporting management of data-objects by making available the standard BREAD operations in a role-specific way. The home pages manage the access to the browse, add, and delete operations. The home pages include a table for each of the data objects accessible for that user role. The table will often only show some of the data items. For instance, in the hiring application applicants can only see jobs application that were submitted by them (c.f. Figure 7).

The data detail pages provide role and state-specific access for reading and editing data elements. Figure 8 shows a data detail page that lets an applicant draft a job application. The current status of the data is 'DRAFTING', which is why, in accordance to the workflow task definition, the data elements are editable. Also the button for submitting the job application is visible, enabled, and indicates the next state (SUBMITTED).

Once the job application has been submitted (i.e. when is not in state DRAFTING any more), the page does not allow editing or submitting of the job application any more (c.f. Figure 9). The input elements in the data detail pages use calls to a custom function (isDataWriteable()) for determining dynamically the access to data and functions in accordance to the workflow task model.

Fig. 7. Applicant Home Page

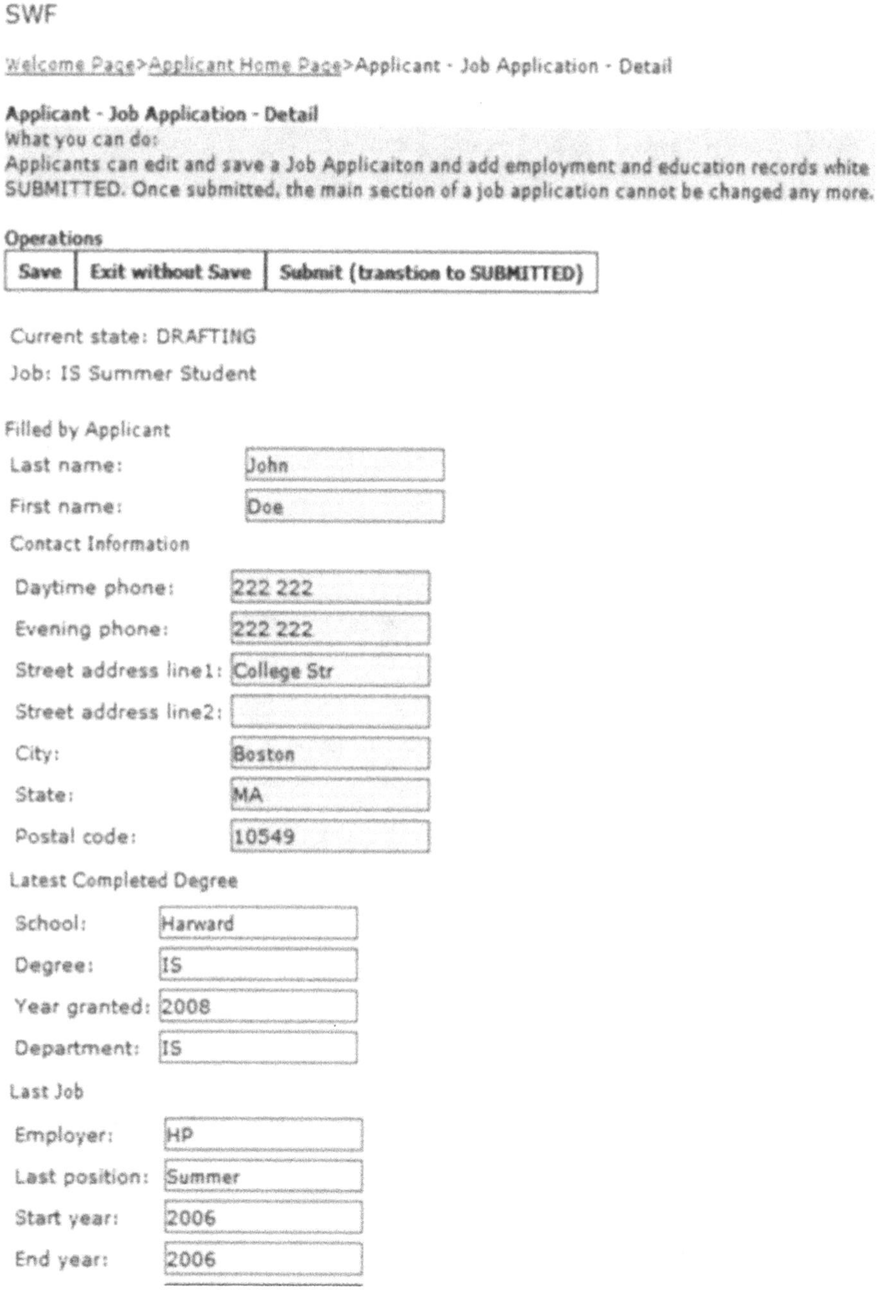

SWF

Welcome Page>Applicant Home Page>Applicant - Job Application - Detail

Applicant - Job Application - Detail
What you can do:
Applicants can edit and save a Job Applicaiton and add employment and education records while SUBMITTED. Once submitted, the main section of a job application cannot be changed any more.

Operations

Save	Exit without Save	Submit (transtion to SUBMITTED)

Current state: DRAFTING

Job: IS Summer Student

Filled by Applicant

Last name: John

First name: Doe

Contact Information

Daytime phone: 222 222

Evening phone: 222 222

Street address line1:   College Str

Street address line2:

City: Boston

State: MA

Postal code: 10549

Latest Completed Degree

School: Harward

Degree: IS

Year granted: 2008

Department: IS

Last Job

Employer: HP

Last position: Summer

Start year: 2006

End year: 2006

Fig. 8. Data Detail Page for an Applicant of a Job Application in State DRAFTING: The data fields are editable as specified in the workflow definition, and the button for submitting the data is enabled and shows the next state

SWF

<u>Welcome Page</u>><u>Applicant Home Page</u>>Applicant - Job Application - Detail

Applicant - Job Application - Detail
What you can do:
Applicants can edit and save a Job Applicaiton and add employment and education records whit
SUBMITTED. Once submitted, the main section of a job application cannot be changed any mor

Operations

Save	Exit without Save

Current state: INVITING

Job: IS Summer Student

Filled by Applicant
Last name: John
First name: Doe
Contact Information

Daytime phone: 222 222
Evening phone: 222 222
Street address line1: College Str
Street address line2:
City: Boston
State: MA
Postal code: 10549

Latest Completed Degree

School: Harward
Degree: IS
Year granted: 2008
Department: IS

Last Job

Fig. 9. Data Detail Page for an Applicant of a Job Application in State SUBMITTED. The data fields are not editable any more; Also, the "Submit" button is not visible any more.

3   Development Process

Occasional developers use the following steps to create a new workflow application:

1. Import a new (empty) template application
2. Create the new data structures and associated data views.
3. Create the XML process definition.
4. Create the role-specific home pages.
5. Create the role-specific data detail pages.
6. Deploy and test the solution.

All of these tasks, with the exception of the editing of the XML process definition, are supported by visual editors. LCD provides a visual XML Schema editor and a visual data view editor to support the tasks in step 2. In step 4 the LCD visual page editor is used to copy and adapt the template home page. The data views defined in Step 2 are placed on the page and page role is specified (c.f. Figure 10). Also for the creation of the data detail pages in Step 5 the visual page editor can be used (c.f. Figure 11). Finally, the application is deployed to a remote portal server by using the LCD application deployment utility. The application is then ready for testing and use once users and their group membership have been defined for the portal.

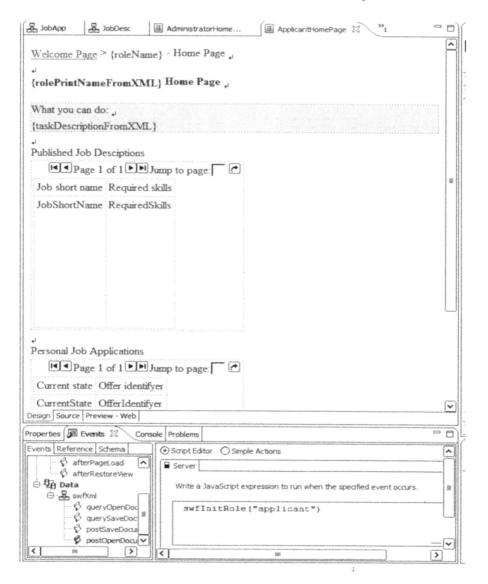

Fig. 10. Creating the Applicant Home Page using the LCD Visual Page Editor

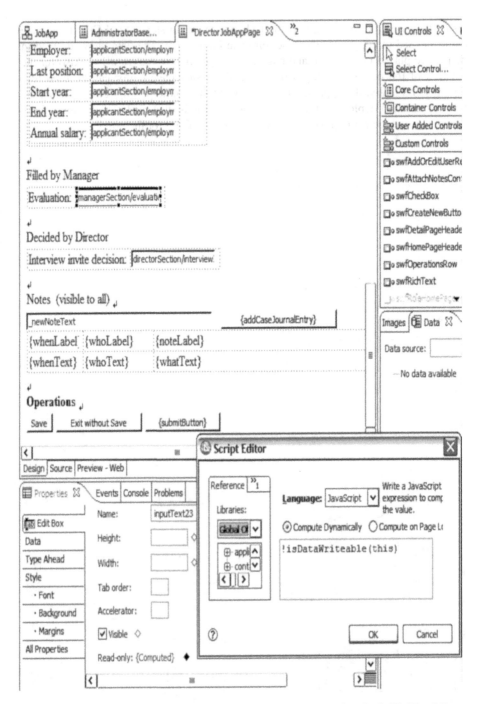

Fig. 11. Creating the Director Job Application Data Detail Page using the LCD Visual Page Editor

4 Discussion and Related Work

BREAD and the related CRUD (create-read-update-delete) patterns have been used as a basis for web-application design before. For example Cachero and Gómez [2], use CRUD explicitly as a basis for web-application modeling. Similarly, WebML [3] a language for modeling web application, is well suited for the design of CRUD web-applications. More recently Bambilla [1] demonstrated that a model-driven compilation approach can be used to create WebML models from workflow models. Similarly, Koehler et al. [4] showed that business process definitions can be transformed into executable web-applications in multiple transformation steps. Task and workflow models have also been used for model-driven development of user-interfaces to web-applications and workflow systems [5, 7].

These approaches differ from the approach presented here in that they target professional software engineers that are well-versed with software engineering notations such as UML and OCL, have no difficulty understanding business process notations such as BPMN, and want to develop their applications in line with Model-Driven Software Engineering approaches [6]. Instead, our goal is to support occasional developers. We extended a graphical web-application development environment with template pages and workflow-specific user-interface components that make it easy to create an initial workflow application. Occasional developers can build workflow applications without programming by modifying the template pages and describing the business logic in the workflow task model. The XML workflow task models are used as a way to eliminate the need for JavaScript programming when creating an initial application. We realize that it will be useful to provide the occasional developers with a graphical editor that reduces the complexities of working directly with the XML workflow task definition. The advantage of providing the workflow support components as template page and adaptable custom extensions to a standard web development environment is that the system can be adapted easily in response to new requirements that are discovered in the course of the system development. The workflow definition can be changed. Content of pages can be changed using the graphical UI editor. And also the workflow-specific UI components can be changed or replaced by finer level components that still reference the same workflow model. The adaptability of the resulting system sets this approach apart from commercial workflow systems that compile a given workflow model into a system that is difficult to adapt.

5 Summary and Future Work

We demonstrate that a workflow-task-model interpreted by custom user interface components facilitates rapid development of interactive workflow applications. Occasional developers can create a workflow application by extending template data objects, adapting template user interface pages including workflow-specific user interface components, and adapting the template workflow task definition that defines the layout and behavior of the workflow-specific user interface components. The system can then be further adapted by further changing the template pages, modifying the workflow custom components, or replacing them by finer-grained UI components that reference the same workflow-task-model. This is an improvement compared to existing workflow systems that use workflow task models to generate a workflow application user interfaces that are difficult to extend. The proposed approach differs from model-driven approaches to workflow web-application development in that it provides a mechanism for application development that does not require knowledge of formal modeling techniques such as UML. This makes the proposed approach more suited for development by occasional developers. The current system can be further improved by providing a graphical editor for the XML workflow task model. Also support for role-specific and person-specific work-list handling, as well as e-mail notification will be useful to add.

References

1. Brambilla, M.: Generation of WebML Web Application Models from Business Process Specifications. In: 6th International Conference on Web Engineering (ICWE 2006), pp. 85–86. ACM press, New York (2006)
2. Cachero, C., Gómez, J.: Advanced Conceptual Modeling of Web Applications: Embedding Operation Interfaces in Navigation Design. JISBD 2002, 235–248 (2002)
3. Ceri, S., Fraternali, P., Bongio, A.: Web Modeling Language (WebML): a modeling language for designing Web sites. Computer Networks 33(1-6), 137–157 (2000)
4. Koehler, J., Hauser, R., Kapoor, S., Wu, F.Y., Kumaran, S.: A Model-Driven Transformation Method. EDOC 2003, 186–197 (2003)
5. Limbourg, Q., Vanderdonckt, J.: Adressing the Mapping Problem in User Interface Design with UsiXML. In: Proceedings of TAMODIA 2004, pp. 155–163. ACM Press, New York (2004)
6. Mellor, S.J., Scott, K., Uhl, A., Weise, D.: MDA Distilled: Principles of Model-Driven Architecture. Addison Wesley, Reading (2004)
7. Stary, C.: TADEUS: Seamless Development of Task-Based and User-Oriented Interfaces. IEEE Transactions on Systems, Man, and Cybernetics 30, 509–525 (2000)
8. WfMC Workflow Management Coalition Terminology & Glossary, WFMC-TC-1011, Document Status- Issue 2.0 (June 1996)
9. zur Muehlen, M.: Organizational management in workflow applications. Information Technology and Management 5(3), 271–291 (2004)

MDA Applied: A Task-Model Driven Tool Chain for Multimodal Applications*

Matthias Heinrich[1], Matthias Winkler[1], Hagen Steidelmüller[1], Manuel Zabelt[1], Alex Behring[2], René Neumerkel[3], and Anja Strunk[3]

[1] SAP AG, SAP Research, Dresden, Germany
{matthias.heinrich, matthias.winkler, hagen.steidelmueller, manuel.zabelt}@sap.com
[2] Department of Computer Science, TU Darmstadt, Germany
behring@tk.informatik.tu-darmstadt.de
[3] Department of Computer Science, TU Dresden, Germany
{neumerkel, strunk}@wwwrn.inf.tu-dresden.de

Abstract. Recently, industry has adopted multimodal, context-aware applications. However, addressing various modalities on heterogeneous platforms implies a demanding development effort. Therefore, we present a task-centric methodology and a tool chain leveraging the development of adaptive multimodal applications.

In order to improve efficiency the tool chain is based on the Model Driven Architecture approach emphasizing two key principles: model-to-model transformations and tool integration.

1 Introduction

During the last decade, capabilities of end-user devices have made a remarkable evolution in terms of multimodality and context-awareness. Nevertheless, the richness of the applications raises development costs, especially in terms of user interface adaptation.

The EMODE project [1] addresses this issue. Since Model Driven Architecture (MDA) also tackles the productivity problem [2], the EMODE tool chain consistently follows the MDA approach.

In contrast to existing projects also proposing a MDA-compliant approach [3], the EMODE project goes beyond the current exploitation of model-to-model transformations and tool integration.

Combining essential tools – model editors, model repository, and transformation engine – in a dedicated design time environment accompanied by a runtime environment drives the tool integration. Furthermore model-to-model transformations using the MDA mapping language QVT [5] accelerate the modelling process. Both assets are the foundation of a cost efficient development lifecycle.

---

* This work was supported in part by the German Ministry of Eduction and Research (BMBF). The project executing organization is the German Aerospace Center (DLR).

M. Winckler, H. Johnson, and P. Palanque (Eds.): TAMODIA 2007, LNCS 4849, pp. 15–27, 2007.

In this paper, we proceed with a brief discussion of related work in Section 2. Section 3 describes the methodology our tool chain is based on. Afterwards a detailed description of the tool chain is given in Section 4. To illustrate the modelling workflow an example demonstrates the required steps in Section 5. Finally we draw the conclusion in Section 6.

2   Related Work

Despite the fact that the MDA approach promises a number of benefits [2], MDA-compliant tool chains supporting the development of multimodal, context-aware applications are rare.

Focusing multimodal, context-aware user interface development, various research projects are centred on UsiXML [6]. Since UsiXML is widely accepted, a growing set of tools is available. In particular the CAMELEON [7] and the SALAMANDRE [8] project made major contributions.

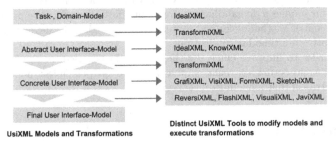

Fig. 1. UsiXML tool chain according to Vanderdonckt [3]

Figure 1 illustrates the variety of tools the UsiXML tool chain consists of. Editing different models on various abstraction levels and initiating transformations requires distinct tools which are not part of an integrating environment. The missing integration hinders a seamless modelling workflow.

While UsiXML and EMODE provide task-centric tool chains to develop multimodal applications, Rousseau et al. focus on tool support for the creation of behavioural models [9]. The behavioural model expressed by a set of election rules represents an algorithm to determine when to use what modality. However, this approach does not provide capabilities to generate user interfaces.

Another model-based approach – the DynaMo-AID project [10] – is devoted to the development of context-aware user interfaces. The DynaMo-AID design time environment provides editors for different models and a model-to-model transformation mechanism. While from a conceptual point of view the MDA principles are satisfied, the tool support is currently considered a "limited prototype" [10].

3   EMODE Methodology

The EMODE methodology, an approach to model multimodal, adaptive user interfaces, is based on the MDA. It is comprised of a number of modelling and development phases, artifacts, transformations, and a conceptual architecture.

MDA encourages the (iterative) refinement of models from an abstract to a platform-specific model [14,15]. EMODE follows the same approach by letting the developer specify models at different levels of abstraction - very abstract at the beginning (e.g. goal model) and more concrete at the end (e.g. the UI model for a specific modality). Among others, the models include goal, concepts, context, user interface and the (for EMODE central) task model (see Section 3.1). As in MDA, the modelling phase in EMODE is followed by a code generation step that produces the application code.

The metamodel for the different models used in EMODE is specified using the Meta-Object Facility (MOF) [4]. This facilitates the use of MOF-based tools, especially model-to-model transformations to support the modelling process, as elaborated in Section 3.2. The EMODE tools presented in Section 4 are implemented on top of the MOF-compliant metamodel and tightly integrated to support seamless development, despite crossing different levels of abstraction.

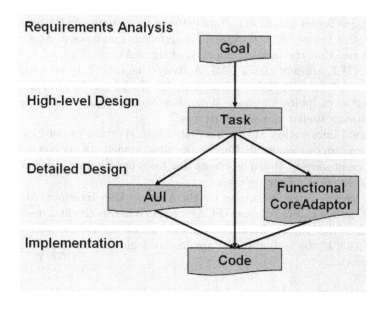

Fig. 2. Phases, Core Artifacts, and Transformations

The modelling process is supported by a number of model-to-model transformations. Models are derived from other models, not only in order to reduce the amount of modelling work which needs to be done, but also to keep the different models consistent with each other. This is of utmost importance, as some of the models are directly connected through mappings. For example, the task model has relations to the Abstract User Interface (AUI) model, describing the applications user interface, and the Functional Core Adapter (FCA) model, which represents the connection to the applications logic. Furthermore, model-to-code transformations have been implemented, generating the concrete user interfaces, controller logic, and method stubs to integrate the application logic. The different phases, models, and transformations are depicted in Figure 2.

The EMODE conceptual architecture describes the components involved in the development process as well as for runtime support. It has been implemented in form of the EMODE tool chain, which is comprised of the modelling infrastructure and runtime components, offering services such as modality handling and processing of contextual information.

3.1   The EMODE Task Model

The central model of the EMODE methodology is the Task model, with which the developer describes the applications behaviour, integrating user and system activities. Task sequencing and parallelism can be modelled, along with a variety of other modelling concepts that can be used by the developer.

Tasks can be classified similar to CTT [16], into *user, interaction, system* and *abstract tasks*. User tasks represent activities the user is performing himself. Interaction tasks represent an interaction between the system and the user. System tasks represent the activities the system is performing on its own. Abstract tasks depict the fact that the task is comprised of subtasks.

Besides CTT, concepts from UML Activity Diagrams [17] were used in the development of the EMODE task metamodel. Tasks can have in and output pins, acting as endpoint for object flows. Furthermore, tasks can be refined by task definitions, similar to UML Activities.

Contextual information can be integrated into the task model by using the EMODE eventing mechanism. Hereby the task model can be connected to a variety of event sources. Based on events new tasks can be started or information can be passed on to a running task.

Closely related to the task model are the Abstract User Interface (AUI) model and the Functional Core Adapter (FCA) model. Whereas the first describes the user interface (i.e. the realization of the interaction tasks), the later describes the connection of the system to the application logic (i.e. the realization of the system tasks).

3.2   Transformations and Mappings

EMODE uses transformations in various ways to support the developer in modelling the application. It is being differentiated between model-to-model and model-to-code transformations. Closely connected to transformations are mappings that link model elements, conveying a meaning [18,19]. Mappings and transformations are an essential part in EMODE to automate development and more tightly integrate the different models with each other.

Model-to-model transformations actively support the developer when modelling, altering his most used artifacts, the models. This improves modelling efficiency by reducing the amount of modelling work that needs to be done. Furthermore, it can be used to keep the different models consistent with each other.

Model-to-model Transformations in EMODE are implemented using QVT-relations [5], a declarative language to specify relations between sets of model elements. EMODE provides the developer with the needed transformations. It would be possible for a developer to adapt the transformations by changing the provided QVT-files. It has to be kept in mind that such changes might have strong implications for the whole development environment and are therefore not recommended.

Mappings between model elements make their relation explicit and provide a meaning to the relation. They are used for example in [18] to improve the consistency of user interfaces. EMODE specifies a number of possible mappings, some of them within one model (e.g. Task-to-Task), others spanning different models, making explicit the connection between more abstract and more concrete models. For example, the task model is connected to the AUI and the FCA model (see Section 4.1).

Model-to-code transformations are used as a final step to produce executable code. This code needs to be extended by the developer in order to integrate business logic. Code extensions will not be overwritten by repeated transformations as long as they are inserted into specially protected sections. Model-to-code transformations have been implemented, generating the concrete user interfaces (from the AUI model), controller logic (from the task model), and method stubs to integrate the application logic (from the FCA model).

4   Tool Chain

The EMODE tool chain is divided into a design time environment and a runtime environment. The design time environment is an integrated modelling environment, which supports the developer modelling the application. Generation and adaptation of code is the last step in using the design time environment. Afterwards, the completed application will be deployed into the runtime environment.

4.1   Design Time

The EMODE design time environment is build as a set of Eclipse plug-ins accompanied by an external repository.

As shown in Figure 3, the repository fulfils two tasks: storing all modelling data and performing model transformations. The modelling environment provides the developer with tools for visualising, editing, and transforming models.

Modelling Environment. The modelling environment consists of a model navigator and multiple editors. The navigator visualises all models at all abstraction levels. Editors for all EMODE models can be opened from within the navigator.

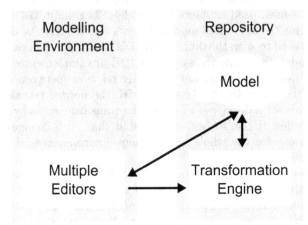

Fig. 3. Design time environment

All editors are based on the Graphical Editing Framework (GEF) [11] and thus provide a common look and feel. The main difference between the individual editors is the set of model-specific tools they provide. The task editor for example supports the developer in connecting tasks to each other via task edges and allows to start model-to-model transformations to AUI or FCA. On the other hand, e.g., the AUI editor lets the developer specify interactors and supports a refinement of the user interface, depending on the set of available modalities.

To seamlessly integrate working at the junction between different models, editors can reference model elements from other models. For example, the task editor allows to specify mappings between task and FCA model by letting the developer associate system tasks to FCA calls. The support is depicted in Figure 4. It shows four central editors of the tool chain. The entire development workflow is controlled from within the modelling environment.

MOF Repository. All models produced by the EMODE editors are stored in an external model repository. This repository and the Java based editors are connected via a MOF-to-CORBA-IDL binding, as proposed by the MOF Specification [4].

Model Transformations. As described in section 3.2, EMODE provides the developer with a set of MOF QVT transformations [5]. These transformations can be triggered by the developer from within the modelling environment. Upon triggering, they are executed in the external repository, which has an integrated QVT-relations compliant transformation engine. After the execution, the editors are updated to be in sync with the repository again.

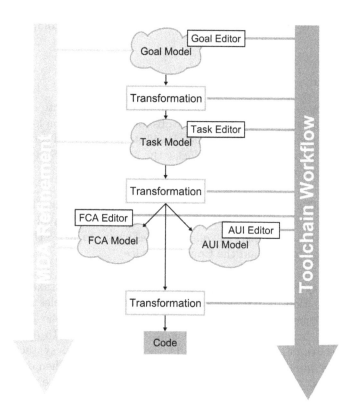

Fig. 4. Models and the support by the design time environment. The developer is supported through all stages of the development workflow: from abstract (goal) models to platform-specific code.

Task-to-AUI and Task-to-FCA transformations are provided. The first transformation maps interaction tasks to interactors, reflecting the hierarchical order of tasks in the hierarchical order of the produced interactors. The later produces a FCA call for each systems task, making sure the FCA call supports the parameters and results in the system task needs. Both transformations automatically set mappings between the source and target elements to depict their relation (which in this case has the semantic "task is realized by").

The task model also plays a key role for the model-to-code transformation. The model-view-controller pattern was applied [12] where the controller is derived from the Task model during a model-to-code transformation. This transformation was implemented using Java Emitter Templates (JET) [13].

While the model-to-model transformations described above, as well as the model-to-code transformations are compliant to the MDA idea, EMODE also supports the direct interpretation of the task model. The task model is interpreted at run time by a process engine, which is part of the EMODE project.

This increases flexibility and removes the need to produce complex code from the model.

4.2   Run Time

In the last transformation step models will be transformed into code. This step includes generation of *controller* code, stubs for the application logic, and different implementations of the AUI model. Besides this generated code, the runtime consists of the two major building blocks: the *Multimodality Service Component (MSC)* and the *Context Service*.

Controller. The controller handles the complete application flow. It is comprised of generated Java code resembling the task model with all its control and data flows. Additionally, the controller provides means to access the Multimodality Services Component and the Context Service.

Multimodality Services Component (MSC). The MSC takes care of adapting the application to different modalities. To this end it selects from the different UI implementations that have been generated from the AUI model. At the same time it supports the use of multiple modalities. To enable the user to switch between multiple available UIs, the MSC supports syntactic input fusion, semantic input fusion and output fission techniques. When deciding which modality to use, the MSC can make use of the Context Service.

Context Service. The Context Service provides appropriate interfaces to applications and other context service clients for utilizing of the runtime context model. This is accomplished in two ways. A query interface provides the possibility to access context information via a declarative language (like SQL). An event mechanism allows clients (e.g. the controller) to register for event notifications.

5   Example Application

This section illustrates the EMODE approach by example. Therefore an application in the area of plant maintenance will be modelled, by using the EMODE design time environment. The final deployment of the modelled application in the EMODE runtime environment creates a fully executable application.

The objective of the application is to support the plant maintenance staff of a large company. Since the plant maintenance staff is responsible for tending to occurring problems as quick as possible, the desired benefit of a multimodal, context-aware application would be an increased efficiency of maintenance order processing.

In the plant maintenance scenario the following IT-Infrastructure is assumed:

- A Product Lifecycle Management (PLM) System, that acts as a central server where all maintenance orders are entered.

– A set of mobile devices serving as a communication interface between the plant maintenance staff and the PLM System.

To outline the modelling process, the listed steps are required to create the application:

1. Create the Task Model
2. Derive the AUI Model using Model-to-Model-Transformations
3. Adapt the generated AUI Model regarding the target platform requirements
4. Derive the FCA Model using Model-to-Model-Transformations
5. Adapt the generated FCA Model regarding the Business Logic requirements
6. Run the Model-to-Code-Transformation
7. Write the Business Logic
8. Deploy the Application

5.1   Create the Task Model

The central Task Model captures the flow of the application and represents the starting point of the modelling process (the optional goal model will not be regarded). Figure 5 defines the flow of the example application.

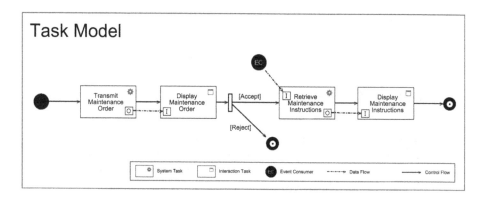

Fig. 5. The Task Model of the Example Application

Starting at the initial node, the control flow defines the execution order of the various tasks. In this example, the PLM System receives a new maintenance order that will be transmitted to a mobile device assigned to a maintenance employee. To map the diversity of tasks, system and interaction tasks are introduced. While system tasks require some kind of computation (e.g. the transmission of a maintenance order), the interaction tasks demand end-user interactions (e.g. read the incoming maintenance order). After receiving the maintenance order, a staff member can decide whether to accept or to reject the maintenance order. In the case of acceptance, the responsible staff member receives detailed instructions, supporting the maintenance task. Note that the system task retrieves data concerning the current noise level from a context service (represented by the event consumer) in order to judge whether instructions are delivered via voice or via a graphical user interface. Afterwards the control flow reaches the final node and the application will terminate.

5.2   Derive the AUI Model Using Model-to-Model-Transformations

In a second step the AUI Model can be derived from the existing Task Model. The mapping is expressed using QVT Relations, a declarative approach for model transformation definitions. The QVT Engine generates an AUI Model requiring the transformation definition and the Task Model. Figure 6 displays the generated AUI Model. Since two interactions tasks are declared in the Task Model, two abstract user interfaces (represented by AUI Interactors) are generated.

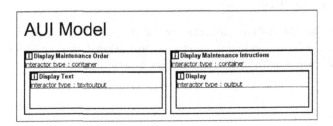

Fig. 6. The AUI Model of the Example Application

5.3   Adapt the Generated AUI Model Regarding the Target Platform Requirements

To meet the demands of distinct modalities and device-restrictions, the AUI Model can be subject to further refinement. Therefore the generated AUIs can be either enriched (e.g. add static content like pictures, text, etc.) or a new version can be derived. The derivation of AUIs is especially important to provide specific UIs for the available set of modalities. In the example application two refined AUI Models were created to reflect UIs for the auditory and the visual modality.

5.4   Derive the FCA Model Using Model-to-Model-Transformations

While counterparts of interaction tasks are laid out in the AUI Model, the correspondents to system tasks are captured in the FCA Model. The initial Model-to-Model transformation creates a FCA Call for each system task. Also input and output parameters of the FCA Call correspond to the incoming and outgoing data flows of a system task. Figure 7 shows the result of Task-to-FCA transformation using the task model from our example application as an input.

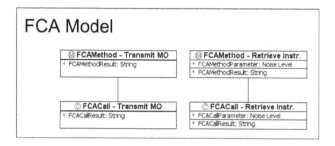

Fig. 7. The FCA Model of the Example Application

5.5 Adapt the Generated FCA Model Regarding the Business Logic Requirements

Apart from FCA Calls, FCA Methods are also an outcome of the Task-to-FCA transformation (see Figure 7). Unlike FCA Calls, which are bound to system tasks, FCA Methods represent methods of the business logic. The benefit of decoupling FCA Calls and FCA Methods is the reuse of existing business logic methods because several FCA Calls can be bound to one FCA Method.

5.6 Run the Model-to-Code-Transformation

After the FCA Model adaptation, the Model-to-Code transformation can be executed. The major return of the transformation is a mapped task model - a so called Controller – and business logic stubs. Both the controller and the business logic stubs are represented as pure Java source code. Only the AUI Model can be mapped to different target languages. Currently, UIs are rendered as Java AWT Frames or as D3ML [20].

5.7 Write the Business Logic

As mentioned beforehand, the Model-to-Code transformation creates Java classes containing method stubs. Therefore Business Logic implementation necessitates filling the marked code blocks. To leverage that task, the Model-to-Code transformation creates a new Java Project within the Eclipse-based design time environment. Consequently all the Java editing facilities provided by the Eclipse IDE are available.

5.8 Deploy the Application

In order to execute the application two steps are requested. At first required libraries need to be added to the encompassed Eclipse Project (e.g. the context service library). Secondly the EMODEApplicaton class has to be executed.

6   Conclusion and Future Work

In this paper, we presented the EMODE tool chain streamlining the development lifecycle of multimodal, context-aware applications. To encourage cost efficient development, the tool chain is MDA-compliant and enveloped by an integrated modelling environment.

The evaluation of the EMODE approach is ongoing. Therefore two demonstrators are currently under development. While the first demonstrator reflects a mobile plant maintenance system, the second deals with an in-car travel assistant. Both applications are implemented using the EMODE and several other tool chains (e.g. the UsiXML tool chain [6]). By means of the developed demonstrators, benefits of the EMODE approach will be carved out.

First feedback by demonstrator developers has been collected and confirms the EMODE idea: Developing multimodal, context-aware applications using one distinct integrated environment facilitates the entire development lifecycle.

Acknowledgement

Contributions from the EMODE partner IKV++ Technologies are gratefully acknowledged.

References

1. Enabling Model Transformation-Based Cost Efficient Adaptive Multi-modal User Interfaces (EMODE) project (2007), http://www.emode-projekt.de
2. Bast, W., Kleppe, A., Warmer, J.: MDA Explained - The Model Driven Architecture: Practice and Promise. Addison-Wesley, Reading (2003)
3. Vanderdonckt, J.: A MDA-Compliant Environment for Developing User Interfaces of Information Systems. In: Proceedings of the 17th conference on Advanced Information Systems Engineering (2005)
4. Meta Object Facility (MOF) Specification (2002), http://www.omg.org/docs/formal/02-04-03.pdf
5. MOF QVT Final Adopted Specification (2005), http://www.omg.org/docs/ptc/05-11-01.pdf
6. Limbourg, Q., Vanderdonckt, J., Michotte, B., Bouillon, L., Florins, M., Trevisan, D.: USIXML: A User Interface Description Language for Context-Sensitive User Interfaces. In: Proceedings of the ACM AVI 2004 Workshop (2004)
7. The CAMELEON Project (2004), http://giove.cnuce.cnr.it/cameleon.html
8. The SALAMANDRE Project (2005), http://www.isys.ucl.ac.be/bchi/research/salamandre.htm
9. Rousseau, C., Bellik, Y., Vernier, F.: Multimodal Output Specification / Simulation Platform. In: Proceedings of the 7th international conference on Multimodal interfaces (2005)
10. Clerckx, T., Luyten, K., Coninx, K.: DynaMo-AID: a Design Process and a Runtime Architecture for Dynamic Model-Based User Interface Development. Engineering Human Computer Interaction and Interactive Systems (2005)
11. Graphical Editing Framework (2007), http://www.eclipse.org/gef/

12. Gamma, E., Helm, R., Johnson, R.E.: Design Patterns - Elements of Reusable Object-Oriented Software. Addison-Wesley, Reading (1995)
13. Java Emitter Templates (JET) Tutorial (2005), http://www.eclipse.org/modeling/emf/docs/2.x/tutorials/jet1/jet_tutorial1_emf2.0.html
14. Miller, J., Mukerji, J.: MDA Guide Version 1.0.1 (2003), http://www.omg.org/docs/omg/03-06-01.pdf
15. Koch, T., Uhl, A., Weise, D.: Model Driven Architecture (2002), http://www.omg.org/docs/ormsc/02-01-04.pdf
16. Paterno, F., Mancini, C., Meniconi, S.: ConcurTaskTrees - A Diagrammatic Notation for Specifying Task Models. In: Proceedings of the International Conference on Human-Computer Interaction (1997)
17. Object Management Group: Unified Modeling Language - Superstructure (2004)
18. Sottet, J., Calvary, G., Favre, J., Coutaz, J., Demeure, A.: Towards Mapping and Model Transformation for Consistency of Plastic User Interfaces. ACM Conference on Computer Human Interaction (2006)
19. Puerta, A., Eisenstein, J.: Towards a general computational framework for model-based interface development systems. In: Proceedings of the 4th international conference on Intelligent user interfaces (1999)
20. Burmeister, R., Pohl, C., Bublitz, S., Hugues, P.: SNOW: A Multimodal Approach for Mobile Maintenance Applications. In: Proceedings of the 15th IEEE International Workshops on Enabling Technologies: Infrastructure for Collaborative Enterprises (2006)

Extending a Dialog Model with Contextual Knowledge

Lode Vanacken, Erwin Cuppens, Tim Clerckx, and Karin Coninx

Hasselt University, Expertise Centre for Digital Media (EDM),
and transnationale Universiteit Limburg
Wetenschapspark 2, B-3590 Diepenbeek, Belgium
{lode.vanacken,erwin.cuppens,tim.clerckx,karin.coninx}@uhasselt.be

Abstract. Designing and exploring multimodal interaction techniques, such as those used in virtual environments, can be facilitated by using high-level notations. Besides task modelling, notations have been introduced at the dialog level such as our notation NiMMiT. For advanced interaction techniques, there is not yet an established approach to decide when to stop detailing the task model and continue modelling at the dialog level. Also, context-awareness is usually introduced at the task level and not at the dialog level. We show that this might cause an explosion in the amount of dialog states in situations where context-aware multimodal interaction is used in one and the same task. Therefore, we propose an approach which attempts to introduce contextual knowledge at the dialog level where transitions are chosen upon context information. We validate our approach in a case study from which we conclude that the augmented notation is easy to use and successfully introduces context at the dialog level.

Keywords: model-based user interface development, multimodal user interfaces, contextual knowledge.

1 Introduction

When developing interactive computer applications, a lot of time is spent designing and implementing the user interface. This is in particular true with 3D multimodal interfaces for Virtual Environments (VEs). The process of creating or selecting interaction techniques for such interfaces is not straightforward. One possible approach is model-based user interface design as described in [1,2,3].

First, in model-based user interface design, the tasks that the user can perform in the application and the tasks that the computer must execute accordingly are modelled in the task model, for example the ConcurTaskTrees notation [4], which orders these tasks in a hierarchical tree with time dependencies. Next, this model is used to define the interaction between the user and the system. An example of such a task is selecting an object in a virtual world. This is one of the basic tasks in 3D multimodal user interfaces. In order to specify this interaction, several high level notations have been introduced: NiMMiT [5], ICO [6], Interaction Object Graphs [7], InTml [8], ICon [9] and CHASM [10].

M. Winckler, H. Johnson, and P. Palanque (Eds.): TAMODIA 2007, LNCS 4849, pp. 28–41, 2007.

Besides being useful for discussion and giving insights into the interaction these models can also be interpreted at runtime such that the interaction can be prototyped. In all these notations we need to assign which devices/modalities should be used during interaction and what events of this device are used, for example the choice between a spacemouse and voice input. In this paper we use the flexibility with respect to interaction metaphors and devices as an example to explain our approach to modelling context at the dialog level.

No consent definition of context exists [11]. In this work we will look at context as influenced by different factors: user, environment, services, and platform as defined in the CoDAMoS context ontology [12]. Dey's definition of context [11] states that context is only relevant when it has an influence on the user's task. About the influence of context on the interaction with the system we can distinguish several distinct levels [13]. Two of these are important for the remainder of this paper:

- **Task Level:** context influences the tasks that are enabled in a certain state of the user interface. A change of context may imply a change of active tasks.
- **Dialog Level:** context influences which state is currently active in the dialog model. Thus, dialog level influence of context may cause a transition to another state of the user interface.

When the assignment of a device/modality is static, the interaction description has to be changed for any situation in the interaction technique where the user would possibly like to switch input devices/modalities. In order to make this switching more dynamic section 3 introduces a combined approach in order to benefit from task level and dialog level context influence.

The validation of our approach will be presented through a case study in section 4. This case study contains some crates that can be positioned by the user. The user can navigate through the environment and *select*, *move* or *rotate* these crates. How the interaction with the environment occurs depends on the setup the user is in. While sitting at a desktop computer, interaction is done by means of keyboard and mouse input but when the user stands in front of a large projection screen he uses a tracking glove in combination with voice input in order to manipulate the scene.

2   Interaction Modelling in NiMMiT

In this section we will discuss NiMMiT ('Notation for MultiModal interaction Techniques'), a diagram based notation intended to describe multimodal interaction between a human and a computer, with the intention to automatically execute the designed diagrams.

Several other high level notations exist for designing interaction, some of them are state driven (ICO [6], Interaction Object Graphs [7] and CHASM [10]) while others use a data flow architecture (InTml [8] and ICon [9]). All these models focus on interaction but only ICO, InTml and CHASM have a similar goal as NiMMiT. They are also oriented towards interaction in (multimodal) VEs. All these notations can be used with several devices/modalities in several context situations but they do not support the integration of changing devices/modalities according to the context of the VE.

In the remainder of this section, we shortly describe the primitives of our notation and will discuss a simple example. For a more detailed description of NiMMiT, we refer to [5].

2.1 NiMMiT Primitives

In NiMMiT, interaction with the computer is considered *event-driven*: users initiate an (inter)action by their behaviour, which invokes events into the system. These events can be triggered by different modalities, such as speech recognition, an action with a pointing device, or a gesture. Interaction is also *state-driven*, which means that not in all cases the system responds to all events. The response to an event, can bring the interaction in another state, responding to other events. Being *data-driven* is another important property of the notation. It is possible that data needs to be shared between several states of the interaction. For example, a subtask of the interaction can provide data, which has to be used in a later phase of the interaction (e.g. touching an object to push it). Finally, an interaction technique can consist of several smaller building blocks, which can be considered as interaction techniques themselves. Therefore, *hierarchical reuse* should be possible within the notation.

Taking the aforementioned considerations into account, NiMMiT defines the following basic primitives: states, events, task chains, tasks, labels and state transitions.

State: A state is depicted as a circle. The interaction technique starts in the start-state, and ends with the end-state. A state defines a set of events to which the system responds.

Event: An event is generated by the framework, based upon the user's input. A combination of events can be multimodal, containing actions such as speech recognition, gestures, pointing device events and button clicks. A single event or a specific combination always triggers the execution of a task chain.

Task Chain: A task chain is a linear succession of tasks, which will be executed one after the other.

Task: A task is a basic building block of the actual execution of the interaction technique. Typically, tasks access or alter the internal state of the application. E.g. when running in a typical 3D environment, a task can be 'collision detection', 'moving objects', 'playing audio feedback', etcetera. Tasks can be predefined by the system, but designers can define their own custom tasks, as well. All tasks can have input and output ports, on which they receive or send parameters or result values. Input ports are required or optional, indicated by a square or circle input port respectively.

Labels: As data can be shared throughout a diagram, NiMMiT needs a system to (temporarily) store values. This is done in 'labels', which can be seen as high-level variables.

State Transitions: Finally, when a task chain has been executed completely, a state transition moves the diagram into the next state. A choice between multiple state transitions is also possible, based upon the value of a certain label.

2.2   Example

By means of figure 1 we will give a brief overview of how the NiMMiT notation should be interpreted. The start-state of this diagram responds to 4 different events (called EVENT1 to EVENT4). When 'EVENT1' *or* 'EVENT3' is fired, 'Taskchain1' will be invoked. 'Taskchain2' however will only be invoked if 'EVENT2' *and* 'EVENT4' occur at the same time, which is defined by the melting pot principle [14].

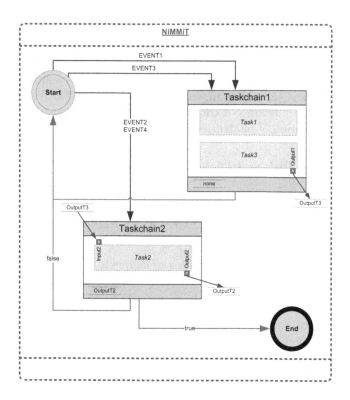

Fig. 1. An abstract NiMMiT Diagram

When a task chain is invoked, all tasks within the chain are executed one after the other (from top to bottom) using each other's output when necessary. The output of a task can be stored in a label in order to be used by a task in an other task chain. In the example the evaluation of 'Taskchain1' will trigger the execution of 'Task1' and 'Task3' of which the last task, 'Task3', results in a boolean value that will be stored in the label 'OutputT3'

When all tasks in the chain are successfully executed, the next state is determined based on the exitlabel of the task chain. In 'Taskchain1' no exitlabel is defined so we return to the 'Start'-state waiting for new events to be fired.

As indicated, 'Taskchain2' will only be executed if 'EVENT2' *and* 'EVENT4' are fired simultaneously. During the execution of 'Taskchain2', the output of 'Task3' (stored in the label 'OutputT3') is used as input for 'Task2', which again results is a boolean value (stored in label 'OutputT2'). Since 'OuputT2' is used as exitlabel for this task chain, the result of 'Task2' will determine the next state of execution: if the value in 'OutputT2' is false, the next state will again be the 'Start'-state; if however, the result of 'Task2' is true, the 'End'-state is reached and the execution of the interaction finishes.

3   Context and NiMMiT

In this section we first discuss briefly two earlier results of our research in the area of model-based design (e.g. in mobile or multi-device developments) that have inspired the approach we use here: (1) incorporating context in task and dialog modelling and (2) adding modality constraints to tasks. We discuss these matters in order to introduce a combination of these two approaches enabling context-aware selection of modalities.

3.1   Context in Task and Dialog Modelling

As discussed before we aim to use context information in order to select the appropriate modality to perform a certain task. Several approaches already incorporate context information at the task level [15,16,17,18]. In our approach we defined the decision task [18]:

Definition 1. *A **decision task** t denotes a junction in the task model where each subtree describes the subtasks of t relevant to the execution of t according to the status of the context. The iconic representation of the decision task is* **D**.

Thus during the runtime of the interactive system exactly one subtree of the decision task is active. In [18] we discussed an algorithm to deduct a corresponding dialog model for each distinct context of use. After the automatic deduction of the dialog models, the designer makes connections between the dialog models to describe when exactly a change of context can introduce a switch to another dialog model.

3.2   Modality Constraints in Task Modelling

In other previous work [19] we have introduced a way to link constraints to the leaf tasks in the task model to specify which modalities are the most desirable to perform the corresponding task. Therefore the designer has to select one

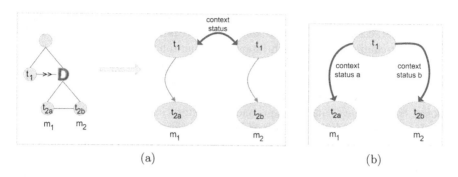

Fig. 2. (a) Combining modality constraints with the decision task notation (task model and dialog model). (b) Merged dialog models.

or more modality categories per task and relate the selected categories with a CARE relation [14]. This enables a runtime selection of a suitable modality with respect to the available interaction techniques surrounding the user at a certain moment in time.

However this is not enough considering the scope of this paper. We would like to take into account more information than the devices populating the VE (application context) to select the appropriate modality. For example in our case study (which will be presented in more detail in section 4) we have 2 different setups (external context) in which we would like to interact with the VE and both setups require other modalities/devices to be used.

One way to overcome this problem is to use the approach we have discussed in section 3.1. This is illustrated in figure 2(a). In this example task t_2 is divided into two distinct tasks t_{2a} and t_{2b}. In this way the designer can attach distinct constraints, m_1 and m_2 to the two tasks. As a result at runtime the task that will be active is chosen with respect to the context status (as shown in the corresponding dialog model in figure 2(a)).

The above described approach works well when just a few tasks require a context-aware selection of the appropriate modality. However when a lot of leaf tasks require a context-aware modality a lot of dialog models are generated and used to describe the same interaction flow. Suppose a task model has got n leaf tasks where a context-aware selection of the appropriate modality is desired and each task is divided into two tasks by means of a decision mode. When the dialog models are extracted from the task specification, all possibilities of context statuses are taken into account resulting in $\binom{n}{2}$ dialog models. It is obvious that n should not be that high to result in an impractical amount of dialog models. This is because the actual purpose of the decision task was to specify different tasks in different context statuses. However in the scope of this paper, the tasks remain the same and for this situation we propose context at the dialog level as a more efficient approach. Note, however, that this way of working can still be combined with context modelling at the task level. This is for instance useful when really different interaction metaphors are offered to the user that do not rely on highly similar task chains. Usually such interaction metaphors are represented as leaf nodes in the task tree, and are modelled with separate NiMMiT diagrams.

A solution to overcome the above mentioned problem of an exploding number of dialog models is to combine the approach of making a distinction between tasks at the task level and the approach of taking care of context at the dialog level. In previous work [13] we showed how transitions in the dialog model can be executed by a change of context information. A combination of the two distinct approaches of context influence at the two levels can be seen as follows. Instead of having two distinct dialog models, we can merge these two together, and make only a distinction between where a difference is made by a context status. This is illustrated in figure 2(b). The two states containing t_1 are merged into one state in the same dialog model, but a choice is made which state will be reached by means of the context status. In this way the decision at the task level is modelled at the dialog level. In the next section we introduce this concept in the NiMMiT notation.

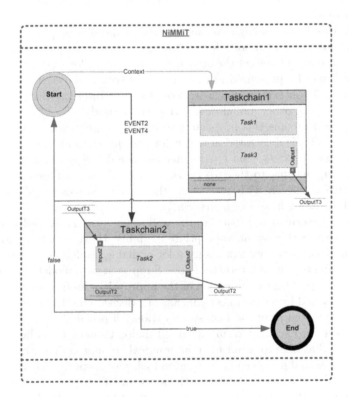

Fig. 3. The context view of an abstract NiMMiT Diagram, 'EVENT1' and 'EVENT3' were added to a specific context

3.3   Context-Aware Modality Selection at the Dialog Level

Remember the NiMMiT example in section 2.2 (figure 1) where in the 'Start'-
state several different events (modalities) could trigger the execution of 'Task-
chain1'. In our new approach we would like to be able to attach a certain context
to a certain event or modality such that depending on this context only those
events belonging to that context will be taken into account when evaluating a
state in the diagram. If for example 'EVENT1' is meant for the expert-users
of the application one can attach the 'expert'-context to the arrow containing
'EVENT1', because here this event is fired by a device such as a spacemouse
which is difficult to handle. Similarly 'EVENT3' could be used in the 'beginner'-
context which is coupled to an easier more common device such as a keyboard.

Adding this contextual knowledge to events transforms the view of the diagram depending onto which context of the diagram we are viewing. The resulting
diagram containing the context arrow is shown in figure 3.

In the following section we will discuss our case study in more detail and
illustrate the context integration in a concrete example.

4   Case Study

4.1   Setup

As mentioned earlier we will illustrate our approach through a case study in
which a simple scene can be manipulated. In the constructed VE it is possible

Fig. 4. Setup of the case study: a wall projection combined with a tracked glove and
speech and a desktop setup with mouse and keyboard

to select, move and rotate some crates onto a plane. To validate our context integration we created 2 setups for this application between which the user can switch at runtime. On one side we have a desktop environment in which the user can interact by means of a keyboard and a mouse, and on the other side we have a large wall projection in which interaction is done using a tracking glove and voice input. The complete setup is depicted in figure 4. For a movie on the case study and our approach see[1].

4.2 Creation

The scene modelling application has been created by a more recent version of Co-GenIVE, a tool supporting the model-based design process depicted in figure 5. For an overview of CoGenIVE and the supported design process we refer to [1,20]. The process starts with the creation of a ConcurTaskTree (CTT) describing the different tasks that are available within the application (figure 6). In this case, some initialisation is done in the 'Load'-task and consequently the 'World Mode'-task becomes enabled. In this task, the user can navigate through the world and manipulate (select, move and rotate) the objects within the environment.

The next step is to define the leaf-tasks of the CTT. The application tasks can be mapped onto system tasks but we have experienced that the user interaction can better be expressed by means of a NiMMiT diagram. Since only the selection and manipulation tasks are context sensitive in this case study, we will focus on

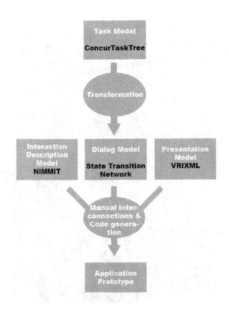

Fig. 5. The model-based design process used in CoGenIVE [20]

---

[1] http://research.edm.uhasselt.be/lvanacken/Tamodia07/Tamodia07.wmv

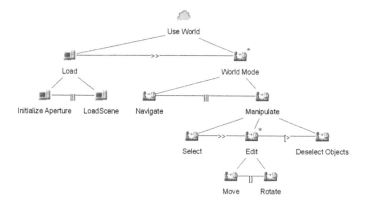

Fig. 6. The ConcurTaskTree of the case study

these tasks in the remainder of the paper. More specific, we will use the select task to illustrate our approach. The NiMMiT diagram of the 'Select'-task will be briefly explained in the remainder of this section and the next section will clarify how context is integrated into the notation.

As shown in the diagrams in Figure 7 the 'Start'-state responds to 2 events (KEYBOARD.MOVE and KEYBOARD.BUTTON_PRESSED.0) for the desktop setup (Figure 7(a)) and 2 events (GLOVE.MOVE and SPEECH.SELECT) for the wall setup (Figure 7(b)). The bottom part of both diagrams is the same and can be seen in figure 8.

When either the keyboard or the glove fires a 'MOVE'-event the right hand task chain will be invoked and all tasks within the chain are executed: first the 'UnhighlightObjects'-task is executed, then the newly collided crates are detected and finally the 'HighlightObjects'-task will highlight the found objects and store these objects in the 'selected'-label. If the chain has been fully evaluated, the diagram returns to the 'Start'-state.

In order to select the highlighted objects the left-hand task chain should be executed. Therefor the user should press a key on his keyboard (in the desktop setup) or issue the speech-command (in the wall setup). Once the 'SelectObjects'-task is executed the diagram gets to the 'End'-state and the interaction technique finishes.

4.3 Context Integration

As indicated in the previous section, for each context a NiMMiT diagram is necessary resulting in n nearly similar diagrams for each task (n being the number of possible contexts). In order to solve this problem we use CoGenIVE to add context information to the NiMMiT diagrams. The possible contexts are provided through an XML-file as defined in [21] and loaded into CoGenIVE. Next, the diagrams in figure 7 are merged, this results in Equivalence [14]. But in our case we would like to enforce a certain modality to a specific context, therefore

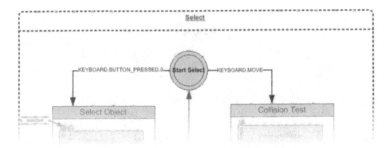

(a) Events active in the Desktop setup.

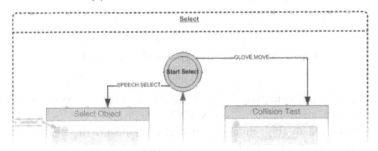

(b) Events active in the Wall setup.

Fig. 7. Active events in the Select interaction

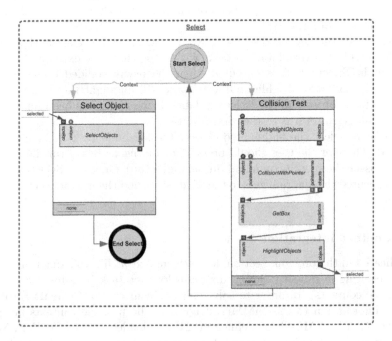

Fig. 8. NiMMiT Diagram of the Select Interaction with the context arrows

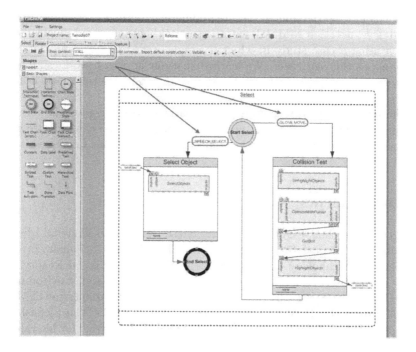

Fig. 9. NiMMiT Diagram of the Select Interaction in the Wall context

to each of the arrows a context specification is added. Within CoGenIVE, arrows with context specifications are automatically replaced by a *context arrow* as shown in figure 8.

In order to interpret these context arrows, the NiMMiT interpreter in our runtime environment has been extended with a simple ContextManagementSystem to indicate the context and a ContextInterpreter to evaluate it and replace the context arrows by the activation events that are specified for the current context.

Further we extended CoGenIVE with a context simulation feature in order to allow the application designer to have a clear view of the NiMMiT diagrams for each context. To do so the user can choose the desired context in a combobox, resulting in a replacement of the context arrows with the activation events that are specified for that context. Figure 9 illustrates the wall setup being chosen and the two Wall context arrows that are shown in the diagram.

5   Conclusion and Future Work

We have shown that context-awareness for high level notations used within multimodal interaction is not always appropriate at the task level where it is usually introduced. As a solution we have presented an approach which attempts to incorporate contextual knowledge into the dialog level for those situations where the task chains keep the same structure in different contexts. We augmented our own high level notation NiMMiT with contextual knowledge and illustrated our approach using a case study in which a simple scene can be manipulated, for a movie about this work see[2]. We learned that our approach works simple and effective and allows designers to use the same interaction descriptions in different contexts.

In the future we plan to try our approach using other context factors such as the user. The user profile (and possibly also user actions) can indicate which modalities are appropriate in certain interaction descriptions expressed in (extended) NiMMiT diagrams.

Acknowledgments

Part of the research at EDM is funded by ERDF (European Regional Development Fund), the Flemish Government and the Flemish Interdisciplinary institute for Broadband technology (IBBT). Both the VR-DeMo (Virtual Reality: conceptual Descriptions and Models for the Realization of Virtual Environments) project (IWT 030248) and the CoDAMoS (Context-Driven Adaptation of Mobile Services) project (IWT 030320) are directly funded by the IWT, a Flemish subsidy organization. The authors would like to thank Tim Tutenel for his valuable contributions in the development of CoGenIVE.

References

1. Cuppens, E., Raymaekers, C., Coninx, K.: A model-based design process for interactive virtual environments. In: DSVIS 2005. Proceedings of 12th International Workshop on Design, Specification and Verification of Interactive Systems, Newcastle upon Tyne, UK, pp. 225–236 (2005)
2. Willans, J., Harrison, M.: A toolset supported approach for designing and testing virtual environment interaction techniques. International Journal of Human-Computer Studies 55, 145–165 (2001)
3. Kulas, C., Sandor, C., Klinker, G.: Towards a development methodology for augmented reality user interfaces. In: Proc. of the International Workshop exploring the Design and Engineering of Mixed Reality Systems - MIXER 2004. CEUR Workshop Proceedings, Funchal, Madeira (2004)
4. Paternò, F.: Model-Based Design and Evaluation of Interactive Applications. Springer, Heidelberg (1999)
5. Vanacken, D., De Boeck, J., Raymaekers, C., Coninx, K.: NiMMiT: A notation for modeling multimodal interaction techniques. In: GRAPP 2006. Proceedings of the International Conference on CG Theory and Applications, Setubal, Portugal (2006)
6. Navarre, D., Palanque, P., Bastide, R., Schyn, A., Winckler, M., Nedel, L., Freitas, C.: A formal description of multimodal interaction techniques for immersive virtual reality applications. In: Proceedings of Tenth IFIP TC13 International Conference on Human-Computer Interaction, Rome, IT (2005)

---

[2] http://research.edm.uhasselt.be/lvanacken/Tamodia07/Tamodia07.wmv

7. Carr, D.: Interaction object graphs: An executable graphical notation for specifying user interfaces. In: Formal Methods for Computer-Human Interaction, pp. 141–156. Springer, Heidelberg (1997)

8. Figueroa, P., Green, M., Hoover, H.J.: InTml: A description language for VR applications. In: Proceedings of Web3D 2002, Arizona, USA, pp. 53–58 (2002)

9. Dragicevic, P., Fekete, J.D.: Support for input adaptability in the ICON toolkit. In (ICMI 2004). Proceedings of the 6th international conference on multimodal interfaces, State College, PA, USA, pp. 212–219 (2004)

10. Wingrave, C., Bowman, D.: CHASM: Bridging description and implementation of 3D interfaces. In: New Directions in 3D User Interfaces Workshop in IEEE Virtual Reality, Bonn, Germany, March 12, 2005 (2005)

11. Dey, A.K.: Providing Architectural Support for Building Context-Aware Applications. PhD thesis, College of Computing, Georgia Institute of Technology (2000)

12. Preuveneers, D., Van den Bergh, J., Wagelaar, D., Georges, A., Rigole, P., Clerckx, T., Berbers, Y., Coninx, K., Jonckers, V., Bosschere, K.D.: Towards an Extensible Context Ontology for Ambient Intelligence. In: Markopoulos, P., Eggen, B., Aarts, E., Crowley, J.L. (eds.) EUSAI 2004. LNCS, vol. 3295, pp. 148–159. Springer, Heidelberg (2004)

13. Clerckx, T., Van den Bergh, J., Coninx, K.: Modeling Multi-Level Context Influence on the User Interface, pp. 57–61. IEEE Computer Society, Los Alamitos (2006)

14. Coutaz, J., Nigay, L., Salber, D., Blandford, A., May, J., Young, R.M.: Four easy pieces for assessing the usability of multimodal interaction: the care properties. In: IFIP Conference Proceedings, pp. 115–120. Chapman & Hall, Sydney, Australia (1995)

15. Pribeanu, C., Limbourg, Q., Vanderdonckt, J.: Task Modelling for Context-Sensitive User Interfaces. In: Johnson, C. (ed.) Interactive Systems: Design, Specification, and Verification, pp. 60–76 (2001)

16. Van den Bergh, J., Coninx, K.: Contextual concurtasktrees: Integrating dynamic contexts in task based design. In: PerCom Workshops, pp. 13–17. IEEE Computer Society, Los Alamitos (2004)

17. Paternó, F., Santoro, C.: One model, many interfaces. In: Kolski, C., Vanderdonckt, J. (eds.) Computer-Aided Design of User Interfaces III, vol. 3, pp. 143–154. Kluwer Academic, Dordrecht (2002)

18. Clerckx, T., Luyten, K., Coninx, K.: DynaMo-AID: A Design Process and a Runtime Architecture for Dynamic Model-Based User Interface Development. In: Bastide, R., Palanque, P., Roth, J. (eds.) Engineering Human Computer Interaction and Interactive Systems. LNCS, vol. 3425, pp. 77–95. Springer, Heidelberg (2005)

19. Clerckx, T., Vandervelpen, C., Coninx, K.: Task-Based Design and Runtime Support for Multimodal User Interface Distribution. In: Engineering Interactive Systems 2007: EHCI/HCSE/DSV-IS (2007)

20. De Boeck, J., Gonzalez Calleros, J.M., Coninx, K., Vanderdonckt, J.: Open issues for the development of 3d multimodal applications from an MDE perspective. In: MDDAUI workshop 2006, Genova, Italy (2006)

21. Clerckx, T., Luyten, K., Coninx, K.: Generating Context-Sensitive Multiple Device Interfaces from Design, pp. 281–294. Kluwer, Dordrecht (2004)

Practical Extensions for Task Models

Daniel Sinnig[1], Maik Wurdel[2], Peter Forbrig[2], Patrice Chalin[1], and Ferhat Khendek[1]

[1] Faculty of Engineering and Computer Science,
Concordia University, Montreal, Quebec, Canada
{d_sinnig, chalin, khendek}@encs.concordia.ca
[2] Department of Computer Science,
University of Rostock, Germany
{maik.wurdel, pforbrig}@informatik.uni-rostock.de

Abstract. The current set of temporal operators is insufficient to make effective use of task models as specifications for user interfaces. Moreover, the predominant monolithic task tree structure does not scale well for sizable applications. In order to overcome these shortcomings, a small collection of practical extensions for task models is proposed. In particular, we define new temporal operators (stop, non-deterministic choice, deterministic choice and instance iteration), concepts in support of modularization and a high-level task diagram notation. Finally, we introduce a new concept for expressing cooperative task models that distinguishes between different roles as well as between actors fulfilling these roles.

Keywords: Task specifications, cooperative task models, modularization, specialization.

1 Introduction

In the domain of human-computer interaction (HCI) task analysis is an effective requirements elicitation device as it helps to gain understanding of how people currently work. According to Johnson, "*the role for the task analysis is to provide an idealized, normative model*" of the tasks users carry out to achieve goals [1].

In recent years, with the advent of model-based UI development [2-5], task models are not only used as analysis models, they are used as a specification of the envisioned user interface as well. Based on a task model specification, more concrete design specifications (e.g. dialog model [5], presentation model [2]) are successively derived until the implementation level has been reached. Within such a model-based development lifecycle, purely idealised task models, as proposed by Johnson, are insufficient since human errors and system errors are not taken into account. Instead, task specifications including failure and error cases are needed in order to obtain a complete specification of the user interface.

Unfortunately the construction of task specifications remains a challenging and cumbersome activity [6]. Based on our experiences while working with task models, we discovered that the current operator set is not sufficient to effectively describe task specifications. For example, CTT—one of the most popular task modelling notations—does not have an operator defining the premature termination of a scenario

M. Winckler, H. Johnson, and P. Palanque (Eds.): TAMODIA 2007, LNCS 4849, pp. 42–55, 2007.

(whether it is due to human or system error). Error handling with the traditional operator set results in an explosion of complexity which diminishes the readability of the task model [6]. Moreover, from a structural point of view, task models are defined as monolithic task trees. Such an approach, does not scale well for applications of medium and large sizes.

In order to overcome these shortcomings we propose a set of practical extensions for task models. The extensions are categorized in three different dimensions: (1) extensions to the operator set, (2) structural extensions, and (3) extensions in support of cooperative task models. The former directly addresses the problem of creating a complete task specifications of the UI by introducing additional temporal operators, namely *stop*, *instance iteration*, *non-deterministic choice*, and *deterministic choice*. In the second set of extensions we propose structural enhancements for task models. A task model is no longer defined as a monolithic task tree but in a modular fashion where a task tree may include references to other sub-ordinate task trees. Moreover we define a *specialization* relation between task models and propose a high-level notation called "*Task Model Diagram*". The third dimension addresses the creation of task models for cooperative applications (e.g. multi-user smart environments). In particular we define a concept of a *cooperative task model*. Within such a cooperative task model the execution of a task of one model may enable or disable the execution of a task in a different task model.

The structure of the remainder of this paper is as follows. Section 2 briefly reviews the task modelling notation CTT and presents relevant related work. In Sections 3 and 4 we propose extensions to the operator set and structural enhancements, respectively. Section 5 presents a new concept for collaborative task models. Finally in Section 6, we draw the conclusion and provide an outlook to future research.

2 Background and Related Work

Various notations for task modelling exist. Among the most popular ones are GOMS [7], GTA [8], HTA [9] and CTT [10]. Even though all notations differ in terms of presentation, level of formality and expressiveness, they share the following common tenet: tasks are hierarchically decomposed into sub-tasks until an atomic level has been reached. In what follows we describe in greater detail the task-modelling notation ConcurTaskTrees (CTT). Within the domain of human-computer interaction, CTT is the most popular notation, as it contains the richest set of operators and it is supported by a tool, CTTE [11], which facilitates the creation, visualization and sharing of task models.

Tasks are arranged hierarchically, with more complex tasks decomposed into simpler sub-tasks. CTT distinguishes between several task types, which are represented by the nodes in the task tree. There are abstract tasks, which are further decomposable into combinations of the other task types including interaction, application and user tasks. CTT includes a set of binary (enabling, choice, order independence, concurrency, disabling, suspend/resume) and unary operators (optional, iteration). The former are used to temporally link sibling tasks at the same level of decomposition whereas the latter are used to identify optional and iterative (unbounded iteration and n-times iteration) tasks. A complete set of the CTT operators together with their interpretation can be found in [10]. We note that most binary operators (except for suspend/resume) have similar (yet not semantically identical) counterparts in LOTOS [12].

In order to support the specification of collaborative (multi-user) interactive systems, CTT has been extended to CCTT (Collaborative ConcurTaskTrees) [11]. A CCTT specification consists of multiple task trees. One task tree acts as a "coordinator" and specifies the collaboration and global interaction between involved user roles. The individual tasks of each user role are, furthermore, specified by separate task trees which contain special activity nodes called "connection tasks". Nodes, of this type exhibit temporal dependencies to connection tasks of other task trees. These temporal dependencies are described in the "coordination" task model. In this paper we further extend CCTT by taken into account that a role is typically fulfilled by several users. For each user we create a copy (instance) of the corresponding role task model. At runtime the various instances of the task model are executed concurrently. Synchronization points between instances are specified in TCL (task constraint language). A coordinator task model, as specified in CCTT, is not needed.

In recent years various attempts were made to extend the CTT notation. In [13; 14] Klug and Dittmar propose additional modelling constructs, namely input/output ports and object dependencies, respectively. Luyten [15] introduces a new node type (decision node) which allows to augment task models with context of use dependencies. Forbrig et al. [16] propose a mechanism which allows the definition of temporal relationships between arbitrary tasks of a task tree—this is in contrast to CTT, where temporal relationships are limited to sibling task, only.

In order to overcome CTT's inability to specify task failures and error cases Bastide and Basnyat introduce the concept of *error patterns* [6]. In this paper, we tackle the same limitation but instead of using error patterns, we define a new temporal operator *stop* which denotes a premature termination of the current scenario. In order to define a consistency relation between use cases and task models, Sinnig et al. [17] suggest that a distinction be made between choices (of two tasks) that happen non-deterministically vs. deterministically from the user's point of view. In this work, we introduce a corresponding temporal operator for both kinds of choice.

In the next three sections, we present our proposed extensions to task models. The extensions are organized into the following categories: extensions to the operator set, structural enhancements, and extensions in support of cooperative task modelling.

3   Extensions to the Operator Set

Task models were originally introduced as analysis artefacts, describing how a user achieves a goal. As such, task models can be seen as idealised descriptions of how the user accomplishes involved tasks; failure of task execution, errors and their consequences were not directly taken into account. Fig. 1 depicts such an idealised description of a login task included in a secure mail system. The task model is idealised as the possibility of login failure is not specified.

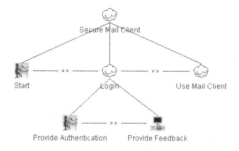

Fig. 1. Idealised Task Model

In recent years, with the advent of model-based UI development, task models have not only been used as analysis models, but also as a requirements specification of the user interface. In model-based UI development frameworks, the task specification typically serves as a starting point for the derivation of more concrete design models such as the dialog and the presentation model [2-5]. Task models used in such a context must not only capture the case of successful task completion but must also cope with failure and error scenarios.

Evidently a purely idealised modelling approach is suitable at the analysis phase, but it is incomplete at the design level, since possible interactions between the user and the system are not captured. In this paper, we argue that with the current set of CTT operators the creation of non-idealised task models is impractical. Work-a-rounds are cumbersome and require a high degree of duplication of tasks and sub-tasks. In what follows, we propose a set of additional temporal operators that ease the modelling of design-task models. Specifically, we present two unary operators (*stop* and *instance iteration*) and two binary operators (*deterministic choice* and *non-deterministic choice*).

Table 1. Additional CTT Temporal Operators

Operator	Syntax	Interpretation
Stop	stop (T$_1$)	Signifies the unsuccessful termination of a task. An unsuccessfully terminated task cannot enable any task.
Deterministic Choice	T$_1$ []$_D$ T$_2$	Deterministic choice composition: either T1 or T2 is performed.
Non-deterministic Choice	T$_1$ []$_N$ T$_2$	Non-deterministic choice composition: either T1 or T2 is performed.
Instance Iteration	T$^\#$	Several "instances" of T may be executed concurrently.

3.1 The Unary *Stop* Operator

Exhaustive modelling of alternatives and error scenarios is indispensable to capturing a full behavioural specification of a user interface. The current set of CTT operators does not support the direct specification of tasks that lead to the premature termination of a scenario. The only work-a-round for this shortcoming is to (artificially) create a high-level choice between the scenarios that terminate prematurely and the scenarios that terminate "normally".

We therefore propose the introduction of a unary *Stop* operator. It signifies the unsuccessful termination of a task. A task "flagged" with the *Stop* operator cannot enable any tasks. The execution of a *Stop* task inevitably leaves the super-ordinate tasks incomplete which eventually leads to the premature termination of a scenario. Syntactically, *stop* is represented by a STOP sign hovering above the affected task.

Fig. 2 illustrates a non-idealised task model of the "Secure Mail Client". It is more detailed than the idealised task model of Fig. 1. In particular, the tasks "Provide Authentication" and "Provide Feedback" have been refined or modified. The former takes into account that the user may "Cancel" the Login task whereas the later takes into account that the login task can fail. Both cases lead to the premature termination of a scenario as the subsequent tasks "Provide Feedback" and "Use Mail Client" respectively will never become enabled.

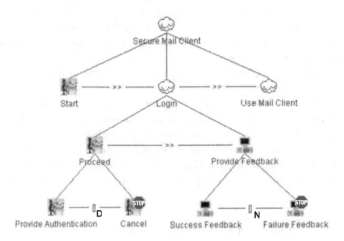

Fig. 2. Non-idealised Task Model

3.2 Deterministic Choice and Non-deterministic Choice Operators

In model-based UI development, task models capture the behaviour of the UI. The system is viewed at a level of abstraction which focuses on input-output interactions and omits internal system operations. These internal system operations are irrelevant for UI design. Opting for such a level of abstraction may lead to apparent non-determinism in the task-model specification. For example, in Fig. 2, the execution of the "Provide Authentication" task may lead to two different system states. In one state the system provides "Success Feedback", whereas in the other the system provides "Failure Feedback". Since internal system states are not part of the model, the choice between the two alternatives, "Failure Feedback" and "Success Feedback", is made internally by the system. The user does not participate in the decision making and views the choice as non-deterministic. In contrast to this, the choice between

"Providing Authentication" or "Cancelling" login is made by the user. Hence, the choice between the two tasks is deterministic.

Based on this observation, we propose to replace the CTT "general purpose" *choice operator* by two operators; one for a *deterministic choice* and another one for *non-deterministic choice*. As depicted in Fig. 2, the former operator is denoted by the symbol $[]_D$ whereas the latter is represented by the symbol $[]_N$. The new operators allow for more expressive modelling of the interplay between the user and system. In addition, a distinction between non-deterministic choice and deterministic choice will help with the definition of a refinement relation between task models. The latter will be described in Section 4.2 in greater detail.

3.3 Instance Iteration

The unary CTT *Iteration* operator (*) specifies that a task may be re-executed after completion. The constraint of task completion before another iteration takes place proves to be too rigid for certain tasks. For illustration purposes let us consider the example of writing e-mails using a mail client. Fig. 3 depicts that in order to send an e-mail the user has to sequentially perform a number of sub-tasks. After he decides to write an e-mail the system displays the input form and the user can compose the e-mail. Finally the user either submits the e-mail or dismisses it. Furthermore, following the paradigm of modern mail clients, the user is allowed to write several e-mails concurrently; i.e. he may interrupt the composition of the current e-mail in order to start with a new e-mail. In other words, another instance of the "Send Mail" task may be executed before the execution of the current instance has terminated.

In CTT it is not possible to directly specify such a form of instance iteration. Due to its frequent applicability (e.g. writing / reading mails, managing calls under waiting, browsing websites, etc.) we therefore propose the definition of a new unary operator *Instance Iteration*.

Definition: (Instance Iteration). The unary operator Instance Iteration (#) is defined as follows: $A^\# = [A ||| A^\#]$.

The behaviour of the operator is optional and is specified as the concurrent execution of the operand task itself and a recursive execution of the instance iteration again. In

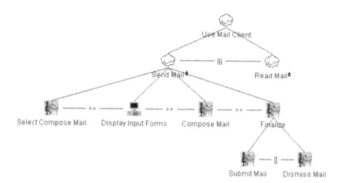

Fig. 3. Task Model of a Mail Client with Instance Iteration

Fig. 3, the tasks "Send Mail" and "Read Mail" are defined using the *Instance Iteration* operator. For sake of conciseness, only the "Send Mail" task has been inflated. As an execution example let us assume that there are two instances of the "Send Mail" tasks that are performed concurrently. Then we can extract the following possible trace of sub-tasks: <<Select Compose Mail$^{(1)}$, Display Input Form$^{(1)}$, Select Compose Mail$^{(2)}$, Display Input Form$^{(2)}$, Compose Mail$^{(1)}$, Compose Mail$^{(2)}$, Dismiss Mail$^{(1)}$, Submit Mail$^{(2)}$>>. We have used superscripts to distinguish between the tasks of the two iterations.

4 Structural Enhancements

In this section we propose two structural operators and a high-level notation for task models. Both result from a research project, which had as its goal the cross-pollination of use-case models and task models. In particular, we define *modular task models* and a *specialization* relationship between task models. The former was found useful in reducing the complexity of task models whereas the latter helps ensuring consistency across multiple UIs. Finally we introduce the graphical notation "*Task Model Diagram*" which can be used to visualize the high-level structure of task models.

4.1 Modular Task Models

In model-based UI development, task models capture the behavioural aspects of the user interface within a single monolithic task tree. A monolithic task tree is suitable for applications of small sizes but becomes unmanageable (in terms of visualization, comprehension and modification) for applications of even moderate size. In order to reduce the complexity of task models, we propose creating models in a modular fashion. More precisely, higher-level models are created through composition of lower-level task models. This becomes possible if we define a task model as a task tree, whose leaves are either *atomic tasks* or *references to other task models*[1].

Even though it is possible to model the entire behaviour of a user interface within a holistic task model without references, we suggest breaking down the overall task model into "sub-task models" which are of manageable size and are reusable in different contexts of use. Examples of generically applicable (sub) task models are "Login", "Fill Form", "Search", "Browse", etc.

It is important to note that the structure of a modular task model is similar to the structure of the use-case model. A use-case model consists of a set of use cases, which are hierarchically organized into summary, user goal and sub-function use cases [18]. Similar to our task model set up, each lower-level use case is a partial specification of the system and a set of use cases is needed to obtain a full specification.

We believe that such a modular set up is a more realistic reflection of how task models are created by the UI developer. It is unlikely that a UI designer develops a task model for an entire UI (which potentially address multiple goals) all at once within a single, holistic task model. Instead, the task model is likely to evolve through

---

[1] Currently CTT only supports references to tasks within the same task tree. A modular construction of the task model out of sub-models is not possible.

a series of steps. First the designer identifies a set of "user-goal" tasks that directly address a goal of the user. Next, task models for each of these user-goal tasks are specified. Note that this step could be carried out concurrently by a team of UI designers. Finally, the various user-goal task models are unified within a single global task model.

4.2 Specialization Between Task Models

With the advent of ubiquitous and mobile devices there has been a shift towards the development of multiple user interfaces. That is, the same application can be accessed through different user interfaces supporting different devices (e.g. laptops, desktops, palmtops, mobile phones, etc.). In such a context it is important to ensure consistency between the various interfaces. Consistency can be achieved on different levels ranging from the way tasks are supported by the system to a consistent presentation and *Look & Feel* across the different UIs. One way to accomplish the former is to develop the underlying task models of the various UIs based on a common coarse grained task description.

For that purpose we propose a *specialization* relation between task models. It links a sub task model to its super task model such that the former is a specialization of the latter. The specialization is possible in two different ways: (1) structural refinement: i.e. breaking previously atomic tasks into sub-tasks; (2) behavioural refinement: i.e. restricting the set of possible scenarios.

Table 2. Valid Task Type Specializations

Task Type in Super Task Model	Valid Task Type(s) in Sub Task Model
abstract	abstract, interaction, user, application
interaction	interaction
user	user
application	application

Structural Refinement. The sub task model may contain more information than its super task model. This can be achieved by further refining the action tasks (tasks at the leaf level) of the super task model. The specialization is deemed valid if the type refinements of Table 2 are preserved. In essence, while abstract tasks can be arbitrarily refined, interaction, user and application tasks must only be refined by subtasks of the same type.

Behavioural Refinement. We define behavioural refinement in such a way that a sub task model does not allow more scenarios than the original task specification. The sub task model may even further restrict the set of scenarios. Such a specialization can be achieved by applying one or many of the following five restrictions:

1. A deterministic choice ($[]_D$) is restricted to either alternative. (Note that a non-deterministic choice ($[]_N$) cannot be further restricted)
2. An optional task [T] becomes obligatory or is removed. (Note that the *optional* operator can be defined as follows: $[T] = T []_D \varnothing$), where the symbol $\varnothing$ is a placeholder for an empty task.

3. A concurrent (|||) or order-independent (|=|) task execution is restricted to a more sequential task execution.
4. Unbounded iteration (*) is restricted to a form of bounded iteration.
5. Instance iteration (#) is bound to traditional iteration (*)

The refinement rules ensure that every scenario for the sub task model is also a valid scenario for its super task model. Moreover, it is guaranteed that all non-deterministic choices are preserved. This is important as we require the UI to *cater for all possibilities that happen non-deterministically*. Main reason for this constraint is to rule out the possibility of a UI stalemate as a result of being incapable to "process" a non-deterministic system response. As an example let us assume we refine the task model of Fig. 2 by excluding the "Failure Feedback" task. As a consequence every case of Login failure (for whatever reason) would lead to a UI stalemate, as the UI is designed to *not* provide failure feedback.

4.3 Task Model Diagrams

In this section, we propose a graphical notation for "Task-Model Diagrams". A task-model diagram conveys the structural properties of task models by highlighting relationships defined among them.

Within a task-model diagram, task models are depicted by ellipses and their relationships are visualized by arrows and lines. Two relationships exist: *Include* and *Specialization*. The former is labelled "include" and it denotes the hierarchical composition of high-level task models from lower-level task models. The high-level task model "Secure Mail Client" (originally introduced in Section 3) invokes the "Use Mail Client" task model and the "Login" task model. In other words, "Login" and "Use Mail Client" are subordinate to "Secure Mail Client"[2]. The *Specialization* relationship is denoted by the UML symbol used for this purpose. It is a relationship that links a task model to its super task model. Hence, for example, "Fingerprint Login" and "Text-based Login" specialize "Login"; i.e. they are specializations of the generic "Login" task model.

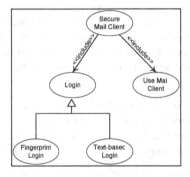

Fig. 4. Task Model Diagram of a Secure Mail Client

---

[2] In contrast to the task model of Fig. 2, "Login" is factored out of from "Secure Mail Client" model (for the sake of increased modularity).

Within the software lifecycle the task models related by virtue of *specialization* are typically build from top to bottom, i.e. first the generic task models are created, which are then further refined. This corresponds to our assumption of Section 4.2 that specialization can be used to ensure consistency in terms of supported tasks across multiple-user interfaces. As a side-effect we also envision that the specialization relation between task models will contribute to the creation of task-model libraries, where recorded task models can be further refined to rapidly and conveniently create specialized task models.

5   Cooperative Task Models

Imagine the following situation of a meeting in a software company, where several persons are involved: *The project manager made an appointment to meet the consultant and the stakeholder and several developers to discuss the forthcoming project. At first the project manager talks about the software company and introduces his employees by showing some slides illustrating their experiences in the stakeholder's domain. After this brief introduction the stakeholder is given the floor and he talks about the basic requirements of the project and his company. Since there has already been a document which describes the basic idea of the project the consultant presents his idea of solving the sketched problem. His presentation is interrupted by questions of the stakeholder which are answered by the plenum.*

This brief example shows, in part, how cooperative work and interaction is performed during a meeting. Several people, fulfilling different roles (e.g. presenter, listener, chairman, etc) interact with each other. Each role has an individual objective, whose accomplishment, however, may depend on the status and actions of other individuals involved in the collaboration. Such a scenario is depicted in Fig. 5. In order to design proactive assistance for such meeting settings the following questions (among others) have to be addressed:

- What is an appropriate assistance in a certain situation?
- How can such an environment be designed or developed?
- What kind of tasks can be assisted and how?
- How can personal devices be used to improve the meeting performance?

In current practice, the analysis phase of a development process for ambient environments is not covered appropriately. Often designs are derived without a thorough understanding of individual goals and tasks of involved actors [19; 20]. We argue that modelling the envisioned scenario in form of collaborative task models is crucial for the development of ambient systems. For example, simulation of the modelled behaviour is able to expose wrong design decisions (at a very early stage).

In the remainder of this paper we present an extension for task models which supports modelling collaborative work and tasks. The main idea is as follows: The behaviour of each user role is modelled by a role task model. At runtime, for each active actor, an instance of the corresponding role task model is created. It represents individual behaviour and captures the enabled task set of a particular actor. Cooperation of actors is defined in terms of a global constraint language. The constraints express temporal dependencies between tasks of different actors, which in

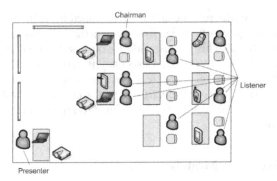

Fig. 5. Ubiquitous Meeting Setting

turn are captured in different instance task models. In essence we define a cooperative task model as a tuple consisting of a *set of roles*, a *set of task specifications* (one for each role), a *set of actors* where each actor belongs to a certain role and a *set of global constraints*. Similar to CCTT, our extension requires the creation of a separate task model for each role involved in the interaction. The role task models for the before-mentioned ubiquitous meeting setting are portrayed in Table 3.

Next and in contrast to CCTT we create, for each actor, an individual copy (instance) of the respective role task model. We denote this process of assigning a task model to an actor as *instantiation* of a role-task model. It is important to note that our approach is based on the assumption that in limited and well-defined domains the

Table 3. Role Task Models

Role	Task Model
Chairman	Presentation: Chairman — Introduces to Session — Manages a Talk* — Finishes Session — Announces Talk — Sits and Listens — Interrupts Talk — [Finishes Talk] — Opens Discussion
Presenter	Presentation: Presenter — Introduces himself — Starts Presentation — Next Slide* — Ends Presentation — Respond to Question — Show Next Slide — Explains Slide
Listener	Presentation: Listener — Sits and listens — Takes Notes — Asks Question

behavioural characteristics of an actor matches, more or less, the stereotypical behaviour captured in its role-task model. Constrains between tasks of different instance task models are defined in a language called Task-Constraint Language (TCL).

Contrary to CCTT, where cooperation between users is specified by another (global) task tree, TCL is not hierarchical structured. As a result, we are able to express constraints between arbitrary tasks of the instance task models. Redundancies and duplications are avoided as the structural breakdown of cooperative tasks does not need to be re-specified. Moreover with TCL is it possible to define constraints between multiple instantiations of the same role task model.

The basic structure of a constraint expressed in TCL is similar to the one of a CTT binary expression. It consists of a left operand, a temporal operator, and a right operand. The operands signify tasks, whereas the temporal operator expresses the type of the constraint. Tasks are identified in two steps: First, we select the instance task model(s) the task belongs to and second we select the task within the model(s).

Fig. 6 shows a constraint expressed in TCL, which can be paraphrased as follows: *After the task OpensDiscussion in any task model instance of role Chairman is executed the task AsksQuestion in all task model instances of the role Listener becomes enabled.* In other words, only if a chairman (there may be more than one) has opened the floor for discussions, listeners are allowed to ask questions. An examination of the operands (Fig. 6) reveals that instances can be identified in two ways. In the case of the left operand, the qualifier "oneInstance" is used to denote that *one* particular instance of the role task model "Chairman" is arbitrarily selected. In the case of the right operand, "allInstances" is used to select all existing instances of role "Listener". Additional sample constraints for the before-mentioned ubiquitous meeting example are displayed in Table 4. We note that the "point notation" used to qualify tasks is similar to the OCL notation for identifying instances of classes [21].

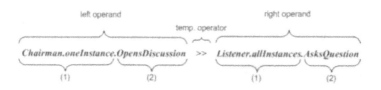

Fig. 6. Sample TCL Constraint

In a non-cooperative model the enabled tasks after an execution trace are easily determined by examining the temporal relationships defined within the model. Within a collaborative task model, however, additionally the global constraints have to be taken into account. A task T is defined to be enabled, if the following holds: T is enabled according to the local temporal relationships *and* T is enabled by virtue of the global constraints. At this point it is important to note that the semantics of collaborative task models allows for the possibility of deadlocks due to conflicting constraints. Intuitively a total deadlock occurs when all enabled tasks of all task model instances are blocked by TCL constraints. A deadlock is partial, if only a subset of the instance task model is affected. For example, a global constraint that makes use of the *Choice* operator causes a deadlock if the operand tasks are obligatory in the corresponding instance task models.

Table 4. TCL Constraints for Ubiquitous Meeting

Operator	Task Constraints (TC)
Enabling (>>)	Chairman.oneInstance.SitsAndListens>>Presenter.oneInstance.StartsPresentation
Choice ([])	Chairman.oneInstance.FinishsTalk [] Presenter.oneInstance.EndsPresentation
Disabling ([>)	Listener.oneInstance.AsksQuestion [> Listener.allInstances..AsksQuestion
Susp/Res. (▷)	Presenter.oneInstance.NextSlide ▷ Chairman.oneInstance.InterruptsTalk

Finally we would like to mention that our approach is based on the assumption that the behaviour of an actor can be approximated through its role. In such a case we argue that modelling and simulating smart environments by using cooperative task models is highly beneficial for the development of proactive assistance. On the one hand cooperative task modelling helps establishing a thorough understanding of the requirements of the envisioned system. On the other hand the cooperative task specification can serve as input for the derivation of probabilistic models, such as Dynamic Bayesian Networks, which are widely used in the research field of proactive assistance in ambient environments [20].

6 Conclusion and Future Research

We have presented a set of practical extensions for task models. The main motivation behind our research was to extend task models such that they can be used as user interface specifications. We reasserted that the original idea of an idealised task model is not sufficient in the context of specifications since errors and failure cases are not covered. Moreover, defining an entire specification within a single monolithic task tree is only suitable for small applications and does not scale for sizable applications.

In order to overcome these shortcomings a richer set of temporal operators as well as structural enhancements were proposed. As for the structural enhancements, we suggested to *modularize* the monolithic task tree into a set of trees which are connected through references. In order to be able to relate task models to each other, we defined a *specialization* relation. *Task-Model Diagrams* were proposed as a notation to convey structural properties of the task specification.

Finally, we detailed a novel approach to model collaborative work of users based on task models. In general, within a cooperative task model the execution of a task of one model may enable or disable tasks in other task models. Within our approach we not only distinguish between different roles but also between different actors fulfilling the roles. Cooperation of actors is defined in terms of a global constraint language called TCL. The constraints express temporal dependencies between tasks of different actors, which in turn are captured in different instance task models.

This paper can be seen as a starting point for more in-depth research for each of the proposed operators and concepts. One future research avenue would be the extension of TCL to be able to specify temporal dependencies based on the state of the actor. Another avenue is the definition of formal semantics for the proposed temporal operators and TCL. The formal semantics can serve as a reference point for the development of tools. We are currently in the process of developing a graphical design tool for collaborative task models and their constraints. In this vein we will also implement a simulator, which is able to interpret TCL. We envision using model-checking techniques to detect deadlocks which are consequences of conflicting constraints.

References

[1] Johnson, P.: Human Computer Interaction: Psychology, Task Analysis and Software Engineering. McGraw-Hill, London (1992)

[2] Berti, S., Correani, F., Mori, G., Paternó, F., Santoro, C.: TERESA: A Transformation-based Environment for Designing and Developing Multi-Device Interfaces. In: Proceedings of Extended abstracts of the CHI 2004, Vienna, Austria, pp. 793–794 (2004)

[3] Molina, P., Trætteberg, H.: Analysis & Design of Model-based User Interfaces. In: Proceedings of CADUI 2004, Funchal, Portugal, pp. 211–222 (2004)

[4] Paternó, F., Santoro, C.: One Model, Many Interfaces. In: Proceedings of CADUI 2002, Valenciennes, France (2002)

[5] Sinnig, D., Forbrig, P., Seffah, A.: Patterns in Model-Based Development. In: Workshop entitled. Software and Usability Cross-Pollination: The Role of Usability Patterns Switzerland (2003)

[6] Bastide, R., Basnyat, S.: Error Patterns: Systematic Investigation of Deviations in Task Models. In: Coninx, K., Luyten, K., Schneider, K.A. (eds.) TAMODIA 2006. LNCS, vol. 4385, pp. 109–122. Springer, Heidelberg (2007)

[7] Card, S., Moran, T.P., Newell, A.: The Psychology of Human Computer Interaction. (1983)

[8] Veer, G., Lenting, B., Bergevoet, B.: GTA: Groupware Task Analysis - Modeling Complexity. Acta Psychologica, 91, 297–332 (1996)

[9] Annett, J., Duncan, K.D.: Task Analysis and Training Design. Journal of Occupational Psychology 41, 211–221 (1967)

[10] Paternó, F.: Model-Based Design and Evaluation of Interactive Applications. Springer, Heidelberg (2000)

[11] Mori, G., Paternó, F., Santoro, C.: CTTE: Support for Developing and Analyzing Task Models for Interactive System Design. IEEE Trans. Softw. Eng. 28, 797–813 (2002)

[12] ISO_8807, Information Process Systems - Open Systems Interconnection - LOTOS- A Formal Description Based on Temporal Ordering of Observational Behaviour (1988)

[13] Klug, T., Kangasharju, J.: Executable task models, chapter In: Proceedings of international workshop on Task models and diagrams, pp. 119–122. Gdansk, Poland (2005)

[14] Dittmar, A., Forbrig, P., Heftberger, S., Stary, C.: Support for Task Modeling - A "Constructive" Exploration. In: Bastide, R., Palanque, P., Roth, J. (eds.) Engineering Human Computer Interaction and Interactive Systems. LNCS, vol. 3425, pp. 59–76. Springer, Heidelberg (2005)

[15] Luyten, K.: Dynamic User Interface Generation for Mobile and Embedded Systems with Model-Based User Interface Development, PhD Thesis in University Limburg (2004)

[16] Forbrig, P., Dittmar, A., Müller, A.: Adaptive Task Modelling: From Formal Models to XML Representations, chapter in Multiple User Interfaces, pp. 169-192

[17] Sinnig, D., Chalin, P., Khendek, F.: Consistency between Task Models and Use Cases. In: Proceedings DSV-IS 2007, Salamanca, Spain (2007)

[18] Cockburn, A.: Writing Effective Use Cases. Addison-Wesley, Boston (2001)

[19] Patterson, D., Liao, L., Fox, D., Kautz, H.: Inferring High-level Behavior from Low-Level Sensors. In: Dey, A.K., Schmidt, A., McCarthy, J.F. (eds.) UbiComp 2003. LNCS, vol. 2864, Springer, Heidelberg (2003)

[20] Franklin, D., Budzik, J., Hammond, K.: Plan-based Interfaces: Keeping Track of User Tasks and Acting to Cooperate. In: Proceedings of IUI 2007, New York, pp. 79–86 (2002)

[21] UML, Unified Modeling Language: Superstructure [Internet] (last Update: 2004) (accessed June 2007), Available from: http://www.omg.org/docs/formal/05-07-04.pdf

Towards Developing Task-Based Models of Creativity

Hilary Johnson[1] and Lucy Carruthers[2]

[1] HCI Laboratory, Department of Computer Science, University of Bath, Claverton Down,
Bath, BA2 7AY, UK
H.Johnson@bath.ac.uk
[2] Foviance, 14 Bonhill St, London, EC2A 4BX, UK
Lucy.Carruthers@foviance.com

Abstract. Modelling creative tasks is a complex activity, yet comprehensive models are needed in order to better understand creativity, and the process of generating creative artefacts. Research on creativity, and how to design useful, usable and engaging creativity support tools, has been one focus of HCI in the last decade. In the present paper we briefly overview selective models of creativity, and distinguish between them on a number of factors. We then outline problems in modelling creative processes in general, and in attempting to create relationships and correspondences between current creativity modelling approaches, in particular. Finally, we consider the role an analytical structure, and task-based models, might play in advancing the state of the art.

Keywords: Creativity, task modelling, Task Knowledge Structures (TKS).

1 Introduction

There are a number of reasons why it is important to develop user interfaces and systems that both enhance, and provide informed and principled support for creativity, and creative processes. One reason is wealth creation. Both industry and governments are conscious of the need for creativity and innovation in our daily lives – and creative products sell. A further reason is that creative problem solutions and the resulting products typically involve pleasure and surprise, humour and fun, and thereby improve the quality of life. Moreover, studying the nature of creativity underpins a primary motivation to generate more creative artefacts. In order to achieve this goal, it is necessary to identify theories, methods and tools across disciplines to provide both a multidisciplinary and interdisciplinary perspective. If this goal were to be achieved then this would serve as a potential leading edge for design, *providing that technological support for creativity is well designed. Thus the role for HCI is paramount.*

There is an opportunity to go beyond the current situation by exploiting the best aspects of research in the different disciplines, but there are also obstacles to advancing the state of the art. Different foci, concepts, semantics and language - terms, labels, and connotations, make working across disciplines a challenge. Additionally, modelling creativity is complex due to the assumed 'magical' or 'creation out of nothing' characteristic that is frequently referred to in communication

M. Winckler, H. Johnson, and P. Palanque (Eds.): TAMODIA 2007, LNCS 4849, pp. 56–69, 2007.

about creativity, but which actually may not be reflected in either reality, or in the activities engaged in.

Creativity has a long history of being modelled, therefore making sense of the *status* of the different models can only be a long-term goal. It would indeed provide a significant new contribution to the literature to be able to relate the different models with respect to the phenomena modelled, and the uses to which the resulting models are put. The focus of the research we are currently undertaking is to understand the different models that exist within and across disciplines, relate those models by identifying commonalities and differences, and finally, identify and overcome what might constitute gaps in the research.

Consequently, we are pursuing both long-term and short-term goals. The long term research goals are to:-

i) identify the different cognitive and behavioural structures, mechanisms and processes of creativity for both individuals and groups across a range of tasks, within different contexts and with different resources, opportunities and constraints;

ii) establish a way of conceptualizing or framing the different models and the mappings between them – this means developing an analytical structure which represents the cognitive and behavioural constituents outlined in i);

iii) consider how current models of creativity relate to the proposed analytical structure;

iv) investigate the role task models might play in providing further understanding and explanation of creative activities; and,

v) investigate the role task models might play in informing creativity support tool design.

Our short-term goals for this paper, given space brevity, are to outline selective models of creativity, distinguish between them, and briefly consider how they can be related. Additionally, the inherent problems experienced in both engaging in this activity, and in applying some of the models, will be outlined. We will then consider the potential benefits and the role task-based models, with a theoretical underpinning, (in this case, Task Knowledge Structures [8]), might play in advancing the state of the art.

The paper is structured as follows: Section 2 selectively reviews models of creativity; Section 3 makes distinctions between various models and outlines problems with modelling in general, in this area. This section also discusses the problems in relating the different models discussed in the paper, and in their application. Section 4 presents a proposal for moving research forward, and the role task-based models of creative tasks might play in this endeavour. Section 5 concludes the paper.

2 Models of Creativity and Creative Processes

There are a plethora of models related to creativity, and creative processes. As an illustration of the magnitude of the problem inherent in reviewing models of creativity we would refer the reader to Sternberg et al, [16]. These authors provide an excellent taxonomy just of the models existing with a psychological foci – these include mystical, pragmatic, psychodynamic, psychometric, cognitive, social-personality and social-cognitive, evolutionary and confluence approaches. Given the extensive literature we are not able to review all approaches in this paper, a more comprehensive review can be found in [6]. Consequently, in this section our goal is to briefly refer to a number of models of creativity and creative processes which are well-known, acknowledged and frequently cited.

The creative process has a long history of being modelled as a series of stages. In 1926, Wallas [17] outlined a model incorporating four creative stages: preparation, incubation, illumination, and verification. The preparation stage involves understanding the problem, and searching for solutions through exploration of conceptual spaces, (see also [2]). The preparation stage is considered to involve 'hard work' and is followed by a more relaxed stage of 'incubation' where people filter information from conscious awareness to the subconscious to be used for creative insight. Creative insight is thought to come in the illumination stage. Tentative solutions which evolved during the illumination stage are then subjected to a verification phase that involves testing, elaborating and developing.

Whilst Wallas's model is still widely cited, the stages have frequently been modified. Kneller [9] introduced a stage before preparation called 'first insight'. Yet other researchers describe the creative process as a generative brainstorming stage followed by an evaluative focusing stage ([4]; [5]).

The stages however are neither as separate nor sequential as some creative process models seem to suggest, but are interdependent and iterative. For example, idea evaluation frequently leads to reformulation of the initial problem, making the process cyclical [5]. Similarly, [10] defines creativity as a cycle of re-representations used for conceptual exploration.

One often-cited model, is provided by [1]. She proposed the following stages as being involved in individual creative processes:

(1) Problem or task presentation
    The task may be one generated by the individual (internally presented) or one presented to the individual (externally presented).
(2) Preparation
    The individual builds or recalls information and solution approaches relevant to the task at hand.
(3) Response Generation
    Alternatives are produced.
(4) Response Validation
    Alternatives are evaluated.
(5) Outcome
    Process terminated with successful outcome, or
    Process terminated in failure with no acceptable solution produced, or
    Individual concludes that some progress has been made and loops back to an earlier step in the model.

This model has provided the basis for research in other disciplines, contexts and spheres of influence.

There are also creative process models within HCI that build upon previous models, such as that of [17]. Shneiderman [15], for example offers a four-phase creativity framework that builds on past models but also departs from them by incorporating some 'social' aspects of creativity. These social aspects relate principally to consultation with peers and dissemination of results. The genex (generator of excellence) proposal consists of four phases:

Collect: Learn from previous works stored in libraries, the web etc;
Relate: Consult with peers and mentors at early, middle and late stages;
Create: Explore, compose, and evaluate possible solutions;
Donate: Disseminate the results.

The four phases are not intended as purely sequential, but as iterative. Shneiderman [15] then proposes eight activities that could be supported by computer tools that occur during the genex phases.

1.   Searching and browsing digital libraries
Searching libraries or other resources accelerates collection of information about previous work. Users may also need to search in order to find consultants, or to decide on candidate communities for disseminating results.

2.   Consulting with peers and mentors
Consultation tools start with email, chat, and instant messenger. However, specialised forms of exchange are needed that guide participants to clarify requests while ensuring credit for and protecting new ideas.

3.   Visualising data and processes
Drawing mental or concept maps of current knowledge helps users organise their knowledge, perceive relationships, identify outliers, recognise clusters, and identify missing elements.

4.   Thinking by free associations
Provide tools that support creative thinking (e.g., brainstorming and lateral thinking) and help people break free from their current mindset.

5.   Exploring solutions – "what if" tools
Enable creative exploration and experimentation to view the implications of decisions and perceive complex relationships.

6.   Composing artefacts and performances
Composition tools include word processors, elaborate music editing programmes, graphics composition tools, slide presentations, and photo editing tools.

7.   Reviewing and replaying session histories
History-keeping is the capacity to record activities, review them, and save for future use. This will allow users to return to previous steps, edit, store frequent patterns of use, and replay histories.

8.   Disseminating results
Finally, when users create something they like, they need to disseminate it. This could include e-mailing to a select group, to all the people whose work was influential and to people who had visited the same websites as they had. Users could create a web page and add entries for others to explore.

The 'Collect, Relate, Create, Donate', creative phases could be accomplished by repeated applications of the eight activities [14] represented below. These eight activities could be further subdivided and could occur during any phase.

GENEX PHASE	PRIMARY ACTIVITY (but can be used in any phase)
Collect	Searching and browsing digital libraries Visualising data and processes
Relate	Consulting with peers and mentors
Create	Thinking by free associations Exploring solutions – what if tools Composing artefacts and performances Reviewing and replaying session histories
Donate	Disseminating results

Fig. 1. Genex phases and the eight iterative activities typically occurring within them

Shneiderman advocates that supporting these eight activities by appropriately designed software and computer tools could greatly facilitate creativity.

Another influential approach, although not widely cited in HCI, is that of Schön. According to [12,13] some activities such as reflection underpin and occur throughout the entire process. He describes the reflective nature of the conversation between the designer and the 'artefact' as a transaction. 'Seeing-drawing-seeing' is one example of a reflective conversation – the designer sees what is there, draws in relation to it, sees what is drawn, which then informs further design. The designer constructs meaning, identifies patterns and gives them 'meaning beyond themselves'.

A designer designs by utilising her/his repertoire of examples, images, understandings and actions from existing knowledge. Making sense of a new situation, means using 'something already present in her/his repertoire'. To see this example as 'that one' means assessing the similarity and difference between the new and the familiar, and this whole process of seeing-as and doing-as may proceed without conscious articulation. The process of creative design ceases when the designer appreciates that a change has resulted in the situation being improved, and given new meaning.

Schön [12] argued that a computer could enable the simulation of a designer's transactions with the design situation by reproducing the following creative process features:-

- the designer's seeing-moving-seeing;
- the construction of figures from marks on a page;

- the appreciation of design qualities;
- the evolution of design intentions in the course of the design process, new design problems being set for solution;
- the recognition of unintended consequences of move experiments;
- the storage and deployment of prototypes, with them being placed in transaction with the design situation; and
- communication across divergent design worlds.

In [6] we extended this model to represent group reflection in collaborative creative tasks, and as a consequence added the following functions that needed *to be supported* to Schön's list:-

- individual, joint, shared and group evaluation;
- individual, joint, shared and group moves and experiments;
- local (individual team members or subset of team members) and global (all team members) reflection and evaluation;
- individual and group design transactions;
- sharing the repertoire of group members;
- different intensities of collaboration in relation to reflection and evaluation;
- alternative means by which talk-back can occur with respect to task context and group composition;
- provide early previews of group solutions.

This is clearly not an exhaustive list and is an initial step in considering how group reflection of creative tasks could be supported. These features necessarily need to be elaborated to incorporate CSCW and HCI requirements for groupware.

In this section we have very briefly referred to models of creativity and creative processes from psychological, HCI and architectural/design perspectives. These instances will demonstrate the difficulty of relating and making correspondences between the different approaches and models. However, it is necessary to establish these relationships and mappings given the divergent sets of requirements generated for supporting creative processes. The next section describes distinctions between a selection of the models referred to in this section, and notes the problems in applying the models.

3   Model Distinctions, and Problems Applying Creative Process Models

For the purposes of this paper the models can be primarily distinguished on the different levels of abstraction, and generality, of the phenomena modelled. Some high-level models describe general psychological capabilities such as reflection [13,14], re-representation and hypothesis testing [10], not limited to creativity. Other models describe rather more specific aspects of creative stages, such as the activities of reviewing alternatives [1], whilst yet others describe general processes of disseminating results [15]. Some of these are high-level phenomena occurring in everyday life. Others, whilst not exclusive to creativity are found particularly frequently in creative processes. Another class of phenomena include the lower level activities not exclusive to creativity which might be considered 'uncreative' but necessary, such as the dissemination of results.

In documenting the different models and approaches it is clear that any one multistage model or approach is insufficient to provide a reasonably accurate representation of creative processes. It is therefore important to devise a means by which to relate the models. This is necessary in order that there is some understanding at different levels of abstraction about what explanatory power each model pertains for explaining different aspects of creative 'behaviour'. For instance, for a particular creative scenario or task, there needs to be an explanation encompassing high-level cognitive processes, how these are harnessed in undertaking the specific creative activities during the task, and the actual behaviour which is observable, (the gestures, utterances, etc. that are associated with that behaviour).

In outlining the problems that modellers and models face, we will adopt both a theoretical and an empirical perspective. The theoretical perspective will highlight, as a result of our understanding of the research from different disciplines, high-level issues to be addressed by modellers of creative processes. On the other hand, the empirical perspective has involved undertaking extensive empirical studies of creative activities and tasks, and applying creative process models to those. These tasks have included musical composition, story development, writing poems, and designing posters, for example.

The theoretical problems we have identified with some of the models include:-

i)   models being little more than superficial generalizations of stages of problem solving;

ii)   models merely labelling or describing procedures within activities, thus affording no prescriptive, predictive or explanatory power. This means any attempt to rationalise improvements on past models is flawed;

iii)   models include activities which may or may not be creative in themselves, without any consideration of the relationship of these to 'creative' activities, and a creative process in general;

iv)   models are frequently not exhaustive, which is not a problem in itself as long as this is recognized, the scope is clearly defined and other complementary models are suggested to overcome the deficiencies;

v)   with respect to iteration - the stage or phases of models are not specified in enough detail to understand what the function of iteration might be. Why are previous activities returned to? What is needed is some understanding or exposition of the causal relationships persisting between the stages;

vi)   there needs to be a better attempt to identify the cognitive structures, mechanisms, resources and behaviour to be utilized in the modelling approach, or in the actual creative episode, activity or task.

There are also a number of issues that have arisen as a result of our application of existing creative process models. In this paper we will highlight problems experienced in applying models to the results of a small-scale study that involved two dissimilar tasks in two distinct domains, with different types of support, [3]. As a consequence of this research, it is clear that three issues of importance need to be addressed by creative process modellers.

The first issue is concerned with devising a means to perceive and interpret, through whatever means, the creative activities and thought processes of study participants. This is not just an issue for creativity and HCI, but also for the behavioural sciences, and consequently there is a relevant literature with the possibility of exploitation.

The second issue is to understand and map the different levels of abstraction within and between models. For example, there is a difference between the generic 'Consult' phase of [15], and the 'more cognitive' phase of 'thinking by free association' and also the 'Response Generation' phase of [1]. Currently differences in level of abstraction are not attended to, but are important when considering tool support.

The third issue relates to mapping observed or reported activities and processes to model stages. Shneiderman [15] has made a very real effort to achieve this in his genex framework.

However, there are a number of sub-issues related to any mapping process:

i)   some activities occur but are frequently not modelled;
ii) stages need to be appropriately labelled, with the chosen labels matching their descriptions and clearly indicating the scope of the stage;
iii) better descriptions and exemplifications of the stages are necessary to avoid under and over-interpretation;
iv) a means to identify on-going, cyclical, iterative, and once-only activities needs to be developed;
v)   the 'same' activities occurring in a number of different stages need to be identified, and whether they have different semantics in each of the activities in which they appear, needs to be modelled;
vi) interdependencies between stages needs outlining;
vii) the 'intensity' of the activities, and the resources expended needs to be modelled.

It is obvious that developing modelling approaches that take account of the theoretical and empirical issues outlined in this section, is a long-term commitment. A first step to achieve this goal is to develop an analytical structure that provides a framework for relating phenomena to models, models to each another, and the mappings between them.

A complementary but different step is to consider the benefits of developing a task-based model of the creative process that builds on current theoretical approaches to task modelling. In the next section we briefly outline the beginnings of an analytical structure for relating models, and discuss the potential benefits of constructing task-based creative process models.

4 An Analytical Structure and Task-Based Models of Creative Activities

4.1 An Initial Analytical Structure

As previously indicated in Section 3, different creative process models represent different phenomena and processes undertaken in developing creative products. The purpose of devising an analytical structure is to provide an early view as to the different levels of abstraction in the models, to situate the models within this space, and to identify gaps in the research.

In this paper we will outline an initial version of this analytical structure. It is important to note that this version of the framework has benefitted from our wide range of studies in different creative domains, and the research undertaken as part of the Designing for the 21st Century creativity cluster involving 26 different disciplines including ten artists from different perspectives. However, it is clear that either more levels or more comprehensive levels will be needed than are presently outlined, and top down theoretical, and bottom up empirical research will both contribute to framework validation, and to the next version of this structure. Therefore, we are currently making no claims about how complete or coherent the structure is, rather we are using the structure to cause us to ask interesting research questions about what each model is representing, and what it contributes to our understanding of either cognitive resources, tasks, activities or actual observable behaviour. Furthermore, the framework will allow us to make judgements about the potential contribution to the state of the art of any future modelling approaches.

The framework itself is not testable but the theories developed within the framework are testable by empirical means. Currently, the analytical structure consists of four layers; cognitive, task, activity and behaviour layers. We are assuming perception has already occurred. The cognitive level consists of psychological structures, mechanisms and processes, and encompasses the ability for example, to problem solve, reflect, decision-make, and so forth. The task layer represents the goal(s) of the activity – e.g. write a poem. The activity layer represents the units of activity, or activities which correspond to Pinelle and Gutwin's [11] taskwork or teamwork mechanics. In the case of individual tasks an activity relevant to creativity might be 'generate ideas', or in the case of collaborative creativity (teamwork mechanics), an example might be 'co-ordinate actions'. The behaviour layer constitutes the low level reported or observed actions which include manipulation of artefacts, for example, drawing, typing, sorting, and communication through whatever implicit or explicit means, for example, utterances, gestures and body language. This is summarized below:-

1. **Cognitive layer** - psychological structures and processes, and abilities, e.g. problem solve, reflect, decision make.
2. **Task layer** - the goal(s) of the activity, e.g. write a poem.
3. **Activity layer** units of activity, e.g. generate ideas, or mechanics, e.g. co-ordinate actions.
4. **Behaviour layer** - low level reported or observed actions.

In addition, there are mappings between these layers, which we have yet to fully develop theoretically, and identify empirically within our existing range of case studies. This will include both top down and bottom up research activities. It is important to do this in order that we can produce more than rich descriptions of behaviour. Explicitly, we are claiming that stipulating the nature of the mappings allows us to generate prescriptions, predictions and explanations that currently do not exist. Once the mappings are fully developed, by observing aspects of behaviour we will be able to traverse through the layers of the analytical structure, enabling us to identify goals and furnish rationales for implicit and explicit behaviour, and also make assumptions about the cognitive activities needing to be supported for goals to be accomplished. Eventually, this will provide a well-informed and principled means to develop creativity support tools.

Attempting to fit current creative process models within this analytical structure is the next step. However, this is a complex undertaking because some models only have representation at one layer whilst others clearly exist at two or three, but not all, layers. Moreover, some modellers emphasize either higher or lower level layers that clearly have implicit relationships, often not postulated, with other layers.

Taking specific examples, 'reflection', as in Schön's [12,13] model fits within the cognitive layer, whilst the activities of designing, and possibly seeing-as and seeing-that within this model fit within the activity layer. Boden's [2] work on conceptual spaces fits within the cognitive layer, but there are clear implications for behaviour. Amabile's [1] model of developing alternatives fits within the activity layer but has implications for problem solving and reflection at the cognitive level, and so on.

Finally, Shneiderman's [15] Collect, Relate, Create, Donate creative phases exist at a number of levels. Collect and Create are activities within the activity layer with appropriate behaviour at the behavioural layer. The Relate and Donate phases include modelling at the task and behaviour levels. However, it is clear that these two phases also have some social, cultural function within the field or domain, which needs to be taken into account in the next version of the analytical structure that will also accommodate collaborative creativity.

An initial and possibly cursory analysis of the fit of models within the analytical structure has suggested to us the paucity of research explicitly discussing purposes, needs, and goals and how these might be fulfilled. Specifically, as discussed in section 3 we have found very few attempts to model the causal links between activities and behaviour that demonstrates priming, cueing, or following on relationships. One possible conclusion is that the task layer for most creative models either does not exist, is not specified in enough detail, or the mappings between this and the other layers are not sufficiently defined to be able to derive any conclusions about what creative 'performers' intended to do, what they will do next, and why. Basically we do not know the derivation of activities and/or behaviours.

A model at the task layer needs to be able to understand when, how and why activities occur, the nature of the causal relationships, and the enabling and resultant states.

One solution is to construct task-based models of the creative process and then objectively assess whether they provide any explanatory purchase. In the next section we briefly consider the benefits of constructing task-based creative process models and consider what might be gained by building TKS models of creative tasks.

4.2 A Task-Based Model of Creative Activities

In the previous section we argued that one possible benefit to constructing task-based models is the potential ability to understand when, how and why activities occur, the nature of the causal relationships, and the enabling and resultant states.

A further benefit is that task models have been used effectively in the past for representing task knowledge and execution, generating requirements and design solutions for everyday simple and complex tasks, supported by technology. Consequently, we believe developing task models will provide a pivotal role in informing the design of computer-based creativity support tools.

Finally, there is a role for task-based models not only in informing design, but also in exploiting the existing theoretical underpinnings. TKS is one of many task modelling approaches benefitting from a theoretical foundation. One question to address is how does it relate to the analytical structure?

The analytical structure's cognitive layer consists of psychological structures, mechanisms and processes. For instance, in the case of memory, the cognitive level consists of knowledge structures and processes associated with learning through experience and undertaking tasks and activities. These processes include acquisition, modifying, categorizing and re-structuring, and retrieving knowledge. This knowledge is represented in either Fundamental Knowledge Structures (FKS, see [7]) or Task Knowledge Structures (TKS, see Figure 2).

FKS represent fundamental psychological knowledge, abilities, and processes that are general, high-level and occur across all tasks and behaviour. These include for example, collaboration, communication and explanation; hypothesizing and problem solving; representation, re-representation, reflection and evaluation; decision-making and risk assessment, and so on. They are fundamental in the sense that they are necessary for the successful functioning of humans in their everyday lives. TKS by contrast represent lower level, task-specific knowledge structures, abilities and processes that relate to specific tasks, such as designing posters, or writing poems.

In the case of creativity, a subset of appropriate FKS knowledge would be recruited in order to problem solve, reflect on solutions, and make decisions about which solution(s) to pursue. In collaborative creativity, the FKS for collaboration [7] would also be instantiated.

At the task layer, the TKS would represent the following knowledge:-

i)   categorization of task artefacts;
ii) structure in tasks – central/important, high priority and typical concepts and activities;
iii) causal relationships between task objects leading to cueing, priming or follow-on task behaviour, and supporting principles of categorical structuring and procedural dependency;
iv) roles; goals; plans within different contexts; current, enabling, conditional, and desired states; strategies; procedures; actions and objects.

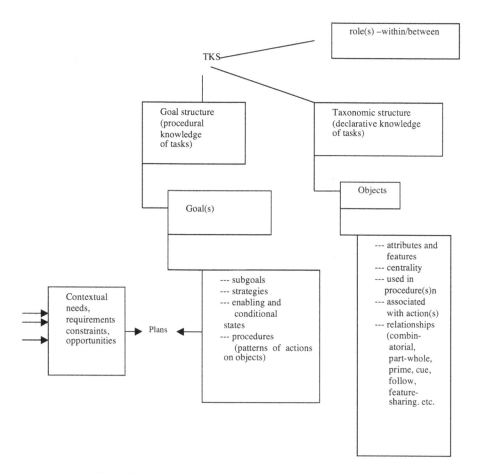

Fig. 2. Knowledge represented in Task Knowledge Structures

It is likely that each of the above elements exist in creative tasks as they do in other everyday simple and complex tasks. As an example related to i) above, in recent funded research, artists in an artist's forum recounted the role categorization, in the form of snippets, photographs, videos, etc. plays in creative inspiration. Therefore, supporting the categorization processes of organizing, storing and re-organising this material effectively, has implications for generating creative ideas and solutions, thus facilitating creative insight and inspiration.

Again, in the case of creativity, there is likely to be central and typical elements of creative artefacts that need to be preserved and which dictate how the task is structured and organised.

In considering the activity layer, this would be comprised of the different task procedures, and the action-object couplings for individual creativity, and collaboration mechanics from [11] if collaborative. Finally, the behavioural layer would include the low level behaviours such as typing, drawing and so on – this is presently not part of TKS and therefore it may be necessary to undertake modifications to the modelling approach.

Current research is developing TKS models of various creative tasks across domains and in different contexts, with different types of resources. The results will be analysed in the light of the analytical structure proposed in section 4.1 and with the aim of providing explanations of creative processes and advancing the state of the art.

5 Conclusion

In this paper we have referred to selective creative process models, and made attempts to relate and apply the models. Theoretical and empirical issues related to modelling creative tasks, such that we are in a position to move beyond description to explanation of activities, have been discussed.

In section 4.1 we outlined an initial analytical structure that represents different levels of abstraction, and provides a means to relate different models.

Finally, we briefly consider aspects of TKS that might constitute a task-based model of creative tasks. A future research agenda includes further development of the analytical structure and its application.

Acknowledgements

We are grateful to the participants of the workshops undertaken as part of the creativity in design cluster.

We are also grateful to AHRC/EPSRC who funded the 'Designing for the 21st century: Enhancing and Supporting Group Creativity in Design' research cluster.

References

1. Amabile, T.M.: The Social Psychology of Creativity. Springer, New York (1983)
2. Boden, M.A.: The Creative Mind: Myths and Mechanisms, Weidenfeld and Nicolson: London (1990)
3. Carruthers, L.: Modelling creativity. Tech Report. University of Bath (2004)
4. Dartnell, T.: Artificial Intelligence and Creativity: An introduction. Artificial Intelligence and the Simulation of Intelligence Quarterly 85 (1993)
5. Dennett, D.: Brainstorms: Philosophical Essays on Mind and Psychology. Harvester Press (1978)
6. Johnson, H., Carruthers, L.: Supporting creative and reflective processes. International Journal of Human Computer Studies 64(10), 998–1030 (2006)
7. Johnson, H., Hyde, J.K.: Towards modelling individual and collaborative construction of jigsaws using Task Knowledge Structures (TKS). Transactions on Computer Human Interaction. December 10(4), 339–387 (2003)
8. Johnson, H., Johnson, P.: Task Knowledge Structures: Psychological basis and integration into system design. Acta Psychologica 78, 3–26 (1991)
9. Kneller, G.F.: The Art and Science of Creativity, Holt Rinehart and Winston, New York (1965)

10. Oxman, R.: Design by re-representation: a model of visual reasoning in design. Design Studies 18, 329–347 (1997)
11. Pinelle, D., Gutwin, C.: Group Task Analysis for Groupware Usability Evaluations. In: Proc. IEEE WetIce 2001, IEEE Computer Society Press, Los Alamitos (2001)
12. Schön, D.: The reflective practitioner: How professionals think in action. Basic books, New York (1983)
13. Schön., D.: Designing as reflective conversation with the materials of a design situation. Knowledge based systems 5(3) (1992)
14. Shneiderman, B.: Codex, memex, genex: The pursuit of transformational technologies. Int. J. Hum-Comput. Interact. 10(2), 87–106 (1998)
15. Shneiderman, B.: User Interfaces for supporting innovation. ACM Trans. on Computer-Human Interaction 7(1), 114–138 (2000)
16. Sternberg, R.J., Lubart, T., Kaufman, J.C., Pretz, J.E.: Creativity. In: Cambridge Handbook of Thinking and Reasoning, pp. 351–369 (2005)
17. Wallas, G.: The Art of Thought. Harcourt Brace: New York (1926)

Articulating Interaction and Task Models for the Design of Advanced Interactive Systems

Syrine Charfi, Emmanuel Dubois, and Remi Bastide

LIIHS – IRIT
118 Route de Narbonne, F-31062 Toulouse cedex 9, France
{charfi, emmanuel.dubois, bastide}@irit.fr

Abstract. Mixed Interactive Systems (MIS) is a generic term encompassing mixed and augmented reality, augmented virtuality, and tangible interfaces systems. The work we present in this paper deals with the design of such systems. Several models have been proposed to describe mixed interactive systems. However, these models neither integrate MIS in the global user activity, nor take into account the dynamics of mixed interactive situations. Task models offer an interesting approach to cover these aspects. The purpose of our work is to contribute to the design of MIS by articulating mixed interaction models and tasks models. This paper presents complementarities and common points between these models, which will be used as the basis for the rules to articulate the task and interaction models.

Keywords: Mixed interactive system, design, mixed interaction models, task models, model driven engineering.

1 Introduction

Mixed Interactive Systems (MIS) constitute an advanced form of interactive systems and result from the fusion of the physical world and the digital world, thus gathering mixed and augmented reality, augmented virtuality, and tangible user interfaces systems [1]. Because of this fusion, multiple objects take part in the user task. Furthermore, the continuous use of digital and physical objects has an impact on the interaction and its dynamic, thus creating new issues in terms of design.

Developing a design process suitable for MIS is an issue for HCI research. To enrich the design approaches dedicated to MIS, we are interested in two complementary design aspects: (1) the description of the global user activity and dynamics aspects of mixed interactive situations; (2) the description of mixed interaction in a way that takes into account the heterogeneity and richness of MIS. These two elements are already partly addressed by specific models such as sequence diagrams or task models for the former, and class diagrams or mixed interaction models for the latter.

The goal of our work is to explore and characterize the articulation of task models with mixed interaction model to contribute to the development of a MIS design process, following a Model Driven Engineering (MDE) approach. For this, we

M. Winckler, H. Johnson, and P. Palanque (Eds.): TAMODIA 2007, LNCS 4849, pp. 70–83, 2007.
© Springer-Verlag Berlin Heidelberg 2007

initially chose a notation of each model: K-MAD for task modelling and ASUR for mixed interaction modelling.

In this paper, we present an illustrative case study RAPACE, an interactive prototype dedicated to be exhibited in a museum of natural history. Then, we position our work according to different design steps of MIS, we briefly introduce the two notations we selected and finally, we present a first set of articulation rules between K-MAD [2] and ASUR [3].

2 Illustrative Case Study

Our case study is a MIS prototype intended to teach cladistics in an interactive way [4]. Cladistics is a philosophy of animal species classification that arranges species according to the evolution of their common ancestral criteria and not by their morphological similarity. Species are then represented in a tree called cladogram. In a cladogram, all species lie at the leaves, and each inner node is the point from which a criteria has evolved.

An educational software based on the WIMP paradigm and coded in Director was initially intended to be used as an interactive exhibition in the museum of natural history. The application is based on a pedagogic method to teach cladistics: the animals are presented by group of three, a reference animal and two comparison animals. The common criteria of the animals are listed and the cladogram, a hierarchical tree representation, structures the result of these comparisons. This approach constitutes an original core to transmit contents in a museal context. But this first prototype does not support an easy explanation of the resulting cladogram, nor does it offer much flexibility such as changing the comparison order. A second prototype has been developed to better support this interactivity. And in order to better integrate the exhibit in the museum, the use of mixed interaction technique has been chosen.

Our case study is based on this second prototype. The user handles physical pictures of animals, an information tool and an insertion tool (Fig. 1 bottom left). To compare two animals, the user brings close together a picture of each animal (Fig. 1 top left). Common criteria between the two animals are displayed. The user can also get information about an animal by bringing close together the picture and the information tool. Finally, the user can insert an animal in the cladogram (Fig. 1 right) either automatically or manually. To insert automatically, the user brings the picture close to the insertion tool. To insert manually, the user choose a node in the cladogram in which he wants to insert the animal. He then turns the picture in front of the node with a movement analogue to screwing. The animal is inserted in the cladogram displayed.

The localisation of the pictures is based on video tracking and marker recognition [5]: a camera tracks markers associated to pictures. The system identifies markers, and two video projectors display respectively the cladogram and the information and comparison results.

We present in the next section our design process and our approach based on metamodels.

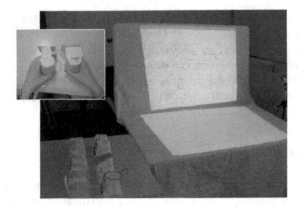

Fig. 1. Projection of the cladogram on the vertical stand, projection of results on the horizontal stand and pictures of animals ready to be used on the left

3 From MDE to Metamodels

This work is in line with the Model Driven Engineering (MDE) approach, by relating notations at the metamodel level. As illustrated in Fig. 2, the design process of MIS can be defined into four levels: the requirement and task analysis, the interaction design, the software design and the implementation. Several models are necessary to cover these four different steps of MIS design and there is so far a lack of means to relay the results from one step to the following. A previous work was already done proposing a link between the interaction design and the software design with ASUR-IL [6]. In this paper we focus on the link between the task analysis step and the interaction design step. The goal of our work is to realise the loop of the Task Analysis, Interaction Design, Refining and Verifying Coherence. A notation used in each step has been chosen, K-MAD for the requirement and task analysis and ASUR for the interaction design. In the following we study metamodels of each notation and establish rules of articulation between the models.

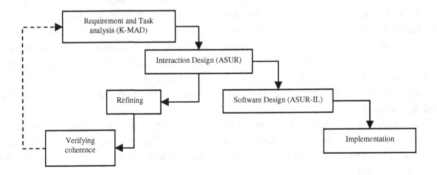

Fig. 2. MIS design process

3.1 Strategy

Our articulating of a task model and a mixed interaction model is based on the K-MAD and ASUR notations. The task model describes the activity on a higher level than the interaction model since it does not describe the interaction.

3.1.1 Task Model K-MAD

To introduce the K-MAD notation [2], we consider one task of our case study: "learn cladistics". This task consists in comparing animals (task "compare animals") then inserting them either manually (task "insert manually") or automatically (task "insert automatically") (Fig. 3 right).

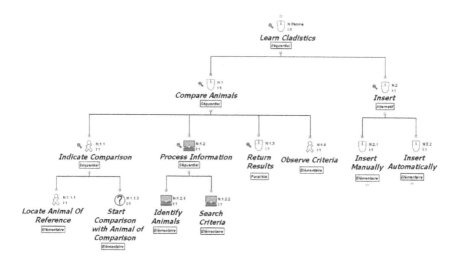

Fig. 3. Task K-MAD "Learn cladistics"

K-MAD (Kernel of Model for Activity Description) is centred on the *task* unit, which can be described according to two aspects, the **decomposition** and the **body**.

1) The **decomposition** of a *task* unit of a given level gives place to several unit tasks of lower level. The decomposition offers *operators* of synchronization, temporal and auxiliary scheduling.

In our example, the task "compare animals" is composed of four subtasks: (1) "indicate comparison" during which the *user* locates the animal of reference and starts the comparison, (2) "process information" during which the *system* identifies the animals and their common criteria, (3) "return results" during which the *system* returns the results of the identification and (4) "observe criteria". Here the temporal scheduling of the decomposed task is described as *sequential*.

2) The **body** supports the characterisation of the *task* and consists of the *core*, the *conditions* and the *state of the world*:

- The *core* gathers a set of textual attributes such as *name, number, priority, goal*, etc: for example, the task "insert" is *number* 2, the task "insert manually" is *number* 2.1 and the task "insert automatically" is *number* 2.2.

- The *conditions* express *pre* and *post-conditions* in a formal way according to a preset grammar: conditions are not required in our case study.
- The *state of the world* allows identifying the various *objects* handled by the *task*: for example, the task "return results" uses the objects animal of reference, animal of comparison and criteria.

K-MAD has his own development environment called K-MADe [7] which has been used to model examples in this paper.

Among the different task modelling approaches, we are particularly interested by those that have been developed to support the design of interactive systems, and not necessarily provides the best support for an in depth analysis of the user-task. We thus focused on CTT [8] and K-MAD that have both editors. Like in CTT, there are different types of *task* and a *task* can use objects. However, K-MAD has its own domain model to describe domain objects. CTT and K-MAD both offer the decomposition of a *task* in tasks of lower level. However, in K-MAD, *operator* of synchronization is an attribute of task unit while in CTT operators are used to link sub tasks.

A concise presentation of this model can be given through its metamodel (Fig. 4). There are three principal concepts in the K-MAD metamodel: the *task*, the *performer* and the *objects*:

- A K-MAD *task* is carried out by a *performer* and uses objects. It can be made up of expressions expressing the constraints: *pre*, *post conditions* and *iterations*. The decomposition is expressed by the attribute *operator* specific to the *task*. A K-MAD *task* is also described by attributes like the *name*, the *number*, the *goal*, etc. It can generate *events* or be generated by events and can belong to a *task-group*.
- The *performer* can be *system*, *unknown* or a *user*. In the latter case the attribute *modality* can be specified as cognitive or motor. A K-MAD *task* is *interactive* when *system* and *user* together perform the *task*. Finally, a K-MAD task can be *abstract*.
- The objects in K-MAD are managed as follows: an abstract object, *object,* has abstract attributes, *attribute*. An instance of an abstract object is a *concrete object* whose *concrete attribute* is an instance of the *abstract attribute*. Each *concrete object* belongs to a group of objects called in the metamodel *object-group*. The objects in K-MAD are involved in the user activity and can define the conditions, but they are not represented on the K-MAD diagram.

The reasons why we chose K-MAD as a starting point in our work are multiple. First it expresses the development of the tasks on a "macro" level. Indeed, it describes two kinds of temporal relations between a parent task and its subtasks: synchronization (parallel, sequential, simultaneous) and scheduling (and, or, alternate). K-MAD also describes the development of a *task* on a "micro" level, by using some of the temporal *operators* (beginning, end, duration). Moreover, the conditions described in the body of task K-MAD allow describing dynamics and tasks relations with *pre* and *post-condition* described in a formal way. Lastly, the management of the world objects supported in K-MAD allows gathering physical and digital objects and defining an *object*'s state before and after *task* development.

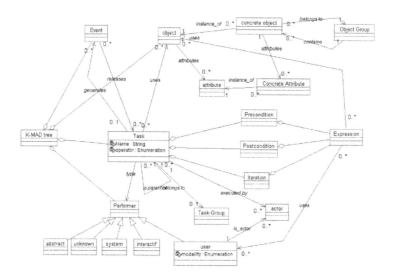

Fig. 4. K-MAD metamodel

3.1.2 Mixed Interaction Model ASUR

ASUR notation (*Adaptor, System, User, Real objects*) [3] adopts a user's interaction point of view on the design of mixed interactive systems. ASUR highlights the key elements that are involved to support the interaction: resources, artefacts and data flows are thus represented. But the dynamic of the combination of these aspects is left out of the ASUR model. To introduce the ASUR notation, we consider the case study, and especially the comparison step. The *user* grabs in hand the picture of the animal of reference and moves it closer to the picture of another animal to perform the comparison and discover the common criteria. The *system* detects the two animals and displays the animals and the common criteria. The corresponding ASUR model is given in Fig. 5.

The first step of the ASUR modelling consists in identifying entities involved in this task:

1) **ASUR Components.** ASUR distinguishes different component types:

- The S_{info}, S_{tool} and S_{object} *components* depict the computer *system*, including computational and storage capabilities and data acquisition and delivery. In our case study the digital animals (animal of reference, animal of comparison and criteria) are three S_{info} Components.
- The *U component* refers to the *user* of the system: the visitor.
- R_{object} and R_{tool} *components* denote physical entities involved when performing the task. R_{object} designates real focus of the *task* such as the animal of reference and, Rt_{ool} plays the role of intermediary entities required to perform the *task*, as animal of comparison or the tool to insert animal in the tree or the lens.
- A_{in} and A_{out} *components* represent *adaptors* conveying data from the physical to the digital world as camera (A_{in}) and video projector (A_{out}).

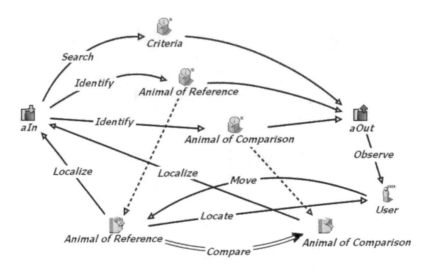

Fig. 5. ASUR modelling of the task "Compare animals"

These components are not autonomous and need to communicate during the task realisation. Such communication is modelled with ASUR relationships.

2) **ASUR Relationships.** We identified three different types of ASUR relationships.

- *Data exchange* (A➔B) means that *component* B may perceive information rendered by *component* A. In our example, the *user* observes the animal of reference (R_{object} ➔ U) and data displayed by the video projector (A_{out}➔U). The camera localizes animal of reference and animal of comparison (R_{object} ➔ A_{in}, R_{tool} ➔ A_{in}), and transmits positions to *system* to identify the animals (S_{info}) and search common criteria (S_{info}). After processing the data, results are sent to the video projector (S_{info} ➔ A_{out}).

- *Trigger* (A⇨B) is always linked to a *data exchange* (C➔D): the data transfer from C to D will only occurs when a specific spatial *condition* is reached between A and B. The *relationship* (A_{in} ➔ S_{info} criteria) occurs when the animal of reference is close to animal of comparison (R_{object} ⇨ R_{tool}). The relation between the trigger and the data exchange that is triggered, is only specified as a trigger property, and is not graphically represented on the ASUR diagram.

- *Physical proximity* (A==B) denotes the physical link that exists between two entities. No such link is used in this model.

3) **ASUR Characteristics.** Additional characteristics are used to refine this modelling:

- *Location* and *perception/action sense* indicate where the *user* has to focus to get the information and through which human sense it is perceivable: *perception* and *action sense* used with animal of reference are *visual* and *physical action*. The *location* is the place where data is projected.

- *Dimension* (1D, 2D, 3D) and *point of view* refine the description of information transfer.

ASUR has his own development environment called Guide-Me [9] which is used to model examples in this paper.

Other mixed interaction notations exist. TAC paradigm [10] and MCPrd [11] architecture describe the elements required in Tangible User Interfaces. Close to ASUR, some notations support the exploration of Mixed Interactive Systems design space [12], [13]: they are based on the identification of artefacts, entities, characteristics and tools relevant to a mixed interactive system. More recent works in mixed interactive systems try to link design and implementation steps by projecting scenarios on software architecture models [14][15] or combining Petri Nets and DWARF components [16].

A concise presentation of the notation can be given through its metamodel (Fig. 6). An ASUR model is composed of *components* and *relationships* to describe a *task*. A *component* can be either a *computer system* - S_{info}, S_{tool}, S_{object} - or a *real entity* - R_{tool}, R_{object} -, or an *adaptor* - A_{in}, A_{out} - or a *user*. Components are connected by relationships. A *relationship* can be either a *data exchange*, a *representation*, a *real association* or a *trigger*.

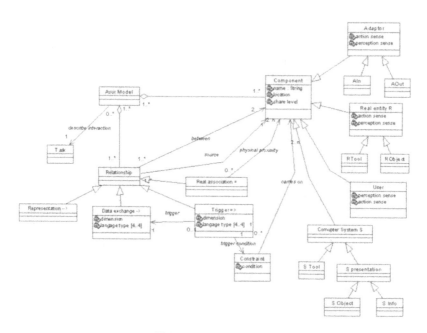

Fig. 6. ASUR Metamodel

The reasons why we chose ASUR are multiple. First, it allows identifying physical and digital entities implied in the task. ASUR notation completes this representation by a detailed description of the role and nature of the entities implied in the interaction, and by identifying a predefine set of types of ASUR *components* and *relationships*. ASUR also contributes to the ergonomic analysis of the system by expressing properties with combinations of characteristics of the components and/or ASUR relationships, as the *perceptual* or *action sense*, *perception place*, *language* etc. It also allows to reason on the interaction independently of all device considerations, by using components such as A_{out} to indicate an *adaptor*, which could be a visual device, sound, haptic…

4 Articulation Between K-MAD and ASUR

We base the presentation of the articulation of K-MAD and ASUR on the metamodels described in the previous section. First, we highlight subsets of the two metamodels that relates to the same concept. Then, we establish articulation rules between subsets of the metamodels.

4.1 Links Between Metamodels

Our study of the two metamodels emphasized articulatory elements between the metamodels: some elements of the metamodel refer to the same concept and constitute direct links of the articulation, while others are specific to each metamodel.

It arises from the analysis of the metamodels that three elements of design are commonly expressed by K-MAD and ASUR: the concept of *task*, *object* and *user*.

L1 The subset of the metamodel gathering *task*, *event* and *task-group* in K-MAD (Fig. 4. left) represents the unit *task* independently of the tree. This subset refers to the same concept than the element *task* of the ASUR metamodel (Fig. 6 left). K-MAD describes the activity of the user in a procedural way, while ASUR describes the interaction of the user with the system for a given task. So K-MAD conveys a global vision of the task while ASUR adopts an atomic vision. An ASUR task thus corresponds either to a K-MAD leaf, or a K-MAD aggregate of subtasks.

L2 The subset of the metamodel gathering the objects in K-MAD, *object, attribute, concrete object, concrete attribute* and *object-group* (Fig. 4 top right) refers to the same concept than the elements *Real Entity* and *Computer System* of the ASUR metamodel (Fig. 6 right). Indeed, K-MAD objects are the domain objects used in the task. Thus, the objects can be physical or digital depending on the conceptual choices. However, the objects are strongly categorised and described in ASUR in a formal way, while K-MAD describes the same objects of the world in a textual way.

L3 The subset in the K-MAD metamodel gathering *user* and *actor* (Fig. 4 bottom right) refers to the same concept than the element *user* of the ASUR metamodel (Fig. 6 right). A user is always required in an ASUR model since the notation describes an interactive task, while in K-MAD a user is only present in user and interactive task. Furthermore, only one user is present in the ASUR models while several actors might be used in K-MAD model.

L4 To a lower extent, we also identify a fourth common element: the subset in the K-MAD metamodel gathering *expression, precondition, postcondition, iteration* (Fig. 4 right) refers to the same concept than the elements *constraint* and *trigger* of the ASUR metamodel (Fig. 6 bottom). The concept carried by these elements is expressing constraints on tasks.

These links constitute a first set of articulation rules that will be useful to study the coherence between a K-MAD model and an associated ASUR model.

There thus remain three elements of the metamodels specific to each metamodel:

- The *performer* is specific to K-MAD (Fig. 4 bottom left) notation: the *performer* does not need to be characterized in ASUR model since with ASUR the task described is always interactive.
- The attribute *operator* and *name* of the *task* are specific to K-MAD (Fig. 4). The *operator* specifies the synchronisation of the tasks. This concept is not used in ASUR which describes an atomic *task*. The *name* is not characterised in ASUR also.
- The *adaptor* is an ASUR *component* (Fig. 6 top right) but is not described as *object* in K-MAD because the goal of K-MAD is not to describe the task at a device level.
- The *relationship* in ASUR (Fig. 6 left) represent the relation between ASUR components and such *relationship* is not represented in K-MAD.

The specific elements of the metamodels will influence the establishing of the additional rules. We present these rules in the following section.

4.2 Studying the Transition from K-MAD to ASUR

As already mentioned K-MAD and ASUR do not share the same design goal and are at different level of abstraction. Thus, arise two essential questions:

- When does the transition from a task model to an interaction model occur, i.e. at which level of modelling should a designer move from K-MAD to ASUR?
- How can the transition from a task model to an interaction model be achieved, i.e. which links can be drawn between elements of K-MAD and ASUR models to facilitate this transition and articulate the two models?

In this section, we first present the rules identifying the level of transition, then the rules of articulation between the subsets or elements of the metamodels (*italic* in the rest of this section).

4.2.1 When Does the Transition to ASUR Occur?

K-MAD describes the *task* in a global way by integrating it in the user activity, while ASUR carries out a description of a specific atomic *task*. The purpose of the study of the border between K-MAD and ASUR is to adapt the type of description according to the level of granularity considered. Since ASUR considers that one *task* involves a unique *user* and a unique *object* of the *task*, we establish here two rules to define this border.

R1   A unique user: to refine the interaction level of a K-MAD description with ASUR, the *user* (Fig. 4 bottom) involved in the K-MAD description must be unique.

R2   A unique task object: to refine the interaction level of a K-MAD description with ASUR, the *object* (Fig. 4 top right) constituting the main focus of the *user* when performing the *task* must be unique.

On the basis of the metamodels, we now need to explain how this transition can be operated with respect to the rules **L1**, **L2**, **L3** and **L4** and by tacking advantages of the richness and complementary of each metamodel.

4.2.2 How Can the Transition to ASUR Be Achieved?

For this purpose we present a set of rules that establish correspondences between an existing K-MAD model and an ASUR model. These rules can be applied to a K-MAD sub-tree, a leaf or a hollow tree, depending on the result of the application of rules R1 and R2 defining the boundaries of the K-MAD model to transform. Their use in a design context would transform a K-MAD tree into an ASUR model or a partial ASUR model i.e. an incomplete ASUR model.

We first present each rule. We then illustrate them on our case study in section 4.3. In the example, both models (K-MAD and ASUR) exist before the application of the rule to explicitly illustrate the effect of the rule. In a design context, the ASUR model would at least partly result from the application of the rule to the K-MAD tree.

Rule associated to the attribute operator of the task in K-MAD

R3   Equivalence of decomposition in K-MAD: the equivalent of a subtask in K-MAD is an ASUR partial model.

In such task, the equivalences in ASUR of the K-MAD elements involved are as follow:

R3.1 The *name* of a K-MAD *task* is the set of values of the attribute *name* and/or the meaning of the *relationship* between the ASUR components. These elements of the metamodels express in different ways the goal of the task.

Rule associated to objects in K-MAD

R4   Equivalence of objects in K-MAD: the equivalent of an *object* used in K-MAD is a physical and/or digital ASUR *component* (*Real entity/Computer System*).

R4.1 The *concrete object* is an ASUR *component* (*Real entity/Computer System*) with a fixed characterization.

R4.2 For each K-MAD *object*, there is at least an ASUR *component* (*Real entity and/or Computer System*).

Rules associated to the performer in K-MAD:

We studied the correspondence rules of a K-MAD user task, a K-MAD system task and a K-MAD interactive task (0).

R5   Equivalence of a K-MAD user task: the equivalent of a *user* task in K-MAD (Fig. 4 bottom) is an ASUR partial model composed of *user*, *Real entity* and/or *Computer System* components intervening in the task and relationships between components (Fig. 6). The rules **R3** and **R4** also apply to K-MAD user task and generate the *Real entity* and/or *Computer System* components and the relationships.

In such task, additional equivalences in ASUR of the K-MAD elements involved are as follow:

R5.1 The *user performer* (Fig. 4. bottom) is the *user component in ASUR* (Fig. 6 right).

R5.2 The *sensory-motor modality*, an attribute of the K-MAD user task (Fig. 4 bottom), is the characteristic *perception/action sense* of the corresponding ASUR *component* (Fig. 6 bottom right) connected to the *user* via a *relationship*.

R5.3 When the *object* of the task is digital, the partial ASUR model equivalent to the K-MAD task contains necessarily an *adaptor* (Fig. 4 bottom right).

R6   Equivalence of a K-MAD system task: the equivalent of a *system task* in K-MAD (Fig. 4 bottom left) is an ASUR partial model composed of *Real entity* and/or

Computer System components intervening in the *task* and relationships between components (Fig. 6). The rules **R3** and **R4** also apply to K-MAD system task and generate the *Real entity* and/or *Computer System* components and the relationships.

In such task, additional equivalences in ASUR of the K-MAD elements involved are as follow:

R6.1 The equivalent ASUR partial model of a K-MAD *system task* using physical objects contains necessarily an *adaptor* (Fig. 4 bottom right).

R7   Equivalence of a K-MAD interactive task: the equivalent of an *interactive task* in K-MAD (Fig. 4 bottom) is an ASUR partial or a complete model composed of *Real entity* and/or *Computer System* components, relationships, *user* and adaptors (Fig. 6). The rules **R3** and **R4** also apply to K-MAD interactive task and generate the *Real entity* and/or *Computer System* components and the relationships. A K-MAD *interactive* task is the fusion of *user* and *system* task. Thus, **R5** and **R6** also apply to K-MAD *interactive* task.

In such task, additional equivalences in ASUR of the K-MAD elements involved are as follow:

R7.1 The equivalent ASUR partial or complete model of an *interactive task* in K-MAD contains at least an *adaptor* (Fig. 6 top right) and at least a *user* (Fig. 6 right).

4.3   Illustrating the Transition from K-MAD to ASUR

To illustrate the rules, we consider the K-MAD *interactive* subtask "compare animals" (Fig. 3). The equivalent ASUR model is presented in Fig. 5. The K-MAD model of the task "compare animal", that is to say the sub tree starting from this *task*, involved only one *user*, the visitor of the museum using this interactive exhibit and one *object* of the *task*, the physical picture representing the animal of reference. According to rules **R1** and **R2**, we can refine the K-MAD model with a unique ASUR description.

According to the rule **R4**, the equivalent to the *object* animal of reference and animal of comparison in K-MAD (Fig. 3) can be in ASUR physical and/or digital object (*Real entity* and/or *Computer System*): in our case the equivalent will respectively be the R_{object} animal of reference, the R_{tool} animal of comparison, the S_{info} animal of reference, animal of comparison and criteria in ASUR (Fig. 5).

According to the rule **R3**, the equivalent to the *name* of the K-MAD task "locate animal of reference" is the *name* and/or the meaning of the relationships in ASUR: in our case the equivalent is the *name* locate of the *data exchange relationship* between R_{object} Animal of reference and the *user*. The equivalent to the *name* of the K-MAD subtasks "identify animals" and "search criteria" are the *names* of the *data exchange relationships* "identify" and "search" (Fig. 5 left).

We then consider the K-MAD subtask "indicate comparison". The task tree describes the activity of the *user* at an abstract level so the subtask "start comparison" has an *unknown performer*. This subtask can be interactive or performed by the *system* or a *user*. We chose in the interaction design level to describe this task as a *user* task. According to the rule **R5**, the equivalent to the *user performer* in K-MAD is the *user component* in ASUR (Fig. 5 right) (**R5.1**); and the equivalent to the *sensori-motor modality* in the K-MAD subtask "locate animal" and "start comparison" is the value of the characteristic *perception/action* sense in ASUR: in our example, the equivalent is respectively the *visual sense* as the value of the *perception sense* and *physical action* as the value of the *action sense* relating to the R_{object} (**R5.2**). Choosing a *system performer* for this task would mean that the *system* is a demonstrator rather than an *interactive* exhibit. As mentioned by **R6.1**, an *adaptor* to display the selected animal would therefore be required.

We consider now the subtask "process information". According to the rule **R6**, the *adaptor* is necessary in the ASUR model since the physical *object* animal of reference is used in the K-MAD *system task* (**R6.1**): in our example, the video projector.

Finally, we consider the K-MAD subtask "return results". According to the rule **R7,** the equivalent to the *interactive* K-MAD task is an ASUR model containing a *user* and an *adaptor* (**R7.1**): in our example, the ASUR model contains *user* and the video projector as A_{out}.

The equivalences expressed previously show that the equivalent to the sub tasks of the K-MAD task "compare animals" is the ASUR partial models (**R3**). For example: the equivalent to the K-MAD *interactive task* "return result" is the ASUR partial model composed of: S_{info} {animal of reference, animal of comparison, criteria} $\rightarrow A_{out}$ $\rightarrow$ *user* (Fig. 5 right).

5 Conclusion and Perspectives

The work presented in this paper is in line with the development process for Mixed Interaction Systems and especially, it focus on the links between the Task Analysis step and the Interaction Design step. To articulate task model and mixed interaction model, we first chose two particular notations: K-MAD and ASUR. Then, by concentrating on their respective metamodels, we highlighted common aspects and links between elements of the metamodels. This first set of rules constitutes a basis for the articulation of the models. We then establish two types of rules to define respectively the boundaries between K-MAD description and ASUR description, and the correspondences between a K-MAD and an ASUR models. This second set of rules supports the articulation of the two complementary models.

Based on the articulation rules, complementary aspects will be useful to investigate additional considerations. Through our illustration we can observe that ASUR does not take into account the order of the subtasks, while the *operators* of K-MAD allow expressing the development of the activity. The study of this complementary point will be done through the sequencing of mixed tasks described in ASUR and managed by K-MAD *operators*. This study is interesting to see the impact of the sequence on the mixed interaction.

Starting from this study, we can define for a high level of a K-MAD model the elements of choice between various ASUR mixed alternatives: the study of mixed interaction sequence will highlights recommendations concerning interaction functionalities and their impact on the user activity. Finally, we have to establish rules to check the coherence between the models and between the rules through the process of development to be sure that there are no incoherencies between the different steps of the development process. This aspect might be based on a further use of the basic links identified between the metamodels. This work also constitutes a first step toward a model-based predictive evaluation of MIS at a design stage.

References

1. Milgram, P., Kishino, F.: A Taxonomy of Mixed reality Visual Displays. Transactions on Information Systems E77-D(12), 1321–1329 (1994)
2. Scapin, D.L.: K-MADe, COST294-MAUSE 3rd International Workshop, Review, Report and Refine Usability Evaluation Methods (R3 UEMs), Athens (March 5, 2007)
3. Dubois, E., Gray, P.D., Nigay, L.: ASUR++: a Design Notation for Mobile Mixed Systems. Interacting with computers 15(3), 497–520 (2003)
4. Ashlock, P., D.: The uses of cladistics. Annual Review of Ecology and Systematics 5, 81–99 (1974)
5. Hirokazu Kato, H., Mark Billinghurst, M.: Marker Tracking and HMD Calibration for a Video-Based Augmented Reality, Conferencing System. In: Proceedings of the 2nd IEEE and ACM International Workshop on Augmented Reality, p.85 (1999)
6. Dubois, E., Gauffre, G., Bach, C., Salembier, P.: Participatory Design Meets Mixed Reality Design Models. In: CADUI 2006. conference Proceedings of Computer Assisted Design of User Interface. Information Systems Series, pp. 71–84. Springer, Heidelberg (2006)
7. Baron, M., Lucquiaud, V., Autard, D., Scapin, D., L.,: K-MADe: un environnement pour le noyau du modéle de description de láctivité. In: Proceedings of the 18th international conference on Association Francophone d'Interaction Homme-Machine IHM 2006 (2006)
8. Paternó, F., Mancini, C., Meniconi, S.: ConcurTaskTrees: A Diagrammatic Notation for Specifying Task Models. In: Proceedings of the IFIP TC13 International Conference on Human-Computer Interaction, pp. 362–369 (1997)
9. Viala, J., Dubois, E., Gray, P., D.: GUIDE-ME: graphical user interface for the design of mixed interactive environment based on the ASUR notation. In: UbiMob 2004. Proceedings of the 1st French-speaking conference on Mobility and ubiquity computing (2004)
10. Shaer, O., Leland, N., Calvillo-Gamez, E.H., Jacob, R.J.K: The TAC paradigm: specifying tangible user interfaces. Personal and Ubiquitous Computing, 359–369 (2004)
11. Ishii, H., Ullmer, B.: Emerging Frameworks for Tangible User Interfaces. IBM Systems Journal 39(3/4), 915–931 (2000)
12. Trevisan, D.G., Vanderdonckt, J., Macq, B.: Conceptualising mixed spaces of interaction for designing continuous interaction. Virtual Reality 8(2), 83–95 (2005)
13. Coutrix, C., Nigay, L.: Mixed Reality: A Model of Mixed Interaction. In: Proceedings of AVI 2006, pp. 45–53. ACM Press, New York (2006)
14. Delotte, O., David, B., Chalon, R.: Task Modelling for Capillary Collaborative Systems based on Scenarios. In: Proceedings of TAMODIA 2004, pp. 25–31. ACM Press, New York (2004)
15. Renevier, P., Nigay, L., Bouchet, J., Pasqualetti, L.: Generic interaction techniques for mobile collaborative mixed systems. In: Proceedings of CADUI 2004, pp. 307–320. ACM, New York (2004)
16. Hilliges, O., Sandor, C., Klinker, G: Interaction Management for Ubiquitous Augmented Reality User Interfaces. Diploma Thesis, Technische Universität München (2005)

A Survey of Model Driven Engineering Tools for User Interface Design

Jorge-Luis Pérez-Medina, Sophie Dupuy-Chessa, and Agnès Front

Laboratory of Informatics of Grenoble
385 rue de la bibliothèque, B.P. 53
38041 Grenoble Cedex 9, France
{Firstname.Lastname}@imag.fr

Abstract. The introduction of new technologies leads to a more and more complex interactive systems design. In order to describe the future interactive system, the human computer interaction (HCI) domain uses specific models and tools. In another way, the Model Driven Engineering (MDE) approach has been proposed in software engineering domain in order to provide techniques and tools for dealing with models in an automated way. MDE approach is based on models, meta-models, models transformation and models weaving and aims to produce productive models, i.e. models concentrated on their generative power. Considering these two domains and the already existing HCI works in MDE, the goal of this paper is to understand actual HCI design needs and to study how MDE tools can support HCI needs. As a first response, it proposes a survey of existing MDE tools in regards to HCI model management.

Keywords: HCI, MDE, model, meta-model, transformation, MDE tools, User Interface Design.

1 Introduction

Model-based approaches aim at helping developers understand user needs and design solutions in an effective way. In the HCI domain, models can be declarative in order to describe the future interactive system, but also generative to (semi-) automate the code generation. If the quality of the generated interfaces can be disappointing [22], models remain interesting for their declarative power. As a matter of fact, interactive systems are more and more complex: they can use everyday life objects to propose tangible interfaces; they can couple the virtual and the physical worlds in augmented reality systems; they can adapt themselves to the user context, etc. They are increasingly difficult to design. So new models appear to represent augmented reality systems [11, 27] or the user context (with a user model, a platform model and an environment model [28]).

In terms of tools, the HCI community uses different tools to support the design of interactive systems, e.g. CTTE [21], GUIDE-ME [32] K-MADe [4], and Teresa [5]. These tools mainly give support to model editing for task models (CTTE, Teresa and K-MADe) or specific models such as ASUR models (GUIDE-ME). In addition, some

M. Winckler, H. Johnson, and P. Palanque (Eds.): TAMODIA 2007, LNCS 4849, pp. 84–97, 2007.

of them [33, 4] allow model simulation. However, many others operations are possible on models, in particular to increase their generative power.

Model management aims at providing techniques and tools for dealing with models in more automated ways. It has been studied independently for years by several research communities in the context of databases, document management and software engineering. Nowadays, a federative approach emerges: model driven engineering (MDE [14]). At the origins of the movement, the Object Management Group proposes the Model Driven Architecture for object-oriented technologies. But this dependence on a technology and the absence of clear concept definitions lead to a more general approach, MDE. In MDE, any kind of models can be taken into account. So MDE is spreading quickly, in particular in the HCI domain as can be seen by the recurring workshop "Model Driven Development of Advanced User Interfaces" at one of the main conferences about MDE, MoDELS.

Based on related work on MDE for HCI, this paper tries to understand the HCI actual design needs related to MDE and proposes a survey of MDE tools for HCI. Our goal is not to identify the best tool for HCI design but to find criteria that could help HCI designers in the choice of a MDE tool.

The paper is organized as follows. Section 2 provides the basic definitions of MDE concepts. Section 3 describes the existing HCI works related to MDE. Section 4 provides a survey of MDE tools for HCI in terms of metamodeling, model transformation and others operations. Finally, conclusions are presented.

2 MDE Concepts

2.1 Models and Meta-models

MDE is a recent paradigm where code is not considered as the central element of software. Code is an element, a model produced by merging different modeling elements. So in MDE, everything can be considered a model. Minsky [20] defines that "To an observer B, an object M* is a model of an object M to the extent that B can use M* to answer questions that interest him about M". This definition shows a model is an object intended to represent a particular behavior, dependent on a particular disciplinary context. In the context of MDE, interesting models are those that can be formalized to make them productive. Some authors integrate this limitation directly into the definition of the notion of model: a model is a description of (part of) a system written in a well-defined language [18]. This definition makes an explicit reference to the notion of well-defined language. In MDE, such a language is described by a meta-model. A meta-model is a specification model that defines the language for expressing a model. It defines the concepts that can be used in the models, which conform to it. In this way, a meta-model allows designers to specify their own domain-specific languages. Models and meta-models are the first main concepts in MDE.

2.2 Model Transformation

Another important concept in MDE is transformation. A transformation permits, from given models, to produce any model [19]. The model produced by transformations can be code, test cases, graphical modeling models, etc. The goal of transformations is double: on the one hand, they capitalize on know-how; on the other hand, they permit to automate this know-how. So transformations provide the generative power of models.

There are several kinds of generation. Classically, code can be generated from given models. But in reverse engineering, the models are produced from the code. There are many examples of translation of a model to another model such as the generation of UML models from formal specifications. In MDE, all these operations on models are considered as transformations. This is one of the key ideas in MDE that permits to consider all the generative operations in the same manner.

A difficulty remains in finding a language to express the transformations. Many different kinds of transformation languages exist: graphical languages like TrML[1]; XML XSLT-based[2] languages; languages based on a programming language (for instance, JMI[3] expresses Java-like transformations); ad-hoc languages like MOLA [17] and MTL [33]; and finally languages based on the OMG standard QVT[4]. QVT principles have been implemented in several languages, of which ATL (ATLAS Transformation Language [1]) that is currently most widely used.

2.3 Model Weaving

MDE is not limited to model transformations. [9] argues that transformations are not sufficient to manage the generative power of models and proposes another operation called model weaving. Model weaving [9, 10] is an operation on models that specifies different kinds of links between model elements. In order to explain model weaving, let us consider the simple information system for a library described in [10]. In this context, an example of transformation of one relational database R1 into its equivalent XML representation X1 is proposed (Figure 1). A model weaving operation is specified to capture the links between both schemas with all the information semantically relevant.

These links are represented in the R1_X1 mapping as illustrated in figure 1. In this example, both schemas represent the same information but distinct data structures are used. For instance, whereas the subjects have a *Name* in R1, they are called *Descr* in X1. The equality between these elements can be represented by the Equals links in the weaving. Moreover, one must also take into account the structure of both schemas: the foreign key constraints and the nested elements are respectively represented by *FK* and *Nested* links.

This example shows that a weaving is specific to a domain. The weaving relationships, e.g. "Equals" or "Nested", depend on the concepts of the models to be manipulated. Thus, a weaving, like any model, must be in accordance with a meta-model. It allows afterward to define transformations from the mapping.

Model management is not limited to model transformation or weaving. Other kinds of operations can be applied to models. Models can be simulated, consistency can be checked between them, etc. If these operations are important to make models more

---

[1] TrML. Transformation modelling language, http://www2.lifl.fr/west/trml/
[2] W3C. World Wide Web Consortium, http://www.w3.org/TR/2007/REC-xslt20-20070123/
[3] JMI. Java Metadata Interface, http://java.sun.com/products/jmi/
[4] Query/View/Transformation. OMG Specification, http://www.omg.org/docs/ptc/05-11-01.pdf

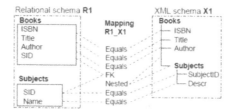

Fig. 1. Links between a relational and an XML schema of a library

useful, they are generally not presented as part of MDE for MDE concentrates on the generative power of models. We can note that it is important that MDE tools can be easily connected to other tools that will provide other operations on models.

3 Existing HCI Works in MDE

Model-based Systems for User Interfaces Design (UIDE) have been addressed using many approaches over the years. Early works on UIDE such as Foley [15] established the foundations for transforming high-level specifications into executable code. Later, various approaches have been developed in the field of model-based design of interactive applications [24]. More recently, works in UI design are using partially the MDE principles. This section describes the existing works in order to identify needs related to MDE tools.

3.1 Models and Meta-models in HCI

Historically, MDA and consequently MDE approaches have been "inspired" by concepts of the UML meta-model and the MOF meta-meta-model. MOF is a model of the meta-models proposed by the OMG. In particular, it is the meta-model of the most used meta-model, the UML one. MDE uses UML class diagrams as notation for the representation of models and meta-models.

In HCI, UML models are not widely used because they are not adequate but also because the HCI domain has developed its own notations such as task models, ASUR models, etc. Several meta-models have been proposed for context-adaptive user interfaces [28, 6, 7]. Generally, they include a meta-model for the task model, but also models related to the user context such as a platform model. For example, Fig. 2 represents a task meta-model proposed in [28]. In this meta-model, the tasks are linked by operators. Logical and temporary operators are considered as binary, whereas the decorations on the tasks are supplied by unary operators.

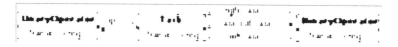

Fig. 2. A task meta-model [28]

The use of MDE and meta-models is not limited to the adaptation of the user interface to its context. Other domains of HCI also define meta-models for specific notations such as ASUR, a graphical notation for augmented reality systems [12] or for specific tools like in [16].

All these meta-models are independent, but they are instances of the same meta-meta-model (i.e. MOF). They are defined from scratch without being the extension of well-known meta-models. Another approach could be to extend an existing meta-model. In particular, UML proposes profiles to extend the UML meta-model to a specific domain. So the meta-models defined as UML profiles take advantage of the already existing semantics of UML and must conform to its semantics. For instance, some extensions have been proposed for HCI through UMLi [25] and for context-sensitive user interfaces [31].

The study of these existing works leads us to conclude that user interfaces design needs MDE tools, which support domain-specific meta-models and models. Unlike for software engineering (SE), there is no consensus on the models for HCI. In addition, even different notations are proposed for task modeling. So the HCI domain must manage several meta-models for task models. This diversity brings the need to use MDE tools that permit designers to create their own meta-model or to modify an existing one.

Finally if designers want to create links between HCI and SE models, all the meta-models must be instance of the same meta-model. As SE and MDE communities use the MOF as the meta-meta-model reference, it is important that the HCI domain conforms to this practice. So the HCI meta-models must be instance of the MOF and they must be represented by an UML class diagram.

3.2 Model Weaving in HCI

Establishing links between model elements can provide numerous application scenarios, such as model comparison, traceability, matching or interoperability. To our current knowledge, model weaving has been used in the HCI domain on the notion of mapping [29]. In this approach, a UI is described as a graph of models and mappings both at the design time and run-time.

The mappings are specified manually in a semi-formal way by the designer, or are created automatically by the system as the result of a transformation function. At design time, the mappings convey some properties that help the designer in selecting the most appropriate transformation function (e.g. the concepts manipulated within a task are grouped together). Either the target element of the mapping is generated using a transformation function. At run-time, mappings are keys for reasoning on usability (e.g. select the appropriate usability framework in the generation of UIs). Mappings models are more than a simple traceability link; they can embed transformation in order to manage models consistency.

The use of model weaving is currently limited in HCI. It is more complex than the direct transformations or comparisons as it requires the creation of a weaving meta-model. But it increases the traceability of model manipulations by explicitly representing links between models. Then transformations or model comparisons can be more easily executed from the weaving links. So the need of weaving models in HCI is important.

3.3 Model Transformations in HCI

More than weaving, transformation operations represent the heart of the MDE. Section 2.2 showed that there are several kinds of transformations and that many languages have been proposed to represent them. In this section, we study how the HCI community uses transformations for user interface design.

3.3.1 Transformation Languages Chosen in HCI

Many transformations languages are currently proposed and still developed in the MDE domain. An important decision consists in selecting a suitable language for transformations. Our study of existing works suggests that transformation languages are currently underused by the HCI community. Most of the work studied does not refer to any transformation language, which suggests that transformations are currently done in an ad-hoc manner or not formalized at all. Nevertheless, there are exceptions. In the domain of web interfaces, the transformation language is XSLT. In other domains, several papers [28, 7, 16] refer to ATL.

So it may be too early to clearly specify the HCI needs in terms of transformation languages. The HCI community seems to follow the standard of use. Nevertheless, the choice of a transformation language requires it to be easy to understand and to use, especially for non-MDE specialists as can be HCI designers. So it is important to note for each MDE tool which kind of language it supports.

3.3.2 Transformations Proposed in HCI

In section 2.2, we identified the needs to generate code from models, models from code or models from models. Even if reverse engineering exists in HCI [3], we did not find any examples of model generation from code using MDE approach.

The idea of transforming one model into another is proposed mainly to bridge the gap between HCI and SE models. [23, 8] propose some informal transformations between activity diagrams and task model. But transformations are more commonly used to produce code. A good example of model transformation can be found in [29]. It describes a complete approach based on transformations with the generation of models from models and of code from models. Because of space limitations, we will comment only one transformation that generates one model from another. The rules are expressed in the same way to generate code.

Based on a case study of a Home Heating Control System (HHCS), this example shows that a final UI can be defined by a set of model transformations that follows the following steps: from the domain-dependent concepts and task models, an abstract UI (Workspace) is derived; this abstract UI is then transformed into a concrete UI (CUI), which is transformed into the final UI. To give a more precise example, we shall concentrate on the transformation from tasks into workspaces. In this example, the tasks are transformed into workspaces; the operators between tasks into chains between workspaces.

Figure 3 presents the meta-models used in the transformation of the tasks into workspaces. In this figure, we see that every task is associated with a workspace and that the binary operator gives rise to chains between workspaces.

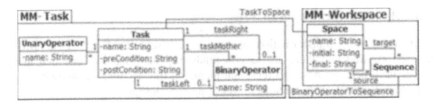

Fig. 3. Meta-models used in the transformation from task to workspace [29]

In the current implementation of HHCS, the mappings between the task model, the workspace and the CUI are expressed in ATL; an example is illustrated in figure 4. The first rule illustrates the generation of a task into a workspace; it consists in creating a space for every task with the assignment of the name of the task. The second rule illustrates the transformation of a binary operator into a chain; it considers only the operator "Or" and is written in two parts: the first one consists in the selection of the binary operators of type "or"; the second describes the access given by the space representing the mother task to spaces representing their two daughters.

```
Module M2A-T to M2A-E {
--Rule 1: The Space takes the name of the task
rule TaskToSpace {from t: M2-T!Task to e: M2-E!Space ( name <- t.name )}
--Rule 2: Management of the operators of type "or"
rule OperatorOrToSequence { from o: M2-T!BinaryOperator ( o.name ="or" )
sequenceLeft : M2-E!Sequence (
    source <- [Task2Space.e]o.taskMother,
    target <- [Task2Space.e]o.taskRight,),
to sequenceRight : M2-E!Sequence (
    source <- [Task2Space.e]o.taskMother,
    target <- [Task2Space.e]o.taskLeft,), }
```

Fig. 4. Example of the transformation Task to Workspace in ATL [28]

In MDE, there is no distinction between transformations: a transformation always generates one model from another. It is assumed that the code or program is also a model. Nevertheless, in the perspective of using MDE tools, one important aspect is to guarantee that the transformation result can be expressed in a recoverable format that is useful for another tool. This implies that the format of the transformation result is important. It is needed to know if the result is a text file that can be compiled or interpreted or if it is a structured file (in XML for instance) that can be manipulated by design tools.

In the perspective of comparing MDE tools according to HCI needs, we note that the existing works in HCI reflects a clear need to realize transformations of HCI models. To go further, the HCI community could define libraries of classic transformations that could be integrated and manipulated by MDE tools. So it is important that MDE tools propose a transformation repository or at least the load of existing transformations. This brings the need to a common language to express transformations but also this adds constraints on the format to permit interoperability between tools. We note that the format of the transformation result is also important to know in order to determine the future operations that can be realized on the resulting model.

4 Survey of MDE Tools for HCI

4.1 Diversity of Tools

Both at the commercial and research levels, several tools for MDE are either available or in development. These tools are designed as frameworks [2] or as plug-in [1]. Several classification works [13, 26] and tool comparisons [30] were proposed. However, no classification estimates the functional criteria that we defined towards our needs, in particular in terms of specific models used in HCI domain.

Table 1 shows a list of tools that we have considered realizing our survey. This list is focused on the MDE tools which could be used in the HCI domain as the manipulated models are not limited to UML models.

Table 1. Survey of MDE Tools

Tool	Version	Description
ACCELEO GPL - Open source	2.0.0	Eclipse and EMF template-based system for MDA generation. http://www.acceleo.org/pages/accueil/fr
AndroMDA Open source	3.2	An extensible generator framework. Models from UML tools will be transformed into deployable components for your favorite platform (J2EE, Spring, .NET). http://galaxy.andromda.org/index.php?option=com_frontpage &Itemid=48
ADT Open source	2.0	ATL Development Tools are a suite of Eclipse plugins including an ATL engine (compiler and virtual machine) as well as an IDE. http://www.sciences.univ-nantes.fr/lina/atl/atldemo/adt
AToM3 Open source	2.2	A Tool for Multi-formalism and Meta-Modelling supporting modelling of complex systems. http://atom3.cs.mcgill.ca/index_html
DSL Tools (Visual Studio 2005 SDK)	4.0	DSL Tools enable the construction of custom graphical designers and the generation of source code using domain-specific diagrammatic notations in Visual Studio 2005. http://msdn2.microsoft.com/en-us/vstudio/aa718368.aspx
Kermeta	0.4.1	A metamodeling language which allows describing both the structure and the behaviour of models. http://www.kermeta.org/
ModFact GPL - Open source	1.0.1	A tool that provides a framework for building application. http://modfact.lip6.fr/
Merlin Open source	0.5.0	A software modelling tool based on model transformation and code generation. http://merlingenerator.sourceforge.net/merlin/index.php
MDA Workbench Open source	3.0	The MDA Workbench is a MDA tool implemented as an Eclipse plug-in based on modelling and code generation. http://sourceforge.net/projects/mda-workbench
MOFLON Open source	1.1.0	A meta modelling framework built as plug-in for the graph transformation tool Fujaba. http://www.moflon.org/
OptimalJ Professional Edition	3.0	Generator of J2EE applications using patterns to translate business models into working applications. http://www.compuware.com/ products/optimalj/
QVT Partners BSD like license	0.1	Tools based on QVT for transformation models to models and code generator. http://qvtp.org/downloads/qvtp-eclipse/
SmartQVT Open source	0.1.4	A model transformation tool based on QVT-Operational language. http://smartqvt.elibel.tm.fr/
UMLX Open source	0.0.2	An experimental concrete syntax for a transformation language. http://dev.eclipse.org/viewcvs/indextech.cgi/gmt-home/subprojects/UMLX/

These tools will be studied according to the needs listed in the previous sections. These needs are general to the HCI domain. Any HCI designer must refine them to choose his MDE tool. So we do not intend to find the best tool but rather to provide relevant information to choose a MDE tool. We will present our survey in terms of the MDE important concepts: models and meta-models, operations on models and other functionalities.

4.2 Tools in Terms of Meta-models and Models Expression

Regarding models and meta-models, the HCI community needs tools that do not just consider UML models, but also specific models. Our list of tools being limited to this kind of tools, any tool in the list can be suitable for HCI in terms of model and meta-model support. Nevertheless, to refine our comparison, we introduce a criterion about the way of expressing models and meta-models: models and meta-models can be represented either textually or graphically. We also note if constraints can be added to complete models and meta-models. Constraints are written in OCL, the constraint language for UML.

Table 2. MDE tools in terms of meta-models and models expression

Tools	Expression (Meta-models)		Expression (Models)	
	Graphical (G) or Textual (T)	Constraints	Graphical (G) or Textual (T)	Constraints
ACCELEO	G, T	OCL	G, T	OCL
AndroMDA	T	OCL	G, T	OCL
ADT	T	OCL	T	OCL
AToM3	G	-	G	-
DSL tools	G, T	-	G, T	-
Kermeta	G,T	OCL	G, T	OCL
ModFact	G	-	G	-
Merlin	G,T	OCL	G, T	OCL
MDA Workbench	G, T	OCL	G, T	OCL
MOFLON	G, T	OCL	G, T	OCL
OptimalJ	G	OCL	G	OCL
QVT Partners	G, T	OCL	T	OCL
SmartQVT	T	OCL	T	OCL
UMLX	G, T	OCL	G, T	OCL

From the previous table, we would recommend that a user interface designer should better choose a tool allowing a graphical expression of models and meta-models, because graphical representations are of course easier to use than textual representations for non specialists.

4.3 Tools in Terms of Model Transformation and Weaving

As mentioned in section 3, HCI needs in terms of operations on models are not limited to transformations. Table 3 lists all the model manipulations proposed by the tools and shows that only ADT provides some part of the infrastructure for the manual creation of weaving models, what is a real advantage on other tools.

Then for transformations, even if there is a standard specification for transformations (QVT), there is no standard language. The majority of MDE tools support QVT so that, in principle, the use of QVT guarantees that the result of a transformation is compatible with another tool that uses QVT. But in practise, the implementations of QVT are different and the compatibility between tools is not guaranteed. We also showed in section 3.3 that XSLT and ATL were nowadays the only two languages used by the HCI community. So to support the creation of transformations libraries for HCI, the tools ADT and UMLX, which support XSLT and ATL, should be preferred in the HCI domain. Moreover ATL is already widely used in the SE domain. So ATL is a good candidate to facilitate links between HCI and SE models.

Moreover it is important to identify the form (text or model) of the generated models in order to identify which kind of tools can manipulate them. In table 3, the word "Text" is used when the result of a transformation is textual. Generally the result is some code written in a programming language (java, C, C++, Cobol, Fortran, VB.net, etc.) that can be compiled or interpreted. The term XMI is used when the result of the transformation is a model in the XMI form (XML Metadata Interchange), which can be loaded in many design tools. Here again ATL and UMLX (with other tools) have an advantage as they provide the XMI and the textual format.

Considering model operations, two tools are good candidates for the HCI domain: ATL that is the solution for works in the SE spirit and UMLX which is more adapted for works with web technologies.

Table 3. MDE tools in terms of models transformation and weaving

| Tool | Transformation | | | | Weaving |
| | Language | Graphical (G) or Textual (T) Expression | Generated model | | |
			XMI	Text	
ACCELEO	QVT, JMI	T	-	Yes	-
AndroMDA	ATL, MofScript	T	Yes	Yes	-
ADT	ATL	T	Yes	Yes	Yes
AToM3	Multi formalism (python)	G		Yes	-
DSL tools	Notation XML	T	Yes	Yes	-
Kermeta	QVT	T	-	Yes	-
ModFact	QVT	T	-	Yes	-
Merlin	QVT, JET	T	-	Yes	-
MDA Workbench	QVT	T	-	Yes	-
MOFLON	JMI	G	-	Yes	-
OptimalJ	QVT	T	-	Yes	-
QVT Partners	QVT	T	Yes	Yes	-
SmartQVT	QVT	T	Yes	Yes	-
UMLX	XSLT, QVT	T	Yes	Yes	-

4.4   Tools in Terms of Other Operations

The studied MDE tools offer good solutions for meta-modeling and transformations. But one may want to reuse models, meta-models or transformations into another tool, so it is very important to know the capacity of a tool to interoperate with other tools.

In sections 3.1 and 3.3, we noted the importance of the format to exchange models and meta-models and to bridge the gap with the SE domain. A great part of the tools is centred on the MOF specification. So they can cover the modelling needs of different domains and especially of HCI. Several implemented formats have been proposed for the MOF: ECore, MDR (Metadata Repository), KM3 (Kernel Meta-

Meta Model), DSL (Domain Specific Language) and CWM (Common Warehouse Meta-model). Nevertheless, DSL does not conform to MOF's implementation. That's why KM3 was created: KM3 is a specialized language to specify meta-models and is used as a bridge between MOF and DSL. The most used format is ECore, which is a simplified version of the MOF. Moreover MDE tools provide many libraries of predefined models and meta-models in ECore. So the choice of a ECore compliant tool is important to guarantee the development and the exchange of reusable models and meta-models.

Regarding model transformation, XMI is proposed for transformations but it is not so widely chosen. As a matter of fact, many other tools prefer textual transformations, in particular for QVT tools. In terms of interoperability, Eclipse proposes de facto methods for the storage and the recovery of models based on XMI. So the great majority of MDE tools is based on Eclipse and can interoperate with other Eclipse tools.

Finally, what is more important in the HCI domain is the interoperability of MDE tools with existing HCI design tools. Generally HCI design tools do not have a known meta-model. However the models produced with them can be saved in an XML format. The interoperability between MDE and HCI design tools can be easily guaranteed by transforming every XML file in a ECore compatible format, so that it could be recovered by the MDE tools that support this format. A longer term solution is that HCI tools incorporate the MDE standards and create mechanisms to import or export information based on the XMI format.

Table 4. MDE tools in terms of other operations

Tool	Repository			Interoperability with others tools
	Metamodeling	Model transformation	Constraints	
ACCELEO	DSL, MDR, ECORE	-	XMI	Eclipse, Netbeans
AndroMDA	MOF, DSL	-	XMI	Eclipse
ADT	DSL, KM3, MDR, ECORE	Text (ATL)	XMI	Eclipse, Netbeans
AToM3	Proprietary graphical multi - formalism			-
DSL tools	DSL - Proprietary notation	XML / XMI	-	Eclipse, Netbeans
Kermeta	ECORE	Text (QVT)	XMI	Eclipse
ModFact	ECORE	XMI	XMI	Eclipse
Merlin	ECORE	Text (QVT)	XMI	Eclipse
MDA Workbench	ECORE	XMI	XMI	Eclipse
MOFLON	ECORE	-	XMI	Eclipse
OptimalJ	CWM, ECORE	XMI	XMI	Eclipse
QVT Partners	ECORE	Text (QVT)	XMI	Eclipse
SmartQVT	ECORE	Text (QVT)	XMI	Eclipse
UMLX	ECORE	XMI, XSLT	XMI, XSLT	Eclipse

5   Conclusion

The goal of this paper is to propose a survey of MDE tools in order to help the HCI community in the choice of a MDE tool. Considering existing works in the HCI domain, we think that the HCI domain shows a clear need for the MDE approach and tools. First, considering models and meta-models, HCI designers use a lot of domain-specific models such as task models, ASUR models, etc. that conform to specific meta-models. Transformation models and weaving models are also needed in HCI domain. In particular, model weaving has been used on the notion of mapping where a user interface is described as a graph of models and mappings both at design time at run-time. Moreover, transformations allow to generate code from models, but also to produce new models from other ones. Two types of transformations are then needed, those that generate code (more generally, a text file that can be compiled or interpreted) and those that generate graphical models (more generally, a structured file that can be manipulated by design tools).

Based on these needs, we draw a survey of several MDE existing tools. Several conclusions can be drawn from this comparison. In terms of modeling, a great part of the tools are centered on MOF and allow to model domain-specific models. In terms of transformations, there is no standard language to use, but it is important to know the language manipulated by the tools and to specify if they are graphical or textual. Moreover, it is important to know the format (text or model) of the generated models in order to identify the kind of tools that can then manipulate them. Our conclusion is that MDE is able to answer the specific needs of the HCI community in terms of models. Nevertheless, the HCI community has to incorporate the proposed standards that MDE is nowadays using. We hope this comparison will be useful to any HCI designer who wants to select a MDE tool based on functional needs in terms of graphical (or textual) expression of domain specific models, models transformation, models weaving and interoperability with specific HCI tools.

Acknowledgments. We would like to express our special thanks to Stéphanie Marsal-Layat for her help in the tool survey. We are also grateful to the Federation IMAG, the Foundation "Gran Mariscal de Ayacucho, the university UCLA-Venezuela" for their financial support.

References

1. Allilaire, F., Idrissi, T.: ADT: Eclipse development tools for ATL. In: Proceedings of the 2nd European Workshop on Model Driven Architecture (MDA) with an emphasis on Methodologies and Transformations (EWMDA-2), Canterbury, UK. England, pp. 171–178. Computing Laboratory, University of Kent (September 2004)
2. Amelunxen, C., Königs, A., Rötschke, T., Schürr, A.: MOFLON: A Standard-Compliant Metamodeling Framework with Graph Transformations. In: Rensink, A., Warmer, J. (eds.) Model Driven Architecture - Foundations and Applications: 2nd European Conference. LNCS, vol. 4066, pp. 361–375. Springer, Heidelberg (2006)
3. Bandelloni, R., Paternó, F., Santoro, C.: Reverse Engineering Cross-Modal User Interfaces for Ubiquitous Environments. In: EIS 2007. Proceedings of the Engineering Interactive Systems Conference. LNCS, Springer, Heidelberg (to appear, 2007)
4. Baron, M., Lucquiaud, V., Autard, D., Scapin, D.: K-MADe: un environement pour le noyau du modéle de description de l'activité. In: Proceedings of 18th French-speaking conference on Human-Computer Interaction (IHM 2006), pp. 287–288. ACM Press, New York (2006)

5. Berti, S., Correani, F., Mori, G., Paternó, F., Santoro, C.: TERESA: A Transformation-Based Environment for Designing Multi-Device Interactive Applications. In: Proceedings of CHI 2004, CHI 2004 extended abstracts on Human factors in Computing Systems, pp. 793–794. ACM Press, New York (2004)

6. Boedcher, A., Mukasa, K., Zuehlke, D.: Capturing Common and Variable Design Aspects for Ubiquitous Computing with MB-UID. In: Proceedings of the International Workshop on Model Driven Development of Advanced User Interfaces (MDDAUI 2005) organized at MoDELS 2005, Jamaica, October. CEUR Workshop Proceedings vol. 159 (2005)

7. Botterweck, G.: A Model-Driven Approach to the Engineering of Multiple User Interfaces. In: Kühne, T. (ed.) MoDELS 2006. LNCS, vol. 4364, pp. 106–115. Springer, Heidelberg (2007)

8. Brüning, J., Dittmar, A., Forbrig, P., Reichart, D.: Getting SW Engineers on board: Task Modelling with Activity Diagrams. In: EIS 2007. Proceedings of the Engineering Interactive Systems Conference. LNCS, Springer, Heidelberg (to appear)

9. Didonet Del Fabro, M., Bézivin, J., Jouault, F., Breton, E., Gueltas, G.: AMW: a generic model weaver. In: Gérard, S., Favre, J.-M., Muller, P.-A., Blanc, X. (eds.) Proceedings of the 1ére Journée sur l'Ingénierie Dirigée par les Modéles (IDM 2005), Paris, France, pp. 105–114 (2005)

10. Didonet Del Fabro, M., Jouault, F.: Model Transformation and Weaving in the AMMA Platform. In: Lämmel, R., Saraiva, J., Visser, J. (eds.) GTTSE 2005. LNCS, vol. 4143, pp. 71–77. Springer, Heidelberg (2006)

11. Dubois, E., D., P., G., Nigay, L.: ASUR++: a Design Notation for Mobile Mixed Systems. Interacting With Computers 15, 497–520 (2003)

12. Dupuy-Chessa, S., Dubois, E.: Requirements and Impacts of Model Driven Engineering on Mixed Systems Design. In: Gérard, S., Favre, J.-M., Muller, P.-A., Blanc, X. (eds.) Proceedings of the 1ére Journée sur l'Ingénierie Dirigée par les Modéles (IDM 2005), Paris, France, pp. 43–54 (2005)

13. Eclipse Modeling Project. Official site (February 2007), http://www.eclipse.org/modeling/

14. Favre, J.-M.: Towards a basic theory to model driven engineering. 3er UML Workshop in Software Model Engineering (WISME 2004) joint event with UML 2004 (October 2004), Available online at: http://www.metamodel.com/wisme-2004/papers.html

15. Foley, J., Sukaviriya, N.: History, Results, and Bibliography of the User Interface Design Environment (UIDE), an Early Model-based for User Interface Design and Development. In: Paternó, F. (ed.) Interactive Systems: Design, Specification, Verification, pp. 3–14. Springer, Heidelberg (1994)

16. Ian Bull, R., Favre, J.M.: Visualization in the Context of Model Driven Engineering. In: Ian Bull, R., Favre, J.M. (eds.) Proceedings of the International Workshop on Model Driven Development of Advanced User Interfaces (MDDAUI 2005) organized at MoDELS 2005, Jamaica (October 2005)

17. Kalnins, A., Barzdins, J., Celms, E.: Model Transformation Language MOLA. In: Proceedings of Model-Driven Architecture: Foundations and Applications (MDAFA 2004), Linkoeping, Sweden, June 10-11, pp. 14–28 (2004)

18. Kleppe, A., Warmer, S., Bast, W.: MDA explained: The model-driven architecture: Practice and promise, p. 192. Addison-Wesley, Reading (2003)

19. Mens, T., Van Gorp, P.: A Taxonomy of Model Transformation. Electronic Notes in Theorical Computer Science 152, 125–142 (2006)

20. Minsky, M.: Matter, Minds, and Models. In: Proceedings of International Federation of Information Processing Congress, New York, United States, vol. 1, pp. 45–49 (1965)

21. Mori, G., Paternó, F., Santoro, C.: CTTE: Support for Developing and Analyzing Task Models for Interactive Systems Design. IEEE Transactions on Software Engineering 28(8), 797–813 (2002)
22. Myers, B., Hudson, S.E., Pausch, R.: Past, Present, and Future of User Interface Software Tools. ACM Transactions on Computer-Human Interaction 7(1), 3–28 (2000)
23. Nóbrega, L., Jardim, N., Coelho, H.: Mapping ConcurTaskTrees into UML 2. In: Gilroy, S.W., Harrison, M.D. (eds.) Interactive Systems. LNCS, vol. 3941, pp. 237–248. Springer, Heidelberg (2006)
24. Paternó, F.: Model-Based Design and Evaluation of Interactive Application. Springer, Heidelberg (1999)
25. Pinheiro da Silva, P., Paton, N.: User Interface Modeling in UMLi. IEEE Software 20(4), 62–69 (2003)
26. Planet MDE, Official site (September 2007), http://planet-mde.org/index.php?option= com_xcombuilder&cat= Tool&Itemid=47
27. Shaer, O., Leland, N., Calvillo, E.H., Jacob, R.J.K.: The TAC Paradigm: Specifying Tangible User Interfaces. In Personal and Ubiquitous Computing 8(5), 359–369 (2004)
28. Sottet, J-S., Calvary, G., Favre, J-M., Coutaz, J., Demeure, A., Balme, L.: Towards Model Driven Engineering of Plastic User Interfaces. In: Satellite Proceedings of the ACM/IEEE 8th International Conference on Models Driven Engineering Languages and Systems, MoDELS/UML 2005. LNCS, pp. 191–200. Springer, Heidelberg (2005)
29. Sottet, J.-S., Calvary, G., Coutaz, J., Favre, J.-M.: A Model-Driven Engineering Approach for the Usability of Plastic User Interfaces. In: EIS 2007. Proc. of the Engineering Interactive Systems Conference. LNCS, Springer, Heidelberg (to appear)
30. Tariq, N., Akhter, N.: Comparison of Model Driven Architecture (MDA) based tools Karolinska University Hospital; A Thesis Document, Sockholm, Sweden, p. 74 (June 2005)
31. Van den Bergh, J., Coninx, K.: Using UML2.0 and Profiles for Modeling Context-Sensitive User Interfaces. In: Proceedings of the International Workshop on Model Driven Development of Advanced User Interfaces (MDDAUI 2005) organized at MoDELS 2005. CEUR Workshop Proceedings, Jamaica, October 2005, vol. 159 (2005)
32. Viala, J., Dubois, E., Gray, P.: GUIDE-ME: Environement Graphique de Manipulation de la Notation ASUR. In: Canals, G., Giboin, A., Nigay, L., Pinna, A.-M., Tigli, J.-Y. (eds.) ACM Proceedings of the French conference: Mobilite et Ubiquite. 2004, Nice, France, pp. 74–78 (June 2004)
33. Vojtisek, D., Jzquel, J.-M.: MTL and Umlaut NG: Engine and Framework for Model Transformation. ERCIM News, Nro. 58, Special Issue on Automated Software Engineering , 42–45 (2004)

From Task to Dialog Model in the UML

Jan Van den Bergh and Karin Coninx

Hasselt University, transnationale Universiteit Limburg,
Expertise Centre for Digital Media
Wetenschapspark 2
3590 Diepenbeek
Belgium
{jan.vandenbergh,karin.coninx}@uhasselt.be

Abstract. Many model-based approaches for user interface design start
from a task model, for which the ConcurTaskTrees notation is frequently
used. Despite this popularity and the importance that has been given to
a close relation with UML, no relation has been established with UML
state machines, which have been shown to be useful for the description of
the behavior of user interfaces. This paper proposes a semantic mapping
of tasks and all temporal relations of the ConcurTaskTrees to UML state
machines which forms the basis for a compact dialog modeling notation
using UML state machines. The proposed approach uses a UML profile
to reduce the visual complexity of the state machine.

1   Introduction

The ConcurTaskTrees notation (CTT) [12] is one of the most popular notations
for hierarchical task modeling used in academia for model-based design of user
interfaces. Since the Unified Modeling language(UML) [11] is one of the most
established modeling notations for software models, several approaches have been
presented to integrate the ConcurTaskTrees notation into UML.

Nunes and e Cunha[10] made a mapping to UML class diagrams as part of
the Wisdom notation. They mapped each task in the task model to a UML
class. The relations between parent and child tasks are represented using aggre-
gation relationships while the relations between siblings are represented using
constraints. All task categories are represented using the same task symbol.

Nobrega et al. [9] present a different approach which emphasizes the fact that
tasks in the ConcurTaskTrees notation represent activities. Therefore, they show
tasks using the UML notation for actions. They also propose new symbols for
the temporal operators of the ConcurTaskTrees. All changes they proposed were
made to integrate the ConcurTaskTrees notation both visually and semantically
into the UML.

In earlier work [16] we opted to extend the class diagram to represent the
CTT but to keep the appearance closer to the original. This resulted in some
notable differences with the approach presented in [10]: The relations between
tasks are represented by stereotyped associations and each task category keeps

M. Winckler, H. Johnson, and P. Palanque (Eds.): TAMODIA 2007, LNCS 4849, pp. 98–111, 2007.
© Springer-Verlag Berlin Heidelberg 2007

its original symbol (and properties), thus keeping the look of the model closer to the original CTT specification.

A close relationship of the CTT with UML state machines has not been established. It has however been shown that (this type of) hierarchical statecharts can effectively be used to describe [3] and generate user interfaces [1,14]. In this work, we extend the state-of-the-art by presenting a semantic mapping of the dynamic aspects of the task model and exploiting this mapping for a compact, powerful dialog modeling notation using UML state machines.

The mapping between CTT and UML state machines is established by giving a behavioral specification for a task using UML state machines and is discussed in section 4 after a short introduction of both notations. This specification is then used in section 5 to express the behavioral semantics of *all* temporal operators. These specifications are used to derive a dialog model from a CTT model. A UML stereotype is used to reduce the visual complexity of the model. The paper is concluded by a discussion of related work and conclusions.

2   ConcurTaskTrees

The ConcurTaskTrees notation [12] is a hierarchical task modeling notation that has a tree-based structure. All nodes in the tree are tasks. There are four task categories, each having its own symbol: abstraction (☺, an abstract task has subtasks of at least two different task categories), interaction (☝, a task performed through interaction of a user with an application), user(☺, a task performed by the user without interaction with the application) and application (☝, a task performed by the application). Siblings in the tree are connected using temporal operators derived from LOTOS [5]. Section 5 discusses these operators into more detail.

Fig. 1 shows a CTT example. It specifies how a user can check the availability of a hotel room. First the user specifies the start and end date of the stay or the start and duration. Next, the user specifies the room type. The application then checks the available hotel rooms (during that period, `Perform Query`) and shows the available rooms to the user. The user can then refine the selection of available rooms by adapting the period and the room type until the refinements are submitted. The check for availability can be cancelled at any time (`Close Availability`).

3   UML State Machines

UML state machines are an object-based variant of Harel statecharts [2]. Both have the advantage over other forms of statecharts and state transition networks that they support concurrent states. This means that when a UML state machine is executed, it can be in multiple states at a given moment in time. Furthermore Harel statecharts as well as UML state machines allow hierarchical composition of states.

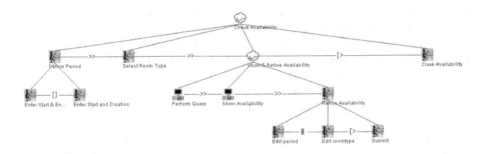

Fig. 1. Example of a CTT specification

Fig. 2 gives an overview of the relevant symbols in this notation. The initial pseudo state and the final state respectively mark the start and the end of a composite state or state machine. An exit point can be used to mark an alternative end point (e.g. due to abnormal behavior). A fork symbol can be used to specify that a single state is followed by two or more concurrent states. A join allows to do the opposite. A choice pseudo state can be used to specify multiple alternative next states. Finally, a small black dot (not shown in Fig. 2 is the symbol for a junction which allows to merge or split transitions (displayed as arrows). For a detailed discussion of UML state machines we refer to the UML Superstructure specification [11].

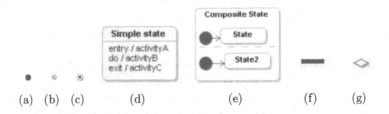

Fig. 2. UML state machine symbols: (a) Initial pseudostate, (b) Exit point, (c) Final state, (d) State with specification of behavior on entry, during and on exit of state, (e) Composite State with two regions specifying concurrent behavior, (f) Fork/join (g) Choice pseudostate

UML state machines have no direct formal mapping, although partial mappings are already specified to stochastic petrinets for UML state machines with the UML realtime stereotype extensions applied [15].

4   Tasks in UML

As mentioned in the introduction, different representations of the CTT in UML have been proposed. Fig. 3 shows the CTT task model of Fig. 1 using the Wisdom notation, proposed in [10]. It clearly shows that each task is represented by the same icon. This icon is related to the stereotype[1]. The task categories are represented by tagged values (shown between brackets such as *application* in Fig. 3) unless they are interactive tasks. Constraints are used to denote the temporal relations. When no constraints are applied between the parent-child relationships of two sibling tasks, these tasks are executed in concurrency.

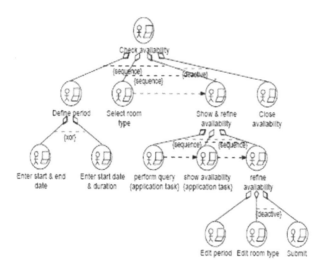

Fig. 3. The example of Fig. 1 using Wisdom notation [10]

In earlier work [16] we presented an alternative representation in UML with a notation that is closer to the original. In fact, the CTT model shown in figure 1 can be modeled using the CTT UML profile[2]. Some differences arise when a task is optional or iterative. These properties are modeled as tagged values, which can be shown when desired.

As both of these approaches use classes to represent tasks and classes can own state machines, a state machine is a natural choice for specifying the behavior of a task. The state machine specification thus complements the specification using classes and gives more details about the behavioral properties of the tasks, while class diagrams can be used to specify the structural properties.

To describe the behavior associated with a task, we model the different states of execution. At the highest level we discern two stages: *active* and *inactive*. These stages can on their turn be subdivided in different states. A task can be considered to be inactive, when it is not yet activated, when it has been successfully *completed* or when it has been *aborted*. The *active* state can be subdivided into two states: *executing* and *sleeping*.

---

[1] Stereotypes are a light-weight method to extend UML metaclasses.

[2] The profile is made in MagicDraw and available at http://research.edm.uhasselt. be/~jvandenbergh/cup/ContextualConcurTaskTrees.mdzip.

Fig. 4 shows the state machine that can be associated with a task T1. Whenever the state T1 is activated (T1 being the name of the task), the task is considered *active*. The inactive states are depicted in Fig. 4 for completeness. They will not be depicted in further diagrams. On entry and exit of the states T1 and Executing, an activity is specified. These activities broadcast an event, which can trigger state changes for other tasks. All these events have an attribute that specifies the source of the event. On entry of the state T1 an event, *activated*, is broadcasted indicating that T1 is *active*. When the actual execution of a task starts an event, *started*, is broadcasted. When an event *stopped* is sent, the task is no longer executing, but the execution might be resumed. The event *ended* indicates that the task has become inactive.

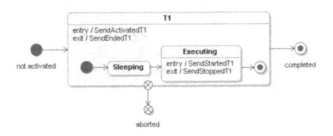

Fig. 4. Task states

The exact meaning of these states depends on the task category and on the platform and context in which the interaction is taking place. Table 1 shows a possible mapping for the states of an interaction task to a concrete context: desktop interaction using a multi-window desktop such as MS Windows or MacOS. The states of an application task presenting data to the user can be described in a similar manner. When the application task is not directly represented on the screen the states might be mapped to the states of the thread or process that executes the task. Giving a concrete description of the states for a user task in general is not as straightforward, although it should be easy to do for user tasks that involve physical activity on a case by case basis.

5   CTT Task Relations and UML State Machines

In this section we discuss how the task representation introduced in section 4 can express the temporal relations of the CTT. For each temporal operator a diagram is discussed that shows the application of the operator to two tasks.

concurrency. The concurrency operator (|||) expresses that two task can be executed in any order and can interrupt each other. It has a straightforward mapping to UML state machines when the state machine definition in Fig. 4 is used. Fig. 5(a) shows that two parallel tasks can be represented by embedding each task representation in a separate region of a complex state.

Table 1. States of task execution for an interaction task on a pc using a graphical user interface

state	description
active	the window containing the user interface controls associated to the task is shown on the screen
sleeping	the user interface controls associated to the task are disabled or not visible
executing	the user interface controls associated to the task are enabled and visible

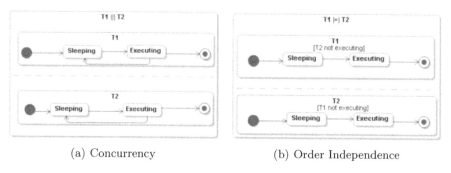

(a) Concurrency   (b) Order Independence

Fig. 5. Concurrency and order independence

order independence. When the order independence operator (|=|) is used between two sibling tasks T1 and T2, these tasks can be executed in any order but not concurrently. This means that when T1 is executing, T2 cannot start execution and vice versa. When one of the tasks is completed, the other can start executing. Fig. 5(b) also clearly shows that the two tasks cannot interrupt each other.

suspend/resume. The suspend/resume operator (|>) suspends one task while another one is executing. Using the terminology introduced in section 4 this means that for the expression T1 |> T2, T1 cannot be in the state `executing` when T2 is in that same state. This is reflected in the diagram in figure 6. The transition from *sleeping* to *executing* is only possible for task T1, when task T2 is not in the executing state. A transition from *sleeping* to *executing* of the task T2 triggers the inverse transition of task T1.

enabling. The main property of the enabling operator is that the tasks that are its operands are executed one after the other. In terms of the proposed state machine for tasks, this means that there is only a constraint on the order of the `executing` state. Fig. 7 thus shows two different state machines that satisfy that constraint. Fig. 7(a) corresponds to the situation where only the tasks that belong to the same enabled task set (ETS) are presented in the user interface. An ETS is a set of tasks that are logically enabled to start their performance during

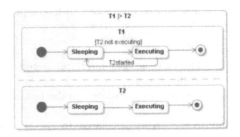

Fig. 6. Suspend/Resume

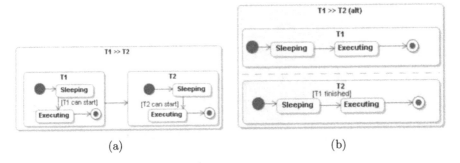

(a)   (b)

Fig. 7. Enabling

the same period of time [12]. Fig. 7(b) corresponds to a situation where two ETSs are merged into a single task set. [13] proposes some heuristics for when such a merge can be desired. Note that unlike many dialog models, Fig. 7(b) still shows that T2 cannot be executed until T1 is finished. This ensures that the dialog model is consistent with the task model, even when ETSs are merged.

deactivation. The deactivation operator ([>) can be used to let one task interrupt the execution of another task and prevent further execution of that task. Fig. 8 shows what this means in terms of our UML state machine representation. T1 [> T2 means that when T2 ends execution, T1 immediately becomes inactive. Note that both diagrams in Fig. 8 result in the described effect. The approach in Fig. 8(a) can be extended to work when T2 has subtasks (although the first subtask of T2 should be used in this case to be compliant with the CTT specification, while the approach in Fig. 8 cannot but offers a simpler syntax instead.

choice. The choice operator ([]) offers the option to choose between two tasks of which only one may be completed. As soon as one of the tasks starts execution, the other tasks become inactive. This prevents that more than one task is executing at the same time. This type of choice is called a "deterministic choice" in

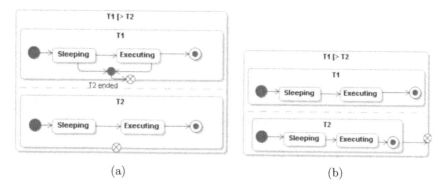

Fig. 8. deactivation

[4]. The same article also describes a non-deterministic choice. This latter type of choice only allows one task to complete; the other options will not become inactive until one of the tasks has been completed (see Fig. 9(b)).

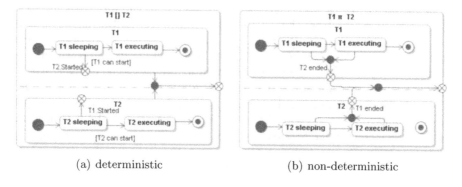

(a) deterministic   (b) non-deterministic

Fig. 9. Choice

task iteration. The two possibilities that are offered by the CTT notation for the expression of iterating task can be expressed as is shown in Fig. 10. Both diagrams using UML state machines clearly show the semantics of the iteration operators in the CTT; the repeatable task has to be completed before another iteration of the task can be repeated.

optional. The state machine representation of an optional task contains an additional transition from the sleeping state to the final pseudo state. The transition is triggered by the completion of a task that triggers a transition to another enabled task set.

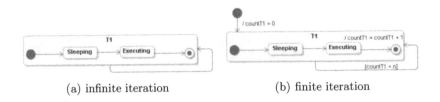

(a) infinite iteration   (b) finite iteration

Fig. 10. Task iteration

6   Towards a Dialog Model

The previous section showed that it is possible to combine the UML state machine description of two (or more) sibling tasks. To create an effective dialog model, however, a complete task model has to be converted into a UML state machine. In this section, we demonstrate by example that it is possible to do so for the task model in Fig. 1.

6.1   The CTT Example

Fig. 11 shows the UML state machine corresponding to the CTT task model in Fig. 1. The hierarchy from the CTT model is preserved in this example. This is however a choice made, not an obligation. Furthermore, one-to-one mapping might not always be possible in the general case but no definitive claims can be made about this without further investigation and in some cases it may be desirable not to copy all abstraction levels from the CTT to the state machine.

We can see that the top-level state is split into four concurrent regions, each corresponding to a direct child of the top-level task in the CTT. The fact that their are four concurrent regions is caused by the choice to use the mapping in Fig. 7(b) for the enabling operator between the tasks **Define period** and **Select room type**, and the tasks **Select Room type** and **Show and refine availability**. For the enabling operator between the tasks **Perform query** and **Show Availability**, the other option was chosen, resulting in a sequence of states within the first region of the task **Show and refine availability**.

When observing the diagram, we can also see the two options to indicate the deactivation operator. The option in Fig. 8(a) is applied for the task **Submit**, while the other option is applied for the task **Close Availability**. It is clear that the choice for the second option reduces the complexity of the overall diagram.

The example in Fig. 11 shows that it is possible to use the proposed notation to map the behavior of the CTT to the UML state machines. The resulting notation is however too complex to quickly understand the meaning of the diagram. To resolve this issue we opted to define a UML profile, which should reduce the complexity of the notation. The profile is discussed into more detail in the following section.

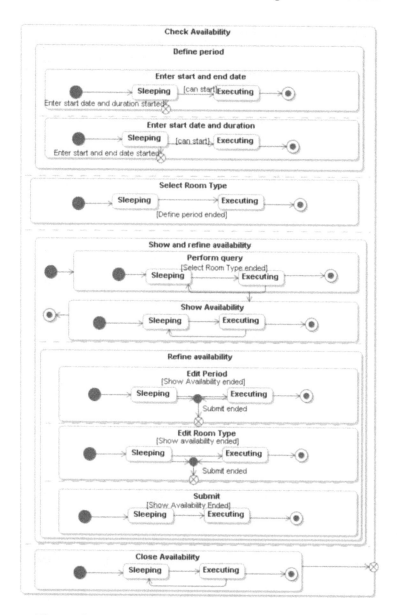

Fig. 11. UML state machine corresponding to Fig. 1 and Fig. 3

6.2   Simplified Notation for a Dialog Model

Fig. 12 gives an overview of the UML profile we defined to simplify the notation for interactive use of the notation. The profile consists of a single stereotype, << task>> for the State metaclass. When the UML-profile is applied to a

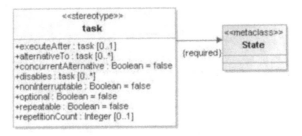

Fig. 12. Proposed stereotype for the *State* metaclass

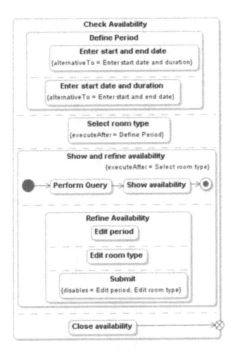

Fig. 13. Simplified notation of Fig. 11 using the stereotype << task>>

UML state machine, the stereotype should be applied to all instances of the metaclass State, i.e. all states in the diagram.

Seven tagged values are defined within the stereotype, which relate to the different temporal operators: executeAfter specifies the task after the completion of which the current task can start executing. It is used in case an overlap in the *active* state of the two tasks is desired as is specified in Fig. 7(b). alternativeTo allows to specify an alternative task. The collection of tasks specified by this tagged value contains one or more tasks when the corresponding task in the CTT is an operand of the choice operator. concurrentAlternative is set to true in case of non-deterministic choice. disables is a non-empty collection of tasks when the corresponding task in the CTT is the right-operand of a deactivation operator and the mapping to Fig. 8(a) is chosen. `nonInterruptable` is `true` when the corresponding task in the CTT is an operand of the operator order independent. `optional` is `true` when the operator optional is applied to the corresponding task in CTT. `repeatable` is set to true when the corresponding task is repeatable. `repetitionCount` can be used to set the number of repetitions.

Fig. 13 shows the simplified version of the state machine in Fig. 11. This diagram is clearly more readable, because the added complexity of the substates and associated transitions of the task state *active* is removed from the diagram. Since all states have the stereotype << `task`>> applied to them, this stereotype is not shown in the diagram. For those states that have a tagged value that contains one or more values, the name of the tagged value as well as the values are shown below the state name between parentheses. For states whose corresponding task is `optional` or `nonInterruptable` or `repeatable` only the name of the tagged value will be shown. Note that there is no such task in this example.

Taking into account the concrete semantics for the task states presented in section 4 and table 1, we can state that we can consider the diagram in Fig. 13 to be a high-level dialog model. A complex state can correspond to a single dialog or window or a part thereof. Fig. 13 can thus describe the dynamic composition of a single window.

7   Related Work

One can find several approaches to define the semantics of the temporal operators of the CTT in literature. Some provide an informal definition of the temporal operators such as Mori et al. [7]. They also present an algorithm to transform the CTT to a set of enabled task sets (ETSs). Mori et al. [8] also propose an abstract user interface model that contains a dialogue model description. This notation is based on task sets and transition tasks.

A more formal definition of the CTT is given by Luyten al. [6] who use these definitions to define an alternative transformation algorithm from the CTT to a set of ETSs. They do not give semantics of the temporal operators except that two of them cause transitions: the enabling and deactivation operators.

Both aforementioned approaches do not support nested states, which means that merging task sets creates inconsistencies between the task model and abstract user interface model.

Nobrega et al. [9] provide a mapping of the CTT to UML 2.0. They define the semantics of most of the operators by defining a mapping to UML 2.0 activity diagrams. In contrast to this work, they do not provide a definition for the suspend/resume operator. They do propose an extension to UML, with a hierarchical task notation, which reuses as much symbols of UML as possible for the newly introduced concepts. This notation is, however, not used to derive further specifications, such as a dialog or abstract user interface model.

Elkoutbi et al. [1] propose a semi-automated approach to derive interactive prototypes from scenarios specified using UML use cases, class diagrams and collaboration diagrams. This approach uses statecharts as an intermediate step to specify the behavior of the interactive prototype. Their approach shows the capabilities of the UML state machines (with nested states) as a specification language that can be used for generation of user interface prototypes.

8   Conclusion

In this paper we proposed a general description of the task execution cycle using UML state machines. We described the influence of the temporal operators on this description. An example that combined the states for a complete task model into one stage machine demonstrated the complexity of the notation for larger compositions. We thus proposed an abbreviated notation for this integrated notation using a small UML profile. This profile adds extra semantics to the states, which can be used to generate the complete specification. The support for nested states offers enhanced expressiveness over other solutions such as state transition networks.

The usage of UML enables the application of proven transformation tools to be applied on the models to generate dialog models at different levels of abstractions and adapted to different contexts of use. Further exploration of this route is planned as future work. Building on the work of [15] would allow to exploit all formal work done on petri nets.

Acknowledgements. Part of the research at EDM is funded by EFRD (European Fund for Regional Development), the Flemish Government and the Flemish Interdisciplinary institute for Broadband Technology (IBBT).

References

1. Elkoutbi, M., Khriss, I., Keller, R.: Automated prototyping of user interfaces based on uml scenarios. Automated Software Engineering 13(1), 5–40 (2006)
2. Harel, D.: Statecharts: a visual formalism for complex systems. Science of Computer Programming 8(3), 231–274 (1987)
3. Horrocks, I.: Constructing the User Interface with Statecharts. Addison-Wesley Professional (1999)
4. Limbourg, Q.: Multi-path development of User Interfaces. PhD thesis, Université Catholique de Louvain (2004)
5. Logrippo, L., Faci, M., Haj-Hussein, M.: An Introduction to LOTOS: Learning by Examples. Computer Networks and ISDN Systems 23(5), 325–342 (1991)
6. Luyten, K., Clerckx, T., Coninx, K.: Derivation of a Dialog Model from a Task Model by Activity Chain Extraction. In: Jorge, J.A., Jardim Nunes, N., Falcão e Cunha, J. (eds.) DSV-IS 2003. LNCS, vol. 2844, pp. 203–217. Springer, Heidelberg (2003)
7. Mori, G., Paternò, F., Santoro, C.: CTTE: support for developing and analyzing task models for interactive system design. IEEE Transactions on Software Engineering 28(8), 797–813 (2002)

8. Mori, G., Paternò, F., Santoro, C.: Design and development of multidevice user interfaces through multiple logical descriptions. IEEE Transactions on Sofware Engineering 30(8), 507–520 (2004)
9. Nobrega, L., Nunes, N.J., Coelho, H.: Mapping concurtasktrees into uml 2. In: Gilroy, S.W., Harrison, M.D. (eds.) Interactive Systems. LNCS, vol. 3941, Springer, Heidelberg (2006)
10. Nunes, N.J., Cunha, J.F.e.: Towards a uml profile for interaction design: the wisdom approach. In: Evans, A., Kent, S., Selic, B. (eds.) UML 2000. LNCS, vol. 1939, pp. 101–116. Springer, Heidelberg (2000)
11. Object Management Group. UML 2.0 Superstructure Specification (October 8, 2004)
12. Paternò, F.: Model-Based Design and Evaluation of Interactive Applications. Springer, Heidelberg (2000)
13. Paternò, F., Santoro, C.: One model, many interfaces. In: Kolski, C., Vanderdonckt, J. (eds.) CADUI 2002, vol. 3, pp. 143–154. Kluwer Academic, Dordrecht (2002)
14. Sauer, S., Dürksen, M., Gebel, A., Hannwacker, D.: Guibuilder - a tool for model-driven development of multimedia user interfaces. In: MoDELS 2006. LNCS, vol. 214, Springer, Heidelberg (2006)
15. Trowitzsch, J., Zimmermann, A.: Using uml state machines and petri nets for the quantitative investigation of etcs. In: valuetools 2006: Proceedings of the 1st international conference on Performance evaluation methodlgies and tools, p. 34. ACM Press, New York (2006)
16. Van den Bergh, J.: High-Level User Interface Models for Model-Driven Design of Context-Sensitive Interactive Applications. PhD thesis, Hasselt University (transnationale Universiteit Limburg) (October 2006)

Towards Method Engineering of Model-Driven User Interface Development

Kênia Sousa, Hildeberto Mendonça, and Jean Vanderdonckt

Université catholique de Louvain, IAG-Louvain School of Management,
Information Systems Unit (ISYS)
Place de Doyens 1, B-1348 Louvain-La-Neuve (Belgium)
{sousa, mendonca, vanderdonckt}@isys.ucl.ac.be

Abstract. Model-driven user interface development environments and their associated methodologies have evolved over time to become more explicit, flexible, and reusable but they still lack to reach a level that allows tailoring a method to the reality of software development organizations and their projects. In order to address this shortcoming, method engineering provides strategies to define and tailor software engineering methods. They should address any usability concerns, which are primordial for the integration of model-driven user interface development methods in the competitive reality of software organizations. To address the issues of explicitly defining a flexible method, we defined a strategy based on method engineering for model-driven user interface development that uses usability goals as a starting point. With the application of this strategy, we aim to help method engineers executing the method with more efficiency when defining or tailoring methods and facilitate the application of model-based user interface development methods in software organizations.

Keywords: model-driven user interface development, methodologies, method engineering, business process modeling, usability.

1 Introduction

Any development method or methodology, whether it is generic or specific for User Interface (UI) for instance, is usually decomposed into three related axes:

1. *Models* that capture different facets of the future interactive application.
2. An *Approach* which governs the actions conducted on the various models.
3. *Software* that supports executing the approach based on the models.

On the one hand, substantive efforts have been devoted to the definition and the usage of models, and extensive development of support software has been achieved. On the other hand, the approach aspect has received less attention over the past decades. Even though, there are many User Interface Development (UID) methods that use task models as a starting point to elicit user requirements and more precisely understand user cognition in order to make UIs more usable. Such a growing interest for models is due to the need to provide a more systematic approach to UID.

Professionals working in systems development usually follow a defined software development process, and when it comes to UID, many professionals do their activities

M. Winckler, H. Johnson, and P. Palanque (Eds.): TAMODIA 2007, LNCS 4849, pp. 112–125, 2007.
© Springer-Verlag Berlin Heidelberg 2007

more empirically because there is still resistance to the application of usability methodologies in software organizations [26], such as resource constraints and lack of knowledge about usability are the factors that most influence professionals. But, a formal UID method requires efficiency to be integrated into software development organizations. Model-based UID comes as a solution to improve efficiency by reusing models, reducing development efforts, among other benefits [3].

To make model-based UID methods applicable in the competitive reality of software development organizations, they need to be explicitly defined with the possibility of easy adaptation when it is necessary to consider constraints pertaining to specific projects [27,33]. Software organizations and their projects have specific characteristics, which require methods to be tailored, for instance, the skills and quantity of professionals affect how the method could be applied. UID is a creative process in which professionals feel the need for flexibility in their work to address the growing complexity of interactive systems. Therefore, a rigid method is no longer desired and there is a need to support method definition and adaptation. In the reality of software organizations and the need for tailoring the method for specific projects, the possibility to reuse pre-defined method specifications aids in accomplishing efficiency.

Considering this scenario, our main research question is: *How can method engineers define a model-based (or model-driven) UID method appropriate for the reality of the software organization and its projects?*

This research work aims to contribute in supporting the application of model-based UID methods efficiently by providing flexibility in its definition. Considering that the existing methods are diffused and applied in different projects around the world, such knowledge and experience acquired can not be taken for granted. Therefore, it is not the intention of this work to define a method nor to compare existing methods because we consider that a more appropriate method is adapted to the problem domain or context of the project, which has been investigated since the early 90's [17,27].

Concerning a possible automation for this support, it is important to address issues related to the creation and maintenance of a method base with propagation of changes in method specifications; how the model editors are integrated with the method tool; collaboration between professionals in the creation of models; the automatic or semi-automatic generation of UIs; coordination of the use of tools; change management of models; and support coordination of cooperative work. Solutions for these issues are appropriately addressed by technology for process automation, which allows executing methods. But such technology requires explaining many details that are not the focus of this work, but subject for another ongoing work.

This paper compares some existing solutions for the definition of methods and points out some shortcomings when considering model-based UID. In the upcoming sections, it proposes an approach for defining a model-based UID method by analyzing goals and activities, and it concludes by presenting the expected advantages and future work.

2 Related Work

A survey performed on Model-Based User Interface Development Environments (MB-UIDE) [16] showed that most of them provide a methodology for UI generation. These environments however support the execution of the methodology by automating some steps to generate a running UI or a specification of the UI; and even though some favor concurrent work or different sequence possibilities, they do not allow adapting the methodology according to the context of the project.

There are many MB-UIDEs that follow a formalized method [6,28,32], but their supporting tools do not provide facilities to change the sequence of the method activities, thus restricting the possibilities to adapt the method. Fig. 1 depicts the level of method flexibility of MB-UIDEs over time: oldest systems in the 90s had no method at all, except perhaps the one induced by the software; old systems like TRIDENT [5] has a very limited method flexibility since the method is completely coupled to the software and no tailoring is possible; TEALLACH [16] offers some flexibility since the design can start from one of the task, domain, and presentation models and evolve to the other models depending on the project; Cameleon-compliant software [10] are much more numerous today ([14,17,22,28,30] among others) and provide some adaptation of the method they rely on.

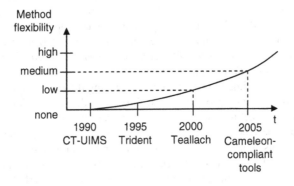

Fig. 1. The evolution of MB-UIDEs

The TEALLACH design process [16] aims to support the flexibility for the designer lacking in existing environments by providing a variety of routes in the process; from one entry point, the designer/developer can select any model to design independently or associate with other models. Even though this is a flexible approach to design UIs, it still hinders a complete flexibility because it is restrictive to the sequence of manipulation of models. Its flexibility is not extended enough to address the entire set of activities, roles, tools, and artifacts. For example, if a software organization aims at applying a method with such characteristic, it is limited by a set of models and activities implemented in the environment. Following, we present an overview of the assessment of model-based methodologies considering three main criteria:

Explicitness. Most methodologies have some kind of method definition, but not all aspects are explicitly defined, such as the association of roles, activities, models, and tools. For instance, some define the lifecycle as a sequence of transformation between models [32], some associate activities with the creation of models, but there is no association with the role responsible for executing them [6], while others have the methodology implemented in the environment, but not explicitly defined. Most of them do not mention tool in the lifecycle because their proposal is an environment to support the lifecycle.

Flexibility. The methodologies that are part of a MB-UIDE are not flexible enough [16], but TEALLACH comes as a solution to fulfill this need. Even though it provides a flexible approach, in the point of view of software development organizations, flexibility has a broader sense, which advocates the ability to change any aspect of the method and integrate with any existing process and tool.

Reuse. Some methodologies in MB-UIDE have a set of activities to be performed, within them, there is usually a set of activities that are not mandatory and can be executed or not, depending on the project's need. But, the idea of reuse is to offer a larger set of activities that provide a wider range of possibilities in different types of projects that could be selected for the method as necessary. This type of strategy is not common in MB-UIDE since the methodology is composed of a small set of activities targeted at a specific goal, such as in the use of patterns [28].

For application in real projects, existing approaches and their environments require organizations to start from scratch to apply the methodology available in the environment. To enhance the effect of methods, we need to adapt existing methods or create a new one that fits to the characteristics of each new project [27].

In a response to this demand, the term method engineering has been introduced as the "engineering discipline to design, construct and adapt methods, techniques and tools for the development of information systems." [7,8]

As an effort to address demands of flexible methods, there are several proposals to automate method engineering, as one of them, *Computer Aided Method Engineering* (CAME) supports building project-specific methods [27]. CAME has two types of tools; the first one is a method editor that creates a method and the second one is a generator of model editors based on the method meta-model to support the created method. This approach to generate CASE tools based on the method description decreases the possibilities of applying the newly created method with external tools, which are currently widely accepted for modeling software systems, as proposed in [17]. This work does not mention how this proposal applies in projects in which the software organization already has standardized a set of tools.

MetaEdit+ offers a CAME environment that allows method specification, integration, management, and maintenance [33]. It focuses on reuse and maintenance aspects for methodology specifications. It provides five strategies when requirements change may affect both the generated models and also the methodology. One detected drawback is that there is still no feature to support the reuse operation in building relationships between methodologies. We envision that during method specification it is primordial to allow integration with other methodologies because software organizations already applying a method may want to accommodate new techniques, in order not to start from scratch with a brand new method.

Decamerone [19] provides a way to adapt and integrate methods stored in a method base. Mentor [29] provides patterns for method engineers to easily design the method. An important aspect is that the generated methods and/or model editors are aimed for information system development, such as database systems, such editors do not address the complexity and creativity necessary in model-based UID.

After analyzing some approaches, the major weaknesses in these approaches is that MB-UIDEs focus on a specific and not so flexible methodology and CAME tools, even though they provide explicitness, flexibility and reuse, they only focus on system development, letting aside the concerns of usability, therefore not fully addressing the definition of model-based UID methods. MB-UIDEs do not allow the definition or adaptation of a method according to the characteristics of the organization and project, which makes them difficult to introduce certain activities that support model-based UID, such as version control. CAME tools are limited to software engineering models and method fragments and since they use a product meta model to generate model editors, they can profit from a meta model for UI models. Therefore, there is a need of interaction between MB-UIDEs and method engineering environments.

In this paper, our goal is to suggest a Model-Based User Interface Method Engineering that can address issues related to method engineering for model-based UID. We shall investigate model-based UID activities to be performed by designers and other usability team members to envision how usability goals specified by stakeholders in the beginning of the project affect the way the usability team works. In other words, we seek to demonstrate the relationship between model-based UID method activities and the desired usability goals and how this association helps outline a method that best suits the context of the project.

3 UID Activities

Considering the evolution of MB-UIDEs and their methodologies over time, it is noticeable the increase in flexibility, as presented in Fig. 1. The Cameleon Reference Framework [10] brings a solution that supports the realization of multiples types of development paths within a single framework. This framework structures a set of models that provide a support for the current user interaction challenges. This framework has 5 models distributed in 4 levels of abstractions in order to express the UID life cycle for different contexts of use. These levels of abstraction are aligned with the model-driven approach, which aims to reduce both the amount of developer effort and the complexity of the models used [18].

The language UsiXML [22] was created as a XML extension to describe UIs for multiple contexts of use, such as graphical, auditory and vocal user interfaces, virtual reality, and multimodal user interfaces. As a language explicitly based on the Cameleon Reference Framework, it adopts four development steps: 1) Task & Concepts, 2) Abstract User Interface (AUI), 3) Concrete User Interface (CUI), and 4) Final UI. The first step generates the task model, domain model and context model, the second step generates the AUI, and the third step generates the CUI. The language does not consider the Final UI as the framework does. The UsiXML methodology is structured as presented in Fig. 2 [30].

Techniques proposed based on UsiXML

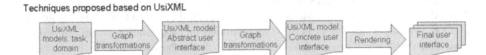

Fig. 2. The distribution of UsiXML models

The UsiXML language will be used to exemplify our proposal in the next sections since it provides the necessary support to represent models in a structured form and it supports the flexibility provided by the Cameleon Framework.

There is a suite of tools, automated techniques, and a framework to support the creation of models, and there is also a running effort to define a detailed model-based UID method. As follows, we explain how we intend to define such a method and how to integrate it with a software development process.

3.1 Theoretical Concepts

In this section, we describe the main theoretical concepts considered as the foundation of our proposal: model-based UID method engineering.

The proposed structure is based on the definition of method content from the Software Process Engineering Metamodel (SPEM), a meta-model for defining software development processes [25]. Considering that SPEM is "limited to the minimal elements necessary to define any software and systems development process, without adding specific features for particular development domains or disciplines" [25], we aim to add specific elements for UID. The main goal is to make usability as a central point not only for UI designers, but even before they come into action during software development processes; making usability also a concern for method engineers.

Fig. 3 depicts a class diagram with the most relevant elements for the definition of a model-based UID method. This proposal shall evolve progressively to address the organization of method activities in a process lifecycle nor does it consider the method enactment (or execution). This proposal extends the basic elements of a method engineering notation by associating usability goals with activities, which will be presented in the next sub-section. In general, a method is defined by describing Activities, which are selected for a Project based on Usability Goals. Activities are performed by Roles, and act upon Work Products using Tools to manage the work products, which can be UI Models.

Usability Goals should be established early in the project to drive professionals into focusing on UID efforts, and to use these goals as precise resources to evaluate their work towards accomplishing these goals. Usability goals can shorten the UID lifecycle, as stated in the Usability Engineering Lifecycle [23]. This methodology establishes usability goals in the requirements analysis phase and uses them to assess UIs during usability evaluation. In our work, usability goals have yet another purpose because they are used in the identification of activities that are appropriate for a specific project. The impact that usability goals can bring to method definition is to provide a manner to make method engineers (as well as project managers) more aligned with usability from the beginning until the end of the project, in order to make sure that all stakeholders value the importance to check whether or not such goals were accomplished in the end.

Projects are composed of activities that are performed to develop a system. *Activities* represent the work that is performed by roles when acting upon work products and using a tool. *Roles* define a set of competencies that professionals must have to execute such role by performing activities and being responsible for work products. *Work Products* are assets or artifacts that are used, produced or updated during the execution of activities using a tool. Work Products can be input or output of activities

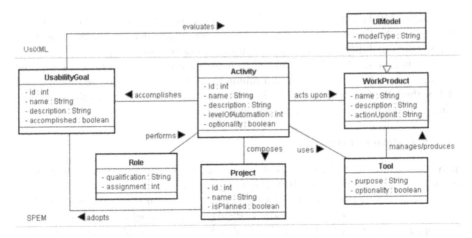

Fig. 3. Concepts for Model-Based UID Method Engineering

performed by roles. For a model-based UID method, the main work products are *UI models*. *Tools* support the execution of activities by managing work products, that is, a tool can manage one or more kinds of work products.

Activities can also be supported by other kinds of implementation besides tools, when it is necessary to implement functionalities that do not need tools or that can be available in more than one tool. In such cases and considering the current technology for process automation, we propose the use of web services.

In general, web services "allow access to a functionality via the web using a set of open standards that make the interaction independent of implementation aspects, such as the operating system platform and the programming language used" [12]. This technology promotes a high level of coherence and a low level of coupling, which contributes to assemble services to compose a method. Business Process Execution Language (BPEL) [4] was defined by W3C to promote assembling services. It has reached a good maturity and it is supported by the main architectures available in the market, such as JEE and .NET.

3.2 Strategy to Define a Method

Aiming at systematizing how a method can be defined and evolved, an evolution driven method engineering approach [2] was defined with two main goals: construct a product model and construct a process model. Focusing on the process model, this approach proposes four strategies to describe a process model:

i) *activity-based*, description of a set of actions to be carried out;
ii) *context-driven*, description considering the context, which is composed of the situation in which the product is undergoing transformation and the intention to be achieved in this situation;
iii) *pattern-driven*, use of a catalogue of patterns with the identification of generic problems and proposal of solutions applicable whenever the problem occurs;
iv) *strategy-driven*, integration of several process models into a complex multi-process model.

We selected the activity-based strategy to help method engineers in identifying activities to construct a method. We have adapted this strategy to the HCI domain, by proposing the identification of usability goals and their association with UID activities that can be included in the method to achieve the desired goals.

Depending on the usability goals presented early in the project specification and system requirements, a set of UID activities could be selected as part of the tailored method. Consequently, the activities performed by the professionals are aligned with the usability goals of the project with two main advantages. First, they are more effective in performing their work because each activity performed has a specific purpose. Second, if any non-planned goal is presented during the UID lifecycle, the method can be adapted with the selection of appropriate activities. A usability goal is a generic specification that can be addressed by one or more UID activities (see Table 1).

Table 1. Association of Goals and Activities

Usability Goal	UID Activity	Description
Design UIs considering users' mental models to perform their tasks	Create task model	Describe tasks in a hierarchical manner.
Design user-centered UIs	Create context of use model	Describe user's characteristics, platform used and environment.
Design UIs focused on the application domain	Create domain model	Describe the manipulated data.
Design for many devices	Create Abstract UI (AUI) model	Specify objects in a UI, independent of device.
Design focused on the look-and-feel of the system	Create Concrete UI (CUI) model	Specify positioning of objects in a UI, considering device constraints.
Adapt the user interaction according to users' personal characteristics	Create context of use model	Specify user's characteristics.
	Create task model	Specify user's tasks according to their specific characteristics.
Automate the generation of UIs considering many devices	Transform task and domain models into AUI model	Receive task model and domain model as input and generate AUI model.
	Transform AUI model into CUI model	Receive AUI model as input and generate CUI model.
Automate the generation of UIs for a specific device	Transform task and domain models into CUI model	Receive task model and domain model as input and generate CUI model.
Automate the generation of specification of UIs	Transform AUI into task model	Receive AUI as input and generate task model.

An activity can be associated with one or more usability goals, which is the case of the UID activity "Create task model". But, this does not mean that once the position and ordering of this activity has been defined, it has to be repeated twice for the different goals to be accomplished. On the other hand, it means that if a project needs to achieve both goals, the execution of this activity addresses both of them.

Depending on the usability goals, activities can be selected independently of each other, which is the case for the activities "Create task model" and "Create context of use model" with their own specific goal. But, in cases of a usability goal triggering more than one activity, their order of execution is clearly specified because one activity has a direct impact on the other, which is the case of executing the activity "Create context of use model" before the activity "Create task model" for the usability goal "Adapt the user interaction according to users' personal characteristics".

In cases when stakeholders state that they want some kind of automation in UID to achieve more productivity, certain activities can be selected depending on the goal. For instance, the activity "Transform task and domain models into AUI model" is appropriate when various devices are considered and the activity "Transform AUI model into CUI model" also aids in the productivity level of designers since they receive UIs with the necessary objects as a starting point to work on the look-and-feel. The activity "Transform task and domain models into CUI model" is useful when one specific device is the aim.

UID activities that are commonly used may already be included in software development processes, such as defining a style guide, prototyping, usability evaluation, among others. But, in cases where such activities are not yet part of the organizational software process, usability goals must be considered to correctly apply these activities. It is our intention to further improve the list in Table 1 with usability goals associated to such activities.

3.3 Tool Support

Tool support for method engineers can be very useful for their productivity when defining or customizing methods. The process of deciding which are the most appropriate activities for specific projects requires knowledge and experience, but tools can help them to maintain a base of experiences and learned lessons, when easily accessed can add value to their work. Therefore, in addition to the strategy presented in the previous section, we selected Business Process Modeling Notation (BPMN) as a standard with available tools to support method engineers.

BPMN was proposed to be applied in the representation of organizational processes [24], and we propose to use BPMN in method definition because: i) it has become a pattern for process modeling; ii) there are many tools available in the market implementing it; iii) it has been intended as a human-readable layer that hides the complexity of designing transactional business processes; and iv) BPMN can be transformed in BPEL to be automated using web services, as described at the end of section 3.1.

There are many tools available that implement BPMN, which provide the necessary support for method engineers that follow a common structure as in the tool presented in Fig. 4. But, after the assessment of model-based UID methods, we noticed the need to use method engineering techniques to improve method definition.

Therefore, we have analyzed the alignment of BPMN with a software engineering notation, more specifically with SPEM. The alignment and complementary aspect is
confirmed by quoting the SPEM documentation [25]: "SPEM 2.0 does not aim to be a
generic process modeling language, nor does it even provide its own behavior modeling concepts. SPEM 2.0 focuses on providing the additional information structures
that you need for processes modeled with UML 2.0 Activities or BPMN/BPDM to
describe an actual development process." Using a process modeling tool to define a
method, we have followed three steps, as pointed out in Fig. 4:

1. *Definition of activities* – we have defined a list of activities for a model-based UID
   method based on the Cameleon Framework.
2. *Association of BPMN and SPEM* – we have associated BPMN elements with
   SPEM elements to give meaning and use business process elements in the method
   engineering domain.
3. *Reuse of activities* – drag and drop activities from the pre-defined list (on the left
   of the tool) and reuse them when defining the method for a specific project, in the
   desired or recommended order.

The method defined on the right side of the tool in Fig. 4 is clearly related with the
concepts defined in Fig. 3. For example, the Role "Usability Expert" performs the Activity "Create AUI" and acts upon (by creating) the Work Product, which in this case
is a UI Model "AUI Model" by using the Tool "IdealXML". To complete, this activity is present in this method because the stakeholders stated the Usability Goal "Design for many devices", which is directly associated with the activity "Create AUI".

After analyzing which activities are important to achieve certain usability goals and
selecting the appropriate ones, it becomes easier to define a method. We must furthermore be able to define methods that are applicable in software development

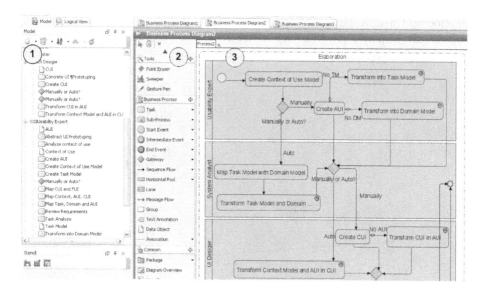

Fig. 4. Activity selection using a process modeling tool [31]

projects and also provide support for model-based UID. Following, we demonstrate an example of integration of model-based UID activities in a software development process.

4 Integration of Methods

In an attempt to make UID methods really effective in real projects, there have been various efforts to bridge the gap between software engineering and HCI. Some proposals focus on user involvement [15], on how to help software engineers execute usability techniques [13], on addressing usability issues using architectural patterns [20], others are product-oriented and adapt an object-oriented notation to support HCI techniques [11], but all aim at making usability techniques applicable in real-life software development projects.

The technique to define project-specific methods from parts of existing methods is called method assembly [8], which can produce a powerful new method. Using this technique, we integrate the best from both domains: activities from a world-wide accepted commercial software development process, the Rational Unified Process (RUP) [21]; and activities for creating UI models. Works, such as [9], demonstrate that the integration with RUP can make model-driven methods in general more accessible to a wider audience of software engineers.

While some HCI methods have specific and unique structures, like the Usability Engineering Lifecycle [23], many proposals that integrate SE and HCI are based on the RUP structure, such as the integration of development activities with usability techniques [13] is based on the RUP process structure; and the UCD [15] creates a new discipline for usability design in the RUP.

This is an example of the integration of a model-based UID method and a software development process. Picture a software organization that already has a well-deployed software development process, such as the RUP and wants to focus on UID. For

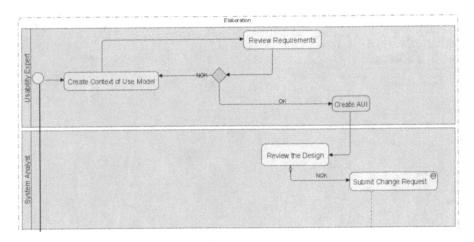

Fig. 5. Integration of software and UID activities

instance, when the organization already has a standard way to do tests, reviews, and controls of change requests, but it wants to increment its way of working with models, it is possible to make a smooth integration. In Fig. 5, we present activities related to model-based UID: create context of use model and create AUI, and SE activities: review requirements, review the design, and submit change request.

Our proposal to support the integration scenario is provided with the association of goals with activities that can be appropriately allocated in the method. For instance, if a new project aims at designing UIs for many devices, the activity "Create AUI" is included in the organizational software process to accomplish this usability goal, as specified in Table 1. In addition, the method engineer might also need support in defining the sequence of the activities; therefore, a proposed model-based UID method that integrates UID activities and RUP activities can be provided as a source of guidance, which is subject for future work.

5 Conclusion

The main goals we intend to achieve with our proposal of a model-based UID method engineering is to aid method engineers when creating methods more efficiently and also to make model-based UID methods applicable in the competitive reality of software development companies.

Method engineers can define a model-based UID method appropriate for the reality of the software organization and its projects using an activity-based strategy. This strategy is founded on usability goals and brings together two different domains: method engineering and UID methods. In other words, when method engineers rely on usability goals to define a method, they also profit from clearly specifying goals that must be accomplished after each activity is concluded.

Our ongoing and future works are related to extending this proposal to address the organization and sequence of UID activities in a process lifecycle, such as the organization of activities in phases and disciplines; to provide guidance for the integration of UID and software engineering activities; to define activities related to UID, but not necessarily to model-based design and associate them to usability goals; and to propose a solution to execute the method and a strategy for model traceability [1].

Acknowledgments. We gratefully acknowledge the support of the Program Alban, the European Union Program of High Level Scholarships for Latin America, under scholarship number E06D103843BR and the Similar network of excellence (http://www.similar.cc), the European research task force creating HCI similar to human-human communication of the European Sixth Framework Program.

References

1. Aizenbud-Reshef, N., Nolan, B.T., Rubin, J., Shaham-Gafni, Y.: Model traceability. IBM Systems Journal 45(3), 515–526 (2006)
2. Ayed, M.B., Ralyte, J., Rolland, C.: Constructing the Lyee method with a method engineering approach. Knowledge-Based Systems 17(7-8), 239–248 (2004)

3. Barclay, P.J., Griffiths, T., McKirdy, J., Kennedy, J.B., Cooper, R., Paton, N.W., Gray, P.: Teallach - a flexible user-interface development environment for object database applications. Journal of Visual Language and Computing 14(1), 47–77 (2003)
4. BEA Systems, IBM Corporation, Microsoft Corporation, SAP AG, Siebel Systems: Business Process Execution Language for Web Services, V1.1 (May 2003)
5. Bodart, F., Hennebert, A.-M., Leheureux, J.-M., Vanderdonckt, J.: Computer-Aided Window Identification in Trident. In: Nordbyn, K., Helmersen, P.H., Gilmore, D.J., Arnesen, S.A. (eds.) Proc. of 5th IFIP TC 13 Int. Conf. on Human-Computer Interaction Interact 1995, Lillehammer, July 1995, pp. 331–336. Chapman & Hall, London (1995)
6. Botterweck, G., Hampe, J.F.: Capturing the Requirements for Multiple User Interfaces. In: Proc. of 11th Australian Workshop on Requirements Engineering AWRE 2006, Adelaide, December 9, 2006, Univ. of South Australia (2006)
7. Brinkkemper, S.: Method engineering: Engineering of information systems development methods and tools. Information Software Technology 38(4), 275–280 (1996)
8. Brinkkemper, S., Saeki, M., Harmsen, F.: Meta-Modelling Based Assembly Techniques for Situational Method Engineering. Information Systems 24(3), 209–228 (1999)
9. Brown, A.W., Iyengar, S., Johnston, S.: A Rational approach to model-driven development. IBM Systems Journal 45(3), 463–480 (2006)
10. Calvary, G., Coutaz, J., Thevenin, D., Limbourg, Q., Bouillon, L., Vanderdonckt, J.: A Unifying Reference Framework for Multi-Target User Interfaces. Interacting with Computers 15(3), 289–308 (2003)
11. Costa, D., Nóbrega, L., Nunes, N.: An MDA Approach for Generating Web Interfaces with UML ConcurTaskTrees and Canonical Abstract Prototypes. In: Proc. of 5th Int. Workshop on Task Models and Diagrams for user interface design Tamodia 2006. LNCS, vol. 4385, pp. 95–102. Springer, Heidelberg (2006)
12. Fensel, D., Lausen, H., Polleres, A., Bruijn, J., Stollberg, M., Roman, D., Domingue, J.: Enabling Semantic Web Services - The Web Service Modeling Ontology. Springer, Berlin (2007)
13. Ferré, X., Juristo, N., Moreno, A.M.: Framework for Integrating Usability Practices into the Software Process. In: PROFES 2005. Proc. of 6th Int. Conf. on Product Focused Software Process Improvement, Oulu, June 13-18, 2005. LNCS, vol. 3547, pp. 202–215. Springer, Heidelberg (2005)
14. Furtado, E., Furtado, J.J.V., Silva, W.B., Rodrigues, D.W.T., Taddeo, L.S., Limbourg, Q., Vanderdonckt, J.: An Ontology-Based Method for Universal Design of User Interfaces. In: Seffah, A., Radhakrishnan, T., Canals, G. (eds.) Proc. of Workshop on Multiple User Interfaces over the Internet: Engineering and Applications Trends MUI 2001 (Lille, September 10, 2001)
15. Göransson, B., Gulliksen, J., Boivie, I.: The usability design process - integrating user-centered systems design in the software development process. Software Process: Improvement and Practice 8(2), 111–131 (2003)
16. Griffiths, T., Barclay, P.J., McKirdy, J., Paton, N.W., Gray, P.D., Kennedy, J.B., Cooper, R., Goble, C.A., West, A., Smyth, M.: Teallach: A Model-Based User Interface Development Environment for Object Databases. In: Proc. of UIDIS 1999, pp. 86–96. IEEE Computer Society Press, Los Alamitos (1999)
17. Grundy, J.C., Venable, J.R.: Towards an integrated environment for method engineering. In: Proc. of IFIP WG 8.1 Conf. on method Engineering, pp. 45–62. Chapman and Hall, Sydney, Australia (1996)
18. Hailpern, B., Tarr, P.: Model-driven development: The good, the bad, and the ugly. IBM Systems Journal 45(3), 451–461 (2006)

19. Harmsen, F.: Situational Method Engineering. Moret Ernst & Young Management Consultants (1997)
20. Juristo, N., López, M., Moreno, A.M., Sánchez-Segura, M.I.: Improving software usability through architectural patterns. In: ICSE Workshop on SE-HCI 2003, pp. 12–19 (2003)
21. Kruchten, Ph.: The Rational Unified Process - An Introduction. Addison-Wesley, New Jersey (2000)
22. Limbourg, Q., Vanderdonckt, J.: UsiXML: A User Interface Description Language Supporting Multiple Levels of Independence. In: Matera, M., Comai, S. (eds.) Engineering Advanced Web Applications, pp. 325–338. Rinton Press, Paramus (2004)
23. Mayhew, D.: The Usability Engineering Lifecycle - A Practitioner's Handbook for User Interface Design. Morgan Kaufmann Publishers, San Francisco (1999)
24. OMG, Business Process Modeling Notation Specification, V1.0 (February 2006)
25. OMG, Software Process Engineering Metamodel Specification, V2.0 (February 2007)
26. Rosenbaum, S., Rohn, J.A., Humburg, J.: A toolkit for strategic usability: Results from Workshops, Panels and Surveys. In: Proc. of ACM Conf. on Human Factors in Computing Systems Proceedings CHI 2000, pp. 337–344. ACM Press, NY (2000)
27. Saeki, M.: Came: The first step to automated software engineering. In: Proc. of the OOPSLA 2003 Workshop on Process Engineering for Object-Oriented and Component-Based Development, pp. 7–18 (2003)
28. Sinnig, D., Gaffar, A., Reichart, D., Seffah, A., Forbrig, P.: Patterns in Model-Based Engineering. In: Proc. of CADUI 2004, pp. 195–208. Kluwer Academic Publishers, Dordrecht (2004)
29. Si-Said, S., Rolland, C., Grosz, G., MENTOR,: A Computer Aided Requirements Engineering Environment. In: Constantopoulos, P., Vassiliou, Y., Mylopoulos, J. (eds.) CAiSE 1996. LNCS, vol. 1080, pp. 22–43. Springer, Heidelberg (1996)
30. Vanderdonckt, J.: A MDA-Compliant Environment for Developing User Interfaces of Information Systems. In: Pastor, Ó., Falcão e Cunha, J. (eds.) CAiSE 2005. LNCS, vol. 3520, pp. 16–31. Springer, Heidelberg (2005)
31. Visual Paradigm. Business Process Visual Architect. Available at: http://www.visual-paradigm.com/product/bpva/
32. Wolff, A., Forbrig, P., Dittmar, A., Reichart, D.: Linking GUI elements to tasks: supporting an evolutionary design process. In: Proc. of TAMODIA 2005, pp. 27–34. ACM Press, New York (2005)
33. Zhang, Z., Lyytinen, K.: A Framework for Component Reuse in a Metamodelling-Based Software Development. Requirements Engineering 6(2), 116–131 (2001)

Modeling Group Artifact Adoption for Awareness in Activity-Focused Co-located Meetings

Christopher Paul Middup and Peter Johnson

Department of Computer Science, University of Bath,
Claverton Down, Bath, BA2 7AY, United Kingdom
{C.P.Middup,P.Johnson}@bath.ac.uk

Abstract. The development of groupware that effectively supports work groups is always limited by how well groups are understood and, consequently, how well they can be modeled to support system design. In this paper we report on an empirical study of groups that has led to the development of a taskwork support model that can be used to aid group awareness. We explain how the adoption of artifacts by work groups influences the division and distribution of tasks within the group, show how this can be observed in co-located group work and suggest how observing groups in this way can be used to support groupware design.

Keywords: Work groups, co-located meetings, knowledge artifacts, groupware, group modeling, SYMLOG.

1 Introduction

Advances in technology over the last twenty years have enabled work groups to become increasingly geographically distributed. However, this is not the way that many small organizations choose to work. Work groups that have co-located meetings to schedule their individual tasks, discuss and progress group objectives and build group knowledge, despite usually working alone or in sub-groups, are a common pattern in reality [21] and the laboratory-based study reported in this paper has been designed to emulate this work pattern. In this paper, we focus on the weekly co-located meetings of the groups in our study.

The development of groupware that effectively supports work groups is always limited by how well groups are understood and, consequently, how well they can be modeled to support system design. A better understanding of group activities would also provide a better basis to determine requirements for collaborative systems [14]. In this paper we report on an empirical study of groups that has led to the development of a taskwork support model that can be used to aid group awareness.

Awareness has previously been taken to mean group members' sensitivity to each other's behavior, whilst engaged in their own activities [10], although sometimes it can be used to describe awareness of more specific elements of group work, such as collaboration [17] or workspace [9]. In this paper we show that awareness of task is as important as awareness of group when complex tasks are attempted.

M. Winckler, H. Johnson, and P. Palanque (Eds.): TAMODIA 2007, LNCS 4849, pp. 126–139, 2007.

A recent meta-review of group models by Ilgen et al. [13] describes how 'structuring models' – those that describe the development and maintenance of group norms, roles and interactions – have been dominated by the constructs of shared mental models and transactive memory.   Shared mental models treat group knowledge as a group level construct, whereas the transactive memory perspective considers it to be a collection of individual perspectives, with a collective shared awareness. We discuss how both perspectives can be used together to model complex task completion in groups. Through negotiation, knowledge artifacts repeatedly shift between being group constructs and individual constructs.   We explain how the adoption of artifacts, including knowledge, by work groups influences the division and distribution of tasks within the group, show how this can be observed in co-located group work and suggest how observing groups in this way can be used to support groupware design for better awareness.

2 Work Groups and Their Tasks

Adair [1] defines a work group as a group whose members have a common task or tasks, explicitly stated, which is the main purpose of the group; the group's leadership is typically competency-based.

When work groups are faced with complex or highly unstructured tasks, they need to organize them into sub-tasks so that they can both be better understood and the work suitably divided between group members.   Some models require this task division to be split down into sub-tasks that can be performed as a single action and are sometimes termed *unit tasks* [4]. The level of granularity required for our model is higher than this, although harder to define precisely.   The groups that we have observed are looking for a level of task division that means each sub-task is fully understood.   To be fully understood, the sub-task must have a specific objective; it must be associated with all the artifacts required to complete it; it must be allocated to a group member or members that are capable of completing it and its outcome must lead to the partial completion of the original complex super-task.

Vogel et al. [25] considered how collections of knowledge as objects could be used to support tasks in distributed groups, both synchronously and asynchronously. Hill and Gutwin [12] also produced a toolkit to support awareness in synchronous distributed groups. In studying distributed groups, however, it is easier for the communication medium to double as a capture mechanism that can be manipulated to support the group, because the overhead of that medium already exists. In co-located settings, this presents a different problem, because capturing the information built in the meeting is an extra group activity.

Carroll et al. [5] identified that there is a cyclic relationship between tasks and artifacts.   Observing and analyzing tasks provides new requirements for artifacts, whereas the introduction of novel artifacts stimulates new ways of approaching tasks. The task-artifact cycle has been widely used to inform and support the development of tangible artifacts.   In this paper we show that it is also a useful model for describing shorter, low-level interactions, which in addition helps the group adopt knowledge.

Stahl [23] suggests that knowledge can be viewed as a type of artifact in group work. Dealing with knowledge in this way presents us with some new challenges. For example, something physical like a mobile phone would generally be identified as a single artifact, and two phones as two artifacts, but with intangibles such as knowledge it is harder to identify this boundary. It is also important to note that there is a hierarchical nature to knowledge, where some knowledge artifacts exist at a meta-level to groups of others, providing such things as organizational information about them. Practically, however, group knowledge is a resource that is used to inform other activities. In the model reported in this paper, the development of group-owned knowledge artifacts supports the understanding of the set task and its sub-division into well-bounded, clearly understood sub-tasks.

Artifacts are adopted into a group through negotiation; a concept that has also been extended to include knowledge and information [24]. Olson and Olson [20] saw this process as one of *clarification*, and split clarification activities according to whether the group was clarifying issues, goals or other activities. The negotiation process can lead to the adaptation of artifacts, as well as their adoption [7], and this process leads to there being a difference between the artifact proposed by a individual and what is finally used by a group. The nature of this adaptation depends upon the physical adaptability of the artifact; if a tangible artifact is not easily adaptable, a group can adapt their understanding of it instead, so that novel uses develop as group emergent knowledge. Rittel and Webber [22] claim that in 'wicked' problems, or those that are essentially unique or ill defined, rebounding the issues is an essential part of the negotiation process. In this paper we also consider the reverse influence of how rebounding the task affects the adoption of knowledge artifacts.

3 Observing Activity-Focused Interaction

To observe how work groups used artifacts to organize their tasks, we set up an empirical study. The study comprised two groups of four people over a four-week period, with the groups being asked to meet together once each week to report their work, fit this into the task and schedule each member's work for the next week.

The group members were all graduate students from the same department of the university campus. They had met previously around the department, but had not worked together in the groupings organized for this study.

The task the groups were asked to perform was to compile a flora and fauna survey of the university campus. The task was deliberately open-ended, so that team members had to balance the demands of breadth versus depth in their survey, given the time constraint upon them. They were required to produce a poster by the end of the fourth week. To encourage the groups to make their best effort at the task there was a small cash prize offered for the survey considered best by two independent judges.

The two groups shared a number of resources: they both used the same meeting room; they both had individual notebook diaries in which they were asked to record their work schedules in the meetings and their findings and intra-group communications between meetings; finally, they shared the same external environment – both as a location for their survey and as a location to use unspecified external resources.

The principal difference between the groups was that one was asked to support their survey and produce a poster only using pen and paper, whereas the other group was asked to maintain their group records and produce the poster on a computer. Both groups' members had individual diaries, in which they were asked to record the work that they undertook during the week in between meetings, as well as any communication with other group members relating to the survey. There were no restrictions placed on the groups as to how they communicated between themselves in between meetings.

At the beginning of each meeting, the room layout was always laid out in the same way for both groups, including the distribution of resources. There was a central table around which the chairs were initially placed; the other resources were distributed around the room, the group record (notepad or laptop) on a desk at one end of the room and the resources to make a poster (desktop, or pens/paper/scissors/glue) on another desk at the other end of the room.

The layout of the room gave the group members three distinct areas in which they could work. In the middle of the room they had their meeting area, and at the two ends they had resource areas. The purpose of defining these spaces was to observe how the group divided its members according to the sub-tasks they wanted to work on at any given time.

There was no restriction placed upon group members as to whether, when or by what means they could communicate between the fixed meetings. If they felt that they required extra meetings, then this was allowed too. In fact, only one extra meeting was requested by one group, and this was during the last week of the study when they preferred to split their work for poster production over two days, into planning and output sessions.

Normally, communication between meetings was limited to e-mails or unplanned face-to-face contact (i.e., bumping into each other on campus). Group members recorded these interactions in their individual diaries and copies of e-mails were forwarded to the researchers. Video recordings were made of all the scheduled co-located meetings, using two fixed cameras and additional cameras or computer output capture, as appropriate, to capture a quad mixed image.

We encoded the verbal and non-verbal communication of group members in the co-located meetings using SYMLOG, a system for the multiple-level observation of groups devised by Bales and Cohen [2]. The system enables an observer to construct messages that describe group behavior. One feature of SYMLOG is that it separates the behavior of the group members towards the target of each interaction from their behavior towards the subject of that interaction, which we have used to analyze interactions specific to taskwork and task development.

In making this coding, we discovered an interesting recurring pattern in the encoded meetings that showed specific periods of activity-focused interaction. We identified this by analyzing the communication instances when the group's task was the subject of the interaction and the target was one, some or all of the other group members. The pattern that recurred was one where a group member had a brief period of clear understanding about part of the task, which they communicated to one or more other group members. Whenever this type of interaction was observed, the group made significant developments in their work towards task completion.

The activity-focused interactions pushed the groupwork between a number of distinct states that gradually broke down the original task into something more manageable. The relationship between these states and interactions forms the basis of the taskwork support model that is described in the next section of this paper.

The drivers for the activity-focused interactions that push the group between states are the artifacts that they use to address the tasks and this in turn shapes the use of physical artifacts, as well as generating new group knowledge artifacts. This low-level, quick looping of the task-artifact cycle [5] is supported by continual artifact negotiation within the group.

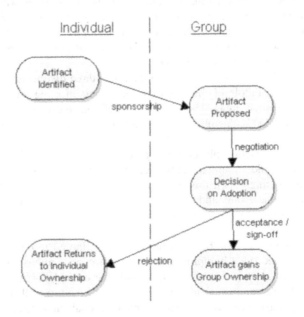

Fig. 1. The negotiation process for group artifact adoption, showing how the artifact's in-group ownership shifts between the individual and group levels

Artifacts were adopted (or rejected) by the groups through negotiation, followed by a 'sign-off'. The negotiation process (Figure 1) begins with an artifact being introduced to the group by one of its members. At this point, the introducer can be considered to be the sponsor of the artifact, and the discussion begins with them making a case for it. Whether the artifact is tangible or not, the case for the sponsor will be linked to how it progresses a sub-task and how it fits with the overall understanding of the main goal at any given time.

How well the proposal meets the needs of the group depends on the common ground [6] that the group members can draw upon to understand a shared perspective. So, in early group meetings these negotiation processes will drive the group towards shared understanding, which in itself is the negotiation and adoption of group knowledge. Later, these knowledge artifacts will help establish group norms as part of the group members' shared history [8], which limit the appropriation of further artifacts to within defined boundaries.

The negotiation process that leads to the group deciding whether or not to adopt the artifact can also lead to the generation of further knowledge artifacts, which are also, implicitly or explicitly, proposed and considered for adoption. This multi-threading is partly responsible for the difficulty that groups have in seeing this process as they perform it. Once group norms begin to be established, the negotiation processes become quicker and more focused, because fewer concurrent negotiations are required to reach a point of common understanding and make a decision.

When the group makes a positive decision to adopt an artifact, the individual has to relinquish control of it. It is no longer theirs to shape in terms of content or use, without reference to the group. By contrast, if an artifact is not adopted by the group, then it is returned to the individual. Often the same artifacts, tangible or otherwise, are re-presented to the group at other times, when the proposer thinks that something has changed in the task understanding to justify another attempt.

4   A Taskwork Support Model

We have analyzed the data to produce a taskwork support model (Figure 2), which explains the behaviors and activities that take place in low-level group work. It can be used by designers to help support the interactions that co-located groups use to understand and complete tasks. Tasks are frequently carried out with various levels of interleaving and interruption [15] and the task of structuring a group's work is no exception. This model restructures the complexity into a series of recurring states, so that it can be better understood. Each of the states in the model represents a key phase of group interaction, through which the group gradually understands and completes their original unstructured, complex task.

The periods of activity-focused interaction that we observed progress the group in a particular state and make it necessary for them to shift states, as shown by the arrows in the model, as it becomes necessary to develop their taskwork in a different context.

The model identifies six key phases within group taskwork that need to be supported. Each of these can be supported by awareness of a group's artifact adoption and how these in turn drive activity-focused interaction.

Understanding the task. This is usually the first problem a new group needs to face, where a complex task needs to be assessed and group members contribute what they think they understand about it. For the flora and fauna survey, both groups first tried to identify skills that they had within the group that might help them progress the task. In terms of artifact negotiation and adoption, the acceptance that someone has a potentially useful skill becomes a group knowledge artifact. The negotiation process involves not only a group acceptance that one of their members has a particular skill, but also that it is relevant and useful to the task and so their perceived understanding of the task increases.

At some point the group members become aware that their understanding of the task has increased to a level where they need to use the new understanding. This is the point as which they shift state with a period of activity-focused interaction, with one or more group members deliberately changing the focus of the group to identify sub-tasks or consider the main task boundary.

This phase was continually revisited in the flora and fauna survey as individual and group knowledge increased, providing new insights into the original requirement. Because none of the participants were experts in flora and fauna, they were forced to continually revise what they knew about extrapolating their observations to the rest of the environment. For example, there is a period early on in the second meeting of one group where a group member, STA, uses his report on his sub-task progress to question the detail that the group is looking for.

STA – "One question I have is how detailed do we go on bugs?"

The nature of this communication shows how the speaker's interaction with the team and task can have different concurrent moods. To the group, he is submissive but friendly: he is genuinely seeking their opinion and his tone suggests that he appreciates their input. At the same time, however, the speaker is demonstrating control over the task – he doesn't know how to overcome his problem, which is why he is asking the group, but he has developed a clearer understanding of what the problem is, and so is taking personal control of the task development by asking the question.

The impact of this statement on the task development is that the group now has to define part of the task more closely and think about how this affects sub-tasks that they have already identified, as well as potential new ones. It also begins a knowledge artifact adoption cycle. Although it isn't fully formed, the knowledge artifact proposed by STA is an entity containing the group's understanding of their requirement with respect to insects.

Bounding the task. In order to limit and focus the work, group members will try to define or redefine the boundary of the task. Such a definition requires the approval of other group members and changes in the boundary definition can lead to a reappraisal of outstanding sub-tasks.

Again, the shared understanding of the task boundary is a knowledge artifact that is proposed, negotiated and then accepted into the group's domain. If the perceived boundary of the task changes, then the next group state will be to focus back on understanding the task within the new domain. It might be that previously accepted knowledge artifacts need to be modified by the group. This is an example of the task-artifact cycle [5] working at the micro level.

In the flora and fauna survey, one of the biggest problems each group had to overcome was deciding what was possible within the four-week survey period. In particular, they had to resolve to competing pressures of breadth versus depth in the survey. The following dialogue comes from one of these discussions:

TIC – "… Common things we can deal with, but obviously there's going to be like a thousand types of plant".
TIH – "I think we should aim at the big things, and not worry about the little details…"

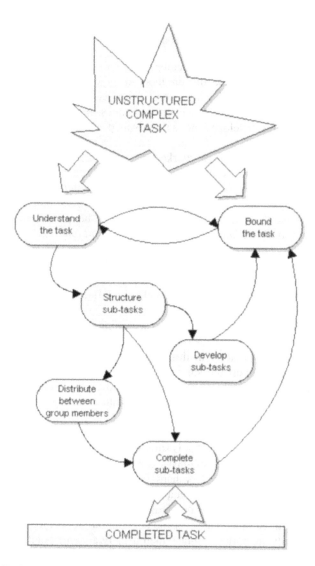

Fig. 2. The Taskwork Support Model, showing the interactions required understand and complete a complex, unstructured task

Although this example shows a more negative attitude towards the task, it still also exhibits awareness of what is required to progress it. TIC has identified a specific problem with the granularity of data that they are trying to gather and, in voicing this issue, is encouraging his teammates to re-evaluate their plans for data gathering. This was negotiated within the groups several times, but each time they would reach a point at which someone decided they had the correct balance and proposed this to the group. Once accepted, this naturally led the group members to reconsider what they now thought the task meant, what they understood and what was still missing. Each of the iterations of this process produces new group-adopted knowledge, which is used as artifacts in the task of trying to understand the complex super-task more fully.

Structuring sub-tasks. As the group members begin to understand their task they start to structure the work as sub-tasks that are more manageable, either by requiring fewer people to complete them or by having a shorter timescale. An example of this is when one group tried to split the data collection into zones. From an initial suggestion by one group member, this developed into a three-way discussion:

ADA – "How would it be if we worked on zones of different types of land? For example, this area here…" *(he points at a campus map they have on the table, and continues to expand on what he thinks the various zones might be)*

DUN – "This says to me why don't we build a system based on plants…"

ADA – "Yeah, so this one and this one are going to be quite similar…" *(He takes this idea on board and continues to build a profile of suitable zones – having the map in front of him gives him great control in this discussion and, although it is effectively a three-way conversation, everything flows though ADA and his use of the artifact)*

STA – "That makes a lot of sense for the presentation, however what maybe <DUN> is suggesting is that we have zones clearly defined … so that we know where we've been…"

ADA – "and it's quite easy to divide it up according to visible landmarks…"

When the group is operating in this state, it needs to manage its repository of artifacts so that they support the sub-tasks as available resources. The negotiation process in the group is aimed at defining meta-level knowledge artifacts that tie together existing artifacts, tangible or otherwise, into a package that supports a low-level goal.

The conversation in this example shows the difficulty that groups have in framing their existing knowledge in a way that is suitably structured for the way they decide to split tasks. In order that some sub-tasks can be performed by individuals or sub-groups, the group has to work very hard so that the correct group knowledge is explicitly tied to the correct sub-task, in a way the whole group agrees upon.

We observed that the outcome or breakdown of this negotiation process could move the group to three other states. If the negotiation process led to agreement that the group had a fully supported sub-task then usually at some point there would be a phase of activity-focused interaction that led the group to move to the state where they negotiated the allocation of work instead. Occasionally, however, someone would identify that the group knowledge development had given the group sufficient resource to complete some sub-task and then the activity-focused interaction would shift the group's state to negotiating sign-off for completed sub-tasks.

At other times, the negotiation of sub-tasks led to the creation of knowledge artifacts that group members identified as important in developing existing sub-tasks and then the new knowledge would be used to shift the group into the state of developing existing sub-tasks.

When a group has co-located meetings as part of primarily distributed work, as in the flora and fauna study, this state is critical to the success of the meeting. Group members leave with a schedule of tasks and a personal mandate to use a subset of the group's artifacts to try to progress or complete those tasks before the next meeting.

Developing sub-tasks. As the group develops its understanding of the main task, they may need to redefine sub-tasks because their needs have changed, or they may see more complexity in a sub-task that shows it needs to be further sub-divided or modified.

In the flora and fauna study, this state was shown to always be a precursor to re-bounding the main task. During the negotiation of how sub-tasks should be defined, a group member always noticed that the new knowledge artifacts created has challenged their existing understanding of the boundary of the task. In our particular study, we often observed that this was triggered by discussions of extra complexity that had been identified during data gathering between meetings.

In the following dialogue, the group is challenged by MAT to define more clearly what their output is going to be. This is an example of how clear activity focus can be generated by group members challenging each other to improve on their ideas. MAT's original question is not itself clearly activity focused – he had no particular insight – but it forced the team to collaborate in defining their approach to the problem more clearly.

MAT – "Have we any thought at all on how we're going to present this? ... if we have any idea now, it might save us hassle further down the line"

ADA – "The way I'd imagined was that we'd draw a map on it, with little lines coming off, but that might incredibly busy, so we might have to get selective with the pictures" *The discussion continues between MAT and ADA, but then DUN says...*

DUN – "I thought we were going to do areas, the areas that we identified as being similar..." *This is controlled by ADA, who shows that the two ideas are the same.*

ADA – "But that would be an elaboration of the map idea, yeah?"

From the progression of this sub-task, the group are now able to re-evaluate what they have been doing individually, and how this now fits into the overall picture. If the sub-task itself is sufficiently complex – it may only be defined as an area of work the group knows it needs to address – then this state becomes a new iteration of the whole taskwork support model, but at a lower level.

This example clearly shows the negotiation process for the adoption of knowledge into a group. ADA starts with a very clear idea of what he believes the group needs and proposes it, but the other group members go to great trouble to modify the idea, until what is finally adopted has been jointly constructed as part of a collaborative exercise.

Distributing work between group members. Early in a group's development, members find it easier to identify sub-tasks that suit their own skills and competencies, and then volunteer to complete them. As group members gain a greater awareness of each other's skills and competencies they are more able to suggest work for other people or shared work.

Group collaboration requires the group members to take responsibility for parts of the shared work [11]. In the flora and fauna study, group members negotiated individual responsibility from the shared pool of identified sub-tasks. Combined with this was the return to individual responsibility for the artifacts previously associated with each sub-task. This cycle of knowledge responsibility is important when it comes to trying to complete sub-tasks. Group members take knowledge that the group has agreed to be usable for a sub-task, attempt the sub-task and then re-present the knowledge back to the group in a revised manner. The negotiation of acceptance of this revision is effectively the group deciding whether to 'sign-off' the sub-task as complete or not. If they are unable to do this, then the group will have to rebound the task again, as they clearly have not all understood the goal for the sub-task in the same way.

In describing the development of the sub-tasks, we discussed a three-way discussion between group members as they tried to identify and define zones on a map that would be a suitable sub-division of the survey. However, it was the fourth member of the group that waited for this discussion to resolve itself, before joining in with an attempt to divide the surveying of these zones among the group.

MAT – "I was going to say, if we're doing it in that way, then it might make sense seeing how I've done woodland here" *(points to map)* "then I might as well do the woodland there, there and there…" *(more pointing)* "because then we don't duplicate stuff…"

This encourages ADA to explain areas he has looked at, and so what he thinks he is more suited to. This interaction leads to a period where a feeling of clear understanding of the task is less apparent. The group is working with the newly formed idea of zones, and so they are trying to feel for a best way to use it. They begin to rely on other group members more, rather than trying to force through their own fully formed ideas.

The group members will try to complete the sub-tasks allocated to them with the artifacts that the group has negotiated to be fit for that purpose. Once the individual owner of a sub-task has made this attempt, they will need to present this to the group, so that acceptance or rejection of the completion can be negotiated.

Completing sub-tasks. For a sub-task to be completed, the work needs to be approved by the whole group in terms of a 'sign-off'. If a sub-task is not signed-off by the group, then group members will have difficulty in integrating that piece of work into the overall work towards completing their main task, forcing the group to re-evaluate what the main task boundary should be.

In the flora and fauna surveys, group members often proposed this 'sign-off' by sharing information that they had collected individually during the week. Because individual information capture is goal-oriented [3], the proposer has a particular purpose in collecting it and presenting it to the group. However, in the negotiation process group members might see a wider scope for the information, or see that it affects the overall understanding of the task boundary. Individuals presenting new knowledge to the group can quickly drive the group from low-level sub-task discussion to high-level main task discussion, because other group members see different things and make different links with the new knowledge artifact. This is another example of an artifact being modified at a low level by the task.

An example of this from the observed data came when a group member had taken some photos and got somebody else to identify the fauna in the photos for him. He tries to get the group to accept that this data is complete, but one other group member refuses to accept it. The discussion continues for about four minutes without being resolved, so in this case the appropriate 'sign-off' has not been made, finishing with:

PET – "I think we've just hit the conflict that this survey was made to encounter, which was depth or breadth"
TIH – "I'm not asking for depth. I'm asking for accuracy."

The discussion does lead to the group then discussing what is good and bad about this data, which then feeds back into their own sub-tasks and their understanding of the overall problem.

5   Conclusion and Future Work

Our study shows that co-located work groups address complex tasks by organizing them into manageable sub-tasks that are both informed and supported through the adoption of artifacts. Although this is a recurring process throughout group meetings, group members are largely unaware of it because it happens at a low level and states shift quickly during activity-focused periods of the meetings.

We have developed a taskwork support model that can be used to help explain the behaviors and activities that take place at a low level in group work. The model can be used to help model groups more effectively, and show how existing approaches should be modified to better support co-located work groups. We believe that the relationship between this process model and group knowledge adoption provides a useful insight into the way in which new groupware for co-located groups could be developed.

Historically, Groupware Support Systems (GSS) have been categorized as Group Decision Support Systems (GDSS) or Group Communication Support Systems (GCSS) [16]. We have shown that in work groups the two categories are fundamentally indivisible, as an awareness of communication is required to fully understand and support decision-making.

Groupware systems that support the development and organization of group knowledge should also support a meta-level awareness, so that the link between group knowledge adoption and task sub-division is apparent to the group members as they work. This would help group members keep in focus their reasons for knowledge adoption.

In many GSS, particularly GDSS, there is a focus on explicit voting on knowledge adoption following a period of negotiation [23]. Although this is possible to support for big decisions, it is impractical at the level reported in this study. The knowledge artifacts are too small and the group's focus changes too quickly; in this case explicit voting would likely be a cause of production blocking.

A promising area of research to find support for these low-level interactions is in knowledge management (KM). Many KM systems use methods to externalize knowledge so that it can be structured in useful ways. However, although many systems exist to capture and structure knowledge, few use this knowledge to tailor the KM system to the group. Mandviwalla and Olfman [19] found that one of the key requirements of groupware was that it should be adjustable to the group's context and, while this has been addressed at a high level, the model presented in this paper shows how lower level group interactions can be structured as useful knowledge artifacts. Malone et al. [18] introduced the idea of 'radical tailorability', where users can easily see and modify the reasoning processes of their support systems, as well as the data captured within them. This is the approach needed to develop the next generation of groupware that deal with interactions at a much lower level than those in existence today.

Additionally, the research area of computer-supported collaborative learning (CSCL) has provided insights into many of the issues facing task-oriented work groups [23], but the generalisability of these findings is often undersold. Learning is just as important outside the domain of formal education and all group development is tightly coupled with learning within the group.

The observations reported here, and the conclusions drawn from them, all relate to synchronous co-located groups and how groupware might better support them. In further work we will look to establish the generalizability of these findings, including how well they model distributed and asynchronous interactions.

Acknowledgments. This research is funded by the Engineering and Physical Sciences Research Council (EPSRC).

References

1. Adair, J.: Effective Teambuilding. Gower (1986)
2. Bales, R.F., Cohen, S.P.: SYMLOG: A system for the multiple level observation of groups. Free Press, New York (1979)
3. Brown, B.A.T., Sellen, A.J., O'Hara, K.P.: A Diary Study of Information Capture in Working Life. In: Proceedings of the International Conference on Computer-Human Interaction (CHI) (2000)
4. Card, S.K., Moran, T.P., Newell, A.: The Psychology of Human-Computer Interaction, LEA, Hillside, NJ (1983)
5. Carroll, J.M., Kellogg, W.A., Rosson, M.B.: The task-artifact cycle. In: Carroll, J.M., Kellogg, W.A., Rosson, M.B. (eds.) Designing Interaction: Psychology at the Human Computer Interface, pp. 74–102. Cambridge University Press, New York (1991)
6. Clark, H.H.: Using Language. Cambridge University Press, Cambridge (1996)
7. Dourish, P.: The Appropriation of Interactive Technologies – Some Lessons from Placeless Documents. Journal of Computer Supported Cooperative Work 12, 465–490 (2003)
8. Feldman, D.C.: The Development and Enforcement of Group Norms. Academy of Management Review 9(1), 47–53 (1984)
9. Gutwin, C., Greenberg, S.: A Descriptive Framework of Workspace Awareness for Real-Time Groupware. Journal of Computer Supported Cooperative Work 11, 411–446 (2002)
10. Heath, C., Svensson, M.S., Hindmarsh, J., Luff, P.: Configuring Awareness. Journal of Computer Supported Cooperative Work 11, 317–347 (2002)

11. Herrmann, T., Kienle, A.: Kolumbus – Context-oriented communication support in a collaborative learning environment. In: van Weert, T.J., Munro, R. (eds.) Proceedings of the Open Conference on Social, Ethical and Cognitive Issues of Informatics and Information and Communication Technology (2002)

12. Hill, J., Gutwin, C.: The MAUI Toolkit – Groupware Widgets for Group Awareness. Journal of Computer Supported Cooperative Work 13, 539–571 (2005)

13. Ilgen, D.R., Hollenbeck, J.R., Johnson, M., Jundt, D.: Teams in Organizations – From Input-Process-Output Models to IMOI Models. Annual Review of Psychology 56, 517–543 (2005)

14. Johnson, H., Hyde, J.: Towards Modeling Individual and Collaborative Construction of Jigsaws Using Task Knowledge Structures (TKS). ACM Transactions on Computer-Human Interaction 10(4), 339–387 (2003)

15. Johnson, P., May, J., Johnson, H.: Introduction to Multiple and Collaborative Tasks. ACM Transactions on Computer-Human Interaction 10(4), 277–280 (2003)

16. Kraemer, K.L., Pinsonneault, A.: Technology and Groups – Assessment of the Empirical Research. In: Galegher, J., Kraut, R.E., Egido, C. (eds.) Intellectual Teamwork, LEA, Hillside, NJ (1990)

17. Leinonen, P., Järvelä, S., Häkkinen, P.: Concepualizing the Awareness of Collaboration – A Qualitative Study of a Global Virtual Team. Journal of Computer Supported Cooperative Work 14, 301–322 (2005)

18. Malone, T.W., Lai, K-Y., Grant, K.R.: Two Design Principles for Collaboration Technology: Examples of Semiformal Systems and Radical Tailorability. In: Olson, G.M., Malone, T.W., Smith, J.B. (eds.) Coordination Theory and Collaboration Technology, LEA, pp. 125–160 (2001)

19. Mandviwalla, M., Olfman, L.: What Do Groups Need? A Proposed Set of Generic Groupware Requirements. ACM Transactions on Computer-Human Interaction 1(3), 245–268 (1994)

20. Olson, G.M., Olson, J.S.: Technology Support for Collaborative Workgroups. In: Olson, G.M., Malone, T.W., Smith, J.B. (eds.) Coordination Theory and Collaboration Technology, LEA, pp. 560–583 (2001)

21. Orre, C., Middup, C.P.: Spheres of Collaboration - People, Space and Technology in Co-located Meetings. In: Proceedings of the Fourth Nordic Conference on Human-Computer Interaction, ACM Press, New York (2006)

22. Rittel, H.W.J., Webber, M.M.: Planning Problems are Wicked Problems. In: Cross, N. (ed.) Developments in Design Methodology, pp. 135–144. Wiley, New York (1984)

23. Stahl, G.: Group Cognition – Computer Support for Building Collaborative Knowledge. MIT Press, Cambridge (2006)

24. Stahl, G., Herrmann, T.: Intertwining Perspectives and Negotiation. In: Proceedings of the International Conference on Supporting Group Work (GROUP). (1999)

25. Vogel, J., Geyer, W., Cheng, L-T., Muller, M.: Consistency Control for Synchronous and Asynchronous Collaboration Based on Shared Objects and Activities. Journal of Computer Supported Cooperative Work 13, 573–602 (2005)

On the Benefit of Synergistic Model-Based Approach for Safety Critical Interactive System Testing

David Navarre[1], Philippe Palanque[1], Eric Barboni[1], and Tomasz Mistrzyk[2]

[1] IRIT, University of Toulouse 3, 118 route de Narbonne
31062 Toulouse, France
{Navarre, palanque, barboni}@irit.fr
[2] University of Paderborn,
33098 Paderborn, Germany
thomek@upb.de

Abstract. This paper claims that the design and construction of safety critical interactive systems require both a task centred approach to support efficiently operator's goals and activities and a system centred approach to increase the dependability of the system. The approach presented proposes a model-based approach integrating tasks and system models. This integration is done at the model level (in a similar way as in [13]) and at the tool level exploiting PetShop environment [3] for the system side and AMBOSS [1] for the task side. The tool level integration describes three different protocols each of them having advantages and limitations. The model-based approaches are introduced through a case study in the field of command and control systems. The application called AGENDA allows operators to define and organize work plan for satellite ground systems.

Keywords: Model-based design, Task modelling, Dialog modelling, Scenarios based simulation.

1 Introduction

Model based approaches have been identified for a long time now as a mean of dealing with the intrinsic complexity of interactive systems [18]. Models are used to organize and store various type of information according to the area of interest of the designer. User models [4] capture information about user capabilities, knowledge or beliefs for instance. Context models aims at capturing information about the various contexts in which a given interactive can be used [8]. Such models are more and more important when dealing with interactive systems that can be used on the move i.e. confronting the users with radically different environmental constraints. Other models like domain models, behavioural models ... are not specific to interactive systems and thus are not addressed in this paper, but approaches like UML [5] are dedicated to model-based design of non interactive aspects of software. Research work in the field of HCI has been trying to extend UML to support the interactive aspects of software (like14]) through various means like inclusion of usability aspects in RUP (the development process associated to UML) or via the extensions capabilities in UML like stereotypes [15].

M. Winckler, H. Johnson, and P. Palanque (Eds.): TAMODIA 2007, LNCS 4849, pp. 140–154, 2007.

This paper focuses on two models of primary importance for interactive systems design: tasks models and system models. Task models gather information related to users goals and activities while system models provide a complete description of system behaviour. As far as interactive systems are concerned, such description must make explicit all the possible states of the system and, for each state, which actions are available to the user on the interface. On the rendering side, the system model must describe, according to any state change how this state change is presented to the user. As the system model describes the actions available to the user and as the task model describes the actions that have to be performed by the user in order to reach a goal, these two models provide two different views on the same elements.

For these reasons, this paper focuses on the possible articulations of task models and system models. This integration is done at the model level (in a similar way as in [13]) as well as at the tool level exploiting PetShop environment [3] for the system side and AMBOSS [1] for the task side. Other approaches such as [7] [20] provide a similar view on the complementarities of tasks and systems descriptions even though they don't address the modelling aspects directly. Other research works, instead of using the complementarity of models, propose the generation from one model to another one such as in [19] and [10] where the authors generates the system model from the task model, or in [9] where the authors do the opposite. The tool level integration describes three different protocols each of them having advantages and limitation (section 3 of the paper). The model-based approaches are introduced through a case study (section 2) in the field of command and control systems. The application called AGENDA allows operators to define and organize work plan for satellite ground systems.

2 Case Study

The work presented in this paper is partly based on the study from both the tasks point of view and the system point of view of the interactive application called AGENDA used in the field of command and control for space-ground systems. AGENDA is a tool that allows an operator from a Satellite Control Planning Facilities such as for SPOT4 or HELIOS1 (SCPF) to monitor the sequence of basic tasks performed by one or more satellite.

2.1 General Context of the Case Study

Fig. 1 presents a snapshot of the application called AGENDA.

The main goals of using the AGENDA in a SCPF are:
- To prepare the daily work plan (called PGT) that consists in defining a sequence of operating tasks.
- To automatically execute the PGT (for pasts SPOT 1, 2 and 3, this was mainly manually done).
- To supervise the execution of operating tasks (e.g. a real time visualisation of the whole activity).
- To control the execution of these tasks (e.g. the operator may intervene on this execution).

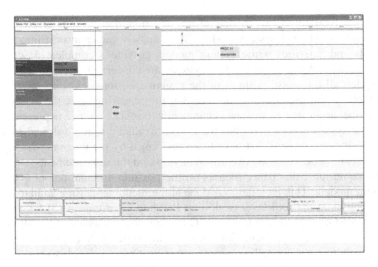

Fig. 1. Snapshot of the AGENDA application

In the following paragraphs, with use terms used from SCPF activities that are explained hereafter:

- An operating task is called a **Procedure**.
- A sequence of tasks is called a **Chain**.
- A working plan is called a **PGT** and is a set of chains that may evolve in parallel.

2.2 Sub Part of the AGENDA Application

Due to space constraints, in the following parts of the paper we only used a very small sub part of the specification of the AGENDA to illustrate our approach, event if the work was done on most of the AGENDA application. This part of the application is based on a simple task which consists in providing a list of conditioning procedures for one procedure. A PGT may be seen as a workflow where basic tasks are procedure, and the possible execution of these procedures may be related to the correct execution of previous procedures. The AGENDA adds some constraints to these conditioning procedures by fixing their maximum number to five.

For this sub part of the AGENDA, the following two sections present first the related task model by recalling basics of the approach called Amboss, and then present the system model using the ICO notation.

3 Two Approaches

This section presents the two approaches used in the work presented in this paper. The choice of these two notations and tools is the result of the cooperation the two groups (from the University of Paul Sabatier and from the University of Paderborn), where both group was trying to find a notation with which a synergistic cooperation should be possible. The work presented here is surely adaptable to others task centred and system centred approaches.

3.1 A Task Centred Approach

There are various approaches that aim to specify tasks. They differ in aspects such as the type of formalism they use, the type of knowledge they capture, and how they support the design and development of interactive systems. In this paper we consider task models that have been represented using the Amboss notation. Amboss [1] is a free tool developed at the University of Paderborn supporting hierarchical task modelling.

In Amboss tasks are described at different abstraction levels in a hierarchical manner, represented graphically in a tree-like format (see **Fig. 2** for an example for both the notation and the tool). Amboss provides a set of temporal relations between the tasks like; **sequential**: The subtasks have to in a fixed sequence, **serial**: where the subtasks have to execute in an unsystematic sequence, **parallel**: in this relation he subtasks can start and end at random relation to each other, **simultaneous**: here the subtasks start in an arbitrary sequence with the constraints that the must be a moment when all tasks are running simultaneously before any task can end, **alternative**: just one randomly selected subtask can execute and the last temporal relation called **optional**: in this case one or no subtask at all can be executed. There almost the same temporal relations which can be found in TOMBOLA. [21] A task node with out any subtasks is automated noted as an **atomic** task.

The software has got distinct additional views of a task model, which can be used for inspecting particular attributes of the tasks. For example if an analyst likes to

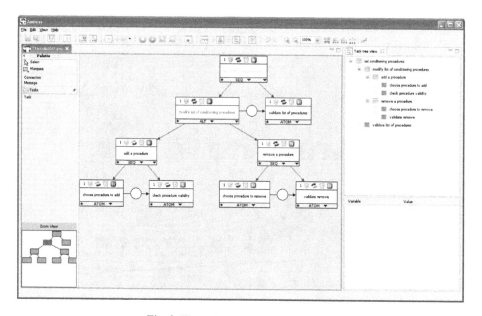

Fig. 2. The task model of the case study

observe what kind of objects (for example procedures from our case study) are manipulated in a system by a particular tasks, he can switch to the object view, take a look over the model and analyse the dependencies between tasks and objects. This tool allows editing as well as directly manipulating the task structure in an easy and intuitive way.

One of the challenges related to modelling socio-technical systems is to involve communication and its parameters into a model. In the model the communication is depicted with white ovals between the tasks.

It is allowed precise description of communication with parameters describing the physical condition using options with respect to the medium of communication, form of message as well as type of transfer. For example if a message is critical for a system, the user can mark the message with a red envelop. In addition the user is able to describe what type of feedback is required in a particular communication process and also if a communication is controlled by a protocol. Both parameters ensure the communication process; additionally control object can be applied to protect information.

The main purpose during the development of AMBOSS was to provide a hierarchical task modelling environment that provides support for developing and analyzing task models in safety critical domains. For modelling tasks in such an environment the model needs to be enhanced with more adequate parameters. Amboss allows specifying parameters like barriers protecting human life or computer systems, riskfaktors estimating the risk and also timing describing the time frame of tasks. Additional the user is able to describe what kind of object is associated to a particular task and what kind of access (read or write) the task does. Furthermore there is a possibility to describe actors related to a task.

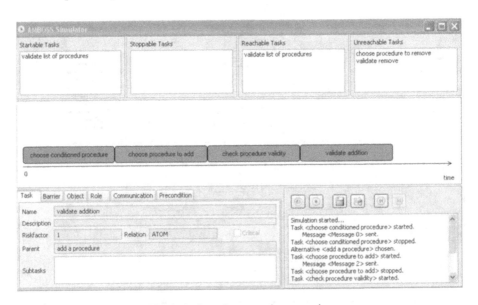

Fig. 3. Amboss for extracting scenarios

By using these parameters it is possible to describe a task model more in detail and have a good overview of the tasks. In order to mark a task as critical the user can change the colours of a task to red. A task modified this way can be easily found in a model.

Similar to other modelling approaches [11] Amboss is able to simulate a task model. The Simulator is depicted on the Fig.4 and shows to the user exactly what happen in a task environment on a particular moment.

A finished task model can be simulated by taking into account the task hierarchy, temporal relations providing the task execution order, communication flow showing messages including their parameters. Additionally during the simulation the user is able to observe the activation and deactivation of barriers, so he can see if a necessary barrier is active or inactive while a critical task is executed. For analysing and reusing different threads of simulation there is a possibility to save scenarios in an xml file.

3.2 System Centred Approach

System modelling is done using the ICO formalism and its development environment is called PetShop. Both of them are presented through the case study. The ICO formalism is the continuation of early work on dialogue modelling using high-level Petri nets [1].

This section recalls the main features of an ICO specification and illustrates them using the case study. The ICO formalism is a formal description technique dedicated to the specification of interactive systems [2]. It uses concepts borrowed from the object-oriented approach (dynamic instantiation, classification, encapsulation, inheritance, client/server relationship) to describe the structural or static aspects of systems, and uses high-level Petri nets [6] to describe their dynamic or behavioural aspects.

ICOs are dedicated to the modelling and the implementation of event-driven interfaces, using several communicating objects to model the system, where both behaviour of objects and communication protocol between objects are described by the Petri net dialect called Cooperative Objects (CO) [1].

In the ICO formalism, an object is an entity featuring four components: a cooperative object which describes the behaviour of the object, a presentation part, and two functions (the activation function and the rendering function) that make the link between the cooperative object and the presentation part.

Behaviour: Fig. 4 presents the behaviour of the case study. The detailed description of this behaviour is partly out of the scope of this paper, but to summarize it, the Petri net may receive events when a procedure is added (or removed) to (from) the set of conditioning procedures. When it is an addition, the behaviour asks the functional core to check if the procedure is a valid as a conditioning procedure or not. The place *availableSlots* initially contains 5 tokens, and every time a procedure is added, a token is removed from this place, and every time a procedure is removed, a token is added. When empty, this place disabled the transition askForAdding (which leads to the popup of the procedure selection window) so that it respects the constraints of maximum 5 conditioning procedures.

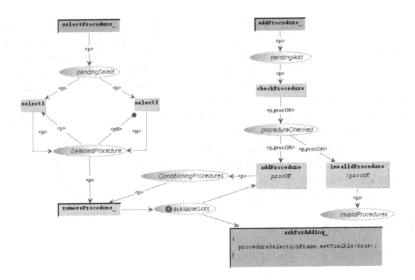

Fig. 4. Behaviour of the application

Presentation part: The presentation of an object states its external appearance. This presentation is a structured set of widgets organized in a set of windows. Even if the method used to render (description and/or code) is out of the scope of an ICO specification, it is possible for it to be handled by an ICO in the following way. The presentation part is viewed as a set of rendering methods (in order to render state changes and availability of event handlers) and a set of user events, embedded in a software interface, in the same language as for the CO interface description.

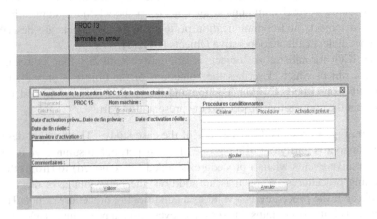

Fig. 5. Window used for editing conditioning procedures

The presentation part is made up of a set of widgets that are used for both rendering information and provides the user with means to interact with the interactive systems.

```
Public interface ConditioningProceduresEdition extends ICOWidget {

    //List of user events.
    public enum Events {select, remove, askAddition}

    //List of activation rendering methods.
    void setAdditionEnabled(Events event, List<ISubstitution> availableSubstitutions);
    void setRemoveEnabled (Events event, List<ISubstitution> availableSubstitutions);
    void setSelectionEnabled (Events event, List<ISubstitution> availableSubstitutions);

    //List of rendering methods.
    void showSelection (IMarkingEvent anEvent);
    void showConditioningProcedures (IMarkingEvent anEvent);
}
```

Fig. 6. Software interface of the presentation part

The layout of the presentation part (Fig. 5) is out of the scope of the ICO specification, but this presentation part is seen as a collection of rendering methods and ways to provide events as shown in Fig. 6.

Activation function: The user actions on the system (inputs) only takes place through widgets. Each user action on a widget may trigger one of the CO event handlers. The relation between user services and widgets is fully stated by the activation function that associates each event from the presentation part with the event handler to be triggered and the associated rendering method for representing the activation or the deactivation.

Fig. 7 present the activation function related to the case study. Each line of this table links one of the events from the presentation part (listed by the enumeration in Fig. 6) to an event handler from the behaviour. For instance, when the user select of procedure in the list, the presentation part triggered the event *select* which finally leads to the firing of the event handler *selectProcedure*. And, when the event handler becomes available (or not) the activation rendering method *setSelectionEnabled* is called with parameters that describe it as available (or not).

User Events	Event handler	ActivationRendering
select	selectProcedure	setSelectionEnabled
remove	removeProcedure	setRemoveEnabled
add	askForAdding	setAdditionEnabled

Fig. 7. Activation function

Rendering function: The system rendering to the user (outputs) aims at presenting the state changes that occurs in the system to the user. The rendering function maintains the consistency between the internal state of the system and its external appearance by reflecting system states changes.

Fig. 8 presents the rendering function related to the case study. Each line links a change of the behaviour state to the call of a rendering method of the presentation part. For instance, when a token enters the place *ConditioningProcedures* (e.g. a procedure has been added), the rendering method *showConditioningProcedures* is called with the marking of the place as a parameter.

ObCSNode name	ObCS event	Rendering method
ConditioningProcedures	token_enter	showConditioningProcedures
ConditioningProcedures	token_removed	showConditioningProcedures
SelectedProcedure	token_enter	showSelection
SelectedProcedure	token_removed	showSelection

Fig. 8. Rendering function

ICOs are used to provide a formal description of the dynamic behaviour of an interactive application. An ICO specification fully describes the potential interactions that users may have with the application. The specification encompasses both the "input" aspects of the interaction (i.e. how user actions impact on the inner state of the application, and which actions are enabled at any given time) and its "output" aspects (i.e. when and how the application displays information relevant to the user).

PetShop: An ICO specification is fully executable, which gives the possibility to prototype and test an application before it is fully implemented [**Error! Reference source not found.**] within the associated environment PetShop.

4 Integration Protocols

The integration framework we have followed takes full advantage of the specific tools that we have been developed initially in a separate manner. One advantage of this separation is that it allows for independent modification of the tools, provided that the interchange format remains the same.

We have previously investigated the relationship between task and system models. For instance in [16] we proposed a transformation mechanism for translating UAN tasks descriptions into Petri nets and then checking whether this Petri net description was compatible with system modelling also done using Petri nets. In [17] we presented the use of CTT for abstract task modelling and high level Petri nets for low-level task modelling. In that paper the low-level task model was used in order to evaluate the "complexity" of the tasks to be performed, by means of performance evaluation techniques available in Petri net theory.

In [13] we proposed a synergistic use of the tools CTTE and PetShop through the exchange of scenarios (provided as files) from CTTE to PetShop. The two notations model slightly different aspects: as CTT is a notation for task modelling whereas ICO is a notation for specifying concurrent systems, an automatic conversion from one notation to the other one would have been difficult. We have preferred a different solution that is easier to implement and better refers to the practice of user interface designers. Indeed, often designers use scenarios for many purposes and to move among the various phases of the design cycle. So, they can be considered a key element in comparing design solutions from different viewpoints.

The **main gap** the user of this framework had to face was the important length of iterations while producing scenarios (i.e. build a scenario and save it as a file), testing it on the system model (i.e. load both the task model and the scenario within the system dedicated tool), change the scenario and/or the task model...

The work presented in this paper is based on the work done in [13] and is basically the investigation of overriding this gap, by first presenting the basic bricks for the integration of the two tools, then by presenting a solution to the gap presented above and finally by presenting a prospective reflection on a stronger integration.

4.1 Tools Inside Notations and Their Associated Environments

As our main interest in this paper is to show it is possible to make task modelling and system modelling cooperate, we present in this section features from each notations and their associated environment as basic tools for the integration framework.

Amboss. As described above, Amboss environment provides a set of tools for engineering task models. For the purpose of integration we only use the interactive tool for editing the tasks and the simulation tool for task models that allows scenario construction from the task models. Thus the two main outputs are a set of task models and a set of scenarios. These two sets are exploited in the following way:

- From the tasks specification a set of human and system tasks is extracted providing a set of manipulations that can be performed by the user on the system and outputs from the system to the user.
- While building a scenario Amboss notifies the evolution of this scenario as Amboss provides an API that allows receiving data from the simulator.

For the case study the interesting tasks are the leaves of the task tree:

Actors	Name	Kind
Human	choose procedure to add	input
Human	choose procedure to remove	input
Human	validate remove	input
Human	validate list of procedures	output
System	check procedure validity	output

ICO. Amongst the features of the ICO environment (PetShop) presented above, the one that is used for the integration is the tool for editing the system model. It allows executing the system model.

From this specification we extract the activation and rendering function which may be seen as the set of inputs and outputs of the system model.

From the case study, we use each line of the activation and rendering functions presented on Fig. 7 and Fig. 8.

4.2 Protocol 1 for the Integration of Notations and Associated Environment

As in the paper [13], the integration protocol is made up with two phases: the definition of the correspondence between the two models and the execution of the system model controlled by a scenario provided by the Amboss simulator.

Correspondence between models. The principle of editing the correspondences between the two models is to put together user input tasks (from the task model) with system inputs (from the system model) and system outputs (from the system model) with system output tasks(from the task model). Correspondence may show inconsistency between the task and system model. The correspondence edition process may be seen as presented on Fig. 9, where each tool provides the correspondence editor with API in order to notify it each time modifications are done one both the task model or the system model.

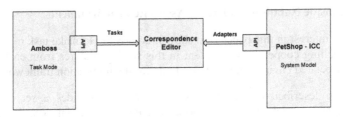

Fig. 9. Correspondence Edition process

The description of the correspondence edition is illustrated hereafter using the case study (see Fig. 10).

Type	Task Items	System Items	Match
Input	choose procedure to add	*add* activation adapter	OK
Input	choose procedure to remove	*select* activation adapter	OK
Input	validate remove	*remove* activation adapter	OK
Output	validate list of procedures	*ConditioningProcedures* rendering adapter	OK
Output	check procedure validity		Not OK
Output		*SelectedProcedure* rendering adapter	Not OK

Fig. 10. Correspondences between the task and system models

While observing Fig. 10, we may see that there are two weak correspondences:

- Task "check procedure validity" does not find any corresponding feedback within the system. It may be a problem because it means that the system does not validate the selected procedure and does not provide any feedback for this. A solution may be to add a new rendering adapter to the rendering function (and a new rendering method to the presentation part), such as:

ObCSNode name	ObCS event	Rendering method
InvalidProcedures	token_enter	showInvalidProcedure

- "SelectedProcedure rendering adapter" is not linked to any task. It means that the system provides extra feedback that is maybe not useful for the user. Such a problem is not necessary a real problem as it is not an extra function provided to the user.

Execution of the system model controlled by the Amboss simulator. The execution of the system model controlled by the Amboss simulator behaves as follow: while building a scenario, if the task performed within the scenario is one of the identified input tasks, an event is sent to the activation function (simulating the corresponding user event), so that it will fire the corresponding event handler from the ObCS of the system model. Fig. 11 presents the architecture of this protocol of integration between tools. The top part of the figure is the correspondence edition part, presented above. The bottom part of the figure presents the architecture of the execution part. The principle is the following one:

- Through an API, the Amboss simulator notifies the Simulation controller of the evolution of the current scenario (it notifies whether a task begins or ends).
- Through another API, the Simulation controller fires the corresponding activation adapter (according to the correspondence provided by the Correspondence editor), simulating a user event.

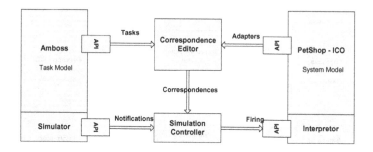

Fig. 11. Protocol 1 for the tools integration

As a scenario may be seen as a sequence of tasks and as we are able to put an input task and an activation adapter into correspondence, it is now possible to convert the scenarios into a sequence of firing of event handlers in the ICO specification.

An ICO specification can be executed in the ICO environment and behaves according to the high-level Petri net describing its behaviour. As the Amboss scenarios can be converted into a sequence of firing of event handlers, it can directly be used to drive the execution of the ICO specification.

The gap identified in the introduction of this section finds a solution as the direct link between the Amboss simulator and PetShop allows a designer to make the two models co-evolve, removing the activity that consists in creating scenario files and in fully separating the two tools.

4.3 Protocol 2 for the Integration of Notations and Associated Environment

We have started a prospective work on how coupling these two tools in a more synergistic way, introducing a communication from the ICO environment to Amboss. The architecture of this second integration protocol is presented on the Fig. 12. The correspondence edition (the top part of the figure) remains the same as in the one described in the previous section. Even if only input aspects are addressed by the first protocol of integration, the correspondence edition links both input and output tasks from the task model with input and output adapters from the system model. The bottom part of the figure proposes a more integrated way to make the two tools communicate. The communication from Amboss to PetShop remains the same (Amboss notifies the Simulation Controller which then ask the firing of the related corresponding adapters in the system model). The addition is the following one:

- Through an extended API, the PetShop interpreter notifies the Simulation controller of the evolution of the current execution of the system model (it notifies rendering changes that comes from both rendering and activation functions).
- Through an extended API, the Simulation controller start or stop the corresponding task (according to the correspondence provided by the Correspondence editor), simulating the user manual action on the Amboss simulator.

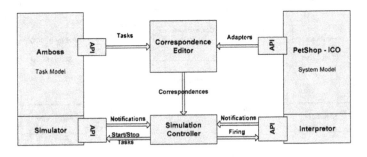

Fig. 12. Protocol 2 for the tools integration

The advantages of this integration protocol a real co-evolution of the two models, as the execution of both tools impacts the execution of the other tool. This integration protocol still provides the designer with shorter iterations in the task and system modelling process in the same way as for the previous protocol. But this protocol may also be an improvement for the final user. The principle would be to use the execution of the system to point out where the user is on the task model. The advantage is to use the task model as an input for providing the user with a partly automated contextual help in two phases:

- As the system model execution point out the corresponding task in the task model, it is easily possible to provide the corresponding task description and attached help.
- Knowing the task on which the user works, it is possible to extract from the task model possible scenarios which start with this task, and then "play" it on the system model as a demonstration of what is possible to do knowing the current context.

5 Conclusion

This paper addressed the issue of integrating task models and system models within a single framework. It claims that modelling approaches for these two critical components of the design of interactive systems provide a valuable mean for managing the complexity of interactive systems. The paper presented on a case study the information that is conveyed by a task model and the one embedded in a system model.

Beyond this modelling level, the paper also presents different ways of relating these two modelling approaches. It presents three protocols that have been identified and describes the advantages and limitation of each of them.

Finally, the paper presents how one of these protocols has been implemented through the coupling of two modelling environments: AMBOSS for the edition and simulation of tasks models and PetShop for the edition and simulation of system models.

The work presented in this paper belongs to a longer term research programme targeting at the design of resilient interactive systems using model-based approaches. Future work targets at exploiting these two models to support the usability evaluation of interactive systems. Indeed, task models provide a unique view on the goals and sequences of actions the users have to perform in order to reach such goals, while system models provide a unique view of the inner behaviour of the system.

Acknowledgments. This work was supported by the EU funded ResIST Network http://www.resist-noe.eu. The work was also partly funded by CNES (Centre National d'Etude Spatial) under contract #00.70.624.00.470.75.96.

References

1. Amboss, http://wwwcs.uni-paderborn.de/cs/ag-szwillus/lehre/ws05_06/PG/PGAMBOSS
2. Bastide, R., Palanque, P., Le, D.-H., Muñoz, J.: Integrating Rendering Specifications into a Formalism for the Design of Interactive Systems. In: DSV-IS 1998, Abingdon, U. K, Springer, Heidelberg (1998)
3. Bastide, R., Navarre, D., Palanque, P.: A Model-Based Tool for Interactive Prototyping of Highly Interactive Applications. In: Tool demonstration. CHI 2002, Minneapolis (USA) (2002)
4. Blandford, A., Butterworth, R., Curzon, P.: Models of interactive systems: a case study on Programmable User Modelling. International Journal of Human-Computer Studies 60(2), 165–216 (2004)
5. Booch, G., Rumbaugh, J., Jacobson, I.: The UML reference manual. Addison-Wesley, Reading
6. Genrich, H.J.: Predicate/Transitions Nets. High-Levels Petri Nets: Theory and Application. In: Jensen, K., Rozenberg, G. (eds.) Predicate/Transitions Nets, pp. 3–43. Springer, Heidelberg (1991)
7. Green, T.R.G., Benyon, D.R.: The skull beneath the skin; Entity-relationship modelling of Information Artefacts. International Journal of Human-Computer Studies (1996)
8. Jameson, A.: Modelling both the Context and the User. Personal Ubiquitous Comput. 5(1), 29–33 (2001)
9. Lu, S., Paris, C., Vander Linden, K.: Towards the automatic generation of task models from object oriented diagrams. In: Chatty, S., Dewan, P. (eds.) Engineering for Human-Computer Interaction, Kluwer academic publishers, Boston (1999)
10. Lu, S., Paris, C., Vander Linden, K., Colineau, N.: Generating UML Diagrams From Task Models. In: proceedings of CHINZ'03, the fourth annual international conference of the New Zealand chapter of the ACM's SIGCHI, Dunedin, New Zealand (July 3-4, 2003)
11. Mori, G., Paternó, F., Santoro, C.: CTTE: support for developing and analyzing task models for interactive system design. IEEE Trans. Softw. Eng. 2(8), 797–813 (2002)

12. Navarre, David, Palanque, Philippe, Bastide, Rémi, Sy, O.: Structuring Interactive Systems Specifications for Executability and Prototypability. In: 7th Eurographics Workshop on DSV-IS 2000, Limerick, Ireland. LNCS

13. Navarre, D., Palanque, P., Bastide, R., Paternó, F., Santoro, C.: A tool suite for integrating task and system models through scenarios. In: 8th Eurographics workshop on Design, Specification and Verification of Interactive Systems, DSV-IS 2001. LNCS, vol. 2220, pp. 88–113. Springer, Heidelberg (2001)

14. Nunes, J.N., Cunha, J.F.: Towards a UML Profile for Interaction Design: The Wisdom approach. In: Evans, A., Kent, S. (eds.) Proceedings of the Unified Modeling Language Conference, UML 2000. LNCS, vol. 1939, pp. 100–116. Springer, Heidelberg (2000)

15. Nunes, N.J., Cunha, J.F.: Wisdom A UML Based Architecture for Interactive Systems (PDF 44.73 Kb). In: Palanque, P., Paternó, F. (eds.) DSV-IS 2000. LNCS, vol. 1946, pp. 191–205. Springer, Heidelberg (2001)

16. Palanque, Philippe, Bastide, R., Sengés, V.: Validating Interactive System Design Through the Verification of Formal Task and System Models. In: EHCI 1995. 6th IFIP Conference on Engineering for Human-Computer Interaction, Garn Targhee Resort, Wyoming, USA, August 14-18, Chapman et Hall, Sydney, Australia (1995)

17. Palanque, Philippe, Bastide, R., Paternó, F.: Formal Specification As a Tool for the Objective Assessment of Safety Critical Interactive Systems. In: Interact 1997. 6th IFIP TC13 Conference on Human-Computer Interaction, Sydney, Australia, July 14-18, 1997, pp. 323–330. Chapman et Hall, Sydney, Australia (1997)

18. Paternó, F.: Model-Based Design and Evaluation of Interactive Application. Springer, Heidelberg (1999)

19. Paternó, F., Breedvelt-Schouten, I., de Konig, N.: Deriving Presentations from Task Models. In: Proceedings EHCI 1998, Creete, Kluwiert Publisher (1998)

20. Sawyer, J.T., Minsk, B., Bisantz, A.M.: Coupling User Models and System Models: A Modeling Framework for Fault Diagnosis in Complex Systems Interacting with computer (1996)

21. Uhr, H.: TOMBOLA: Simulation and User-Specific Presentation of Executable Task Models, Paper. In: Human-Computer Interaction: Theory and Practice (Part I), Proceedings of HCI International 2003, pp. S263–267. Lawrence Erlbaum Associates, Mahwah, NJ (2003)

Remote Evaluation of Mobile Applications

Fabio Paternò, Andrea Russino, and Carmen Santoro

ISTI-CNR, Via G. Moruzzi, 1,
56124 Pisa, Italy
{Fabio.Paterno, Andrea.Russino, Carmen.Santoro}@isti.cnr.it

Abstract. In this paper we present a method and a supporting environment that allows remote evaluation of mobile applications. Various modules have been developed in order to gather contextual data about the usage of such applications in different environments. In addition, issues related to how to visualise usability data have been addressed in order to support the designers' work in analysing such data.

Keywords: Remote usability evaluation, Usability in Mobile Applications, Representation of Usability Data.

1 Introduction

In remote usability evaluation, evaluators and users are separated in space and possibly time during the evaluation [1]. This type of evaluation is becoming increasingly important for the number of advantages it offers. Indeed, it allows the collection of detailed information on actual user behaviour in real contexts of use, which is especially useful in contexts in which it is not possible (or convenient) having an evaluator directly observing or recording the session. In addition, the fact that the users carry out the evaluation in their familiar environments contributes to gain more 'natural' users' behaviour.

In order to have a complete picture of what users did during the session and derive consequent conclusions about the usability of the application, it is crucial for the evaluators to reconstruct not only the interactions that users carried out during the session, but also the contextual conditions that might have affected the user interaction itself. Indeed, if such conditions are not completely known, the evaluators might draw incorrect conclusions about the usability of the considered application. This problem becomes even more difficult to address when dealing with mobile applications. Indeed, while for desktop applications the lack of co-presence between users and evaluators can be compensated to some extent by equipping the test environment with devices such as web cams, mobile applications require different solutions that are able to flexibly support evaluation in different contexts without being too obtrusive on the user side. When dealing with remote applications for mobile devices, there are some additional problems that make it more difficult to gather data to remotely evaluate such applications. For instance, we have to take into account the more limited capability of mobile devices, which imposes constraints on the kinds of techniques to be used for tracking user interactions. In addition, there is

M. Winckler, H. Johnson, and P. Palanque (Eds.): TAMODIA 2007, LNCS 4849, pp. 155–169, 2007.

the further problem of detecting the environmental conditions in which the session takes place.

In this paper we discuss a novel extension of a tool able to remotely process multimodal information on users interacting with desktop applications. The new solution is enriched with the possibility of tracking and evaluating also user interfaces of mobile applications, including the detection of environmental conditions that might affect user interaction (e.g.: noise in the surrounding environment, battery level consumption, etc.). The new tool, MultiDevice RemUsine, is able to identify where users interactions deviate from those envisioned by the system design and represented in the related task model. In addition, we also improved the graphical representations that are provided to the evaluators for visualizing the gathered data. Indeed, especially when dealing with a large amount of information, it is very important to use effective representations highlighting relevant information so as to enable evaluators to better identify potential issues and where they occur.

The structure of the paper is the following one: in the next section we discuss related work, and next we introduce our general approach. Then, we present the main features of the additional component (Mobile Logger) we developed for supporting the detection of user interactions with mobile applications and environmental conditions that might affect the performance of user's activity. In the following, we also discuss the issue of more effective visualisation techniques for representing the data that have been collected regarding the user activity. Lastly, we conclude with some remarks and indications for future work.

2   Related Work

Interest in automatic support for usability evaluation is rapidly increasing [2], especially as far as the remote evaluation is concerned, because, on the one hand, it is important that users interact with the application in their daily environment, but, on the other hand, it is impractical to have evaluators directly observe users' interactions. In [1] one of the first examples of remote-control evaluation is described. The remote-control method checks a local computer from another computer at a remote site. Using this method, the evaluator's computer is located in the usability lab where a video camera or scan converter captures the users' actions. The remote users remain in their work environment and audio capture is performed via the computer or telephone. This is an example of a flexible technique for asynchronous remote evaluation which is restricted to be used on desktop systems due to some software limitations.

Other studies [3] have confirmed the validity of remote evaluation in the field of Web usability. The work by Lister [4] has been oriented to using audio and video capture for qualitative analysis performed by evaluators on the result of usability testing. Other works have highlighted the importance of performing a comprehensive evaluation able to take into account data derived from multiple sources, and the consequent need to provide analysts from a variety of disciplines (each using distinct sets of skills to focus on specific aspects of the problem) to work cooperatively, in order to adequately gain insight into large bodies of multisource data [5]. A more recent work [6] compares three methods for remote usability testing and a conventional laboratory-based think-aloud method. The three remote methods are a remote synchronous condition, where testing is conducted in real time but the test monitor is separated spatially from the test subjects, and two remote asynchronous conditions, where the test monitor and the test subjects are separated both spatially and temporally. The authors claim that the two methods identified almost the same number of usability problems, and users spent the same time completing the tasks. The asynchronous methods are more time-consuming for the test subjects and identify fewer usability problems, yet they may still be worthwhile because they relieve the expert evaluators from a considerable amount of work, and enable collection of use data from many participants.

Since most applications have been developed for the desktop, the majority of remote evaluation methods have addressed this type of platform. Only a few proposals have been put forward for remote evaluation of mobile applications. An example in this area is the paper by Waterson et al. [7], where the authors discuss a pilot usability study using wireless Internet-enabled personal digital assistants (PDAs), in which they compare usability data gathered in traditional lab studies with a proxy-based logging and analysis tool. They found that this remote testing technique can more easily gather many of the content-related usability issues, whereas device-related issues are more difficult to capture. In [8] the authors describe a usability evaluation study of a system that permits collaboration of small groups of museum visitors through mobile handheld devices (PDAs). As usability evaluation methodology, they propose a combination of a logging mechanism and an analysis tool (the ColAT environment [9]), which permits mixing of multiple sources of observational data, a necessary requirement in evaluation studies involving mobile technology, when users move about in physical space and are difficult to track. The museum system evaluated is based on a client–server architecture and an important characteristic of the application is that the server produces a centralized XML log file of the actions that occur during the visit, and this log file can be combined with a video recording of the visit allowing evaluation of activity during the visit. The methodology was able to deliver data useful for deriving quantitative information (e.g. total and average times for solving the puzzles, etc.), aspects related to group activities (number of exchanges between the group, strategies used for solving the puzzles, ..), behavioural patterns of participants. In general, while logging tools for mobile devices have already been proposed [10], we wanted to develop a novel solution for this purpose able also gather data useful to better identify the context of use related to aspects such as environmental conditions, connectivity and so on.

Another emerging need in this area concerns tools able to support effective representations for enabling the evaluators to analyze the evaluation data collected. To aid analysis of the gathered usability test data, the WebQuilt [11] visualization provides filtering capabilities and semantic zooming, aiming to allow the designer to understand the test results at the overall view of the navigation graph, and then drill down to sub-paths and single pages. A first attempt to provide visual representations linking task models and log data was provided by Maly and Salvik [12]. In this paper, we present a representation sharing similar goals that is based on our experience in order to provide useful information for evaluators.

3 General Approach

Our approach is mainly based on a comparison of planned user behaviour and actual user behaviour [13]. Information about the planned logical behaviour of the user is contained in a (previously developed) task model, which describes how the tasks should be performed according to the current design and implementation. The task model can be built in various way. It can be the result of an interdisciplinary discussion involving end users, designers, application domain experts, and developers. There are also reverse engineering techniques able to build automatically the system task model of Web pages starting with their implementation.

The data about the actual user behaviour are provided by the other modules (eg: the logging tools), which are supposed to be available within the client environment. An overview of the general approach is described in Figure 1. A logging tool, which depends on the type of application considered, stores various user or system-generated events during the user session. In addition, other sources of information regarding the user behaviour can be considered, such as Web Cams showing the actual user behaviour and face expressions or eye-trackers detecting where the user is looking at.

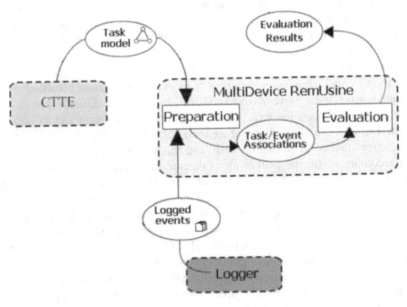

Fig. 1. The architecture of Multi-Device RemUsine

As for the expected user behaviour, CTT [14] task models are used to describe it by their graphical representation of the hierarchical logical structure of the potential activities along with specification of temporal and semantic relations among tasks. It is worth pointing out that, with the CTT notation used, the designer might easily specify different sequences of paths that can correspond to the accomplishment of the same high-level task: this is possible thanks to the various temporal operators available in the CTT notation, which also include, for instance, the specification of *concurrent*, multitask activities, or activities that *interrupt* other ones. On the one hand, for the designer is quite easy to specify in a compact manner even a complex behaviour, on the other hand the behaviour of such operators is automatically mapped by the underneath engine into all the corresponding possible paths of behaviours.

In order to enable an automatic analysis of the actual user behaviour identified by the sequences of actions in the logs against the possible expected behaviours described by the task model there is a preparation phase. In this phase the possible log actions are associated with the corresponding basic tasks (the leaves in the task model). Once this association is created then it can be exploited for analysing all the possible user sessions without further effort. In this way, the tool is able to detect whether the sequence of the basic tasks performed violates some temporal or logical relation in the model. If this occurs then it can mean that either there is something unclear on how to accomplish the tasks or the task model is too rigid and it is not able to consider possible ways to achieve user goals. Thus, by comparing the planned behaviours (described within the task model) with the information coming from log files, MultiDevice RemUsine is able to offer the evaluators useful hints about problematic parts of the considered application. To this regard, it is worth pointing out that the tool is able to discriminate to what extent a behaviour deviates from the expected one (for instance, whether some additional useless tasks have been performed but they did not prevent the user from completing the main target task, in comparison with other cases in which the deviation led to unsuccessful paths).

4   Mobile Logging

With mobile interaction there are some contextual events that should be considered since they can have an impact on the user's activity. Among the relevant events that might be taken into consideration there are the noise of the environment, its lightness, the location of the user, the signal power of the network, as well as other conditions related to the mobile device, e.g. the residual capacity of the battery.

When we deal with usability evaluation in which stationary devices are used, the contextual conditions under which the interaction occurs and involving the location of the user remain unchanged over the experiment session. In this case, the information about user interaction might be sufficient. When we consider interaction with mobile devices, since the interaction occurs in an environment that can considerably change not only between two different executions, but also within the same execution, this is no longer valid. Thus, it is important to acquire comprehensive and detailed information about the different aspects of the context of use in which the interaction currently occurs since they might have an impact on the user's activity.

Each of these variables, as well as combinations of them can affect the user interaction, and in our tool we developed a separate module for detecting to what extent each of these components can affect the user interaction. Currently, we consider aspects connected with the current position of the user (the position itself, together with the noise and lightness of the surrounding environment, according to such a position) together with other variables, which are more connected to objective,

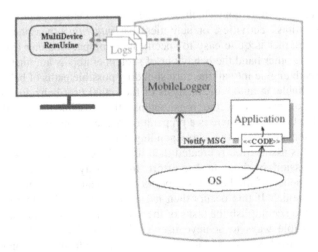

Fig. 2. The architecture of the logging system

technological requirements for enabling/disabling features involving the PDA overall working (battery level and network signal). Differently from the latter ones, the impact of the first aspect has to be put in relation with how the users might subjectively perceive the user interface, therefore, managing them could be harder.

The general architecture of the tool is shown in Figure 2. The core of the logging tool is the Mobile Logger, which is in an intermediate position between the application to be evaluated and MultiDevice RemUsine. Indeed, on the one hand it has to communicate with the operating system to detect events and track the user's activity, and, on the other hand, it has to record and communicate the logged data to the evaluation tool. In the following sub-sessions we will detail both aspects in more depth.

4.1 Tracking the User's Activity: Events and Messages

The task of tracking the activity of the user is carried out by a procedure that is executed by the application evaluated, which uses libraries included in the operating system to detect events, and which exploits an inter-process communication model based on exchanges of messages. The execution of an interactive graphical application is driven by events, notified in Windows systems by means of messages. Indeed, WindowsCE, like other Windows systems, is an operating system based on the "push" mechanism: every application has to be coded to react to the notifications (namely: messages) that are received from the operating system. Each window has a window procedure that defines the behaviour of the component.

Therefore, it is theoretically possible to derive all the information associated with the interaction from such messages. However, it is worth noting that not all messages received by the window procedure of a window/component are useful to reconstruct the user interaction. Indeed, there are messages that do not directly regard the user interaction, for instance the WM_PAINT message forces the refreshing of the display of a certain component, but it is not triggered by the user. As a consequence, only a subset of the messages is considered for our purposes. Such set includes, for instance: WM_LBUTTONDOWN, a message that is received from every component as soon as a click event is detected on it; WM_KEYDOWN, a message that is sent to the component that currently has the focus as soon as the user presses a key on the keyboard.

The functionality to track and save all the interactions of the user with the system is not centrally delegated to a single module but instead distributed over multiple modules that track the activity of the user according to a specific aspect:

- **NoiseMod:** It is the module that has to track possible conditions that might interfere with the user activity on the audio channel. In order to track the conditions on the audio channel, this module executes at regular intervals of time a sampling of the audio. Depending on the samplings recorded, the value to be recorded in the log file is calculated.
- **PowerMod:** It is the module that monitors the battery consumption of the device. The values are saved as they are provided by the system, without performing any calculation on them.
- **LightMod:** It is the component that is in charge of tracking conditions that might interfere on the visual channel, for instance variations on the brightness of the surrounding environment.
- **SignalMod:** Some applications might depend on the availability of a communication network and on the intensity of the signal. In these cases, the task of recording the power of such a signal is delegated to this module.
- **PositionMod:** Some applications might be affected by the current position of the user. In this case, this module will track the location of the user and how it changes over the time.

These modules have been identified taking into account the possibilities opened up by the sensing technologies of current mobile devices. Such modules for gathering environmental data are dynamically loaded only if a logging session is started and the activation of these specific components is requested. They record events using a sampling frequency algorithm, which is able to *adapt* the frequency at which the sampling is taken.

Therefore, the sampling is not carried out at fixed time intervals. It starts with setting an initial interval of time in which events are acquired. Then, it proceeds in the following way: if, in the last interval of time no variation has been registered, the interval of time to be considered for the next acquisition becomes larger, otherwise it decreases (following an exponential law). This choice is based on the consideration that using a fixed interval of time for the sampling frequency might not be a good solution. For instance, if the sampling frequency is much smaller than the frequency at which the environmental condition changes, a more flexible algorithm can avoid the activation of useless event detection during some intervals of time, saving battery consumption, which is not an irrelevant aspect for mobile devices.

4.2 Saving the Logged Data

The tool receives notification messages from the application to be tested, and delivers XML-based log files in which the events are saved according to a specific structure that will be detailed later on in the section.

Therefore, Mobile Logger communicates with Multi-Device RemUsine through the log files: in such files the logging tool records the detected events, and from such log files Multi-Device RemUsine gets the information needed to reconstruct the user's activity.

The log file is an XML-based file, and it is structured into two main parts: a header and the list of events that have been registered by the logger. The header contains information related to the entire evaluation session, for instance, the username of the tester, the temporal interval spent performing the test, the application tested, the list of contextual aspects that have been registered and the related parameters of sampling.

The events are recorded according to the following structure: (temporal event, type of event, value), and they have been categorised into different classes: *contextual* events (all the events that have been registered as a consequence of a contextual condition); *intention* event (which is used to signal that the user has changed the target task, which has to be explicitly indicated); *system* event (the events generated by the system for replying to a user's action); *interaction* event, further specialised into different categories like: click focus, select, check, scroll, edit.

As an example, we can consider an application of the tool focusing on the use of information regarding noise and battery power. In this case, the tested application was a museum guide available on a PDA device. When the tool is activated it appears as shown in Figure 3(a): the user is supposed to fill identification information, then specify the aspects of the environment s/he is interested to consider, and also specify the target task (intention) that she wants to achieve (Fig. 3c), by selecting it from a list of high-level tasks supported by the application (Figure 3-b).

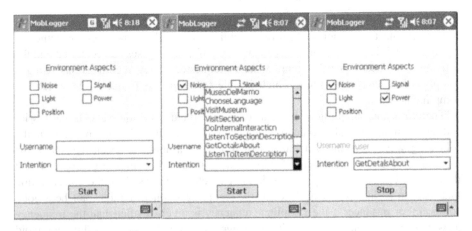

Fig. 3. The logging tool: (a) when it starts; (b) after selecting the environmental conditions of interest; (c) after selecting the intention

Then, after selecting the "Start" button the log file regarding the user's activity is created. Figure 4 shows an excerpt of the log file indicating the detection of the noise with an initial frequency of 500 ms and an increment factor of 50 ms. In addition, only variations not less of 3dB with respect to the previously detected values will be tracked. As for the battery level, the temporal parameters used are similar apart that the resolution is of only 1 percentage point.

Fig. 4. An excerpt of log file recorded by the MobileLogger

During the session evaluated, the user is supposed to interact with the application. Figure 5 shows an excerpt of the log file highlighting some events that have been registered and referring to the abovementioned scenario. From top to bottom, we have highlighted two environmental data regarding battery and noise; then, we have the notification of a system event (the loading of a window in the application), lastly, we have the notification of the selection of the target task (intention) made by the user.

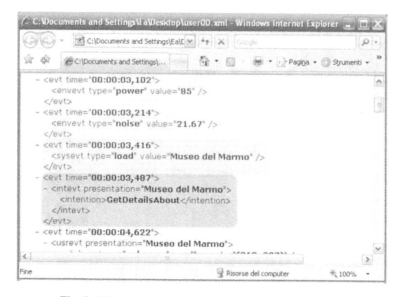

Fig. 5. Different types of events recorded by the Mobile Logger

5   Representing Usability Data

Usability evaluation is strictly connected to how the gathered data are represented and provided to the evaluator. Therefore, the choice about the particular representation to use is important for enabling an effective assessment by the evaluators. Indeed, the data that are gathered might produce a large amount of information, which, if not adequately represented, might become a burden for the evaluators rather than facilitating their work. A previous version of the tool (see [13]) already provided the possibility to visualise the data gathered during the evaluation session, so that the evaluators could analyse them and derive their results accordingly.

However, the evaluation reports were mainly textual, and therefore they were not able to highlight the main aspects effectively (see Figure 6-top part). The new version

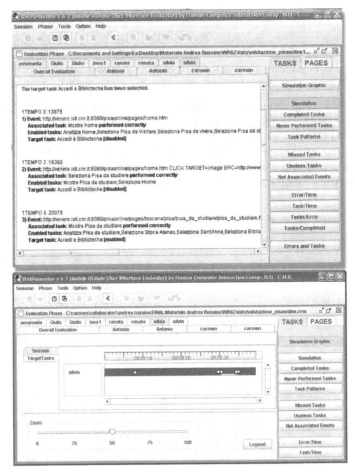

Fig. 6. Representing the evaluation results in the previous version of the tool (top) and in the new version (bottom)

of the tool offers graphical visualisations of the data gathered, which can be managed more easily by the evaluators (an example is shown in Figure 6-bottom part), thereby representing a step forward with respect to the previous visualisation technique. The new graphical representations will be described in further detail in the next sections. One of the most important points to bear in mind when deciding the technique to use for representing evaluation data is that such representation should make it easy to identify the parts of the application where users encounter problems. Therefore, the information represented is effective insofar as it is able to highlight such information, and consequently enable the evaluator to draw conclusions about the usability of the application. One relevant aspect for effectively reconstructing a user session is providing data according to its evolution over the time. In addition, evaluators should be able to easily carry out comparisons between the behaviour of different users; therefore, the use of graphical representations (rather than e.g. lengthy text-based descriptions) can also provide the evaluators with an overview of the collected data and allow them to compare data on different users.

Such considerations led to the type of representation we have investigated to represent usage data, the *timelines*. In particular, we identified three types of timelines:

- *Simple Timeline*: linear representations of the events that have been recorded;
- *State-timeline*, which is an extension of the first one, enriched with information about the current state of the target task, which is represented through different colours associated with *disabled*, *enabled* or active;
- *Deviation-timeline*, which is a representation of the registration over three different parallel levels, in which squared elements indicate the level of deviation from a sort of "ideal" path.

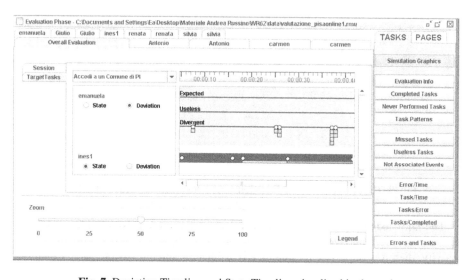

Fig. 7. Deviation Timeline and State Timeline visualized in the tool

In particular, we developed a number of panels in which not only whole sessions but also segments of them are represented both in relation to a single user and group of users. Figure 7 shows an example of both representations (the white circles identify the temporal occurrence of basic tasks whose performance is detected by an analysis of the log file), each one associated with a different user. The lines contained within the State Timeline identify the evolution of the state of the target task that has been selected: *disabled, enabled, active*, which are represented in different colours. For the Deviation timeline (see Figure 7), each square represents a degree of deviation from the ideal path which was supposed to be followed by the designer.

As Figure 7 shows, the evaluators can select the preferred type of representation and specify if they are interested to visualise data associated with a whole session or associated with single tasks. The two solutions are basically similar, but the second one is especially useful when the evaluator wish to perform some comparisons, because the selection of a single task provides information independent of absolute times. In this way, a target task explicitly selected by a user after a certain period of time from the start of the session will be perfectly lined up with another one from a different user, which started exactly at the beginning of the session. Within the timelines it is possible not only to identify when the task occurred, but also the type of task that occurred, through the use of a particular colour (see Figure 8).

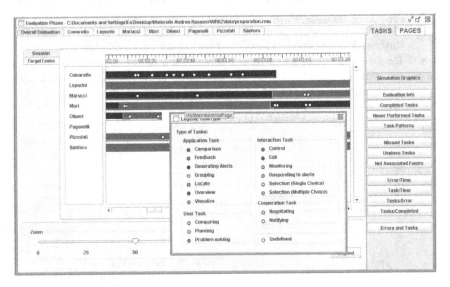

Fig. 8. The different types of intentions represented through different colours

The knowledge about the different contexts in which the user session evolved is relevant for deriving whether any condition might have interfered with the user's activity, then it is important for completely reconstructing the conditions in which the experiment took place. Contexts that are relevant for the evaluation might physically correspond to a certain place and situation, but they might also be associated with the variation of some specific aspects (for example, noise or light) even if the user is still in the same position. Then, two basic manners for defining contexts can be considered: on the one hand, there is the possibility to explicitly list the contexts that are judged relevant and define each of them in terms of the various contextual dimensions we are interested in. For instance, it might be the case that we are interested to only two specific contexts, one characterised by high level of noise, light and network connectivity (such as the office), another one characterised by low levels of noise, medium level of light and low level of network connectivity, which might be at home. On the other hand, we might wish to specify in other cases just the variations that determine the change of context, e.g. the variation of a certain parameter beyond a specific threshold value or percentage. For instance, we might want to investigate the impact on the usage of the application whenever a reduction/increase of 30% in light is registered in the environment.

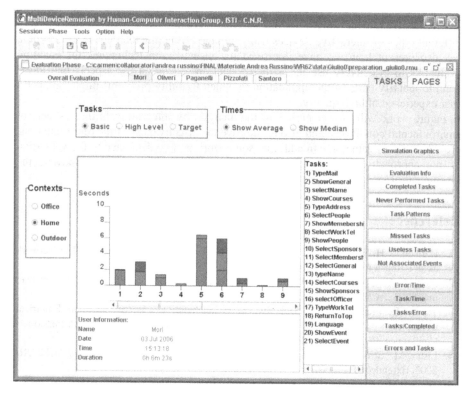

Fig. 9. Possibility of selecting task performance information related to a specific context of use

Once the different contexts have been identified, various aspects can be analysed by the evaluator. For instance, if the achievement of a certain goal is obtained by carrying out the related activities partially in an environment and partially in other environments, it might be interesting to see how the performance of a certain task evolves. In other cases, it might be interesting for the evaluator to carry out an analysis that takes into account a specific context and understand the evolution of the sessions in that specific context. For instance, it might be useful to understand the amount of time the user has spent in a specific environment and the number of tasks that have been completed in such an environment. In Figure 9 the time spent for carrying out a certain task in a specific context is visualised: the evaluator can select the specific context ("Home" in Figure 9) and then the tool shows how much time was needed by the user in order to carry out the tasks in that specific context.

6 Conclusions and Future Work

In this paper we describe an extension of a tool for remote usability evaluation. The extension aimed at supporting the evaluation of mobile applications through a logging tool also able to detect some environmental conditions that might affect the user interaction, which can be useful information for the evaluator. The resulting environment is able to support usability evaluation of applications that are executed in different types of interactive devices using a range of logging techniques. In addition, we also present how we have improved the visualization techniques for enabling evaluators to effectively use the gathered data and focus on the aspects that allow them to identify parts of the application in which usability problems might hamper a user experience of high quality.

Future work will aim at enriching the analysis by integrating further aspects of environmental conditions, and also to improve the effectiveness of the representations provided to the evaluator. In addition, some work will be dedicated to the validation of the approach and tools, for instance on the usability diagnosis power, the assessment of evaluator support, etc.

References

1. Hartson, R.H., Castillo, J.C., Kelso, J.T., Neale, W.C.: Remote Evaluation: The Network as an Extension of the Usability Laboratory. CHI 1996, 228–235 (1996)
2. Ivory, M.Y., Hearst, M.A.: The state of the art in automating usability evaluation of user interfaces. ACM Computing Surveys 33(4), 470–516 (2001)
3. Tullis, T., Fleischman, S., McNulty, M., Cianchette, C., Bergel, M.: An Empirical Comparison of Lab and Remote Usability Testing of Web Sites. Usability Professionals Conference, Pennsylvania (2002)
4. Lister, M.: Streaming Format Software for Usability Testing. In: Proceedings ACM CHI 2003, Extended Abstracts, pp. 632–633 (2003)
5. Tennent, P., Chalmers, M.: Recording and Understanding Mobile People and Mobile Technology, E-social science (2005)
6. Andreasen, M., Nielsen, H., Schrøder, S., Stage, J.: What happened to remote usability testing?: An empirical study of three methods. In: CHI 2007, pp. 1405–1414 (2007)
7. Waterson, S., Landay, J.A., Matthews, T.: In the lab and Out in the wild: remote web usability usability Testing for Mobile Devices. In: CHI 2002, Minneapolis, Minnesota, USA, pp. 796–797 (April 2002)
8. Stoica, A., Fiotakis, G., Simarro Cabrera, J., Frutos, H.M., Avouris, N., Dimitriadis, Y.: Usability evaluation of handheld devices: A case study for a museum application. In: Bozanis, P., Houstis, E.N. (eds.) PCI 2005. LNCS, vol. 3746, Springer, Heidelberg (2005)

9. Avouris, N., Komis, V., Margaritis, M., Fiotakis, G.: An environment for studying collaborative learning activities. Journal (2004)
10. Serrano, M., Nigay, L., Demumieux, R., Descos, J., Losquin, P.: Multimodal interaction on mobile phones: Development and evaluation using ACICARE. In: Proceedings of the 8th Conference on Human-Computer Interaction with Mobile Devices and Services, Mobile HCI 2006, Helsinki, Finland, pp. 129–136 (September 12-15, 2006)
11. Waterson, S., Hong, J., Sohn, T., Heer, J., Matthews, T., Landay, J.: What Did They Do? Understanding Clickstreams with the WebQuilt Visualization System. In: Proceedings of the ACM International Working Conference on Advanced Visual Interfaces, Trento, Italy (September 12-15, 2002)
12. Maly, I., Slavik, P.: Towards Visual Analysis of Usability Test Logs Using Task Models (Paper in Conference Proceedings). In: Coninx, K., Luyten, K., Schneider, K.A. (eds.) TAMODIA 2006. LNCS, vol. 4385, pp. 24–38. Springer, Heidelberg (2007)
13. Paganelli, L., Paternò, F.: Tools for Remote Usability Evaluation of Web Applications through Browser Logs and Task Models, Behavior Research Methods, Instruments, and Computers. The Psychonomic Society Publications 35(3), 369–378 (2003)
14. Paternò, F.: Model-based design and evaluation of interactive applications. Springer, Heidelberg (1999)

Defining Task Oriented Components

Grégory Bourguin[1], Arnaud Lewandowski[1], and Jean-Claude Tarby[2]

[1] LIL, Université du Littoral Côte d'Opale, France
{Gregory.Bourguin, Arnaud.Lewandowski}@lil.univ-littoral.fr
[2] LIFL, Université des Sciences et Technologies de Lille, France
Jean-Claude.Tarby@univ-lille1.fr

Abstract. For many years, tailorability has been identified as a very important property of system design in order to take care of the emerging users needs towards their working environments. In the same time component-based approaches have been revealed as an interesting solution for tailorability, allowing dynamic integration of components in global environments supporting specific tasks. However, component technologies still face some drawbacks mainly due to a semantic problem. In order to palliate these lacks we propose in this paper a new solution that tends to merge tasks models, from the HCI research field, and existing component models. It particularly consists in a new design approach — the Task Oriented (TO) approach — supported by STOrM, a tool dedicated to the creation and manipulation of Task Oriented Components (TOCs).

Keywords: Component, integration, task, modeler.

1 Introduction

For the past years and building their experience on multidisciplinary, many different research fields related to the HCI (Human Computer Interaction) research domain have demonstrated that tailorability is a key concept that has to be taken into account while designing software applications [27]. In the same time and following the growth of the Internet, the need for global environments supporting complex and eventually cooperative activities has been identified. In this track, CSCW (Computer Supported Cooperative Work) researchers have shown that component-based approaches could support tailorability in global environments [15].

As defined by Szyperski and Pfister [25], "Components can be deployed independently and are subject to composition by third parties". The fact that a component should be designed for use by third parties implicitly raises questions about its integration in the environment where it will be used: this integration should not be realized by its developers but by its users.

We have been working for many years in the CSCW research domain while creating groupware systems like CooLDev (Cooperative Layer supporting software Development) [11]. This work leads us to identify a strong issue in existing component-based technologies regarding their integration means. In this paper, we will firstly show that this issue is closely linked to a semantic loss. The second part will propose a new

M. Winckler, H. Johnson, and P. Palanque (Eds.): TAMODIA 2007, LNCS 4849, pp. 170–183, 2007.

solution corresponding to an augmented software component model inspired by Object Oriented (OO) approaches but putting the user task in the center of the component design process: the Task Oriented Component (TOC) approach. The third part will define the five main steps helping to create TOCs. We will also introduce the STOrM (Simple Task Oriented Modeler) Eclipse plug-in that is designed to support this TOC creation process. The fourth part will present the benefits resulting from the TOC approach regarding the integration issue. The fifth part will describe some collateral development showing that this approach is part of a global thinking that goes beyond the facet presented in this paper. The last part will present our conclusions and perspectives.

2   The Component Integration Problem

In order to illustrate the type of integration we are interested in here, we now introduce the work we have realized in the CooLDev project. CooLDev is a global, cooperative and integrated environment designed to support Software Development (SD) cooperative activities. This exemplification will help us to underline the lacks existing in the current means for component integration.

2.1   The CooLDev Project

Briefly described, CooLDev is a distributed environment that aims at proposing an integrated space for the use of diverse tools serving its users activities. From this point of view, it can be compared to existing environments like SourceForge [1], also dedicated to support SD activities, or even Moodle [7] widely used in the distance-learning domain. This paper does not aim at listing all the concepts and properties that differentiate CooLDev from existing platforms. The reader may find more information about this in [11]. We will just underline here the fact that in CooLDev, the client part of the environment is not supported by Web browsers, but is realized as an extension of the Eclipse platform that is widely used by the community of software developers.

Anyway, these environments aim at providing a sort of portal allowing their users to access a set of tools that have been integrated in it. This way, thanks to Sourceforge or CooLDev, users can directly and concurrently use a forum tool, a chat, a CVS, a bug-tracking system, etc., because these tools have been put together in order to support global SD activities. We can consider that each of these tools is a component that has been integrated and contextualized for supporting the global and specific user's activity. For example, a chat tool is not a priori dedicated to a particular application domain but, once contextualized into CooLDev, it is automatically connected to the discussion project's channel and the user's community. Without the global environment, each user would have to furnish her/his connection parameters for each tool and in each specific project. Thanks to CooLDev, the user only has to identify her/himself once and the platform controls and configures each integrated tool in order to automatically propose a coherent working environment. Moreover, this integration also allows managing some synergy between the components supporting the same activity. For example, in CooLDev, we can imagine that realizing a CVS "commit" will trigger an automatic message in the chat tool, thus warning the community about the changes, and that it will dynamically modify the users' rights regarding other tools/components thus for example allowing the "testers" to evaluate and annotate the new software version.

Finally, it is important to remember that platform tailorability is a strongly required property [27][16][28]. Tailorability involves that the components supporting a particular activity do not know each other a priori: in other words, the chat and the CVS have not been created by the same developers and do not know that they will be involved in such a synergy. In the same time, CooLDev cannot anticipate the future needs of its future users and thus, it cannot know in advance which components it will eventually integrate. The main issue is then to propose the means making these components open enough and well designed to be easily and finely integrated in order to support the mechanisms that we have just presented.

2.2 Existing Integration Means

Component integration is a complex research domain. Many technical solutions try to propose solutions to the many aspects of this problem. For example, components like JavaBeans, Corba, EJB, and Web Services are designed to be integrated. Their different integration methods generally follow the same principle: it is possible to dynamically find objects over the Internet, to create instances of them, to study them using introspection [13], to discover their public methods and their event channels, and finally to use them. Even if these mechanisms are useful in order to finely and dynamically integrate components, they mainly address the technical part of the problem. We can also notice that these means are exclusively directed to experienced developers [9].

The dynamic and fine integration of a component supposes that we can use it, but also and moreover that we can understand how to use it. Integrating a chat in CooLDev is a typical example of this problem. CooLDev is partially realized over Eclipse and then, the chat is an Eclipse plug-in that follows, among others, the Javabean model. A CooLDev user that needs to design a particular activity support that integrates the chat will be able to download it (as a "jar" file for example) and to discover its integration means allowing to dynamically create an instance of it, to discover its methods and to call them. Supposing that the chat has been designed as an open component, it will certainly propose a set of methods allowing its control like sendMessage, connect, disconnect, or even changeUserInfo. Even if the name of these methods may appear explicit enough, it is often hard to know what to do with these latter. In order to palliate this first semantic problem, Object Oriented (OO) technologies propose some support for their comprehension. We can cite as an example the WSDL [3], a Web Services description language, or the Javadoc, a Javabeans documentation mean. This documentation will usually be shaped as the one presented in Fig. 1.

However, even if useful, this kind of documentation mainly succinctly describes the methods, and does not really help in knowing how and when to use them. Every developer has been faced to this problem, raising many questions in which the main is probably: *"in which order the integrating application has to call these methods in order to make the component work properly?"* For example, in the case of our chat, a direct call to sendMessage will raise an error at run-time because the connect

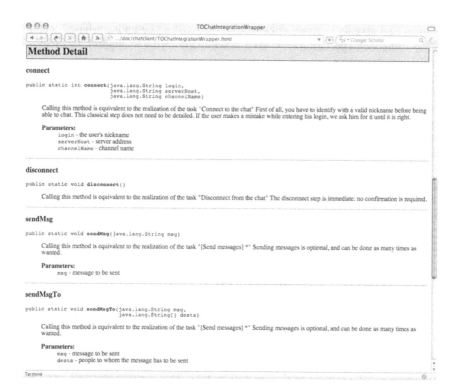

Fig. 1. A chat component Javadoc sample

method that effectively registers the user in a server channel should have been called first. Of course, in the chat example, one can imagine that someone integrating the component and discovering `connect` and `sendMessage` will certainly understand that authentication has to be performed *before* sending messages. This can be explained because this corresponds to a well-known and stereotyped task (a kind of pattern), thus also explaining why we have chosen this example in this paper. However, comprehension is less evident while considering the `changeUserInfo` method. One can imagine that if the user's data like her/his nickname or icon are stored in her/his own computer, it is possible to call `changeUserInfo` without a preliminary connection step. On the other hand, one can imagine that if the data are centralized in the server, the `connect` method has to be called first... From the component user, the ambiguity exists and the question cannot be solved without proceeding to fastidious tests, or without having to explore the component implementation, if available. More generally, and considering more complex and less stereotyped examples, with components proposing method names making sense for their designers but not necessarily for their users, it appears that the components comprehension allowing their appropriate integration is still a strong issue.

For all these reasons, only very motivated developers are usually capable to really integrate most of the components emerging from the Internet because, by studying existing source code, they have to mentally reconstruct almost all the functioning mechanisms of the tool they need to integrate. This issue limits reuse to very specialized users and reveals a strong drawback in the existing component-based technologies regarding the expectation they have generated in trying to support the creation of tailorable environments.

This analysis let us think that the difficulties encountered in component integration mainly come from a semantic loss in their documentation. In fact, the interested research community has already noticed this semantic lack and some work trying to propose new solutions is already in progress [10][14]. However, and considering the existing models, even computer scientists have difficulties in integrating external components to create their applications. This explains why we can notice that these new propositions are still directed to experienced developers. In our own work regarding tailorability [4], we have shown that facilitating the fine and dynamic component integration would also be very valuable for less experienced users. However, one point seems important for guiding our work: these users, computer scientists or not, are not necessarily familiar with the involved technology, but they all are guided by the task they need to perform.

3   Task Oriented Components: TOCs

Because we have been working for many years in the HCI research domain, particularly in the CSCW (Computer Supported Cooperative Work) research field, we have adopted this particular viewpoint: each tool or component can be considered as supporting a more or less generic and complex user task. From this viewpoint, a tool like Firefox supports the generic 'web exploration' task. This is a complex task that can be decomposed in (sub-)tasks like the 'bookmark management' or even the 'string search inside a web page'. An instance of this generic task may correspond to 'collecting information for writing a research paper for TAMODIA'. In the same way, the generic task that is supported by the chat component is distant and synchronous discussion that will for example support a particular debate activity during a global software design activity supported by CooLDev. It then appears that contextualizing a component means putting its task in the context of a more global one: the integrating environment's task. This contextualization will then be realized by creating links between the integrating task and the component's one.

The task notion takes a more and more important place inside software engineering, mainly in the HCI domain where a lot of work aims at expressing the users' tasks. This task-oriented approach is generally used in the early or in the last stages of the development process [6][12][21]. However, if these methods propose to start component design by a tasks modeling, the task notion progressively disappears during the development process and is finally replaced by the Object Oriented (OO) paradigm. This classical design approach tends to transform tasks models into object models from which results the class-based structure of the component (cf. Fig. 1, upper part). The component tasks model is then implicitly drowned in the complexity of the produced code. In fact, the (user) task notion is mostly not used during the design and development cycle, i.e. after the requirements analysis. Moreover, the existing tools used by software engineers like IDEs (Integrated Development Environments – supporting coding and test phases) or CASE tools (Computer Aided Software Engineering – supporting the whole design process like Rational Rose) do not integrate

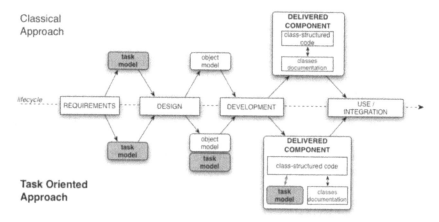

Fig. 2. Classical Object-Oriented design approach versus Task-Oriented approach

task-oriented approaches, even if several propositions have tried to palliate this lack [5][18][20][23]. Unfortunately, we can only observe the lack of concrete results in recent software development teams' tools.

Thus, it appears that the tasks model used in preliminary phases of the design process is progressively diluted in the implementation and is not explicitly accessible anymore in the delivered component. This mainly explains why, as we mentioned before, the integrators have to go in the component's code to try and extract the functioning and especially the use logic [22]. In other words, the integrator has to mostly completely and mentally reconstruct the underlying tasks model in order to make it explicit again.

This is why we propose to better use the components' tasks models that can be seen as a kind of missing link disappearing between the design phase and the produced code. We call Task Oriented Component (TOC) this new software component type. As shown in Fig. 1 (lower part), the basic principle behind a TOC is that it contains its classical OO documentation and is explicitly augmented by the tasks model describing its use logic. In this approach, some parts of the functional code (component methods) are linked to the tasks model they come from, thus allowing TOC contextualization from a higher abstraction level.

Moreover, we can notice that tasks models – when created – already serve as shared objects facilitating a better communication between the different actors (including end-users) involved in the complex design process. Thus, the TOC approach should also serve as a better support for collaboration between these actors.

4   Creating TOCs

4.1   The Approach

As a beginning, we have chosen a top-down approach for creating TOCs. We propose a method and design means supporting the creation of TOCs. This process defines several steps in which the five most important are the following:

1. Ideally, the development process should include an early task-modeling phase in order to describe the expected behavior of the future component. The resulting model will be the starting point of the TOC creation. The ergonomist collaborating with other design process actors like developers or future end-users constructs a task tree. Each task can be annotated in order to make the tasks model well understood by all the actors and serve as a shared representation of the TOC.
2. The tasks model is then augmented by the computer scientist while specifying methods that will be directly linked to the tasks and annotations that have been brought to the fore.
3. Implementation and documentation skeletons can then be directly deduced (automatically generated) from the augmented tasks model.
4. Skeletons are implemented (using a classical OO approach) while following the specifications of the augmented tasks model.
5. The component is delivered with its classical OO documentation, but also with its hybrid model linking the user's task and the component's code, thus forming the TOC documentation.

The integration activity needs an access point allowing the tierce environment to communicate with the component: when a TOC instance is created, it should provide a reference with which the integrative application will interact. This front object, also called "wrapper", proposes a set of methods making possible the control of the component by another application by replacing or "simulating" the component's user. These methods in some way allow to automatically realize or "shunt" some user tasks defined in the TOC model: for example, in our chat, calling the connect method replaces the fact that the user has to fill in a dialog box asking for his/her connection parameters; it is CoOLDev that performs the chat connection to the good server instead of its user and by using the known information about this user and about the global software development task in which the chat is involved.

These particular methods are thought for the external component's integration and control. Their implementation calls other methods that are internal to the component. The technical solution consists in generating the wrapper skeleton as an additional class that will serve as a mediator between the tasks model and the component code. This is illustrated in the Fig. 3.

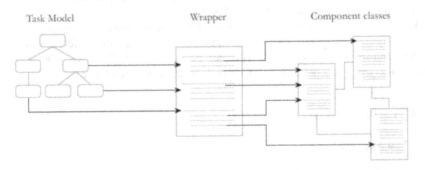

Fig. 3. Linking tasks model and implementation code through the integration wrapper

4.2 STOrM: A TOC Design Tool

4.2.1 An Augmented Task Modeler

Because the TOC development process is intimately linked to its augmented tasks model definition, we have developed a modeler supporting this activity. This tool has been called STOrM (Simple Task Oriented Modeler) (cf. Fig. 4).

STOrM has been realized as an Eclipse plug-in for many reasons. Proposing an Eclipse plug-in dedicated to software user tasks modeling that maintains strong links between user tasks models and implementation code appears as a first step towards the effective integration of user tasks modeling inside widely used development tools. Moreover, we have already underlined that a TOC development results from a close collaboration between different actors of the design process and that CooLDev aims at better supporting this collaboration. This environment being itself partially realized over the Eclipse platform, we want to involve STOrM inside the collaborative activities supported by CooLDev.

The concepts we have used to create and represent tasks models are both inspired by CTTE [17] and K-Made [2]. The reason is that we wanted to be able to freely create tasks models with, for example, isolated tasks (i.e. without parent), eventually untyped tasks, etc., things that are somehow not globally possible with only one of these formalisms. We also wanted to augment them with new elements directly inspired from our specific approach. These choices result from many years using these modeling tools with very diverse publics like computers scientists (students, teachers, developers), simple computer users and ergonomists. We then decided to select interesting elements issued from each formalism like the CTTE tree view, the K-Made icons and "unknown" task concept. We also mixed the temporal operators, merging the "unknown" temporal operator from K-Made with those from CTT, etc.

4.2.2 Creating a Chat TOC

To illustrate the use of STOrM for creating TOCs, we will once again consider the chat example that has been described since the beginning of this paper. Thus, STOrM is used to create the tasks model of the future chat TOC. This model is partially presented in Fig. 4. Using STOrM, the developer can augment the produced tasks model while specifying the basis of the component's functional code. As mentioned before, a tierce environment will use these integration methods to create shunts over desired user tasks. This explains why the developer takes benefit in reasoning on the component's tasks model to identify the tasks that may serve this mechanism. STOrM supports this extension phase by providing the means to augment each task while defining the public methods signatures that will make the augmented tasks accessible from a tierce environment. The augmented tasks model of the chat component is shown in Fig. 4 where one can notice that the developer has for example augmented the *Connect to the chat* task, thus making possible for a tierce environment like CooLDev to automatically configure this component by taking the place of its user in providing the adequate connection data. This is characterized by the existence of the connect method. If an integrating environment calls connect while providing the required parameters, the connection task is directly realized. If the parameters are not provided, the component will open a dialog box requiring a user interaction. Finally,

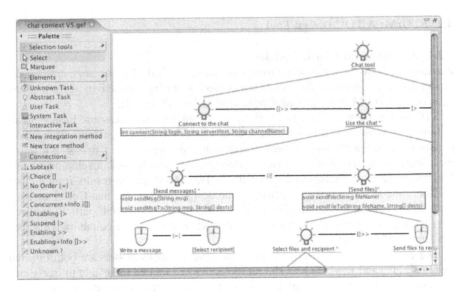

Fig. 4. The chat tasks model augmented by integration method signatures

it is important to notice that, with this augmentation, the designers clearly indicate that `connect` is the first method to be called when the chat is instantiated.

4.2.3 An Implementation Skeleton Generator

Once the tasks model has been augmented, STOrM is able to generate the corresponding implementation skeletons. More precisely, a Wrapper (java) class is generated on

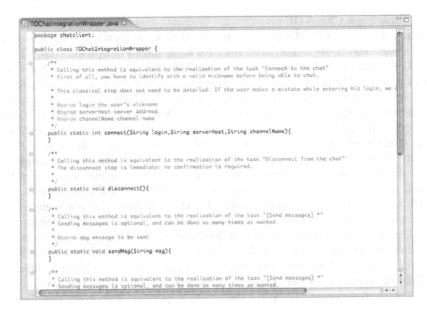

Fig. 5. Sample code of the generated wrapper class

demand. This class provides the entry points that will be involved in the future TOC integration. Considering the chat augmented tasks model already introduced, the `ChatIntegrationWrapper` class has been generated and is shown in Fig. 5. A Javadoc embryo is also generated, taking benefit from information (e.g. annotations) available in the task associated to each method. This skeleton is a basis element that the development team will "just" have to complement while implementing the methods bodies and the Javadoc from its point of view.

5 Using TOCs

Even if the classical OO introspection mechanism is still available, the TOC provides a new viewpoint over its integration methods because its tasks model is delivered with the component. This way, opening a TOC in STOrM (or any future compatible tool) provides a new introspection type that helps in discovering the integration methods, not only through a simple list, but now through the task that is supported by the component. This new viewpoint palliates the semantic problems we exposed before. Considering the chat example (cf. Fig. 6), it is now possible to easily study it's functioning and to quickly discover its functions that have been judged as key elements by its designers. Each possibility offered by the component regarding integration corresponds to an augmented task that is contextualized in the frame of the global task supported by the component. The integration methods are linked to these tasks. Thanks to this, the ambiguity described before and introduced by the `changeUser-Info` method directly disappears because the augmented tasks model, with the task transition semantics, clearly indicates that the connection task has to be realized first. The integrator does not need to know where data are stored: the tasks model is clear

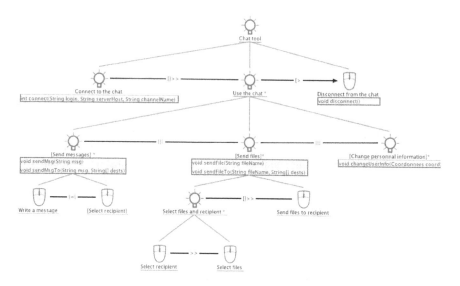

Fig. 6. TOC introspection facilitating its integration

enough. Finally, we will underline that, going further in displaying the different aspects of the TOC, STOrM can simultaneously display the component's augmented tasks model and each method's Javadoc. This contextualizes classical information, coming from a lower abstraction level like comments about the method's parameters, in the frame of the task higher abstraction level.

6 Collateral Development

In this paper and due to a lack of space, we have limited our demonstration to the components' integration issue. However, we also would like to briefly underline another point closely linked to our approach. Another issue about component-based technologies is related to the means to verify how a component effectively supports the task it has been designed for. More precisely, we are interested in finding solutions that help to generate and analyze components' use traces.

From this point of view, our work uses the Aspect Oriented Programming (AOP) [8] to generate traces [26] reflecting the component's use: its execution involves method calls that support the interactions between the user and the component; tracing these methods help to analyze the task performed by a user with the component. This technique offers several benefits that we will not describe here. However, without our TOC approach, one drawback is that the ergonomist wanting to trace a component has to browse the code to identify and select the methods that have to be traced. Due to the semantic loss we have described in this paper, this work can only hardly be realized since an ergonomist is usually not a computer scientist and because the available implementation methods do not easily correspond to the user tasks he needs to trace.

This further explains how the TOC approach also truly tries to take care about the ergonomist's needs, and how this method should amplify and favor a balanced cooperation: in the first step of the method, while creating the tasks model, the ergonomist also describes the tasks he want to trace later. While augmenting this tasks model in step 2, the computer scientist then also defines key methods for tracing. These methods are not necessarily integration methods constituting the wrapper, but correspond to the core implementation code of the component, i.e. the component's classes that may be involved in the wrapper's implementation as described in Fig. 3. Using a tool like STOrM, the corresponding skeleton can be generated and implemented according to the augmented tasks model. Thus, thanks to the TOC technology, an ergonomist can more easily create aspects that will generate the expected use traces. He does not have to hardly browse the component's code anymore. He now just has to identify the tasks he wants to trace, which corresponds to his/her abstraction level. Since the tasks model is directly connected to the corresponding methods, STOrM can help in generating the aspects over the (implicitly) selected methods.

7 Conclusion

As demonstrated by many years of multidisciplinary research involved in software design, tailorability has to be an intrinsic property of new interactive systems in order to take into account the inevitable emerging users' needs. It has been shown that tailorability can be supported by component-based technologies. However, we have demonstrated in this paper that existing component models still present semantic problems. This lack hardens component integration. To palliate this problem, we have proposed a new Task Oriented (TO) design approach trying to marry HCI tasks models and existing Object Oriented (OO) component models. We have noticed that user tasks models are poorly involved in current software design. In the TO approach, the tasks model become the center around which components are constructed while federating the expertise of the different actors involved in the design process. This approach defines five main steps that guide the creation of Task Oriented Components (TOC).

The main advantage of a TOC is that it contains its tasks model that has been augmented by key methods signatures providing concrete means for its integration in a tierce environment. These methods are used to generate an integration wrapper skeleton. TOCs then augment the classical OO introspection mechanisms by adding the semantic linked to their tasks model. This facilitates the component discovery and comprehension, thus easing its integration because the tasks model contextualizes the methods that enable its control and indicates which tasks can be called and/or shunted by an integrating environment.

The TO approach is now partially supported by STOrM (Simple Task Oriented Modeler), a tool dedicated to the creation and manipulation of TOCs. STOrM, as this TO approach, is still subject to evolutions but these first results are opening several exciting perspectives. One of them is to further develop STOrM in order to support graphical components integration. As we said, integrating a component in a specific environment corresponds to contextualizing its generic task in the frame of a more global one. We strongly believe that component integration will then be possible by graphically linking tasks models together. We hope that this mechanism will make component integration more accessible, maybe even to end-users, thus better supporting the tailorability principle.

Finally, we have shown in the last part of this paper that the TOC approach aims at facilitating more than component integration. This is why STOrM has been realized as an Eclipse plug-in that can be integrated in the CooLDev environment. CooLDev is precisely dedicated to the support of global cooperative software development activities like the one we have described in this paper for creating TOCs. This should help us to test and further develop this work that takes place in a global research approach dedicated to better software design and complex application development support.

Acknowledgments. The authors would like to thank the Direction de la Recherche for the ACI CooLDEv, the TAC program financed by La Région Nord/Pas-de-Calais and the french estate in the frame of the CPER for the MIAOU and EUCUE projects.

References

1. Augustin, L., Bressler, D., Smith, G.: Accelerating software development through collaboration. In: 24rd International Conference on Software Engineering, pp. 559–563 (2002)
2. Baron, M., Lucquiaud, V., Autard, D., Scapin, D.L.: K-MADe: Un environnement pour le noyau du modéle de description de l'activité. In: 18éme Conf. Francophone sur l'Interaction Homme-Machine IHM 2006, pp. 287–288 (2006)

3. Booth, D., Liu, C.K.: Web Services Description Language (WSDL) Version 2.0. (2006)Avalaible at: http://www.w3.org/TR/wsdl20-primer
4. Bourguin, G., Derycke, A., Tarby, J.C.: Beyond the Interface: Co-evolution Inside Interactive Systems - A proposal Founded on Activity Theory. In: Blandford, Vanderdonckt, Gray. (eds.) Interaction without Frontiers, Proc. of HCI 2001. People and Computer, pp. 297–310. Springer, Heidelberg (2001)
5. Bruins, A.: The Value of Task Analysis in Interaction Design. In: Task to Dialogue: Task-Based User Interface Design Workshop, CHI 1998 (1998)
6. Clerckx, T., Luyten, K., Coninx, K.: DynaMo-AID: a Design Process and a Runtime Architecture for Dynamic Model-Based User Interface Development. In: 9th IFIP Working Conference on Engineering for Human-Computer Interaction. Pre-Proceedings, Hamburg, Germany, July 11-13, pp. 142–160 (2004)
7. Dougiamas, M.: Moodle: open-source software for producing internet-based courses (2001), Available at: http://moodle.com
8. Filman, R., Elrad, T., Clarke, S., Aksit, M.: Aspect-oriented software development. Addison-Wesley, Reading (2004)
9. Heineman, G.T., Councill, W.T.: Component-based software engineering: putting the pieces together. Addison-Wesley Longman Publishing Co., Inc, Boston, MA (2001)
10. Kiniry, J.R.: Semantic Component Composition. In: Cardelli, L. (ed.) ECOOP 2003. LNCS, vol. 2743, Springer, Heidelberg (2003)
11. Lewandowski, A., Bourguin, G.: Supporting Collaboration in Software Development Activities. In: 10th International Conference on Computer Supported Cooperative Work in Design (CSCWD 2006), May 3-5, 2006, vol. 1, pp. 381–387. IEEE Press, Los Alamitos (2006)
12. Lu, S., Paris, C., Vander Linden, K., Colineau, N.: Generating UML Diagrams From Tasks models. In: CHINZ 2003, Dunedin, New Zealand (2003)
13. Maes, P.: Concepts and experiments in computational reflection. In: Object-oriented programming systems, languages and applications, New York, USA, pp. 147–155 (1987)
14. Medjahed, B., Bouguettaya, A., Elmagarmid, A.K.: Composing Web services on the Semantic Web. The International Journal on Very Large Data Bases 12(4), 333–351 (2003)
15. Mørch, A.: Three levels of end-user tailoring: customization, integration, and extension. In: Method and Tools for Tailoring Object-Oriented Applications: An Evolving Artifacts Approach. PhD thesis, Dept of Informatics, University of Oslo, pp. 41–51 (1997)
16. Mørch, A.I., Stevens, G., Won, M., Klann, M., Dittrich, Y., Wulf, V.: Component-based technologies for end-user development. Communications of the ACM 47(9), 59–62 (2004)
17. Mori, G., Paterno, F., Santoro, C.: CTTE: Support for Developing and Analysing Tasks models for Interactive System Design. IEEE Transactions on Software Engineering 28(8), 797–813 (2002)
18. Nunes, N., Cunha, J.F.e.: Towards a UML pro-file for interaction design: the Wisdom approach. In: Evans, A., Kent, S., Selic, B. (eds.) UML 2000. LNCS, vol. 1939, Springer, Heidelberg (2000)
19. Object Technology International, Inc.: Eclipse Platform Technical Overview (2003), Available at: http://www.eclipse.org
20. Pinheiro da Silva, P.: Object Modelling of Interactive Systems: The UMLi Approach. PhD Thesis, University of Manchester, United Kingdom (2002)
21. Reichart, D., Forbrig, P., Dittmar, A.: Tasks models as basis for requirements engineering and software execution. In: [24], pp. 51–58 (2004)
22. Richard, J.F.: Logique de fonctionnement et logique d'utilisation. Rapport de recherche INRIA n° Avril 202 (1983)

23. Scogings, C., Phillips, C.: Linking Task and Dialogue Modeling: Toward an Integrated Software Engineering Method. In: Diaper, D., Stanton, N. (eds.) Handbook of Task Analysis for Human-Computer Interaction, pp. 551–566. Lawrence Erlbaum Associates Pubs, Mahwah, NJ (2004)
24. Slavík, P., Palanque, P.: Proceedings of the 3rd Int. Workshop on Tasks models and Diagrams for User Interface Design - TAMODIA 2004, pp. 15–16. ACM, New York (2004)
25. Szyperski, C., Pfister, C.: Workshop on component-oriented programming, summary. In: Cointe, P. (ed.) ECOOP 1996. LNCS, vol. 1098, Springer, Heidelberg (1996)
26. Tarby, J.C., Ezzedine, H., Rouillard, J., Tran, C.D., Laporte, P., Kolski, K.: Traces using aspect oriented programming and interactive agent-based architecture for early usability evaluation: Basic principles and comparison. In: HCI International, Beijing, P.R. China. LNCS, vol. 4550, pp. 632–641. Springer, Heidelberg (2007)
27. Vicente, K.J.: HCI in the global knowledge-based economy: Designing to support worker adaptation. Communications of the ACM 7(2), 263–280 (2000)
28. Won, M., Stiemerling, O., Wulf, V.: Component-Based Approaches To Tailorable Systems. In: Lieberman, H., Paternó, F., Wulf, V. (eds.) End-User Development. Human-Computer Interaction Series, pp. 115–142. Kluwer Academic, Dordrecht (2005)

Patterns in Task-Based Modeling of User Interfaces

Frank Radeke[1] and Peter Forbrig[2]

[1] Information Systems 2
European Business School
Schloss Reichartshausen
65375 Oestrich-Winkel, Germany
frank.radeke@ebs.edu
[2] Software-Engineering Group
Institute of Computer Science
Albert-Einstein-Str. 2
18059 Rostock, Germany
peter.forbrig@uni-rostock.de

Abstract. The development of user interfaces is influenced by various challenges in recent years. These are foremost caused by increasing complexity of the underlying applications and the use of these applications on different devices, by different user types and in changing environments. Model-based user interface development approaches have been shown to be suitable to face these challenges. However, creating, transforming and linking the various included models are complex tasks. Employing patterns can avoid these disadvantages and provide an advanced concept of reuse. In this paper a general framework is introduced that describes how model-based approaches can be extended with patterns. The implementation of the framework is exemplarily shown in order to derive a concrete pattern-driven model-based approach for user interface development. A case study is used to illustrate the derived approach.

Keywords: Pattern, Model-based User Interface Design, Pattern Notation.

1 Introduction

User interfaces have to handle increasing challenges. They convey the output of the underlying application and the input from application users and hence have to cope with the complexity of both sides [6], as Fig. 1 illustrates.

On the one hand the increasing complexity of software applications in general influences the user interface design, since the application functionality has to be accessed via the user interface.

On the other hand the user interface needs to accommodate different types of users, ranging from computer novices to computer experts. Additionally, a wide spectrum of new devices beside the desktop PC, like PDAs or mobile phones, has caused a growing demand for device spanning applications in the last years. However, running the application on different devices often meant developing a user interface for each of the devices. Eventually different and dynamically changing environments, where the applications are used in, have to be considered.

M. Winckler, H. Johnson, and P. Palanque (Eds.): TAMODIA 2007, LNCS 4849, pp. 184–197, 2007.

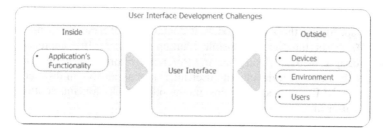

Fig. 1. User interface development challenges

Model-based user interface development has gained momentum in the recent years. Various development approaches have been suggested. However, they often differ in the underlying models, the modeling method and the modeling notation used to describe the models. Beside the benefits of model-based user interface development, creating the models and linking them to each other is still a time-consuming activity. Furthermore the approaches lack an advanced concept of reuse.

To avoid these disadvantages patterns may be employed. Patterns describe recurring solutions in a generic form, so that they are applicable in different contexts while adapting the solution to the given situation. Since the solution has to be specified only once when creating the pattern, patterns provide an advanced concept of reuse. Furthermore patterns are suitable to reduce complexity of model-based approaches, because they provide a more aggregated perspective in the development.

In this paper an approach for integrating model-based and pattern-driven approaches for user interface development is introduced. In the next chapter related work is discussed. Following, in the third chapter, a framework is introduced that describes the general idea of how model-based approaches for user interface development can be extended with patterns. Afterwards, in the fourth chapter, it is shown exemplarily how to implement the framework in order to derive a concrete pattern-driven model-based approach. The capability of the derived approach will be illustrated by presenting a case study within the fifth chapter. Finally the concepts introduced in this paper will be summarized and future avenues will be outlined.

2 Related Work

The idea of model-based development of user interfaces is to describe the user interface by a set of models, whereby each specifies a certain aspect of the user interface. For this purpose various model-based approaches have been suggested in recent years. Usually each approach contains a *modeling method* that describes which models have to be created in order to specify the final user interface and a *modeling language* that is used to specify the single models.

The left box in Fig. 2 highlights exemplarily three model-based approaches. The *Mobi-D* (Model-based Interface Designer, [13]) approach includes a modeling method that is based on a user-task, a domain, a user, a dialog and a presentation model. Furthermore XIML (Extensible Interface Markup Language, [23]) is included in the approach in order to specify the single models. The "*One Model Many Interfaces*" [12] approach suggests task, abstract and concrete models for user interface modeling. It aims to support the development of multimodal user interfaces. For the purpose of specifying the single models it contains the Teresa XML notation [16]. The *UsiXML* (User Interface Extensible Markup Language, [9]) approach is structured according to the Cameleon Unifying Reference Framework [5] that attempts to characterize the process of developing user interfaces applicable in different contexts of use. The UsiXML approach contains among others task, domain, context, abstract and concrete user interface models.

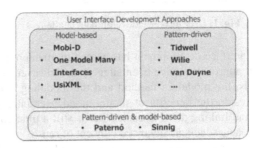

Fig. 2. Model-based and pattern-driven approaches for user interface development

Patterns, pattern languages and a process of pattern application were first proposed by Christopher Alexander in the domain of urban architecture [1, 2]. According to Alexander a pattern describes "... a problem which occurs over and over again in our environment, and then describes the core of the solution to that problem, in such a way that you can use this solution a million times over, without doing it the same way twice." [2].

The pattern concept was quickly adapted to other domains. First references to Alexander's work in user interface related papers were published in "User Centered System Design" [10]. However, interest in pattern languages for interaction design has gained momentum only in recent years [3]. As outlined on the right hand of Fig. 2 user interface patterns have been suggested in form of pattern collections and pattern languages. *Van Duyne* et al. [19] focus on patterns that describe solutions in costumer-centered web design. Thereby the authors follow closely Alexander's format of pattern representation. *Tidwell* [17] defines a pattern language that may be employed in user interface design for desktop applications as well. While emphasizing on how and why usability is improved by employing their patterns, *Wilie* et al. [21] focus on providing user-centered solutions for user interface design. The patterns in the mentioned languages are mainly described in a textual or graphical notation.

Patterns in the context of user interface modeling are a rather new and rarely examined research field. Such patterns encapsulate solutions for the creation of the single user interface models. In [11] *Paternó* suggests task and architectural patterns. The task patterns capture a high level description of recurring activities performed while interacting with the application. For describing the patterns a textual pattern notation is used. Additionally the task structure of the task patterns is described using the CTT (ConcurTaskTree, [11]) notation. In line with task patterns the architectural patterns describe recurring system components used to support interaction with the user independent of the implementation language. Some task patterns based on the suggested approach are introduced in [4].

Sinnig [15] proposes a framework for employing patterns in model-based user interface design. The framework includes a set of models, a model-based user interface development method for constructing these models and a set of user interface patterns that can be used in this construction. The patterns are described in a uniformed textual and graphical notation. For the task patterns TPML (Task Pattern Markup Language) a machine-readable notation was proposed.

3 General Pattern Application Framework

In this section a general pattern application framework is introduced that describes how model-based development of user interfaces can be extended while employing patterns. The framework abstracts from a concrete *model-based approach*, a concrete *pattern language* and a concrete *pattern notation* for specifying the single patterns in order to be applicable for different underlying model-based approaches.

Fig. 3 shows the architecture of the framework. It contains three general phases. The user interface designer is involved in all these phases. It also shows the three

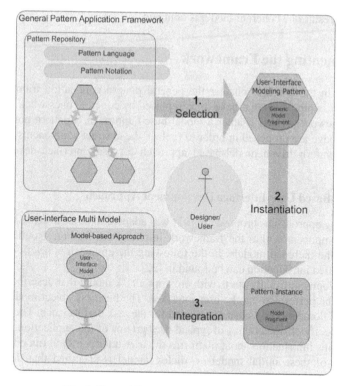

Fig. 3. General Pattern Application Framework

abstract components of the framework. The abstract components are specified when the framework is implemented. In what follows the framework's phases, its main elements and the abstract components are discussed in more detail.

During the pattern *selection* phase the designer selects an appropriate *user interface pattern* that shall be applied to the *user interface models*. The pattern is chosen out of the *pattern repository* which contains the available patterns of the *pattern language*. Within the pattern language the patterns are hierarchically structured into patterns and sub-patterns. Each pattern in the pattern language is specified according to a specific *pattern notation*. A user interface modeling pattern in the framework contains a model fragment that describes the pattern solution. Compared to concrete user interface models the model-fragment is *generic* in order to be applicable in various contexts and to allow the pattern to be instantiated in multiple ways.

The generic parts of the selected pattern are concretized during the *pattern instantiation* phase. This interactive process results in a *pattern instance* derived from the original pattern. Since all generic pattern parts are concretized the resulting pattern instance does not differ in its structure from a concrete user interface model.

Eventually the pattern instance is integrated in the user interface models. This is done in the pattern *integration* phase. First the model fragment of the created pattern instance is integrated into the corresponding model. Next the model elements contributed by the pattern instance are linked with the existing elements of the user interface model. As a result one coherent model is obtained.

4   Implementing the Framework

As outlined in the previous chapter the general pattern application framework contains abstract components that have to be replaced by concrete ones when implementing the framework. In this chapter a model-based approach, a pattern notation and a pattern language are proposed in order to replace the abstract components. As a result a concrete pattern-driven model-based approach for user interface development is achieved.

4.1   Model-Based User Interface Development Approach

The modeling approach as proposed in [22] was adapted in order to serve as modeling approach component within the framework implementation. Fig. 4 outlines the approach and the included models. In the following the approach is briefly introduced. A more detailed introduction can be found in [22].

The development usually starts with creating a task model that describes the tasks, which shall be performed via the user interface. The business object model describes properties of domain objects that are needed for the task performance. The user model is used to specify characteristics of typical user groups of the application. The device model contains information about platforms the user interface shall run on. Following the creation of these initial models, a dialog model is specified that describes the navigational structure of the user interface in form of views and transitions between these views. Using the information of the models created so far an abstract user interface model is generated automatically, which is interactively refined into the final concrete user interface model afterwards.

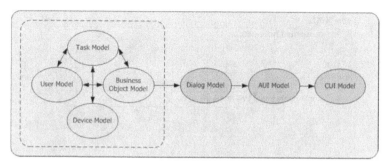

Fig. 4. Model-based approach as suggested by Wolff et al. [22]

4.2 Pattern Notation

Patterns contained in pattern languages suggested so far describe the single patterns mainly in a textual and graphical form. This information helps the developer to determine whether a specific pattern is applicable in a concrete design situation. In the following it is referred to this kind of information as *contextual* information. However, the patterns usually do not contain machine-readable information about the solutions captured by them. Thus implementing the solutions is usually left up to the developer. Including this information in the pattern would enable computer support for the entire pattern application process. Such machine-readable information is referred to as *implementational* information in the following.

In the context of the pattern application framework the UsiPXML (User Interface Pattern Extensible Markup Language) has been developed. It allows describing as well contextual *and* implementational information for a pattern. The composition of UsiPXML is illustrated in Fig. 5.

The contextual information in UsiPXML is structured according to the format as suggested by PLML (Pattern Language Markup Language, [8]). PLML was an output of the CHI 2003 (Conference on Human Factors in Computing Systems) workshop with the goal to define a common structure for patterns. Up to that point most authors used their own format for describing their patterns. PLML contains common elements, like for instance the pattern name, the problem and the solution, that can be found in most of the patterns suggested so far.

As mentioned before user interface modeling patterns describe the solution in form of model fragments. In order to specify these fragments in a machine-readable way UsiPXML is based on UsiXML (User Interface Extensible Markup Language, [18]). Since UsiXML is suitable for user interface model specification it is as well suitable for description of the pattern solution captured in form of a model fragment. However, by definition patterns describe the solution in a *generic* way. Thus the solution can be applied in different contexts. In order to describe the solution in a machine-readable but generic way UsiXML has been extended with pattern-specific components as outlined in the lower part of Fig. 5. These components are structure attributes, variable declarations and assignments and pattern references and interfaces. These extensions will be introduced in the following using an illustrative example. A more detailed description of the extensions can be found in [14].

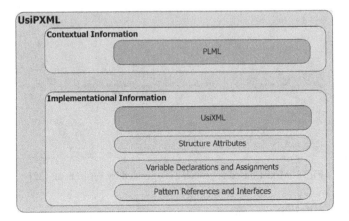

Fig. 5. Composition of UsiPXML

Fig. 6 (a) shows the UsiPXML structure of the "Form Pattern" [15]. It can be employed in situation where the user shall enter a set of related values. Fig. 6 (b) shows a possible instance generated from the pattern. A first concept that can be found in UsiPXML are structure attributes. Structure attributes are used to assign the numbers of allowed occurrences to elements that are contained in the pattern structure. The minimum and maximum number of allowed occurrences of an element is indicated in brackets behind the element. For instance the element "Box: Single Input (0, unbound)" that can be found in the middle of Fig. 6 (a) is allowed to occur arbitrarily often in the final pattern instance. The concrete occurrence number of the element is determined by the designer during the pattern instantiation. In the instance shown in Fig. 6 (b) the single input element occurs five times.

Furthermore variables can be defined within patterns. They serve as placeholders for concrete values. During the pattern instantiation the designer is prompted to assign values to all variables that occur within the selected pattern. The "Form Pattern" contains for instance a variable "introductionText" that allows to specify an introduction text, which is displayed in top of the form as shown exemplarily in Fig. 6 (b). Variables are evaluated by assignment elements in the pattern. This evaluation returns a value that is assigned to attributes of pattern elements. To summarize, variables represent the design decisions of the user interface designer. Assignments evaluate these decisions and according to this evaluation adapt the structure of the pattern solution.

A last concept that can be found in UsiPXML are pattern references and pattern interfaces. Pattern references allow employing sub-patterns in order to refine a pattern solution. As shown in the lower part of Fig. 6 (b) the "Form Pattern" refers to the "Unambiguous Format Pattern" [15, 20] as a sub-pattern. The purpose of the "Unambiguous Format Pattern" is to provide a single input element depending on the type of information that is entered in this input. Therefore the type of information that shall be entered in the input is passed to the sub-pattern via its pattern interface. The sub-pattern evaluates this information and provides the appropriate input element.

It can be summarized that UsiPXML allows describing contextual and implementational information of a pattern. The implementational information describes the pattern solution in a machine-readable, generic way.

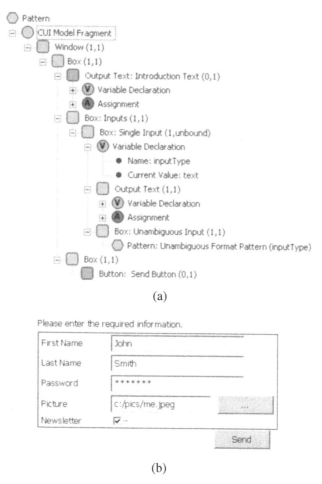

(a)

(b)

Fig. 6. UsiPXML structure (a) of the "Form Pattern" and a pattern instance generated from the pattern (b)

4.3 Pattern Language

A last component that has to be specified in order to implement the pattern application framework is the pattern language. It contains the available patterns and relations among these patterns. For this purpose a set of patterns in UsiPXML format has been developed and has been integrated into the "User Interface Modeling Pattern Language". Fig. 7 shows that the language is divided in four pattern classes.

Task patterns describe recurring tasks in a generic manner. A set of task patterns has already been specified by Sinnig [15] in the TPML (Task Pattern Markup Language) pattern notation. Some of these patterns have been transformed to the UsiPXML pattern notation and have been integrated into the pattern language as displayed in the top left of Fig. 7. Dialog patterns describe recurring navigational structures of user interfaces. They are employed in the creation of the dialog model.

Layout patterns capture recurring solutions for the layout of user interface elements. Examples are the positioning of elements or setting layout attributes like size, color or font. Presentation patterns describe recurring concrete user interface structures. That may be groups of concrete user interface elements or single user interface elements in more specific patterns. In the next chapter some patterns will be introduced using an illustrative example. The entire pattern language can be found in [14].

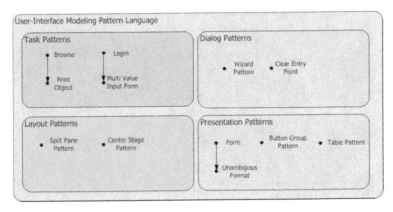

Fig. 7. User Interface Modeling Pattern Language

5 Tool Support and Case Study

The UsiPXML pattern notation allows the description of the patterns in a machine-readable format. Thus the pattern application can be supported by software tools. Such tools have been developed in order to implement the concrete pattern-driven model-based approach that has been derived in the last chapter. The tools are developed as so called plug-ins for the Eclipse [7] environment. They strictly follow the three steps of the pattern application process proposed by the framework introduced above: Pattern selection, pattern instantiation and pattern integration. The designer can browse the pattern hierarchy and retrieve contextual information for each of the patterns in order to *select* an appropriate pattern. The *instantiation* of a selected pattern is afterwards supported by an "Instantiation Wizard". It helps to determine the structure of the pattern instance and to assign values to variables that occur within the pattern. The *integration* of the resulting pattern instance into a target model is finally supported by an "Integration Wizard". The tools summarized in the pattern plug-in work closely together with Eclipse plug-ins that support the model-based approach.

In order to validate the functioning of the pattern tools a case study has been conducted. The user interface for a "Maintenance Support System" application shall be developed. The supposed system shall assist the technicians of greater enterprises or organizations in managing the maintenance jobs that arise. In the following the development of a user interface for the desired application using the pattern-driven model-based approach will be briefly outlined. The entire case study is discussed in more detail in [7].

5.1 Task Modeling

The task modeling is started with creating an initial task model as outlined in Fig. 8. It shows that the user has to authenticate himself before he can access the main functionality. After having accessed the main functionality he can concurrently perform the "Manage Service Schedule", "Find Documentation" and "Assemble Maintenance Jobs" tasks.

Fig. 8. Initial task model

For the further refinement of the initial task model task patterns are employed. Exemplarily the application of the "Login" [15] task pattern for refining the "Authenticate" task is shown. The "Login Pattern" is applicable when the user needs to identify himself in order to access secured data or perform authorized operations. The "Login Pattern", as outlined in Fig. 9 (a), employs the "Multi Value Input Form Pattern" [11, 15] as a sub-pattern.

The "Multi Value Input Form Pattern" can be used when the user has to provide a set of related values. In the context of the "Login Pattern" it is employed to specify, which coordinates have to be provided to authenticate the user. Fig. 9 (b) shows the pattern instance that has been achieved while instantiating the "Login" and its sub-pattern for the "Maintenance Support System" application. In the next step this pattern instance is integrated into the initial task model while replacing the "Authenticate" task. In a similar way the other task may be refined by applying appropriate task patterns. This shall not be discussed here any further.

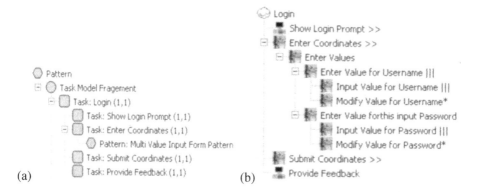

Fig. 9. "Login Pattern" (a) and instance (b)

5.2 Dialog Modeling

A dialog pattern that can be employed in the creation of the application's dialog model is the "Clear Entry Point Pattern" [17]. It suggests a navigational structure where, starting from an entry view, transitions to all main sub-views are provided. The user thus can easily overlook the provided content and navigate to the desired sub-view. Fig. 10 (a) shows the UsiPXML structure of the "Clear Entry Point Pattern".

In the creation of the dialog model for the "Maintenance Support System" application the "Clear Entry Point Pattern" is employed to design a "Main View" from where the user can navigate to a "Manage Schedule View", "Find Documentation View" and "Assemble Maintenance Jobs View". The resulting instance is shown in Fig. 10 (b).

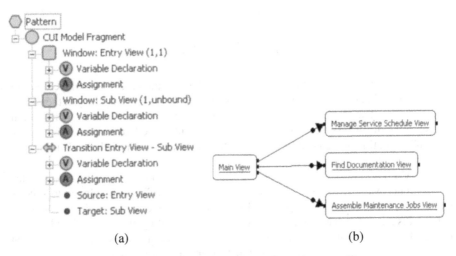

(a)   (b)

Fig. 10. "Clear Entry Point Pattern" (a) and instance (b)

5.3 Layout and Presentation Modeling

Presentation and layout patterns are employed to refine the abstract user interface model as described in 4.1. In order to keep the example simple it will be focused on refining the "Assemble Maintenance Jobs" window, which was automatically derived from the corresponding view.

Within the "Assemble Maintenance Jobs" window the technician can select single jobs, retrieve detailed information or send this information to the PDA. Therefore the window is split in two panes. One pane contains a list of maintenance jobs and the second provides interaction elements needed to perform the actions described above. To split the window in different panes the "Split Pane" layout pattern is employed. The structure of the pattern is outlined in Fig. 11 (a). The first variable declaration assignment pair allows determining the orientation of the single panes. The second pair allows setting the size of each single pane. The instance may contain an arbitrary number of such panes. Fig. 11 (b) shows two possible instances of the pattern. The

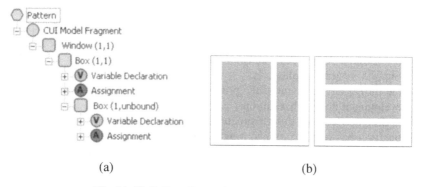

(a)   (b)

Fig. 11. "Split Pane Pattern" (a) and instances (b)

instance that has been instantiated to split the content of the "Assemble Maintenance Jobs" window is similar to the instance on the left-hand side of Fig. 11 (b).

The "Table" presentation pattern is employed to fill the left pane provided by the "Split Pane Pattern" instance. It may be used when multiple records of similar structure have to be listed in a user interface. In the context of the maintenance support system it is applied to display the maintenance jobs information.

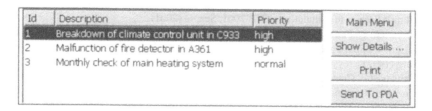

Fig. 12. Content of the "Assemble Maintenance Jobs Window"

In order to fill the right pane provided by the "Split Pane Pattern" instance the "Button Group Pattern" is instantiated. The pattern provides a group of buttons that may be employed to access related functionality. During instantiation of the pattern the number, orientation and labeling of the buttons can be determined. Fig. 12 shows the resulting content of the "Assemble Maintenance Jobs Window".

6 Summary and Outlook

In this paper a framework has been suggested that integrates model-based and pattern-driven development of user interfaces into one approach. The framework is sufficiently abstract in order to be applicable for different underlying model-based approaches. The implementation of the framework in order to derive a concrete pattern-driven model-based approach for user interface development was shown exemplarily. In this context the UsiPXML pattern notation has been suggested that allows describing patterns in a generic but machine-readable way and thus enables tool support for the pattern application process. Furthermore the "User Interface Modeling Pattern Language" was introduced that contains the patterns, which can be applied to models. Finally the capability of the derived pattern-driven model-based approach was demonstrated with a case study of developing the user interface of a "Maintenance Support System" application.

For the further development of the proposed pattern-driven model-based user interface development approach additional patterns have to be specified in order to provide the designer for each design situation with a sufficient set of available patterns. Additionally it has to be examined how the application of patterns on one modeling level influences the application of patterns on other model levels. For instance the application of the "Multi Value Input Form Pattern" at the task level tends to employ the "Form Pattern" on the presentation level. Prospective patterns could integrate both pattern solutions. Eventually a way to identify already applied patterns in models in the context of reengineering has to be examined.

References

1. Alexander, C.: The Timeless Way of Building. Oxford University Press, New York (1979)
2. Alexander, C., Ishikawa, S., Silverstein, M., Jacobson, M., Fiksdahl-King, I., Angel, S.: A Pattern Language. Oxford University Press, New York (1977)
3. Borchers, J., Thomas, J.: Patterns: What's In It For HCI. In: Proceedings of Conference on Human Factors in Computing (CHI) 2001, Seattle (2001)
4. Breedvelt, I., Paternó, F., Severiins, C.: Reusable Structures in Task Models. In: Proceedings of Design, Specification, Verification of Interactive Systems 1997, Springer, Heidelberg (1997)
5. Calvary, G., Coutaz, J., Thevenin, D., Limbourg, Q., Bouillon, L., Vanderdonckt, J.: A Unifying Reference Framework for Multi-Target User Interfaces. Interacting with Computers 15(3), 289–308 (2003)
6. da Silva, P.: User Interface Declarative Models and Development Environments: A Survey. In: Palanque, P., Paternó, F. (eds.) DSV-IS 2000. LNCS, vol. 1946, pp. 207–226. Springer, Heidelberg (2001)
7. Eclipse 2007. Eclipse - An open development platform. Internet Resource. Accessed at (January 2007), http://www.eclipse.org
8. Fincher, S.: CHI 2003 Workshop Report - Perspectives on HCI Patterns: Concepts and Tools (introducing PLML). Interfaces 56, 26–28 (2003)
9. Limbourg, Q., Vanderdonckt, J., Michotte, B., Laurent, B., Murielle, F., Trevisan, D.: USIXML: A User Interface Description Language for Context-Sensitive User Interfaces. In: Proceedings of ACM AVI 2004 Workshop Developing User Interfaces with XML: Advances on User Interface Description Languages, Gallipoli (2004)
10. Norman, D.A., Draper, S.W.e.: User Centered System Design: New perspectives on Human-Computer Interaction. Lawrence Erlbaum Associates, Hillsdale, New Jersey (1986)
11. Paternó, F.: Model-based design and evaluation of interactive applications. Springer, Berlin (2000)
12. Paternó, F., Santoro, C.: One Model, Many Interfaces. In: Proceedings of: CADUI 2002, Valenciennes, France (2002)
13. Puerta, A., Eisenstei, J.: Towards a General Computational Framework for Model-Based Interface Development Systems. In: Proceedings of IUI 1999: International Conference on Intelligent User Interfaces, Los Angeles (1999)

14. Radeke, F.: Pattern-driven Model-based User-Interface Development, Diploma Thesis in Department of Computer Science, University of Rostock, Rostock (2007)
15. Sinnig, D.: The Complicity of Patterns and Model-based UI Development, Master's Thesis in Department of Computer Science, Concordia University, Montreal, Canada (2004)
16. TeresaXML 2007: XML languages of Teresa. Internet Resource. Accessed at (January 2007), Available from: http://giove.cnuce.cnr.it/teresa/teresa_xml.html
17. Tidwell, J.: Designing Interfaces - Patterns for Effective Interaction Design. O'Reilly, Beijing (2005)
18. UsiXML 2006: User Interface Extensible Markup Language. Internet Resource (accessed at December 2006) Available from: http://www.usixml.org
19. van Duyne, D., Landay, J., Hong, J.: The Design of Sites - Patterns, Principles and Processes for Crafting a Customer-centered Web Experience. Addison Wesley, Boston, USA (2005)
20. Welie, M.: Patterns in Interaction Design. Internet Resource (accessed at January 2007), Available from: http://www.welie.com/
21. Welie, M., Trætteberg, H.: Interaction Patterns in User Interfaces. In: Proceedings of Pattern Languages of Programs (PLoP 2000), Monticello, Illinois, USA (2000)
22. Wolff, A., Forbrig, P., Dittmar, A., Reichart, D.: Linking GUI Elements to Tasks - Supporting an Evolutionary Design Process. In: Proceedings of TAMODIA 2005, Gdansk, Poland (2005)
23. XIML 2006. XIML: A Universal Language for User Interfaces. Internet Resource (accessed at October 2006), Available from: http://www.ximl.org

Towards Activity Representations for Describing Task Dynamics

Anke Dittmar and Peter Forbrig

Rostock University, 18055 Rostock, Germany
ad@informatik.uni-rostock.de, pforbrig@informatik.uni-rostock.de

Abstract. Activity representations are proposed as an extension to traditional task models. Basically, an activity representation describes fragments of knowledge about several tasks and how to interleave or merge them. Knowledge about single tasks is spread over several representations at different levels of abstraction. Lower-level models are more ephemeral and help people to organise their day-to-day activities. On the one hand, their creation is supported by more stable representations reflecting goals, activity rhythms, domain knowledge etc. On the other hand, situated action is necessary to create such (task) knowledge.

We show that higher-order activity representations provide a better explanation of some task-related aspects than monolithic single task models. For example, they support re-/on-the-fly planning and contribute to dispel the belief in complete and consistent task descriptions. The paper focuses on task redefinition, task grouping and polymotivated actions, activity spaces, goal elaboration, and the interplay between habits and learning. Some conclusions for interaction design are given.

Keywords: dynamically planned on-the-fly activities, collaborative and multiple tasks, cognitive task models, task modelling, activity representations.

1 Introduction

Task analysis and task modelling are well-known techniques in HCI. They are mainly used for designing and evaluating user interfaces. Basically, a task is considered as an activity undertaken by one or more agents to achieve a certain change of state in a given domain. It is assumed that "task knowledge is represented in a person's memory... which is assumed to be activated during task execution" [20]. It is furthermore assumed that the underlying mental activity of work can be elaborated, analysed, and represented as cognitive task models. The comparison in [24] reveals that most existing task analysis approaches like HTA (Hierarchical Task Analysis, [2]), GOMS (Goals, Operators, Methods, Selection rules, [6]), TKS (Task Knowledge Structures, [20]), and CCT (Concur Task Trees, [27]) characterise tasks in terms of goals, actions, operations, task domain objects, roles etc. Although there are differences in the use of basic concepts and the level of detail task structures are decomposed hierarchically and temporal dependencies between sub-tasks are described.

M. Winckler, H. Johnson, and P. Palanque (Eds.): TAMODIA 2007, LNCS 4849, pp. 198–212, 2007.

Though task analysis approaches claim to support a task-oriented and user-centred interaction design they are often criticized for explaining actual working practices insufficiently. Traditional approaches have concentrated on single users and single tasks. They fail to model dynamically changing situations, task interruption [25] as well as multiple and collaborative tasks [36]. The position papers of the workshop on the temporal aspects of tasks [36] also show that existing approaches do not allow a more fine-grained consideration of temporal aspects (e.g. activity rhythms) and of triggers which direct the task process (see also [15]). In [31], task models are seen as idealised and normative. They are criticised as "treating tasks as discrete, isolated chunks of behaviour as if they were representations of how the work is actually done". In other words, task models might reflect what Dourish calls a "narrowly cognitive perspective". It is more or less assumed that the mind is "the seat of consciousness and rational decision making, with an abstract model of the world that can be operated upon" and that the objective, external world is "a largely stable collection of objects and events to be observed and manipulated according to the internal mental states of the individual" [16]. In contrast, approaches like ethnography (e.g. [1]) try to explain human behaviour as shaped by the interaction with the actual situation rather than by abstract mental models or plans. As a consequence they propose to support work with resources rather than automating 'work flows' on the basis of formal models of work routines.

However, a dichotomy between planned and situated actions is rejected by Bardram and others. Plans are seen as cognitive or material artifacts "which support the anticipatory reflection of future goals for actions, based on experience about recurrent structures in life" [3]. Bardram's understanding is based on activity theory which considers consciousness "as the product of an individual's interactions with *people* and *artifacts* in the context of everyday practical activity" and provides a better explanation of dynamic aspects of human activity [22]. However, an advantage of cognitive task models is their elaborated notion of task. Payne suggests in [30] that cognitive task models might (still) help to understand the balance between planned and responsive behaviour that characterises any complex activity which is collaborative in its nature.

In this paper, we explore the limits of task representations and how they might be better dealt with. *Activity representations* are suggested as an extension to traditional task models in order to achieve a richer task understanding. Activity representations are models at different levels of abstraction. The formation of models at a higher-level is rather driven by goals, values, and beliefs. These models help to trigger certain internal or mental actions in order to produce or manipulate other mental representations. In the case of planning activities this can result in more situated models. Reflection activities might result in new goals or in discarding goals. Models at a more concrete level help to trigger certain external or physical actions in an actual situation. Their development is rather resource-driven (time, location, collaborators, available artifacts etc.). Activity representations reflect our idea that people do not hold monolithic task models for each single task. Instead, a task is represented by a set of models at different levels of abstraction. However, one activity representation reflects not only one single task but a 'state of merging' of multiple tasks at a certain level of detail. Humans never develop 'complete plans' containing all possible alternatives of how to achieve a certain goal but elaborate them to a great deal on demand. Plans are seen as means that people use to (try to) direct their behaviour. However, human actions imply constant refining of plans as well as re- and on-the-fly planning activities. We believe that this is supported by maintaining of and operating on activity representations with different grades of stability. In this paper, a description of models is assumed, which is grounded in existing approaches. We still focus on goal-oriented or intentional behaviour which is controlled by feedback. However, by proposing activity representations as an open system we emphasise the interplay between mental and physical actions to enable humans to adapt to unforeseen changes of the environment (to be in harmony). We focus on the following aspects of multiple and collaborative tasks: task redefinition (Sect. 2.2), task grouping and polymotivated actions (Sect. 2.3), activity spaces (Sect. 2.4), and goal elaboration and abstraction (Sect. 2.5). We further explore the interplay between externalised and internalised task descriptions. We discuss the higher-order property of activity representations and the interplay between habits and learning (Sect. 3). Finally, we show how an enriched task understanding can influence the understanding of interaction design (Sect. 4).

2   Activity Representations: Basic Ideas and Related Work

In this section, we use an example scenario to introduce our approach and to relate it to other work in this area. The task domain is a software engineering (SE) course at a university. Collaborators are the professor who gives the lecture, the assistants who give tutorials and supervise the work of project groups, and the students who attend the lecture, the tutorials, and who work on projects.

2.1   "Traditional" Task Models

Fig. 1 shows two CTT-like task models describing the tasks of giving a tutorial and of supervising a project. Equations in the boxes specify temporal relations between sibling sub-tasks. It is said that an assistant has to meet the professor. Afterwards, he has to prepare and give the tutorial and so on. For reasons of brevity, a task domain description is omitted in most of the examples (for more details see e.g. [13]). But in a meeting, the assistant gets information about the last lecture and proposals for exercises and homework (sub-task T1). In sub-task P3 he deals with source code, user documentation etc.

Wild says in [36] "that tasks are about writing papers, developing courses or collaborating to run something like a conference. Not a key press or mouse movement. Overall there is something in the work patterns around us that we can point to and say, that's a task, sub task, project etc." This might be in line with Dowell and Long who distinguish between work systems and application

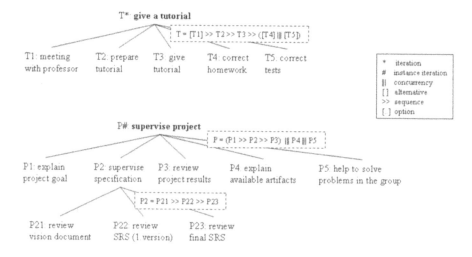

Fig. 1. CTT-like task models for an assistant

domains (see Fig. 2a). They consider tasks as "means by which the work system changes the application domain. Goals are desired future states of the application domain that the work system should achieve by the tasks it carries out" (in [11]).

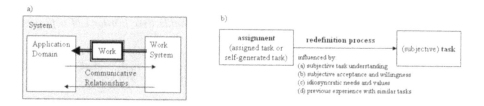

Fig. 2. a) General model of work (in [11]), b) Task redefinition according to [19]

In this sense, task models like those in Fig. 1 are external representations of normative task knowledge. This is not a problem as such. Human behaviour is determined by division of labour, existing artifacts and norms. It becomes problematic if norms are drawn from dogmatic visions of life. One can use a task description to convey domain knowledge. However, one can also use them to gain control over others by imposing one's orders on them (e.g. [33]). But this is a general problem with any artifact. Humans are always responsible for what they create and how they use it. In our example, we could imagine that an assistant whom we call Paul got the task descriptions in Fig. 1 from his professor. Now he has to internalise these assignments to be able to accomplish his work. This is an active process called task redefinition.

2.2   Task Redefinition in Collaborative Tasks

The idea of *task redefinition* is introduced in [19]. Hackman says that a task may be assigned to a person or a group by an external agent or it may be self-generated. But either way, it has to be interpreted. Fig. 2b) illustrates this process and the distinction between external task descriptions and their subjective internalisation. The concept of self-generated tasks suggests that humans not only redefine external task representations but also act upon internal ones. This supports our idea of higher-order representations as introduced in [12].

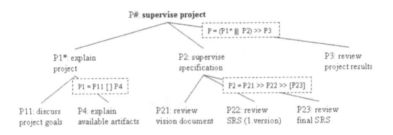

Fig. 3. Pauls redefinition of assignment *supervise project* of Fig. 1

In the example, let us assume that following points refer to Paul's understanding and attidudes concerning the task of supervising projects.

- *If the first version of the SRS (Software Requirements Specification) of a project group is okay they don't need to supply a revised version.*
- *Project goals cannot fully be explained at the beginning. They have to be developed over time. Their elaboration depends strongly on available tools and skills.*
- *Project groups have to solve their problems by themselves.*

The model in Fig. 3 describes Paul's redefinition as a snapshot. It does not explain why and how Paul developed his task understanding. Furthermore, we can also discuss whether it is an expressive description of above mentioned points but it is one. And it illustrates the following points.

- Temporal relations are modified. For example, sub-task P23 is optional, P1 is iterative and is performed at any time before P3.
- Sub-tasks are discarded (e.g. P5).
- Sub-tasks are refined (e.g. P1).
- The task hierarchy is re-structured. For example, P4 is now a sub-task of P1.

Now imagine we ask Paul why he doesn't help students who have trouble to work together. He answers: "I know the professor expects me to do that but it makes me sick to mediate between people." Take note that although Paul acts upon his redefined model the underlying assignment is still there and influences his acting. He might feel a tension between it and his redefinition caused by the image of himself and the belief to have to fulfill his professor's assignments.

Tasks have to be accomplished by actions of individuals who, typically, work in several domains and groups. Their collaboration is, among other things,

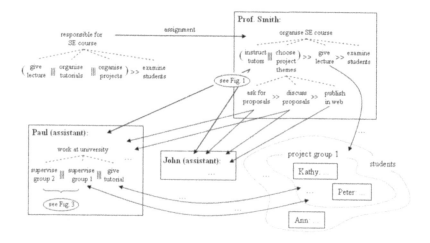

Fig. 4. An illustration of some collaborative aspects in the example

characterised by task delegation as illustrated in Fig. 4. Models in boxes are actual redefinitions. Only some of the assignments (indicated by arrows) are specified.

2.3   Task Grouping and Polymotivated Actions in Multiple Tasks

Most task analysis approaches have concentrated on single tasks and related goals. However, "a person can also perform an action on the basis of unrelated goals" [11]. In [3] actions are seen "as usually *polymotivated*; two or more activities can temporarily merge, motivating the same action". In addition, goals can be prioritized differently in different contexts and, often, a combination of goals is needed to trigger some behaviour [11]. McFarlane remarks that it "is unusual for a person to be engaged in only a single activity from start to finish to the exclusion of all other tasks" [25]. England and Du propose in [36] to consider the management of interleaved tasks and of interruptions as necessary in multitasking as tasks themselves. This further supports our assumption of higher-order representations related to tasks.

Like most approaches, we assume that humans develop representations for single tasks. Such goal-oriented plans focus on an object of interest. Associated ordered actions are intended to manipulate this object in a desired way. However, we further suggest that humans develop additional models with a shift of focus from objects of interest to objects describing the actual environment such as people, locations, actual time constraints, available artifacts etc. This is in line with task grouping by deadline, by location, by participants, or by role as proposed in [35]. However, Wild et al. do not consider grouping strategies as tasks themselves and they do not elaborate possible consequences on task structures.

Though we assume activity representations structured like existing task models we coined a new term for several reasons. First, task models are often associated with properties like completeness or consistency (see e.g. [8]). Even if complete and consistent descriptions were possible it would not necessarily be useful. For example, the absence of 'gaps' in plans and a too detailed description of action sequences can interfere with the ability of a person or a group to cope with interruptions. Second, an activity representation at one level of abstraction describes *fragments of knowledge* about several tasks and how to interleave or merge them in a hopefully effective, efficient, and sustainable way. In consequence, the description of a single task is spread over several representations. We suggest that activity representations at a lower level of abstraction are more ephemeral. They help people to organise their day-to-day activities. Take note, they are still explicit representations that people hold when planning and executing tasks. Certainly low-level activities can have patterns that are very persistent like habits or proceduralised action sequences. The creation of lower-level models is supported by more stable, higher-level representations reflecting the "recognition of *recurrent structures* in the world" [3] (goals, values, beliefs, but also activity rhythms as mentioned in [36], domain knowledge in general).

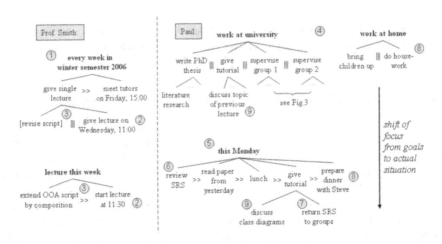

Fig. 5. Prof. Smith and Paul: Activity representations at different levels of abstraction

In Fig. 5, example representations are sketched to show the general idea. In addition, the heighlighted points should be considered in more detail.

1. Activity representations can reflect temporal patterns or rhythms. Here, a weekly rhythm over a certain period of time concerning a lecture is described.
2. More concrete representations can contain 'inconsistencies' to more stable ones reflecting actual conditions. In the example, the lecture starts this week at 11:30, though normally it starts 11:00.
3. Most ad hoc plans and close to moment plans are basically structured linear plans. The "this Monday" plan in Fig. 5 is another example. One reviewer suggested that humans are pretty bad at modal thinking. So, much beyond short 'extensions' from the main plan (in their head) will be hard.

4. This is an example of multiple tasks.

5. An example for interleaving multiple tasks and also for grouping by time. Parts of tasks are woven into the daily rhythm (indicated by lunch and dinner).

6. An example for grouping by deadline (that is for prioritising and sequencing) though not described explicitly. If possible, Paul uses the morning hours for doing research. But this Monday, he has to return the SRS to the project groups. Because the review for the second group is not finished yet he wants to complete it this morning. Another aspect might also be interesting. More concrete plans often contain "abbreviations", which are clear in their context. In the example, it is clear to Paul that he reviews the first version of the SRS of the second group (though several versions are described explicitly in Fig. 3).

7. A grouping by location and people: Paul intends to use the tutorial to return the SRSs to both project groups.

8. Paul plans to prepare a dinner together with his son. A polymotivated action: while doing some housework he 'teaches' his son how to do that.

9. Sub-task *deal with class diagrams* is an 'instance' of *deal with topic from last lecture*.

Let us assume that Paul realised this Monday morning while reviewing the SRS that the students didn't really understand statecharts. Although he has prepared a tutorial about class diagrams (point 9 in Fig. 5) he decides to discuss statecharts again. He puts away the paper from yesterday and starts to read in a paper about statecharts & task modelling instead. Maybe he can also find some examples for his tutorial this afternoon... This is a typical example for interrupting the actual activity and for re-planning as a response to unexpected changes in the environment. Here, Paul's assumptions about the skills of his students have changed. (Take note, that the reading of the 'statecharts paper' is also polymotivated: for literature research and for preparing the tutorial).

Re-planning and on-the-fly planning is supported by the concept of activity representations rather than by single task models. First, it is easier to give up actual plans, and then to use more stable representations to create new or modify actual plans. Second, it allows 'inconsistencies' between representations (e.g., point 2 in Fig. 5). This supports an acting, which is rather guided but not fully controlled by norms. Third, it is easier to add (or remove) an activity representation. It can reflect a more fine-grained interleaving of multiple tasks (elaboration) as necessary e.g. to cope with interruptions. It can also abstract from non-relevant aspects with respect to a single task.

One of the reviewers of a previous attempt to explain our task modelling ideas criticised that this approach is "based on perspective that the interaction is completely structured and structurable". Of course, we do not believe that human acting is completely structured and structurable (a description of their actions is probably somehow). However, people plan and reflect their behaviour (anticipatory reflection). They think in and by action. Mental representations are a resource for but also a result of human acting. By doing actions again and again habits are developed and mental models are 'fine tuned'.

2.4   Task Environments as Activity Spaces

The authors of [15] criticise that task models consider objects of a task environment always as "second class". However, task activities are not only centered around the creation of artifacts they can only be accomplished by interacting with them. The role of triggers in timing and pacing a task is, for example, well explored in [15]. In the literature, it is often distinguished between *physical artifacts* which are important in sequencing, triggering and closure of tasks, and *cognitive artifacts* as physical objects made by humans for the purpose of aiding, enhancing, or improving cognition (Spillers in [36]). Kirsh coined the term *activity space* to emphasise that not the environment itself is important but how people deliberately alter it according to their goals (in [32]).

The question when things in their environment really become artifacts for humans still remains open. In our example, it is probably not only the fact that this paper about statecharts & task modelling is lying on his desk that lets Paul re-plan this Monday in the way described in Sect. 2.3. There must be 'internal counterparts' to such external clues that let them work as artifacts. Paul must have internalised the assignment of reading research papers. The concept of *functional organs* in activity theory might give an explanation of this phenomenon. They are "created by individuals through the combination of both internal and external resources. Functional organs combine natural human capabilities with artifacts to allow the individual to attain goals that could not be attained otherwise" [22]. Human eyes in combination with eyeglasses are an example.

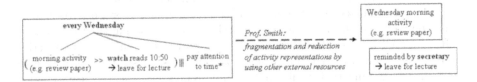

Fig. 6. Prof. Smith reduces the cost of his mental operations by task delegation

In Fig. 6, we emphasise the dynamics inherent in functional organs. On the left side, an activity representation of Prof. Smith is shown, which might or might not work in combination with a watch ('watch reads 10:50' is the intended trigger for action 'leave for lecture'). The representations on the right side are the result of delegating the task of paying attention to time to the secretary. Generally, such *fragmentations* of plans into more situated plans by using artifacts are necessary to successfully accomplish tasks. Take note that fragmentation processes often involve task delegation and require the creation of new artifacts including task representations (assignments) to support a shared task continuity. Take also note that a person is skilled if their (fragmented) plans reflect a deep understanding of the environment, in particular of own and other people's habits. Prof. Smith might know that he usually 'forgets the time' and that his secretary as reminder is a more safe trigger to interrupt his morning work and to leave for the lecture. He might also know that his assistants are more engaged in supervising projects if they can propose some themes (see Fig. 4). Or that most students (in his culture) only do their homework if they get some points. But of course everything changes, and so do human habits. Maybe, lists with points and marks for homework will not be necessary some day ;) To summarise, there is a constant learning and a constant adaptation of mental models to actual situations.

2.5   Goal Elaboration and Abstraction

The concept of goals is one of the most vague in task analysis. Goals are mostly defined as desired states of task domain objects. That is they seem to be given once and for all. However, we suggest to consider goals as active processes constituting a context for actions which are focused on a common object of interest (OoI in Fig. 7). However, humans do not only need to elaborate actions describing their understanding of *how* to achieve goals. They also need to shape their understanding of *what* they want, why they want it and how they can establish such desired states. Again, they do it by acting. Often, a goals' object of interest constitute the range of future goals. If the goal is achieved, the object of interest is shaped more clearly. This is illustrated in Fig. 7. While 'teach students *modern* SE' is a rather abstract goal, it becomes more concrete with 'teach students object-oriented ideas'.

By considering goal elaboration as occurring over several steps and involving several activity representations we can explain the fluidity between motives and goals as they become consciously perceived and then forgotten (see e.g. [22]). In the example, Prof. Smith might have forgotten why he explains object-oriented ideas because goal 'teach students *modern* SE' works as a motive after its elaboration. However, what happens when new promising concepts emerge? Maybe he can remember why he deals with OOA/D techniques and will restructure his lecture. Or maybe he will change his goals...

The processes of elaboration and abstraction of goals and action plans become more intertwined by frequent repetition of actions (including deliberate alterations

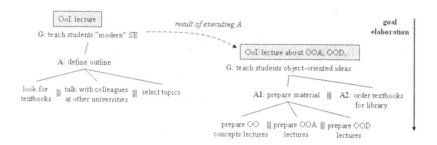

Fig. 7. Prof. Smith: Two elaboration steps to shape the goal understanding

to the environment, see Sect. 2.4). On the one hand, this may result in polymotivated actions, and then in routines or habits as recurrent, often unconscious patterns of behaviour which are honed in such a way that "the most minimal of actions [often shared between two or more people] has a wealth of significance and well understood mutual accountabilities" [34]. On the other hand, it may result in more stable goals and values as well as in deeper domain knowledge.

3   Activity Representations and the Dynamic of Action

In the last section, the idea of activity representations was introduced and integrated in existing work. It was argued that humans develop activity representations by collaborating and, generally, by acting in the world. Deep knowledge ('fine tuning' of models) can only be acquired by doing actions over and over again, by reflecting processes and results, by empathising with collaborators and so on. It was also argued that tasks belonging to certain work systems and application domains (Fig. 2) are typically represented by several activity representations at different levels of abstraction. Higher-level representations rather reflect single tasks. They are more stable and developed over a longer period of time. Lower-level, more ephemeral representations rather describe an interleaving of fragments of multiple tasks which seems to fit a concrete situation.

To summarize, activity representations are seen as mental configurations humans develop in the hope that they 'evoke' adequate mental or physical responses when confronted with certain cues in a situation. This argumentation is in line with Rorty who says that knowledge "[is not] a matter of getting reality right, but rather... a matter of acquiring habits of action for coping with reality" (cited in [22]). It is also in line with Hacker who speaks of "Wissensinseln" (islands of knowledge) [18]. Activity representations are such islands. They are constantly evolving, neither 'complete' nor 'consistent'. On the contrary, inconsistencies between different representations are seen as important in order to cope with actual situations. Humans constantly make exceptions to rules.

In [26], Naur points out that "[d]escribing people in terms of 'knowledge' or 'mental models' has the consequence that the dynamic of thought, the way thoughts develop, tend to be ignored. In particular the all-pervading importance of *habit* on all human activity is lost from sight." This view on thoughts as results of habitual thought processes might be better supported by activity representations. Though they are still mental models the related higher-order approach does not emphasise task structures as such (as in traditional task analysis) but also their development and use. Generally, a combination of an activity representation and a cue triggers a certain habit. However, activity representations do not only trigger physical behaviour in combination with physical cues. They can also serve as cues themselves for other representations to trigger a certain mental behaviour. They may guide elaboration steps like sequencing, refinement, merging to create polymotivated actions, interleaving to support task grouping in multiple tasks, or creation of assignments to support task delegation. They may guide abstraction activities like selection, generalisation (e.g. of temporal

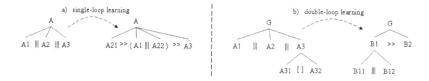

Fig. 8. Abstract examples for manipulating activity representations in learning

constraints), extension (e.g. by new alternatives), or modification. While elaboration is important to initiate (intended) behaviour, abstraction is important to develop behavioural alternatives to be better prepared for possible future worlds.

In [5], single-loop learning, double-loop learning, and learning to learn are proposed as three fundamental levels of human learning. Perhaps, these categories and Fig. 8 help to clarify our understanding of mental activities.

- *Single-loop learning* serves and refines habits. It involves modifications of activity representations by mental activities like sequencing, refinement, or merging.
- *Double-loop learning* changes habits because they no longer serve a certain goal. It involves mental activities like extension or new action grouping to explore alternatives for achieving the same goals.
- *Learning to learn* as the third level changes how we change habits. This learning might include how humans develop goals (Sect. 2.5), how they create polymotivated actions (Sect. 2.3), and how they create artifacts (Sect. 2.4)[1].

4   Some Conclusions for Interaction Design

A 'classical' application area of task modelling is model-based design (MBD). Mostly, task models are used to derive user interface specifications (e.g. [28]). As a consequence of single task models, most approaches concentrate on single applications. Even extensions like [29] or [9] dealing with multiple devices or context-aware systems use basically CTT models. Further limitations of existing MBD approaches like the 'myth' of generalised task models or the weak conceptual understanding of differences between task and dialog models are discussed in [14]. There are two application areas that we want to explore more deeply in the future.

Activity-Based Computing. In [21], interactive systems focussing on higher-level user activities are discussed. Such systems support the *activity-based computing* paradigm which was proposed in [4] to complement the prevalent application- and document-centred computing paradigm. Activity-based computing aims to support the management of parallel activities and interruptions. Hence, the basic computational unit is no longer a file or an application but the activity of

---

[1] The interplay between learning and habits is well described in [5]:"Paradoxically, habit is both the product of learning and the escape from learning. We learn in order not to learn. Habit is efficient; learning is messy and wasteful. Learning that doesn't produce habit is a waste of time. Habit that does not resist learning is failing in its function of continuity and efficiency."

a user. We think that activity representations can help to elaborate and refine this approach. In particular, the idea of goal elaboration and abstraction and of polymotivated actions could serve as foundation for developing tools to help users organize their activities.

Activity Representations as Sketches. Carroll points out in [8] that traditional task analysis not only assumes correct and complete structural task descriptions but also that they are always desireable. It is, furthermore, assumed that the objective is optimal performance. However, all representations including task models foster certain ways of thinking and acting. They also reflect power relations and are used to convince others of one's own views (see e.g. [23]). Hence, Carroll is certainly right when saying that detailed normative descriptions of existing work can support the interests of managers because other aspects of work are typically not in the focus. In addition, our own experiences confirm that task models as used in MBD do not really support reflection and a 'provocative' discussion but a more specification-driven design process. There are questions concerning action sequences and answers like "In order to achieve goal G the user has to perform A1 first, and then A2 or A3." But one rarely hears questions concerning underlying motives, assumptions, or interests. Carroll points out that traditional task analysis might hinder the stakeholders to bring in their own values into the design process. In [14], we propose not only to accept the fragmentary character of task models but to use such fragments and representations created in complementary analysis and design approaches in a creative way. Activity representations can further enrich our task understanding. We argue that humans do not hold mental models of single tasks but that tasks are reflected in several, more or less stable activity representations at different levels of abstraction, which are neither complete nor necessarily consistent to each other and which are under constant development by shaping the environment. With such an understanding, activity representations may also be used as sketches in the design process[2] and may contribute to a more creative use of task modelling in interactive design.

Acknowledgements. The first author would like to thank Jörgen Dahlke for discussing task grouping and the participants of RE course 23054 2006 for inspiring the example. We are particularly grateful to an anonymous reviewer for their feedback.

References

1. Anderson, B.: Work, Ethnography and System Design. In: Kent, A., Williams, J.G. (eds.) The Encyclopedia of Microcomputers, vol. 20, Marcel Dekker (1997)
2. Annett, J., Duncan, K.D.: Task analysis and training design. Occupational Psychology 41 (1967)

---

[2] In [17], Fallman points out that sketching is not only useful for communicating with other designers and stakeholders. It is "not simply an externalization of ideas already in the designer's mind, but on the contrary a way of shaping new ideas." Sketching supports the idea of design as a dialogue, a reflective conversation.

3. Bardram, J.: Plans as situated actions: An activity theory approach to workflow systems. In: Proc. of the 5th ECSCW (1997)
4. Bardram, J.: Support for Activity-Based Computing in a Personal Computing Operating System. In: Proc. of CHI 2006 (2006)
5. Brand, S.: How Buildings Learn: What happens after they're built, Penguin (1994)
6. Card, S.K., Moran, T.P., Newell, A.: The Psychology of Human-Computer Interaction. Lawrence Erlbaum Associates, Hillsdale, New Jersey (1983)
7. Carroll, J. (ed.): HCI Models, Theories, and Frameworks - Toward a Multidisciplinary Science. Morgan Kaufmann Publishers, San Francisco (2003)
8. Carroll, J.M.: Scenarios and Task Analysis as Design Methods. In: Workshop on Exploring Design as a Research Activity, CHI 2007, http://www.chi2007.org/attend/workshops.php
9. Clerckx, T., Vandervelpen, C., Luyten, K., Coninx, K.: A Prototype-Driven Process for Context-Aware User Interfaces. In: Coninx, K., Luyten, K., Schneider, K.A. (eds.) TAMODIA 2006. LNCS, vol. 4385, Springer, Heidelberg (2007)
10. Diaper, D., Stanton, N.A. (eds.): The handbook of task analysis for human-computer interaction. Lawrence Erlbaum Associates, Mahwah (2004)
11. Diaper, D.: Understanding Task Analysis for Human-Computer Interaction. In: [10]
12. Dittmar, A., Forbrig, P.: Higher-Order Task Models. In: Jorge, J.A., Jardim Nunes, N., Falcão e Cunha, J. (eds.) DSV-IS 2003. LNCS, vol. 2844, Springer, Heidelberg (2003)
13. Dittmar, A., Forbrig, P., Heftberger, S., Stary, C.: Tool Support for Task Modelling - A Constructive Exploration. In: Bastide, R., Palanque, P., Roth, J. (eds.) Engineering Human Computer Interaction and Interactive Systems. LNCS, vol. 3425, Springer, Heidelberg (2005)
14. Dittmar, A., Gellendin, A., Forbrig, P.: Requirements Elicitation and Elaboration in Task-Based Design Needs More than Task Modelling: A Case Study. In: Coninx, K., Luyten, K., Schneider, K.A. (eds.) TAMODIA 2006. LNCS, vol. 4385, Springer, Heidelberg (2007)
15. Dix, A., Ramduny-Ellis, D., Wilkinson, J.: Trigger Analysis: Understanding Broken Tasks. In: [10]
16. Dourish, P.: Where the Action Is. MIT Press, Cambridge (2001)
17. Fallman, D.: Design-oriented Human-Computer Interaction. In: Proc. of CHI (2003)
18. Hacker, W.: Allgemeine Arbeitspsychologie, Bern: Huber (1986)
19. Hackman, J.R.: Toward understanding the role of tasks in behavioral research. Acta Psychologica 31 (1969)
20. Johnson, P.: Human computer interaction: Psychology, task analysis, and software engineering. McGraw-Hill Book Company, New York (1992)
21. Kaptelinin, V.: UMEA: Translating Interaction Histories into Project Contexts. In: Proc. of CHI 2003 (2003)
22. Kaptelinin, V., Nardi, B.A.: Acting with technology: Activity theory and interaction design. MIT Press, Cambridge (2006)
23. Latour, B.: Drawing Things Together. In: Lynch, M., Woolgar, S. (eds.) Representation in Scientific Practice, MIT Press, Cambridge (1990)
24. Limbourg, Q., Vanderdonckt, J.: Comparing Task Models for User Interface Design. In: [10]
25. McFarlane, D.: Interruption of People in Human Computer Interaction: A General Unifying Definition of Human Interruption and Taxonomy. Technical Report NRL/FR/5510-97-9870, US Naval Research Lab, Washington, DC (1997)

26. Naur, P.: CHI and human thinking. In: Proceedings of NordiCHI 2000 (2000)
27. Paterno, F., Mancini, C., Meniconi, S.: ConcurTaskTrees: A notation for specifying task models. In: INTERACT 1997 (1997)
28. Paterno, F.: Model-Based Design and Evaluation of Interactive Applcations. Springer, Heidelberg (2000)
29. Paterno, F., Santoro, C.: One Model, Many Interfaces. In: Proc. of the Fourth International Conference on Computer-Aided Design of User Interfaces, Kluwer Academic Publishers, Dordrecht (2002)
30. Payne, S.J.: Users' Mental Models: The Very Ideas. In: [7]
31. Randall, D., Hughes, J., Shapiro, D.: Steps towards a partnership: Ethnography and system design. In: Jirotka, M., Gougen, J. (eds.) Requirements Engineering: Social and Technical Issues, Academic Press, San Diego, Ca (1994)
32. Spillers, F.: Task Analysis Through Cognitive Analysis. In: [10]
33. Suchman, L.: Do categories have politics? The language/action perspective reconsidered. Computer-Supported Cooperative Work (CSCW) 2 (1994)
34. Tolmie, P., Pycock, J., Diggins, T., MacLean, A., Karsenty, A.: Unremarkable computing. CHI 2002
35. Wild, P.J., Johnson, P., Johnson, H.: Understanding Task Grouping Strategies. In: Proc. of HCI 2003: Designing for Society, pp. 3–20. Springer, Heidelberg (2003)
36. Workshop on the Temporal Aspects of Tasks. HCI 2003, http://www.cs.bath.ac.uk/~hci/TICKS/temporalaspects.html

A Framework for Light-Weight Composition and Management of Ad-Hoc Business Processes

Todor Stoitsev, Stefan Scheidl, and Michael Spahn

SAP AG, SAP Research CEC Darmstadt, Bleichstr. 8,
64283 Darmstadt, Germany
{todor.stoitsev, stefan.scheidl, michael.spahn}@sap.com

Abstract. The increasing importance of unstructured, knowledge-intensive processes in enterprises is largely recognized. Conventional workflow solutions do not provide adequate support for the management and optimization of such processes. Therefore the need for more flexible approaches arises. This paper presents a conceptual framework for unobtrusive support of unstructured, knowledge-intensive business processes. The framework enables modeling, exchange and reuse of light-weight, user-defined task structures. In addition to the person-to-person exchange of best-practices, it further enables 'outsourcing' of dynamic task structures and resources in personal workspaces and organizational units where these are managed according to local domain knowledge and made available for reuse in shared repositories. The delegation of tasks enables the generation of enterprise process chains, spreading beyond the boundaries of a user's personal workspace. The structures emerging from user-defined tasks, task delegations and on-demand acquisition of dynamic, externally managed tasks and resources adequately represent agile, human-centric business processes. Thereby the framework facilitates effective knowledge management and fosters proactive tailoring of underspecified business processes through end users in a light-weight, unobtrusive manner. The presented concepts are supported within the Collaborative Task Manager (CTM), a novel prototype for email-integrated task management.

Keywords: Task management, ad-hoc workflow, computer supported cooperative work, knowledge management, human computer interaction, agile business processes.

1 Introduction

The amount of unstructured, knowledge intensive processes in organizations is increasing. Conventional workflows do not provide sufficient flexibility to reflect the nature of such processes and to provide adequate support for their optimization [3], [18]. Therefore the need arises to elaborate more flexible approaches, able to represent and manage underspecified, highly dynamic user tasks. This is accompanied with the increasing demand to facilitate effective Knowledge Management (KM) in organizations, which could increase the efficiency of business users, engaged in non-routine tasks and which could enable them to better shape their everyday work through application of shared best-practices [12], [20].

M. Winckler, H. Johnson, and P. Palanque (Eds.): TAMODIA 2007, LNCS 4849, pp. 213–226, 2007.
© Springer-Verlag Berlin Heidelberg 2007

The presented paper focuses on intrinsic flexibility and KM aspects, concerning ad-hoc, knowledge-intensive processes. The described framework aims to deliver a generic conceptual base for a software system, which is able to support light-weight, unobtrusive composition and management of underspecified processes in different enterprises from various business domains. The concepts are supported within the Collaborative Task Manager (CTM), a novel prototype which enables proactive tailoring of ad-hoc business processes through end users.

The paper is organized as follows. Section 2 provides an overview of related work in the area of software support for agile business processes. Section 3 describes the basic solution approach behind the framework. Sections 4, 5, 6 and 7 describe the basic framework entities and the associated functionalities. In section 8 conclusions and future research directions are given.

2 Related Work

Software support for unstructured, knowledge-intensive processes has been in the focus of extended research in the last years. The reuse of emerging task hierarchies within a global enterprise infrastructure is often described as one of the major possibilities to support such processes. Riss et al. [17] discuss the challenges for the next generation business process management by suggesting the generation, recognition and application of reusable '*task patterns*' and '*process patterns*' as an alternative to static workflows. The task pattern technique is further considered by Grebner et al. [9], who describe basic directions for the utilization of task-based approaches to support users engaged in intensive, unstructured knowledge work. Within the presented paper a task is generally referred to as a self contained unit of work, which can be refined through an arbitrary number of sub tasks and aims to achieve a certain business goal. Thereby the focus is set on high-level tasks, representing single steps in ad-hoc business processes, and the notion of task patterns presented in the above studies is used. In the literature '*task patterns*' are discussed also regarding reusable structures for task models in the field of interactive systems design [8], [14], [15]. However, such observations focus on low-level interactive activities like e.g. searching, browsing or providing generic system input, and are beyond the scope of the presented paper.

A comprehensive approach, addressing the gap between completely ad-hoc processes, which are in the focus of Computer Supported Cooperative Work (CSCW), and rigid, predefined business processes, which are well supported through conventional workflow solutions, is provided by Bernstein [7]. This approach provides "*contextual basis for situated improvisation*" by enabling delivery of "*process models, process fragments, and past cases*" for tasks and providing shared, distributed-accessible, hierarchical to-do lists, where different process participants can access and enrich task resources and information. An extended state of the art study in the area of flexible workflows and task management and a further approach for integrating ad-hoc and routine work is presented by Jorgensen [13]. He reveals major issues concerning business process flexibility and how it can be facilitated through interactive processes models.

Approaches focusing on completely ad-hoc processes are also known. A case-based approach for enabling business process flexibility, where *"the knowledge worker in charge of a particular case actively decides on how the goal of that case is reached"* is provided by van der Aalst et al. [2]. A further solution of supporting completely ad-hoc processes is presented by Holz et al. [11]. It provides document-based and task-based proactive information delivery, which enables evaluation of similar cases and instance-based task reuse. Thereby it is suggested that frequently recurring tasks, relevant for an enterprise, are modeled more formally using process types if the enterprise is willing to make an investment into process modeling. Advanced techniques for building personal knowledge spaces and wiki-based collaborative document spaces are also integrated in the latter solution.

The major difference of the framework presented in this paper to the above mentioned approaches is that it focuses on the unobtrusive support for ad-hoc business processes. It enables users to act as close as possible to their usual work practices without confronting them with new working environments or upfront process definition tools. Thereby a software system supporting this framework should be able to provide added value by unfolding emergent process structures behind the scenes in an unobtrusive, implicit manner. The motivation behind this approach is that enterprise processes are generally executed by multiple actors, who have different level of technical skills and different attitude towards maintaining process data. At the same time analysis, reuse and adaptation of knowledge-intensive processes is often desired in a way similar to conventional workflows. The framework therefore enables end users without advanced technical expertise or process understanding to manage tasks in personal to-do lists, which are integrated in a common software working environment. As such the framework uses email, which plays a central role for the exchange of tasks and task-related information in organizations [6], [10], [19]. Behind the scenes, personal task hierarchies of multiple process participants are reconciled to overall enterprise processes in central repositories, where context information and resources are provided on-demand to advanced users and process analysts. Thereby no formal process modeling, explicit definition of rules or user roles is required.

3 Solution Approach

This study is based on intra-organizational knowledge sources accumulating customer requirements as well as on dedicated site visits and interviews at companies representing predominantly small and medium enterprises from various industries (automotive, software, textile), and builds on the state-of the art research in the areas of task management, flexible workflows and CSCW.

Unstructured, knowledge-intensive processes are generally executed through *'situated actions'* [4]. Within this paper we assume that tasks can be executed, cancelled or completed without meeting any pre- or post-conditions. Thereby the process flow is determined solely through the sequence of the task execution, which is decided by the end users according to their current work situation. This raises various flexibility and KM issues, related to the overall process structure and context information. Van der Aalst et al. [1] discuss business process flexibility by stating that: *"Workflows are case-based, i.e., every piece of work is executed for a specific case: an order, an in-*

surance claim, a tax declaration, etc. The objective of a workflow management system is to handle these cases (by executing tasks) as efficiently and effectively as possible." The authors further describe, that a task is executed through specific resources which might be e.g. a tool or an employee and suggest three basic dimensions of a workflow – *"case", "process"* and *"resource"* dimension. Human activities thereby comprise cases, which are handled with corresponding tasks using the appropriate resources. Unpredictability of human activities hence implies deviations in case handling and dynamic adaptations of tasks and resources. The framework presented herewith focuses on intrinsic flexibility and KM aspects considering these basic issues.

As a concrete solution approach, the framework suggests tracking of user actions, which are executed on personal workspace level in a common user working environment, and unobtrusive (implicit) replication of task data on central enterprise repositories. This process is further referred to as *externalization*. Externalized task structures and the accompanying data of different users are integrated in the repositories to overall enterprise processes. Furthermore, logically unconnected tasks from different processes and users can be associated in the central repositories based on different criteria to provide advanced KM. Concretely, the CTM prototype uses Microsoft Outlook as an office integration environment by exploiting the fact that tasks and email are provided in the same office application. Web services are used to track user actions, executed in the CTM Outlook Add-In, on a CTM back-end application. It is based on the Java Platform Enterprise Edition and deployed on a JBoss server. The tracked data is persisted in a MySQL Database (DB), which provides the repository functionality for the basic framework entities. The CTM prototype is not explicitly discussed in this paper as the focus here is set on generic flexibility and KM concepts for supporting dynamic resource and task adaptations and for handling case deviations in unstructured, knowledge-intensive processes. These concepts are implemented through the basic framework entities, described in the following sections. Certain CTM functionalities are mentioned as clarifications to the discussed concepts.

4   Artifacts

An artifact refers to a file, e.g. a text document, a spreadsheet or an executable file, which is associated (attached) to a task. Artifacts generally represent resources (cf. Sec. 3), which are used or generated during task execution. The presented framework provides three basic types of task artifacts. These are described in Fig. 1. The depicted entities are designed equally in all figures in the paper.

4.1   Externally-Managed Artifact (EMA)

An EMA is an artifact, the content of which is managed by a user or a user group outside of the scope of a user task. An EMA can be e.g. a document, which is being elaborated by multiple users as part of a concrete process. Collaborative authoring techniques are known in the literature (cf. [11]) and are not discussed in this paper. Another type of EMA could be a document, which is provided as a template from a company department and is used in various processes throughout an enterprise. Such could be e.g. an employment contract template provided by a Human Resources (HR) department. The user or user group managing the artifact content, e.g. HR employee(s), is referred to as *external artifact manager(s)* (see Fig.1). The latter can edit the artifact content in their workspaces and submit a consolidated EMA version to a globally accessible artifact repository. It can be e.g. file system or DB based and should be able to maintain artifact history. References to an EMA can be added in user tasks. Within the presented framework an EMA reference in a task stores a unique identifier and a version number of the EMA. Changes to an EMA increase its version on the repository and trigger notifications to all referring tasks. An owner of such a task can thereby switch the reference to the updated version or preserve the current reference.

In the CTM prototype, the artifact repository is realized through an artifact table in the MySQL DB, containing paths to actual artifact files on the server file system. Users are able to view different artifacts and artifact versions and submit an EMA through an Artifact Repository Explorer component which is part of the CTM Outlook Add-In. This component enables also setting of references to an EMA in a user-defined task and EMA reference handling upon notifications.

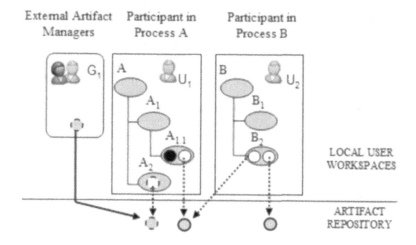

Fig. 1. User-defined *tasks (gray ellipses with a black outline)* reside with their sub task hierarchies in the *workspaces (top layer denoted on the right)* of users (U_1 and U_2). A group of *external artifact managers (G_1)* edit an *Externally-Managed Artifact (gray circle with a black, dotted outline)*, in the following referred to as *EMA*, in their local *workspaces* and submit it to a central *artifact repository (bottom layer denoted on the right)*. An *EMA reference (a white circle with a black, dotted outline)* can be set in a user-defined *task (A_2)*. An artifact, emerging as a common *user* attachment to a *task* is either explicitly protected as *Locally-Managed, Non-Externalized Artifact (black circle in $A_{1.1}$)* or implicitly replicated to a central *artifact repository* as *Externalized Artifact (a gray circle with a black outline)*, in the following referred to as *EA*. The *task* preserves a *local EA representation (white circles with a black outline in $A_{1.1}$ and B_2)*, comprising a local copy of the attachment and a reference to the *EA* in the repository.

4.2 Externalized Artifact (EA)

An Externalized Artifact (EA) is contained in the local task definition of a user and is additionally replicated on a central enterprise repository (see Fig.1). The software infrastructure supporting the presented framework should do this in an unobtrusive manner, without additional user effort by tracking user actions on tasks in the local workspace and replicating task attachments to a central artifact repository. Tasks are themselves replicated to a task repository (cf. Sec. 6). During artifact externalization a single artifact copy, identified in a unique manner, should be created in the artifact repository for artifacts with the same name and the same content. As a consequence a one-to-many relation can be created from a single EA to multiple tasks, which are using it. In Fig. 1 task $A_{1.1}$ and task B_2 use the same EA in two independent processes. Furthermore, queries with different criteria can be executed in the central repositories to retrieve similar artifacts and the referencing tasks. Externalization hence enables unobtrusive detection of recurring tasks and recognition of global optimization possibilities based on usage of similar resources in dispersed, independent processes.

The second consequence from task externalization is that in case of extraction of a Task Pattern (TP) (cf. Sec. 7) from a user-defined task containing an artifact, a resulting TP document can contain only a short reference to the EA in the repository. This prevents from any explicit encoding of binary content, which could result in increased TP document size, and further provides a system dependent representation of artifacts within reusable task structures. Consequently, artifacts will not be provided outside of the system context and the appropriate artifact access policy. When a TP is reapplied for reuse artifact content can be retrieved upon request from the central artifact repository based on the unique identifier and according to the repository access policy.

4.3 Locally Managed, Non-externalized Artifacts

The access policy for artifacts in the artifact repository might not suffice the privacy needs of end users in different business domains and occupation areas. The framework hence provides possibility to store artifacts in a local, non-externalized manner (see task $A_{1.1}$ in Fig.1). Tasks using such kind of representation however do not benefit from the unobtrusive KM and data protection enabled through EA and extended flexibility provided through EMA.

5   Human Actors

The framework uses a light-weight representation of human actors, associated to tasks. In related literature human actors are considered resources for tasks (cf. [1], [13]). The representation of human actors within the framework has mainly the purpose to store knowledge about the person, who has expertise related to a given task. This knowledge is important for unstructured, ad-hoc work. Ribak et al. state for example that *"employee's key asset is their network of contacts and those people they can approach for advice or help"* [16].

To avoid the need of introducing domain-specific roles, which may harm the generic character of the framework, two basic roles for human actors are currently provided – *owner* and *recipient*. The *owner* of a task is a person, who's to-do list contains the task, i.e. who is or was responsible for the task execution. If a task owner decides to delegate a task to another person, recipient information is additionally stored in the owner task. The *recipient* is a person, who has received a task through a delegation from other system user. Thereby we generally suggest that delegations are handled by creating a copy of the requester task at recipient site. The recipient task, generated through this, holds the same context information and artifacts as the requester task and can be further adapted by the recipient. A requester task hence contains two human actor representations: owner – referring to the requester; recipient – describing the recipient of the task delegation. The recipient task holds a single human actor – an owner referring to the recipient. On the lowest level human actors in both roles are represented through an email address and a human-readable name. In the current CTM implementation such representations are stored within the user-defined tasks, where an owner is always set when a task is inserted in a personal to-do list and a recipient is set when a delegation is triggered. User data is also replicated in a central user repository during task tracking. In CTM the repository is a user DB table.

6 Tasks

Within the presented framework enterprise processes emerge as dynamic, user-defined task hierarchies, where tasks are represented through system objects, described through certain attributes like e.g. subject, description, owner, due date, status etc. Artifacts and human actors are associated to tasks as described in the above sections. The framework enables association of tasks according to the collaborative flow in human-centric processes and association of tasks of logically independent processes for KM purposes.

6.1 Task Delegation Graph (TDG)

In a collaborative process tasks can be delegated between different process participants. An overall enterprise process can be therefore observed as a Task Delegation

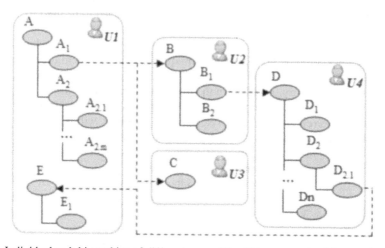

Fig. 2. Individual task hierarchies of different *users* (U_1 - U_4) are contained in *users' personal workspaces* (*dotted-line areas*). In collaborative processes tasks are distributed between *users* through *delegations* (*dotted line arrows*), which enable interconnection of personal task hierarchies to an overall Task Delegation Graph (TDG).

Graph (TDG), which emerges through the evolution of user-defined task hierarchies beyond personal workspaces (see Fig. 2). A TDG has the purpose to integrate individual task hierarchies to a complete, end-to-end process structure. Within the presented framework a TDG is generated through tracking of user actions, which are executed on tasks in the personal user workspace, on a shared enterprise repository. The individual task hierarchies of multiple users are integrated through tracking of email exchange for task delegation. As a consequence task hierarchies, defined by end users in the personal workspace, are replicated with all context, artifact and human actor information and connected to overall enterprise processes in a central task repository. The structure of these processes is determined by the adaptations of the individual task hierarchies (to-do lists) within the local workspace of each process participant, and by the collaborative flow for task delegation. No further process modeling or definition of rules is required.

6.2   Externally-Managed Task (EMT)

While a TDG connects task hierarchies with respect to process flow, tasks may be related in process independent manner for KM purposes. Such relations are enabled through EMT (see Fig.3). Similarly to an EMA, an EMT is managed according to specific expertise by one or more users, in the following referred to as *external task manager(s)*. While an EMA enables reuse of resources, an EMT addresses the reuse of others' process knowledge for the elaboration of the individual tasks. Two major types of EMT can be distinguished. To the first type belong tasks, which are part of concrete processes. Referencing such a task in a task from another process, results in cross-process references which allow peering of related (parallel) tasks. An EMT of the second type represents a recommendation of best-practice. Such a task can be created e.g. by a Quality Assurance (QA) department in a software company to describe routines, which need to be executed by developers prior to code submissions. This task will represent certain organizational policy and will need to be used by all developers for the organization of their personal tasks.

An EMT is generally provided in a shared task repository. The tracking of tasks used for the generation of TDG has the consequence that all system users are implicitly external task managers to their own tasks. Therefore the task tracking repository is also an EMT repository. An EMT in the repository can contain further references to other EMT, which provides recurring task flexibility. An EMT can contain artifacts of all presented types (cf. Sec. 4). However, only EMA and EA will be externally accessible. An important note is that the artifacts, contained in tasks in the local workspace of users U_1 and U_2 in Fig. 3 also have references to artifacts in the artifacts repository (see Fig. 2), which are not shown for simplicity reasons.

When an EMT reference task is declared in a local user workspace, it may be synchronized with the repository to copy locally the complete EMT structure and context information. In Fig. 3 no sub tasks are given for A_2 and $B_{2.1}$ for simplicity. When an EMT is updated or removed, notifications are sent to all owners of reference tasks. An owner can accordingly update a changed reference task, remove it or release the EMT reference and preserve the currently used local copy. The latter operation corresponds to an apply pattern operation (cf. Sec. 7) and will generate the corresponding ancestor/descendant references.

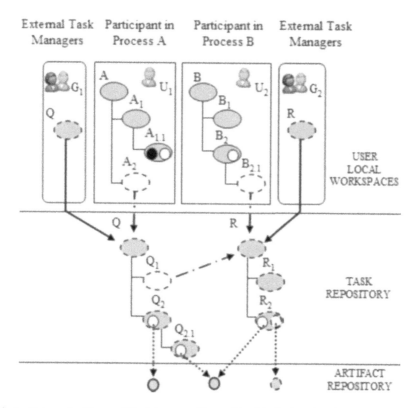

Fig. 3. An *Externally-Managed Task (a gray ellipse with a black, dotted outline – see Q and R)*, in the following referred to as *EMT*, is defined and edited in the workspace(s) of one or more *external task managers (G₁ on the left and G₂ on the right)* and submitted for reuse in a *central task repository (middle layer denoted on the right)*. Users, including *external task managers*, may reuse an *EMT* through an *EMT reference task (a white ellipse with a black, dotted outline – see A₂ and B₂.₁)*. A reference chain ends with an *EMT* without further references.

7   Task Patterns (TP)

In the presented framework cases are handled through user-defined tasks, which hold attributes with context information, associated artifacts and human actors. Tasks can be extracted with their complete context, artifact and actor information to a Task Pattern (TP). A TP provides explicit best-practice recommendation for handling of recurring cases as introduced in [17] and clearly refers to the case dimension (cf. Sec. 3).

7.1   Overall Functionality

An overview of the TP functionality is given in Fig. 4. A TP can have different granularity. Such can be extracted from an arbitrary item in a task hierarchy, contained in a local user workspace. Furthermore, a TP can be extracted from the task tracking repository and represent a complete TDG. The central repository with tracked user tasks

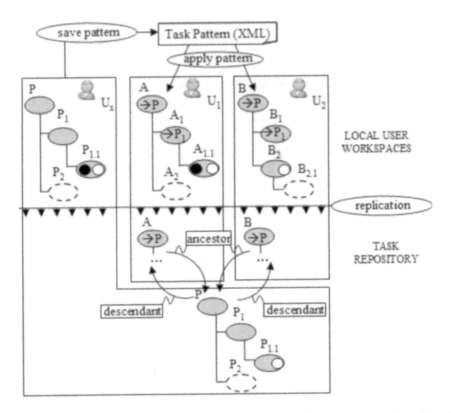

Fig. 4. A task *P* with a sub task hierarchy is created by user U_x and exported as a *Task Pattern* (TP) in XML format. The task *P* from the TP is applied in the workspaces of users U_1 and U_2 respectively on tasks *A* and *B*. Thereby the complete content and structure of *P* is applied to tasks *A* and *B* and replicated in the central task, artifact and user repositories. The replicated structures and the artifact and user repositories are not explicitly represented for simplicity reasons. The initial TP structure under task *B* has been changed by user U_2. To enable tracing and evaluation of such deviations *ancestor/descendant* relationships are set when the TP is applied.

is hence implicitly also a TP (case) repository. The current CTM implementation enables search, extraction and editing of TP in a Task Pattern Explorer/Editor component. A TP can be exported in XML format. The TP format represents the generic task model for the framework (cf. Sec. 7.2). All entities contained in the TP structure preserve their type – EMA and EA are represented through unique system identifiers and may not contain any binary content. An EMT can be included only through a unique task identifier without explicit task structure and context information.

Changes in reusable best-practice might often be required to adapt it to the current work situation. In Fig. 4 task A has preserved the same structure as P. However, user U_2 has changed the initial TP structure of task B. The framework provides advanced KM techniques, which help to evaluate deviating solutions for similar cases. This is accomplished through *ancestor/descendant* relationships, which emerge when a TP is applied. Ancestor references are set iteratively for all tasks in a task hierarchy. In Fig. 4 an ancestor reference to task P ($\rightarrow$P) is set in tasks A and B, an ancestor reference to P_1 is set in A_1 and B_1 etc. Therewith it is guaranteed that ancestor information will be available also for fine-grained extraction of a TP from a sub task. Furthermore, repeated extraction and application of TP can generate complex ancestor hierarchies. If user U_2 declares a TP from task B, a task resulting from the application of the latter TP will have an ancestor reference to B, which will have ancestor reference to P etc.

While an ancestor relationship enables tracing of the case history backwards, a descendant relationship enables tracing of task adaptations in different application cases for tasks, which have been extracted as a TP. In Fig. 4 users U_1 and U_2 have reused the TP originating from task P. The framework suggests storing of descendant relations to tasks A and B in the repository instance of task P. Hence a one-to-many relation from a single ancestor task to multiple descendant tasks is maintained. In the current CTM implementation this is done in the task DB repository, whereby descendants can be retrieved upon request through the CTM front-end.

7.2 TP Format – Task Model Implementation and Structural Overview

The format for TP documents is described in a XML schema definition as shown in Fig. 5. This schema provides also an implementation and an overview of the task model used in the framework.

Representation of artifacts is defined through the 'artifact' complex type. An 'artifactName' element holds a human-readable artifact name e.g. the name of a file attached to a task. A choice element enables representation of different artifact types. The 'content' element enables local, non-externalized artifact representation through inclusion of artifact content as base64 encoded binary data. The 'artifactId' element provides a system-generated identification of an EA. A group element containing an 'artifactRefId' element and a 'version' element provides EMA representation.

The 'user' complex type defines the representation of human actors. It is currently highly simplified and might be extended in the future to contain e.g. role information. This type contains a 'personId', which holds unique user identification like e.g. an email address, and a 'personName', which specifies a human-readable user name.

Task delegations are defined through the 'delegation' complex type, which contains a 'recipient' and a 'task' element. The latter provides the possibility to store a complete TDG through iteratively storing recipient tasks which have emerged from task delegation.

Finally, the 'task' complex type describes the structure of a task, where the 'taskName' is the only required user-defined field in a task. We suggest that under-specified task definition is important as users may often record tasks in highly simplified manner e.g. by only writing down several keywords [5]. Tasks are generally identified through a system-generated id, which is stored in the 'taskId' element. An EMT is additionally referred through a 'taskRefId'. The 'description' element provides a human-readable description of a task whereas a suggested task execution time is given in a 'time' element. An 'owner' element represents a task owner (cf. Sec. 5) whereas recipients are contained in a 'delegation' element, complying with the delegation complex type. The ancestor and descendant references (cf. Sec. 7.1) are represented accordingly with an 'ancestor' and 'descendant' elements. A task can have multiple artifacts, which are described in 'artifact' elements. Sub tasks within a task definition are represented through nested 'task' elements.

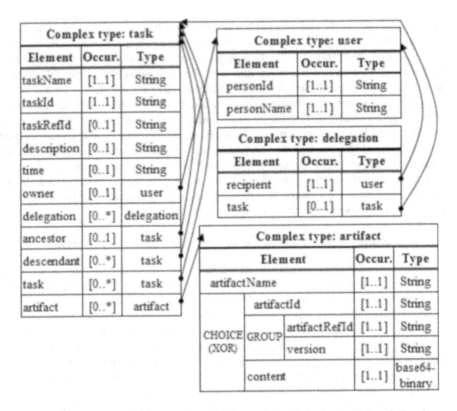

Complex type: task

Element	Occur.	Type
taskName	[1..1]	String
taskId	[1..1]	String
taskRefId	[0..1]	String
description	[0..1]	String
time	[0..1]	String
owner	[0..1]	user
delegation	[0..*]	delegation
ancestor	[0..1]	task
descendant	[0..*]	task
task	[0..*]	task
artifact	[0..*]	artifact

Complex type: user

Element	Occur.	Type
personId	[1..1]	String
personName	[1..1]	String

Complex type: delegation

Element	Occur.	Type
recipient	[1..1]	user
task	[0..1]	task

Complex type: artifact

Element			Occur.	Type
artifactName			[1..1]	String
CHOICE (XOR)	GROUP	artifactId	[1..1]	String
		artifactRefId	[1..1]	String
		version	[1..1]	String
	content		[1..1]	base64-binary

Fig. 5. The XML schema definition provides the format for Task Pattern (TP) description documents and an implementation and an overview of the task model used in the framework. Each complex type is described with its *elements*, which are given with their name, followed by *occurrence ([1..1] required; [0..1] optional; [0..*] zero or more; [1..*] one or more)* and a *content type*. While simple types like *String* and *base64binry* provide implementation specifics, the presented *complex types* depict basic model building blocks, which refer to the framework entities described in the previous sections – *artifact, user* (human actor) and *task*.

8 Conclusions and Future Work

The offered framework provides adequate support for agile business processes and appropriately reflects the dynamic nature of unstructured, knowledge-intensive work. The solution focuses on email-based, human-to-human cooperation, where the collaborative flow determines the enterprise process flow. The users are the main drivers of enterprise processes. As such, they are enabled to shape and share best-practices in a light-weight, ad-hoc manner. The value of reusing previous experience on a personal level is expanded by integrating personal task hierarchies in overall enterprise process structures, exceeding users' personal workspaces. Such processes are generated dynamically an unobtrusively on a central enterprise repository through tracking of user activities on personal tasks and collaborative message exchange related to these tasks. As a result the solution facilitates effective KM through rich process mining capabilities, and enables end users to proactively tailor underspecified business processes.

The next steps in our research will include the evaluation of the framework through the CTM prototype by conducting user tests with real end users from partner companies. The prototype and the generic framework may then be extended according to the received user feedback and its detailed analysis.

Acknowledgments. The work, this paper is based on, was supported financially by the German "Federal Ministry of Education and Research" (BMBF, project EUDISMES, number 01 IS E03 C). We thank all participants in the customer studies for their time and cooperation.

References

1. Aalst, W.M.P.v.d., Basten, T., Verbeek, H.M.W., Verkoulen, P.A.C., Verhoeve, M.: Adaptive Workflow: On the interplay between flexibility and support. In: Proceedings of the first International Conference on Enterprise Information Systems, Setubal, Portugal, pp. 353–360 (1999)
2. Aalst, W.M.P.v.d., Weske, M., Grünbauer, D.: Case Handling: A New Paradigm for Business Process Support. Data and Knowledge Engineering 53(2), 129–162 (2005)
3. Abbott, K.R., Sarin, S.K.: Experiences with Workflow Management: Issues for the Next Generation. In: Proceedings of the ACM Conference on Computer Supported Cooperative Work, pp. 113–120. ACM Press, New York (1994)
4. Bardram, J.E.: Plans as Situated Action: An Activity Theory Approach to Workflow Systems. In: Proceedings of the European Conference on Computer Supported Cooperative Work, Lancaster, UK, p. 1732 (1997)
5. Bellotti, V., Dalal, B., Good, N., Flynn, P., Bobrow, D.G., Ducheneaut, N.: What a To-Do: Studies of Task Management towards the Design of a Personal Task List Manager. In: Proceedings of the SIGCHI Conference on Human Factors in Computing Systems, pp. 735–742. ACM Press, New York (2004)
6. Bellotti, V., Ducheneaut, N., Howard, M., Smith, I.: Taking Email to Task: The Design and Evaluation of a Task Management Centered Email Tool. In: Proceedings of the SIGCHI Conference on Human Factors in Computing Systems, Ft. Lauderdale, Florida, USA, pp. 345–352. ACM Press, New York (2003)
7. Bernstein, A.: How Can Cooperative Work Tools Support Dynamic Group Processes? Bridging the Specificity Frontier. In: Proceedings of the ACM Conference on Computer Supported Cooperative Work, pp. 279–288. ACM Press, New York (2000)
8. Gaffar, A., Sinnig, D., Seffah, A., Forbig, P.: Modeling patterns for task models. In: Proceedings of the 3rd annual Conference on Task Models and Diagrams, pp. 99–104. ACM Press, New York (2004)
9. Grebner, O., Ong, E., Riss, U., Brunzel, M., Bernardi, A., Roth-Berghofer, T.: Task Management Model (Last visited September 01, 2007), http://nepomuk.semanticdesktop.org/xwiki/bin/view/Main1/D3-1
10. Gruen, D., Rohall, S.L., Minassian, S., Kerr, B., Moody, P., Stachel, B., Wattenberg, M., Wilcox, E.: Lessons from the ReMail Prototypes. In: Proceedings of the ACM Conference on Computer Supported Cooperative Work, pp. 152–161. ACM Press, New York (2004)

11. Holz, H., Rostanin, O., Dengel, A., Suzuki, T., Maeda, K., Kanasaki, K.: Task-based process know-how reuse and proactive information delivery in TaskNavigator. In: Proceedings of the 15th ACM International Conference on Information and Knowledge Management, pp. 522–531. ACM Press, New York (2006)
12. Jennex, M.E., Olfman, L., Addo, T.B.A.: The Need for an Organizational Knowledge Management Strategy. In: HICSS 2003. Proceedings of the 36th annual Hawaii International Conference on System Sciences, p. 117.1. IEEE Computer Society, Washington (2003)
13. Jorgensen, H.D.: Interactive Process Models. Ph.D. Thesis, Norwegian University of Science and Technology, Trondheim, Norway (2004)
14. Palanque, P., Basnyat, S.: Task Patterns for Taking into Account in an Efficient and Systematic Way Both Standard and Abnormal User Behaviour. In: IFIP 13.5 Working Conference on Human Error, Safety and Systems Development, Toulouse, France, pp. 109–130 (2004)
15. Paternó, F.: Model-Based Design and Evaluation of Interactive Applications. Springer, Heidelberg (2000)
16. Ribak, A., Jacovi, M., Soroka, V.: "Ask Before You Search": Peer Support and Community Building with ReachOut. In: Proceedings of the ACM Conference on Computer Supported Cooperative Work, pp. 126–135. ACM Press, New York (2002)
17. Riss, U., Rickayzen, A., Maus, H., van der Aalst, W.M.P.: Challenges for Business Process and Task Management. Journal of Universal Knowledge Management 0(2), 77–100 (2005)
18. Schwarz, S., Abecker, A., Maus, H., Sintek, M.: Anforderungen an die Workflow-Unterstützung für wissensintensive Geschäftsprozesse. In: Proceedings of 1st Conference for Professional Knowledge Management (WM 2001), Baden-Baden, Germany (2001)
19. Siu, N., Iverson, L., Tang, A.: Going with the Flow: Email Awareness and Task Management. In: Proceedings of the ACM Conference on Computer Supported Cooperative Work, pp. 441–450. ACM Press, New York (2006)
20. Wiig, K.M.: People-focused knowledge management: How effective decision making leads to corporate success. Elsevier Butterworth–Heinemann (2004)

Model-Based User Interface Design in the Context of Workflow Models

Renate Kristiansen and Hallvard Trætteberg

Department of Computer and Information Science,
Norwegian University of Science and Technology,
Sem Sælands vei 7-9, N-7491 Trondheim, Norway

Abstract. Within ERP systems, workflow models are used by business analysts to specify which business processes the system supports. The workflow model specify which actors that performs what activity in what sequence and the required resources. Within user interface (UI) design task models are used to develop task-centric user interfaces. Task-centric UIs can increase systems' usability as it focuses on the end-user. In this article we will show how task models together with other models used in the field of model-based UI design can be created within the context of already existing workflow models. We show how standard tasks can be defined as editable UI components allowing role-based composition of the UI with support from the workflow model.

Keywords: ERP, MBUID, Workflow, Task modeling.

1 Introduction

Enterprise Resource Planning (ERP) systems are off-the shelf business applications providing a tightly integrated solution to organizations' information system needs [27]. ERP benefits include best practice business processes, real-time access to information and shared practices across the entire enterprise. One important characteristic of ERP systems is the fact that they are pre-built software packages designed to meet the general needs of a business sector instead of the unique requirements of a particular organization [1]. To be able to deliver such huge software packages, ERP vendors use different business process models in their overall description of the system to describe the supported processes and organizational structures together with the structure of data and objects [13]. The reference models are founded upon what the vendor considers being the industrial best practices, that is, the most efficient way the business processes should be structured [5]. SAP uses Event Process Chain (EPC) models to document the system's functionality [12] while Microsoft uses Business Process Modeling Notation (BPMN) to describe the business domain. These are descriptive models documenting the existing software (in contrast to prescriptive models that are used as a specification of what to create) [15].

In this article we use models and information collected from a large company developing ERP systems and show how prescriptive task models can be connected to descriptive workflow models. The company currently runs a project

M. Winckler, H. Johnson, and P. Palanque (Eds.): TAMODIA 2007, LNCS 4849, pp. 227–239, 2007.

where the ERP system's functionality is modeled using workflow modeling. The intention is to use the models as documentation in implementation projects. In addition there is an interest in investigating how these models can be reused in other contexts. We want to show how they can take advantage of model-based user interface design (MBUID) to allow flexible role-centered composition of user interfaces in the context of the workflow models. Role-based access and portal solution is considered the answers to the severe usability problems identified in ERP systems [7].

A challenge with role-based systems is how to keep the number of roles on a manageable level. When new functionality is added, should this result in the creation of a new role? A single person typically fulfills several roles, and the combination of roles users have differs among companies. Flexibility in creating user interfaces (UI) for various combinations of roles is therefore important. We will explore a systematic way to define what needs to be included in the UI for one particular user based on her participation in the workflow process. The workflow model defines what tasks need to be fulfilled and their possible ordering; hence the workflow model is suitable as a 'frame' for creating task models. A task model typically focuses on modeling the work of an individual user.

A short introduction to task and workflow modeling is given in section 2, and we discuss how MBUID and workflow models by virtue of coming from different research traditions have differences in concepts, focus and pragmatics. Our work take advantage of existing modeling languages proved useful in one context, and proposes how they can be combined to add value in an industrial context. Section 3 describes relevant aspects of the ERP vendor organization, and describe our approach by showing a practical example. In section 4 we explain how to make use of pattern structures to compose role-oriented user interfaces so that the highly detailed, executable dialogue models can be wrapped into easier to work with lesser detailed components. We have discussed our approach with the user interface developers in the company and report some of their first-hand comments. Finally, in section 5 we conclude and give some notes on future work.

2   Different Modeling Traditions and Their Relation

We will give a short introduction to task modeling and explain how task models relate to other models used in MBUID. Workflow modeling is then introduced before the relationship between task modeling and workflow modeling is discussed. Based on our discussion we argue for the choice of modeling languages used in the case study.

2.1   Task Models and Model-Based User Interface Design

Task modeling is often used first in the analysis phase to understand and communicate the problem domain (resulting in a descriptive model), and later on as a prescriptive task model for the system to be designed (as e.g. the DUTCH method using GTA [33]). Examples of task modeling languages are: Méthode Analytique de Description des tâches (MAD)[26], Task Knowledge Structure (TKS) [11], GroupWare Task Analysis (GTA) [32] and ConcurTaskTrees(CTT)[19] which all support designers by hierarchically decomposing tasks, defining objects manipulated and the role responsible for performing the task.

The vast number of task modeling notations results in semantic and syntactic differences which are discussed by e.g. [14] and [35]. Based on their analysis a uniform task model is created which includes concepts like: task and goal hierarchies, operators that express temporal constraints between task, some role concept to deal with co-operative aspects, and objects with possible actions.

Task models are considered one of the viewpoints in the model-based community [20]. Viewpoints are related to both abstraction level and focus of the model. Is the level of detail high and is the focus on the task or on the UI? Models with different viewpoint are:

1. *Task model and object model* represent the highest level of abstraction and their focus is on user's goals, tasks and what objects that are manipulated (the object model is often referred to as a domain model).
2. The second layer is the *abstract user interface* describing the structure and behaviour of the user interface [29].
3. The third level involves building a *concrete user interface* specification defining the platform dependent look and feel of the interface.
4. The fourth level is the *final user interface* which is the running interface implemented on a specific software environment.

Model-based user interface design (MBUID) processes often start with a task related model that is evolved through an incremental approach to the final UI [4]. In each of the transformation phases the designer has the possibility to manually change the generated artefact, and the modification is preserved when regenerating the UI.

The concept of tasks is very similar to that of processes (in a workflow); the difference is mainly that of scope and focus. Processes typically relate directly to organizational goals, while tasks focus on the goal and actions of individual users playing a role. Hence, a task model may be seen as a refinement of a process model, in the context of a specific user role [28].

2.2 Workflow Modeling

Workflow models focus on how work is done to accomplish some organizational goals. It defines how documents, information and tasks are passed between human or other actors in the enterprise [25]. Important workflow characteristics are tasks/activities that are performed by role-playing persons using supporting tools that give access to various shared information resources [17] [2].

In the literature there is confusion about the differences on business process models and workflow models. According to [10] a business process is defined by a process definition and managed by a workflow management system. Hence the process model includes the workflow model.

Many workflow modeling languages have formal semantic built on Petri nets [25]. A Petri net is a directed graph with a mathematical formalism facilitating visual modeling on the one hand and formal analysis, verification and validation of the model on the other. An example of such a language is Yet Another Workflow Language (YAWL) [31]. Informal workflow modeling languages includes Event-Process Chain (EPC) [12], Action Port Model (APM) [2] and Business Process Modeling Notation (BPMN) [8]. BPMN is defined by the Object Management Group and offers a rich notation for workflow modeling. The notation supports decomposition of processes into sub-processes and tasks. A task is an atomic activity and cannot be decomposed further. A task can usually be performed by an end-user and/or an application [8].

2.3   The Relation Between Models

We will use a two-dimensional representation framework to discuss how different modeling notations used by different research traditions relate to each other. The representation space is shown in figure 1. The problem/requirement-solution/design dimension say something about how tight the model is connected to the final design. While problem-oriented notations describe goals and requirements to the design in abstract manners, solution-oriented notations describe aspects of the artifact we are designing and give specific details on the environment the artifact will act in. Along the problem-solution axis models have different granularity, which is the second dimension. Business processes (BP) have high granularity as they describe the activities businesses undertake to reach their business goals. Workflow models (WF) need to include more details to be executable by a workflow management system. The task model (TM) is partly overlapping the workflow model since the lowest level of workflow models usually is a task performed by one actor. A task performed by one actor is typically the highest level in a task model describing which sub-task that must be completed to reach the goal of its parent task. Dialogue models (DM) add details of the functionality and the interaction that the UI provide. Dialogue models and task models together cover the same area of the problem-solution axis as workflow models, but have lower granularity. A model of the concrete interaction (CIM) is very close to the final system, and has a low granularity specifying both visual details (e.g. layout, widget usage, etc.) and interaction (keyboard and mouse).

As we have explained, different modeling notations cover different areas of the representation space. We emphasize the following differences between workflow and task modeling:

- **Different research tradition:** Workflow models have their origin in organizational theory. Hammer stated in [9] that usability was a "second order issue" and should only be considered when all other functionality has been considered. "The important thing for automated office application were: (1) functionality; (2) functionality; (3) nothing; (4) functionality; and only then, (5) everything else" [6, page 119]. Task models come from the field of human

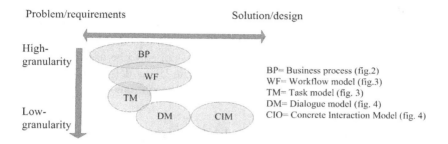

Fig. 1. A representation framework for classification of modeling languages

factors [21] and are used with the aim of increasing usability of computerized systems. This naturally leads on to the second difference:

- **Difference in focus:** In workflow models the focus is on how to reach organizational goals. In task modeling the focus is on the goals of individual users. It is important to be aware of the difference between organizational goals, the individual goals and how they are related as they might not be aligned [34].
- **Differences in concepts:** Section 2 pointed to the mixture in concept definition between task models, and the same mixture is present if we consider concepts across task models and workflow models. As [21] point out, a concept defined in a task model can be used in a workflow model with a different meaning. This gives a pragmatic problem across modeling languages.

When a combination of workflow models and task models are considered these differences must be taken into consideration. In the next section we choose which modeling languages we will use in our case study.

2.4   Selection of Modeling Languages

Our case study company use BPMN for workflow modeling, so these models are kept and used directly. Because of the considerable overlap in workflow and task modeling concepts, we have considered the possibility of extending BPMN so that it also can be used for task modeling. However, because of the difference in focus and use of concepts, we think that it is useful to have two separate notations and instead emphasize that the focus shifts from being about organizational goals to considering individual users' goals. BPMN uses swimlanes for modeling the responsibility of actors, which generally is problematic when it comes to decompositions. For these reasons we have chosen to use Taskmodl [29] which is a task modeling language with its origin both from the workflow tradition and the tradition of task modeling and analysis. It was created with the aim to narrow the gap between workflow and task modeling and it is based on the workflow modeling language APM [2]. The main APM concepts are interpreted in the context of task modeling [29] resulting in a notation supporting the traditional hierarchical sequence-oriented style typical for task modeling languages.

Taskmodl supports decompositions of BPMN tasks into user-centric task hierarchies, specify resources, actors and sequence constraints. To model the user interface we will use Diamodl [29] [30] which is an executable modeling notation for abstract user interface specification developed to be used together with Taskmodk. Central for our approach is that the UI models should be editable and result in a running UI. Diamodl satisfies this requirement.

3   Models from a Real World Company and Their Relation to MBUID

We will show how a workflow model developed at a large international ERP vendor can be used as a starting point for creating a task-oriented user interface. We call the vendor ProERP and explain the models they currently use in their developing organization before we show how a MBUID approach can be pursued in connection to this information.

To aid the software development ProERP uses a model of the business domain as a common point of reference. The model is split into two representations:

- **User and Organizational Model** has the individuals and their organizational relationship as focus. The users are described using Personas [3] [24]. A Persona is an archetype of an actual user and included in the Persona description is information stating what roles a Persona can take and what tasks he or she is responsible for. The numerous Personas are grouped into departments, and each department is illustrated by organizational charts.
- **Business Process Model** has a supply chain perspective and is decomposed into the activities involved in the business process. The processes are grouped together and placed within departmental borders, showing which department is responsible for which processes. The business process shown in figure 2 is one of seven business processes grouped under the "Operations" department.

The two model representations describe the same world, but with different perspective. The information used in this case study is based on this generic model together with documentation that was provided by two other projects. ProERP had a project that decomposed the business process model into BPMN diagrams and the uppermost diagram in figure 3 is from that project. In addition, documentation from a user interface development project lead by the UI design team is used.

When new functionality is designed, the Personas that should participate are identified and used as leading actors when developing scenarios [22] describing the functionality. Detailed information concerning the business domain and what is required for the new functionality is provided by domain experts participating on the design project. The UI design specification consists of sketches of the user interface drawn with a drawing tool and supplemented by textual description of the interaction. For usability evaluation Powerpoint slides are used.

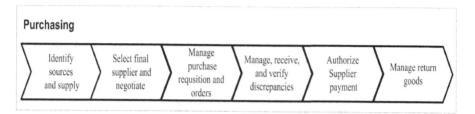

Fig. 2. Example of business process

The process steps in figure 2 are further decomposed into BPMN diagrams showing which activities that are carried out to execute the process. In topmost diagram in figure 3 one of the decompositions under "Manage purchase requisitions and orders" is shown. Sara (which is a Purchaser) first creates a purchase order (PO). The PO is then transferred to the stack of outgoing, awaiting PO's and she can choose when she wants to communicate the PO by sending it to the supplier. The supplier must send an order acknowledgment before a pre-defined time has elapsed, otherwise a rule triggers and the PO is put into the stack of PO's awaiting for order acknowledgment. A reminder should then be sent to the supplier.

Each of the boxes in the BPMN model is a task suitable for one person and can be considered the highest level in a task model hierarchy modeled in a task modeling language. The decomposition of the Create PO task is shown in the task structure in the lower part of the figure 3. The rounded rectangles are tasks, with an identifier and a name in the top compartment. The lower compartment is optional and contains the resources necessary for the task and the actor performing the task (shown in the parent task). A middle compartment can be added with a task description, but we have not used this compartment in this figure. The resources that are sent between tasks are flow resources triggering the execution of the following task (e.g. PO and Product). The circle enclosing the arrow means that the tasks need to be executed in a fixed sequence. To create a purchase order Sara has to find the products, add them to a requirement list and then generate a purchase order from the requirement list. How to accomplish a task is a question of design and requires domain knowledge and knowledge about constraints in the software. In the current user interface design process, the designers in ProERP create scenario descriptions and sketches of the user interface to describe the functionality.

The task model describe "what to do" but does not include the "how to do it" knowledge describing how users accomplish a task in the UI using interaction objects, state and data flow specification. This is information typically specified in a dialogue model. Dialogue models are suitable for representing abstract interaction tasks as selecting an element from a set of elements or pushing a button to trigger some functionality. We have developed dialogue models for each of the leaf node tasks of the Create PO tasks tree in figure 3 based on the UI designers description of how the UI should look like and behave. As it seems to be essential for the user interface designer to have complete control of the design process, we have not pursued a more formal derivation of the dialogue model from the task model as done e.g. by [16].

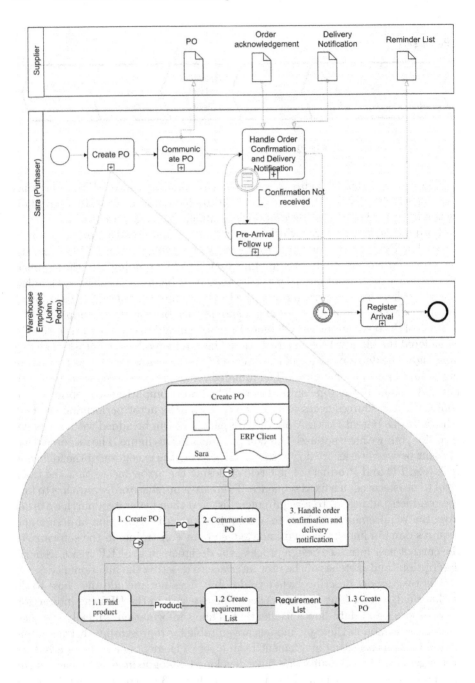

Fig. 3. Workflow model showing the process in which a PO is manually created and a task model that show the decomposition of one of the tasks

The abstract user interface model is drawn using DiaModl notation, and figure 4 shows the dialogue model for the task 1.1 Find Product. *Interactors* are drawn as rectangles with a name describing their functionality. Attached to the interactor's left side are *gates* which define user input (pointing outwards) and output to the user (pointing inwards). The free floating triangle is a computation with functionality as indicated by the description (match). The edges between elements are connections, and define flow of data. The Product object is from the domain model. To find a product the user first search for the product by typing the product number. For each digit the user types, a match function filters the product list and highlights the first product that match. Some of the attributes of the supplier and product object is displayed to the user.

The dialogue model shows an abstract model of the interaction which can be used as a specification for the concrete implementation of the UI. The interactor's input/output signature determines a set of concrete interactor objects (e.g. a set of standard widgets) that can replace the abstract user interface component. The lower model in figure 4 show how the abstract interactors are replaced with concrete ones matching their input/output signature.

4   A Role-Oriented Approach to Dialog Composition

When creating a homepage for a specific user with a different role composition than the ones in the pre-defined Persona description, the BPMN diagram can be used as a starting point for creating task models. Using task models, the necessary steps for solving the BPMN tasks identified in the workflow model can be modeled in a user-centric way. Our experience from the case study indicate that each of the BPMN tasks are candidates for being the top level of a task structure accessible directly from the employee's personal homepage.

Since the low-level tasks encapsulate a dialogue structure, a task-oriented user interface can be created by assembling the dialogue fragments for the required set of tasks. As noted by [18] modeling the user interface of an interactive system in sufficient details to be "run" soon becomes an overwhelming task - and an abstraction mechanism is required to get the "big picture" of the system. To reduce this complexity we suggest using task model components as patterns for how standard tasks can be solved. Patterns give a generic solution to a problem and should be adapted to the specific problem [19]. Composing a UI then will consist of defining which tasks are needed, plug together the dialogue fragments and do possible adaption to the standard structure. For example if a specific user needs to search for a product using supplier name instead of product number as the abstract dialogue model in figure 4 prescribe, it is possible to edit the model to support search on supplier name by adding the supplier object as a resource in the interactor.

In large software development organizations like ProERP, UI designers and developers work in different, disperse teams. The designer wants to be in charge of the UI design, but as paper prototypes "do-not-fly" in ProERP, they need to spend much time drawing the UI and "implementing" the interaction using

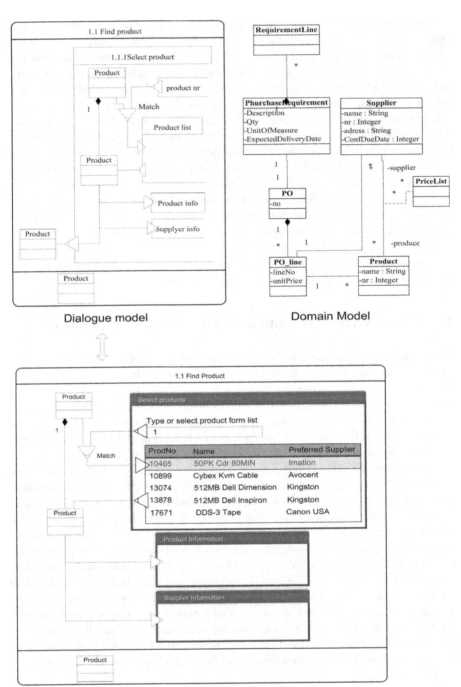

Fig. 4. Dialogue model of the task "1.1 Find Product", the domain model and a concrete UI specification of the abstract dialogue model

power-point slides. On the developer side it is required to have a précis description of the UI and what specific business objects that are used. Having a library of standard UI components will make it quicker for the UI designer to create a prototype of a running UI which can both be used in usability testing and as design specification to developers. It is important that the designer is still in charge of the UI design and has complete control of the model.

Presenting our approach to UI designers at ProERP they suggested that if they could be in charge of designing and testing such standard components, the developers could implement them and return them to the UI design team. The design team could then use the components as a resource when designing new UIs. Since designers and developers are grouped into two disperse teams the UI design ideas are communicated through scenarios for some illustrative example cases that demonstrate the principles the UI should follow. The information is supplemented with design guidelines handed over to the developing team. As a consequence the UI designers have not complete control over the look-and-feel of the final UI. Having a library of standard UI components for solving common tasks will help assure consistence across different UIs.

In this paper the approach is presented as a linear process moving from the workflow diagram towards the final user interface using several models along the way. However, this is done purely for explanatory reasons. For UI designers, it is also relevant to move from a concrete UI design towards the abstract design. After all, people tend to prefer to think in concrete terms instead of abstract terms. It is equally relevant to support starting with a concrete design for thereafter specifying its abstract and formal structure and behavior.

It is important that models are used as design aid for the UI designers. We do not believe that an automation of the design process will be appreciated. Presenting this approach to the UI designers in ProERP they commented that having a library with standard tasks (designed by them) that are editable would be a feature, not a limitation for their work.

5   Conclusion and Future Work

In an ERP domain many of the same or similar tasks are performed by different people having different subsets of roles within an organization. We have proposed an approach where models from the field of model-based user interface design are used in the context of workflow models to allow role-centric composition of ERP systems' UI. As the suggested UI components are defined using an executable modeling notation, they can be edited and thereby allowing tailoring of the UI. Typical cases where editing would be relevant is when a user should be allowed to take shortcuts compared to what is considered the standard process (e.g. create a purchase order without getting a requisition from the manager).

In the suggested approach the transition from a task model to a dialogue structure is a matter of design decisions from the UI designer. We do not provide design support for determining a useful mapping from the task model to the abstract user interface model as done in the methodology proposed by [23].

They provide a decision tree for selecting an abstract interaction object fitting the task. We need to consider whether such support would be appreciated by the UI designers in the ERP domain. Also, the appropriate size of the UI components needs to be investigated further.

References

1. Brehm, L., Heinzl, A., Markus, M.L.: Tailoring erp systems: A spectrum of choices and their implications. In: Proceedings of the 34th Hawaii International Conference on System Sciences (2001)
2. Carlsen, S.: Conceptual Modeling and Composition of Flexible Workflow Models. PhD thesis, Norwegian University of Science and Technology (1997)
3. Cooper, A.: The inmates are running the asylum: Why high-tech products drive us crazy and how to restore the sanity. Sams Publishing (1999)
4. Cuppens, E., Raymaekers, C., Coninx, K.: A model-based design process for interactive virtual environments. In: Gilroy, S.W., Harrison, M.D. (eds.) Interactive Systems. LNCS, vol. 3941, pp. 225–236. Springer, Heidelberg (2006)
5. Curran, T.A., Ladd, A.: SAP R/3 Business Blueprint: Understaning Enterprise Supply Chain Management. Prentice-Hall, Englewood Cliffs (2000)
6. Diaper, D., Sanger, C.: Tasks for and tasks in human-computer interaction. In: Interacting with Computers, vol. 18, pp. 117–138. Elsevier B.V, Amsterdam (2006)
7. Gilbert, A.: Business apps get bad marks in usability (2003), Accessed at: http://news.com.com/2100-1017-980648.htmlon8/12/2006
8. Object Management Group. Business process modeling notation specification, final adopted specification dtc/06-02-01 (2006)
9. Hammer, M.: The oa mirage. Datamation 30, 36–46 (1984)
10. Hollingsworth, D.: Workflow management coalition -the workflow reference model. Document Number TC00-1003 (January 1995)
11. Johnson, P., Johnson, H., Waddington, R., Shouls, A.: Task-related knowledge structures: Analysis, modeling and application. In: People and Computers IV, pp. 35–62 (1988)
12. Keller, G., Taufel, T.: SAP R/3 Process-Oriented Implementation. Addison-Wesley, Reading (1998)
13. Klaus, H., Rosemann, M., Gable, G.G.: What is erp? Information Systems Frontiers 2(2), 141–162 (2000)
14. Limbourg, Q., Vanderdonckt, J.: Comparing task models for user interface design. In: Diaper, D., Stanton, N. (eds.) The Handbook of Task Analysis for Human-Computer Interaction, vol. 6, pp. 135–154. Lawrence Erlbaum, Mahwah (2003), http://citeseer.ist.psu.edu/limbourg03comparing.html
15. Ludewig, J.: Models in software engineering an introduction. In: Software and Systems Modeling, vol. 2, pp. 5–14. Springer, Heidelberg (2003)
16. Luyten, K., Clerckx, T., Coninx, K., Vanderdonckt, J.: Derivation of a dialog model from a task model by activity chain extraction. In: Jorge, J.A., Jardim Nunes, N., Falcão e Cunha, J. (eds.) DSV-IS 2003. LNCS, vol. 2844, pp. 203–217. Springer, Heidelberg (2003)
17. Marshak.: Workflow: Applying automation to group processes. In: Coleman, D. (ed.) Groupware - Collaborative Strategies for Corporate LANs and Intranets, pp. 143–181. Prentice Hall PTR, Englewood Cliffs (1997)

18. Paquette, D., Schneider, K.: Interaction templates for constructing user interfaces from task models. In: Jacob, R.J.K., Limbourg, Q., Vanderdonckt, J. (eds.) Computer-Aided Design of User Interfaces IV, pp. 223–234. Springer, Heidelberg (2004)

19. Paternó, F.: Model-Based Design and Evaluation of interactive Applications. Springer, Heidelberg (2000)

20. Paternó, F.: Model-based tools for pervasive usability. Interacting with Computers, 1–25 (2004)

21. Pontico, F., Farenc, C., Winckler, M.: Model-based support for specifying eservice egovernment applications. In: Coninx, K., Luyten, K., Schneider, K.A. (eds.) TAMODIA 2006. LNCS, vol. 4385, Springer, Heidelberg (2007)

22. Preece, J., Rogers, Y., Sharp, H.: Interaction Design: beyond human computer interaction. John Wiley & Sons, Chichester (2002)

23. Pribeanu, C., Vanderdonckt, J.: A methodological approach to task-based design of user interfaces. Studies in Informatics and Control 11, 145–158 (2002)

24. Pruitt, J., Grudin, J.: Personas: practice and theory. In: DUX 2003: Proceedings of the 2003 conference on Designing for user experiences, pp. 1–15. ACM Press, New York (2003)

25. Salimifard, K., Wright, M.: Petri net-based modelling of workflow systems: An overview. European Journal of Operational Research 134, 664–676 (2001)

26. Scapin, D., Pierret-Golbreich, C.: Towards a method for task description: Mad. In: Work With Display Units (WWU 1989) (1989)

27. Shehab, E.M., Sharp, M.W., Supramaniam, L., T.A.: Spedding. Enterprise resource planning: An integrative review. Business Process Management Journal 10(4), 359–386 (2004)

28. Trætteberg, H.: Modeling work: Workflow and task modeling. In: CADUI 1999 (1999)

29. Trætteberg, H.: Model-based User Interface Design. PhD thesis, Norwegian University of Science and Technology (2002)

30. Hallvard., Trætteberg.: A hybrid tool for user interface modeling and prototyping. In: Computer-Aided Design of User Interfaces V. Springer Science+Business Media B.V. (2006)

31. van der Aalst, W.M.P., ter Hofstede, A.H.M.: Yawl: Yet another workflow language (revised version). Information Systems 30, 245–275 (2005)

32. van der Veer, C.C., Lenting, B.F., Bergevoet, B.A.J.: Gta:groupware task analysis-modeling complexity. Acta Psycologica 91, 297–322 (1996)

33. van der Veer, G., van Welie, M.: Task based groupware design: putting theory into practice. In: Proceedings of DIS 2000 (August 2000)

34. van Welie, M.: Task-based User Interface Design. PhD thesis, Vrije universiteit (2001)

35. van Welie, M., van der Veer, G.C., Eliëns, A.: An ontology for task world models. In: Proc. Int'l Eurographics Workshop Design, Specification, and Verification of Interactive Systems (DSV-IS 1998), pp. 57–70 (1998)

The WebTaskModel Approach to Web Process Modelling

Birgit Bomsdorf

University Hagen, Germany
birgit.bomsdorf@fernuni.hagen.de

Abstract. Task modelling has been entering the development process of web applications. However, modelling web processes from a usage-centred perspective is still challenging due to the strong distinctions of traditional interactive systems and state-of-the-art web applications. This paper proposes the Web-TaskModel approach, by which task model concepts are adapted for the purpose of modelling interactive web applications. The main difference to existing task models is the introduction and build-time usage of a generic task lifecycle. Hereby the descriptions of exceptions and error cases of task performance (caused by, e.g., the stateless protocol or Browser interactions) are on the one hand appended to the task while, on the other hand, being clearly separated.

Keywords: usage-centred design, task model, model-driven development, task lifecycle.

1 Introduction

Current solutions (platforms, protocols, frameworks, etc.) are well-suited for the development of traditional web-sites, but cause problems in realizing state-of-the-art web applications. Modelling the special requirements of web processes is still a critical point. State-based task sequences, for example, have to be implemented based on the stateless HTT Protocol. A further problem results from interactions enabled by Web browsers that allow the user to backtrack to an earlier sub-task of a sequence, bookmark an interaction and come back to it later to finalize the task. This situation comes along with an increasing occurrence and importance of processes in web applications in general. Task modelling has been entering the development process to face the problems. Both Web Engineering (WE) and Human-Computer-Interaction (HCI) contribute to this but with different emphasis on various aspects in each community due to the respective origin and background.

Traditional interactive systems (desktop applications) and web sites of the first days (content-driven web sites) are quite different. Their characteristics are contrasted in Table 1, whereby the focus is on usage related aspects. Web applications are in-between the two, as shown by the grey fields marking their key features. A single application, however, might cover a feature with different intensity. For example, when a customer visits an online book store information about books and relations between them may be in the foreground. Once the customer wants to check out, the activities to be performed are dominating. From the users' point of view, however, the distinction between content-oriented interactions (accessing the information space)

M. Winckler, H. Johnson, and P. Palanque (Eds.): TAMODIA 2007, LNCS 4849, pp. 240–253, 2007.

and process-oriented interactions (accessing the function space) is of no interest. They simply want to reach their goals easily – which has to be accomplished by an appropriate design.

Table 1. Comparison of traditional interactive systems and content-driven web-sites (grey fields mark characteristics of web applications)

	Traditional interactive systems	Content-driven web-sites
target groups	agentive persons	visitors / consumers
	known users	most of the time unknown, heterogeneous users
purpose / goals	users want to execute task	site visitors want to search, browse, and explore information site providers want to inform, advertise, …
primary subject of design	functionality and access to it through a user interface	information and access to it through web pages
documentation	detailed handbooks	hardly, most of the time no printed material
central paradigm	interaction	navigation
state information	state is meaningful important: task/interaction completion	stateless important: current position
control	system has control	user has control
interactivity	complex	simple
metaphor	direct manipulation	navigation
genres	isolated dedicated applications	interlinked applications of different genres
basic design principles/claim	usability and utility	user experience

An adequate modelling approach demands the combination and adaptation of both UI models and web site models in different combinations. Whereas some areas (subsites, pages, or even areas within a page) are dominated by the tasks and their structures, other areas might be structured according to the content or user roles. Therefore, a web modelling approach has to facilitate emancipated specification of task-driven, role-driven and content-driven views.

The WebTaskModel (WTM) presented in this paper is a part of a broader modelling approach, within which the task, the object and the role models are loosely linked but strongly related to each other. It allows the developer to switch and alternate between them so that none of the concepts is dominating the construction of the application and its user interface. In [3] we have been showing the derivation of an initial task-based navigation model and its combination with content-driven domain and navigation models. The focus in this paper is on the extensions aiming at the description of usage-oriented processes of web applications. In section 2 we first clarify different perspectives taken during modelling of the processes to point out where our approach fits in. Task model concepts cannot be applied straightforwardly due to the differences between traditional user interfaces and web applications. The second part of section 2 introduces basic concepts by means of an example. Section 3 goes on with the WTM presentation detailing the description of behavioural aspects. Afterwards, section 4 depicts the connections to role, object and context models. This is followed by the introduction of a first WTM simulation tool in section 5.

2 Basic Concepts of WebTaskModel

2.1 Different Perspectives of Modelling Web Processes

Since the build-time usage of task state machines leads from time to time to misunderstandings, we first reflect different modelling perspectives. Web applications, as considered here, are characterized by three kinds of processes:

Usage-oriented processes represent from the perspective of the users how they perform tasks and activities by means of the web application.

Domain-oriented processes result from the domain and the purpose of the web application. Examples of such processes are business processes in e-commerce or didactical design in e-learning. The process specification reflects the view point of the site owner and his goals.

System-based processes are specified from the perspective of the developer aiming at implementation. The description is conditioned by, e.g., business logic and system internal control information. This group of processes also includes the models of web services which are specified by business processes as well.

Both WE and HCI provide answers of how to model such web processes but with different emphasis of the usage perspective and different utilization of the resulting specifications in subsequent design steps. The inclusion of process specification in existing modelling approaches leads to the adoption and adaptation of different models, whereby business processes (OO-H and UWE [9], OOHDM [14], workflow (WebML [6]) or user task models (WSDM [7], CTT [11]) are most commonly utilized. In principle they provide similar concepts, but usage in existing approaches differs.

As a rule of thumb, task models concern mainly usage-oriented processes, whereas business process models and workflows are more used to cover the domain- and system-oriented perspective. Generally, process/workflow models focus more on responsibilities and task assignment, whereas the concept tasks relate more to user goals. Control structures used in process/workflow models are basically adopted from programming languages, whereas constructors in task models are more influenced by the domain and the users. The prevalent focus in modelling differs as well. Task models put the decomposition structure into the foreground which is typically denoted by means of a hierarchical tree notation. Process models lay the primary focus on the sequencing information, formulated in most cases in terms of UML activity diagrams.

Each model is dedicated to one perspective or a mixture. All perspectives and their relations are needed (separation of concerns). The WebTaskModel (WTM) describes web processes from the perspective of using a web application, whereby it provides clear interfaces to link task with additional process descriptions.

2.2 Basic Task Description

WTM enhances our previous work on task based modelling [5]. Since that approach was from the beginning similar, but not identical to other task models it can not make use of existing tools and notations, such as CTTE [11]. In our current work we extend the modelling concepts to account more appropriately for characteristics of interactive web applications. In contrast to other approaches of task modelling, we assume the developer not to describe the complete application by means of a connected task model; instead task modelling can be applied whenever usage-centred aspects are under investigation. In the case aspects of the information space (objects and their semantic relations) are dominating the modelling focus, the well-known models and notations (such as UML and Entity-Relationship diagrams) are applied. The resulting specification consists of several task models, interrelated and linked to data-centric model parts. Since from this a first navigation structure is derived [3], neither the task nor the content structure dominates the entire web user interface but only those parts where appropriate.

As an example of task modelling, Figure 1 shows parts of a model of an online travel agency.[1] As in general, the task hierarchy, showing decomposition of a task into its subtasks, and different task types are modelled. In the specification of high-level usage behaviour we distinguish cooperation tasks (represented by ▢) to denote pieces of work that are performed by the user in conjunction with the web application; user tasks (▢) that denote the user parts of the cooperation and are thus performed without system intervention; system tasks (■) to define pure system parts. Abstract tasks (▢), similarly to CTT are compound tasks the subtask of which belong to different task categories.

Figure 1 depicts three separate task models specifying the login/logout procedure, the booking of a flight and a hotel, and the single-task model *get tourist information*. We define no dependency between these models to allow a user to switch between the tasks, e.g., to perform the login process at every point within the booking process. At this modelling stage, all isolated task models are conceptually related by the web application (here *Flight Application*). The position in the final site and thus inclusion of the related interaction elements into pages depends on the navigation and page design.

The number of task executions is constrained by cardinalities of the form (min,max), whereby no label indicates mandatory performance, i.e, card=(1,1). The task *perform login process* is marked with (1..*) to denote that the user can repeat it as often as he wants. Labels indicating min=0 define optional tasks (in the example *alter shipping data* and *alter payment data*). Additionally, the label *T* is used to define transactional tasks, i.e., task sequences that have to be performed completely successfully, or not at all (*payment* in the example).

The order of task execution is given by temporal relations, which are assigned conceptually to the parent task so that the same temporal relation is valid for all of the subtasks. Relations typically used in task models are *sequential* task execution,

---

[1] The representations are used here to explain the concepts but not to introduce a new notation.

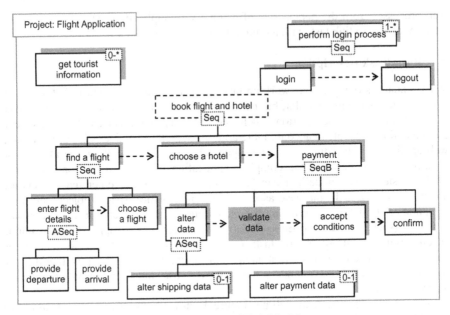

Fig. 1. Examples of Task Models

parallel task execution, and *selection* of one task from a set of alternative tasks. Further relations are described in [11] and [5]. In the notation used in Figure 1, temporal relations are denoted by abbreviations. The tasks *find a flight, choose a hotel* and *payment* have to be performed strictly one after the other (denoted by *Seq*) in the specified order (denoted by ➝).

Tasks of an arbitrary sequence, such as *provide departure* and *provide arrival* or *alter shipping data* and *alter payment data*, are performed one after the other in any arbitrary order (denoted by *ASeq*), so that at one point in time only one of the tasks is under execution. *SeqB* is an extension we made to describe task ordering that often exists in web applications: going "back" systematically to an already executed task of a sequence. Hereby, the results of that task or of the complete sequence up from that task are rolled back and the tasks can be performed again. In the example, the user is guided through the tasks of *payment*. Before he accepts the conditions or confirms he is allowed to go back to re-perform *alter data* and *accept conditions*, respectively. Since *validate data* is a system task, the user cannot step back to it, but it is performed automatically after each execution of *alter data*. Guided tours as traditionally implemented in web sites provide similar behaviour but the effect is different. Visitors are guided through an information space enabling them to leave the tour at any arbitrary point without any effect on the information space or domain model.

The example shows some extensions made by WTM; further extensions are presented together with the task state machine, which is used as an explicit build-time concept.

3 Generic Task Lifecycle

Tasks undergo different state changes while they are performed. The states are also significant to users since in their planning of follow-up activities they take into account current task situations. It is important to a user, whether he can start to work on a task (*initiated*) or not because of unfulfilled conditions, or if he is already performing a task and thus its subtasks (*running*). Further task states and the possible transitions between them are given in Figure 2. All in all, the behaviour of each task is represented by its state machine aiming at task control at run time [2, 4]. The static task model is transformed into a hierarchy of task state machines for this purpose. Conditions and temporal relations are translated into specifications of the transitions, e.g., preconditions are linked to the transition from *initiated* to *running*, so that a task can only be started if the conditions are fulfilled. Subtasks are coordinated by the superior task state machine, e.g., their state machines are invoked if the superior is running.

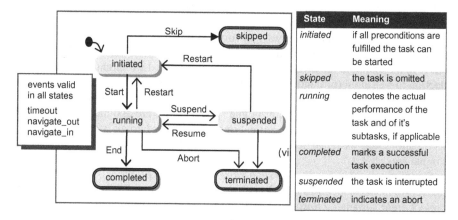

Fig. 2. Generic Task State Machine

We applied our extended task model in small projects (in industry as well as in students' projects) before implementing an editor. The experiences show that the models are more structured and concise in the cases the developers could make use of the task state machine directly. Although we do not regard this as a representative evaluation, it motivated us to re-design our first editor conception. As a result, the main task structure is modelled as before by means of a hierarchical tree notation but additional behaviour can be assigned explicitly to states and transitions.

3.1 Task Behaviour

States and transitions can be extended by additional behaviours, which are specified by triggers and actions. The actions of a behaviour may affect tasks, objects, roles and/or conditions as well as context information. An action affects

- a task by sending a global or specific task event to it (task-action),
- an object by sending an event to the object (object-action),
- a role by sending an event to the role model (role-action),
- the context by sending an event to the context model (context-action)
- a condition by setting its value (condition-action).

The actions are triggered
- either by a global task event or a specific task event (event-trigger),
- or by entering or leaving a state (on-entry, on-exit) or while the task is in the state (state-trigger).

As an abbreviation we use here the notation: task.task-state.task-event → action where task-event is either an event-trigger or a state-trigger, and action is a task-action, an object-action, a role-action, a context-action or a condition-action. Let us consider the case of an interruption as a first example of refining task behaviour.

A further extension of our web-task model is given by the explicit specification of interruptions from the users' point of view[2]. Here we distinguish three phases: The *prologue* description contains the information presented to the user and the required behaviour when the task is going to be suspended. Similarly, the *epilogue* (phase of resuming a task) description shows the information to be presented to the user and required behaviour to continue. The phase of the interruption is called *within interruption*. If in the example the task *find a flight* gets interrupted we might want the current selection to be stored (prologue). Once the task is resumed, the selection and the message "Flight selection incomplete" should be provided to the user (epilogue).

Referring to the task life cycle, prologue specifications are assigned to the *Suspend* transition, *within interruption* specifications are assigned to *in_state* and epilogue specifications are assigned to *Resume* transition. The resulting behaviours for the example are:

select flight.running.Suspend → send *store* to object *myFlight*
select flight.suspended.Resume → send *restore* to object *myFlight*
select flight.suspended.Resume → send *flight_selection_incomplete*
                                   to object *message*

3.2 Specific Task Events

The specific events *Start, End, Skip, Restart, Suspend, Resume* and *Abort* can be used on the one hand to represent internal system events influencing task execution. Hereby we realize the coordination of the usage-oriented processes with the domain-oriented and system-based processes. On the other hand, the specific task events can be used to represent events resulting from user interactions. Within the runtime system the task control layer is complemented by a dialog layer that controls the user-system dialog and forwards interactions events to the task control component [2, 4]. At build time the developer has to specify, which interactions should match a task event.

The screen fragments in Figure 3 show two possible implementations of the same task description, whereby the screen shots were taken after the execution of the first

---

[2] This extension is also useful in the context of tradition interactive applications.

task. On the right hand a solution with two selection lists (drop down boxes) is shown. The lower list is customized according to the current selection resulting from the *From*-selection. On the left hand the tasks are implemented by means of an interactive map presenting all supported airports. Each time the mouse cursor is positioned upon a city name all existing connections are visualized by means of lines. After activating the left mouse button, they are fixed (as shown by the screenshot of the example) and the user can perform the subsequent task by a mouse click on the destination. We could take those solutions to implement the dialog for the example task *enter flight details*, whereby the subtasks are to be performed in strict sequential order. The realization of a strict sequential dialog would impose a restriction, but would not violate the predefined *ASeq* access specification. In the resulting web user interface different interaction possibilities are provided for performing the same task. Thus, the respective events are bound to the same task events, e.g., both the selection from the list and the mouse click on the map are bound to the *End* event of *provide arrival*.

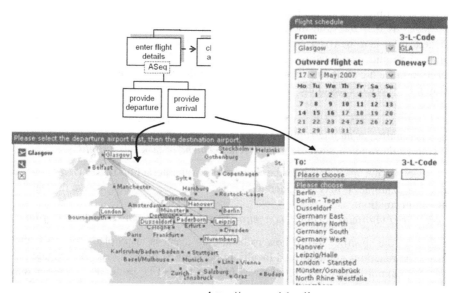

http://www.airberlin.com

Fig. 3. Possible implementations of the task *enter flight details*

Events resulting from interactions and task events can be mapped arbitrarily to each other. Although all specific events can be linked to interactions, *Start*, *End* and *Skip* are particularly significant in designing the web user interface since they signalize the need for interaction elements. However, there is no need to define an explicit interaction for each task event. For example, often a task is skipped by just performing another one. The optional subtasks of *alter data* (Figure 1) might be, for example, skipped by accepting the conditions, i.e., by an interaction assigned to another task.

3.3 Unexpected User Navigation and Timeout: Global Task Events

The global events *timeout*, *navigate_out* and *navigate_in* are generated from the "outside" and are valid for all states but the end states (*skipped*, *completed* and *terminated*). The *timeout* event is a pure system event introduced here to deal with the occurrence of session timeouts. In contrast to user interfaces of traditional applications the Client/Browser provides additional navigation interactions (e.g., Back-button, navigation history). The WebTaskModel provides the events *navigate_in* and *navigate_out* to deal explicitly with unexpected user navigations by which he leaves or steps into a predefined ordering of task execution. Such user behaviour as well as session timeouts have to be considered at the level of task modelling since they may significantly impact the predefined processes. Online shops are often exemplified in this context, e.g., the Orbitz Bug (actual bug in the flight-reservation program of Orbitz.com) as reported in [10].

First of all the relevance of a global event for a specific task is to be decided: Should something happen at all or should a global event cause no special behaviour of the "task". If it is relevant, the impact on further task executions and on the results reached so far is to be fixed: Should a task be aborted, be interrupted or should occur nothing? Should modifications on objects remain or is a rollback to be performed? Reaction in each case is in general a matter of application design (examples are given below). Furthermore, as in the case of a specific task event, the related trigger is to be defined.

In our example we want to treat a navigate_out, occurring while the task *select flight* is running, as an interruption, which is formulated by

select flight.running.navigate_out $\rightarrow$ send *Suspend* to task *select flight*

The specification does not describe from what user interaction the *navigate_out* results. For example, it may be generated because the user starts to browse through the tourist information:

get tourist information.running.on_entry $\rightarrow$ send *navigate_out* to task *select flight*

In general, the specification of how to handle an event is uncoupled from its occurrence. The reactions are described locally in the context of each task. A navigate out, however, cannot be detected in all cases (due to the HTTP protocol). The user may navigate to an external web site leaving the current task process open. At a predefined point in time the web application server will terminate the user session, whereby the *timeout* event is generated. We could make use of this event to formulate the same behaviour as defined for *navigate_out*:

select flight.running. timeout $\rightarrow$ send *Suspend* to task *select flight*

However, if the user is not logged in we do not know how to assign to him the data collected so far. So we model a system task *handle timeout* that differentiates the cases:

select flight.running.timeout $\rightarrow$ send *Start* to task *handle timeout*

Another irregular navigation transition is given by requesting a page assigned to a task whose previous mandatory tasks were not carried out. All in all, there are diverse causes and different ways of detecting navigations beyond task sequencing. It can be specified at task level as well as at user interface level, e.g., supported by the JStateMachine framework that handles allowed and forbidden UI state transitions [1]. As shown by these few examples, the task life cycle model can be used in a flexible way to describe complex behaviour of high level tasks. The events *timeout, navigate_out* and *navigate_in* are used only if they impact high-level behaviour. If, for example, two tasks are represented and accessible, respectively, by the same page, it is rather useless to attach reactions to the *navigate_out* and *navigate_in* events. Furthermore, a simple structured task, e.g. entry of a word, does not require control by means of all states of the generic life cycle. Our experience so far shows, that in particular *navigate_out* specifications are not very often defined at the task abstraction layer, but if so they are effective in keeping the web application behaviour consistent over all web pages presenting the same task.

4 Relating Object, Roles and Context

We make use of simplified object models as well as of detailed models describing conceptual domain objects. The descriptions are detailed as needed during modelling of abstract behaviour, refined and completed in subsequent development steps. A simplified object model is used particularly for describing task objects. Such objects represent information units as observed and used by the user (i.e., by the different roles) during task performance. They are not considered as irredundant information sources, but rather as views on the information and function space.

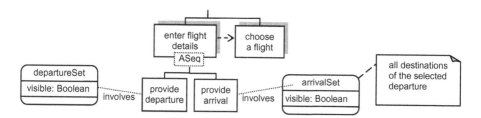

Fig. 4. Examples of Task Objects

In the example, the customer should be able to choose the departure from a set and afterwards the destination depending on the selected departure. Thus sets for the two selection tasks are provided (see Figure 4). The connections between tasks and task objects are denoted by *involves* relations, which are defined by the specifications of object-actions (see above). Additional information, such as constraints or derivation from the domain objects, is attached informally. In the example, in the underlying database we would provide a relation between departure and arrival entities, based on which the second set can be dynamically derived and inserted into a web page.

Properties of task objects and task object types, respectively, are described by means of attributes while their life cycles are specified by means of a finite state machine. Hereby, only those aspects are modelled that are relevant to the user while performing a task and interacting with the system, respectively. Later on in the process, we apply UML diagrams by which the model can be described in a very detailed way and with ongoing refinement the object-actions are replaced by, e.g., method invocations.

Role and context models are linked in the same way: Roles as well as context objects are described by attributes and state machines for specifying role and context changes, respectively. Role change in web applications is often more dynamical than in traditional desktop applications. For example, a user requesting the start page of the online travel agency is unknown. Taken this role he is allowed to choose a flight and a hotel. The task can be finalized only if he is logged in, adopting the role of a registered user. Role changes resulting from task execution as well as determination of a task space resulting from a role change occurs more often than in traditional interactive applications. In addition, contextual changes have to be handled likewise. In WTM, these interplays are modelled by the actions resulting from state transitions and events triggered from elements of the task, role, object, and context model.

Long-term dependencies are modelled by conditions. Task execution mostly depends also on business rules, context information and results of tasks performed so far. These dependencies are specified by pre- and post-conditions. A pre-condition is a logical expression that has to hold true before starting the task. Once it is started the condition is no longer checked. A post-condition is a logical expression which has to be satisfied for completing the task. In contrast to pre- and post-conditions, temporal relations decide on ordering of task execution. Once a task could be performed because of the sequencing information, the conditions can be evaluated to determine if an execution is actually enabled and may be finalized, respectively. In WTM structuring and composition of conditions are separated from their usage in task performance (as well as from roles, objects, and context). A condition may be relevant for more than one task, possibly assigned to a task as a pre-condition while being a post-condition for another one. Since conditions are formulated separately from tasks, objects, and roles they can be attached flexibly to the respective model.

5 Simulation of Usage-Oriented Web Processes

Due to the diverse interrelations of the task, role, object and context model the overall behaviour can become difficult to check. Following the tradition of simulating task models [5, 8, 11] we currently work on a WTM simulation that takes into account the various models. Figure 5 shows a first prototype of the tool.[3]

Each task is represented by an icon showing static and dynamic information about the task (such as the task type, temporal relations, and the current state). The current state of a task is indicated by means of the state name and a dedicated colour. A task icon context menu enables to trigger one of the events that are defined by the generic task state machine and are currently valid (i). The detailed specifications as resulting from the task model can be viewed as well within an additional window (not shown here).

The hierarchical task structure is presented on the left side (ii). The views (iii) and (iv) list all tasks that can be started and ended at a current point in time, respectively. (The *Endable Leaf Task* view is empty in this example because the option for ending a task automatically by the tool is activated.)

---

[3] Again we are not going to propose a new notation; the "nice" ellipses will be replaced.

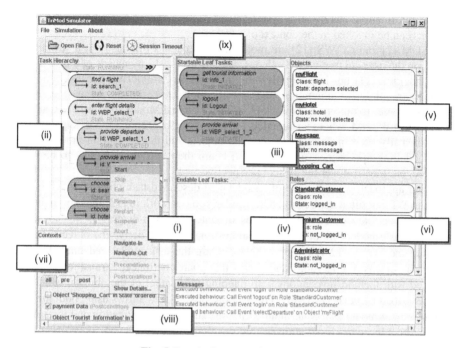

Fig. 5. Proof-of-concept simulation tool

The simulator provides not only the simulation of the tasks, theirs behaviours and interdependencies, but also task performance in conjunctions with the other model specifications. The object area (v) on the right side shows the task objects and their manipulations during task execution. Similarly, the role area (vi) depicts all roles and their states specified, allowing investigating role changes resulting from task execution as well as disabling and enabling of tasks because of role changes. The context area (vii) represents the context specification, which is empty in this example. Likewise in the case of the role, task, and object models effects on context settings can be tested and the reactions to context changes.

The condition area (viii) presents the conditions and their value changes resulting from modifications occurring in the role, task, object and context model. All in all, the mutual dependencies of all the models can be investigated. In addition, the special case of a session timeout can be tested. A respective event is sent to all tasks if the Session Timeout button is activated (ix).

6 Conclusion

The task model enhancements presented in this paper aim particularly at developing web applications but are applicable to traditional interactive systems as well. The main extension introduced by the WebTaskModel is the explicit description of task performance by means of state information at build time. Application specific rules can be added to the generic task behaviour and are used at run time as part of the control information. Hereby also system functionality required for handling the interruptions can be invoked in the context of a task.

WSDM [7] and OOWS [12] are modelling approaches that also put a strong emphasis on the user-centred view; both describe the user tasks by means of a task model (CTT notation [11] but in a slightly modified version). In OOWS the task model is used for requirement elicitation and specification concerning system operations, which is similar to our previous work [13]. The WebTaskModel approach, in contrast, is similar to WSDM, where task models are part of the conceptual modelling and thus more formally used in deriving the domain objects and the navigation model. Other web modelling approaches, e.g., UWE [9] claim their activity diagrams to be user-oriented, but mostly cover the system perspective.

In our approach we make use of less detailed described task objects, which is different to WE but often applied in HCI. Similarly to our work in [13] the modifications on task objects are described by means of state-transition-diagrams. In that work, however, task models are only used as an informal input to derive the objects' transitions. In the WebTaskModel approach we retain the task model and bind it to the objects by means of conditions and events that guard the objects' transitions. This is replaced with method invocations with ongoing refinement of the objects, which are then described by means of UML. This is more flexible and allows using both the task and the object model as formal input within the subsequent navigation and interaction design [3]. First experience showed that developers tend to favour only one of the object types at a time depending on their background.

The general objective of our work is to provide a modelling and runtime support for multiple user interfaces. One of the steps towards this direction is the presented link to context models, which will be refined in a follow-up work. The WebTaskModel is used at build time to generically define the task and domain specific behaviour of the site. The tasks can be refined down to the dialog level, e.g., as done in WSDM. Alternatively, the dialog can be described by a separate dialog model, as for instance introduced in [16]. Currently, we investigate both directions. In [2] a refined WebTaskModel is combined with so-called Abstract Dialog Units. The resulting models are transformed into a runtime system, whereby the task state machines become part of the controller [4]. All in all, we make multi-use of runtime task models: as a small scale workflow system within an e-learning application, as a generic extension of the application architecture, and within the simulation of task models. Hereby, modelling the task-related behaviour has been gaining importance. In our work on the WebTaskModel so far we concentrate mainly on its concepts and their applications in projects. First proof-of-concepts editors and simulation tools have been implemented as part of Bachelor theses and are currently developed further.

Acknowledgements

The author would like to thank Sebastian Schuth for implementing the first simulation tool and also the reviewers (particularly "Reviewer 2") for their valuable comments about this paper.

References

1. Anderson, D., O'Byrne, B.: Lean Interaction Design and Implementation: Using State-charts with Feature Driven Development. In: Proceedings of the 2nd International Conference on Usage-Centered Design - ForUse 2003 (2003)
2. Betermieux, S., Bomsdorf, B.: Finalizing Dialog Models at Runtime. In: 7th International Conference on Web Engineering - ICWE 2007. LNCS, vol. 4607, pp. 137–151. Springer, Heidelberg (2007)
3. Bomsdorf, B.: Modelling Interactive Web Applications: From Usage Modelling towards Navigation Models. In: Proceedings of the 6th International Workshop on Web-Oriented Software Technologies - IWWOST 2007, pp. 194–208 (2007)
4. Bomsdorf, B.: First Steps Towards Task-Related Web User Interface. In: Proceedings of the 4th International Conference on Computer-Aided Design of User Interfaces - CADUI 2002, pp. 349–356. Kluwer, Dordrecht (2002)
5. Bomsdorf, B.: A Coherent and Integrative Modelling Framework for Task-Based Development of Interactive Systems (in German), PhD Thesis, Heinz-Nixdorf-Institut/Universität Paderborn (1999), http://pi1.fernuni-hagen.de/bomsdorf
6. Brambilla, M., Ceri, S., Fraternali, P., Manolescu, I.: Process Modeling in Web Applications. In: ACM Transactions on Software Engineering and Methodology (TOSEM) (2006)
7. De Troyer, O., Casteleyn, S.: Modeling Complex Processes for Web Applications using WSDM. In: Proceedings of the International Workshop on Web-Oriented Software Technologies (IWWOST 2003) (2003)
8. Klug, T., Kangasharju, J.: Executable task models. In: 4th Forth International Workshop on Task Models and Diagrams for User Interface Design - TAMODIA 2005, pp. 119–122 (2005)
9. Koch, N., Kraus, A., Cachero, C., Meliá, S.: Integration of business processes in web application models. Journal of Web Engineering 3(1), 22–49 (2004)
10. Licata, D.R., Krishnamurthi, S.: Verifying interactive web programs. In: Proceedings of the IEEE International Conference on Automated Software Engineering, pp. 164–173. IEEE Computer Society Press, Los Alamitos (2004)
11. Paternó, F.: Model-based Design and Evaluation of Interactive Applications. Springer, Berlin (1999)
12. Ruiz, M., Pelechano, V., Pastor, Ó.: Designing Web Services for Supporting User Tasks: A Model Driven Approach. In: Proceedings of the International Workshop on Conceptual Modeling of Service-Oriented Software Systems - CoSS 2006, pp. 193–202 (2006)
13. Szwillus, G., Bomsdorf, B.: Models for Task-Object-Based Web Site Management. In: Forbrig, P., Limbourg, Q., Urban, B., Vanderdonckt, J. (eds.) DSV-IS 2002. LNCS, vol. 2545, pp. 267–281. Springer, Heidelberg (2002)
14. Schmid, H.A., Rossi, G.: Designing Business Processes in E-commerce Applications. In: Bauknecht, K., Tjoa, A.M., Quirchmayr, G. (eds.) EC-Web 2002. LNCS, vol. 2455, pp. 353–362. Springer, Heidelberg (2002)
15. Vilain, P., Schwabe, D.: Improving the Web Application Design Process with UIDs. 2nd International Workshop on Web-Oriented Software Technology (2002)
16. Winckler, M., Vanderdonckt, J.: Towards a User-Centered Design of Web Applications based on a Task Model. In: International Workshop on Web-Oriented Software Technologies - IWWOST 2005 (2005)

Exploring Usability Needs by Human-Computer Interaction Patterns

Markus Specker[1] and Ina Wentzlaff[2]

[1] Siemens IT Solutions and Services, C-LAB, 33102 Paderborn, Germany
markus.specker@c-lab.de
[2] University Duisburg-Essen, Software Engineering, 47057 Duisburg, Germany
ina.wentzlaff@uni-duisburg-essen.de

Abstract. Covering quality aspects such as usability through the software development life cycle is challenging. These "-ilities" are generally difficult to grasp and usually lack an appropriate quantifiability, which would ease their systematic consideration. We propose a pattern-based development method supporting the identification of usability requirements and their proper specification. By taking usability principles from Human-Computer Interaction (HCI) design patterns and incorporate them into patterns for software analysis (problem frames), we obtain a new kind of patterns applicable for requirements engineering: *HCI*Frames. They are used for exploring usability needs of a given problem situation.

1 Motivation and Related Work

Patterns for developing software have become popular for quite some time. They support reuse of development knowledge, which has proven of value, and can assist developers to build software efficiently. A common approach is using design patterns, which represent best practice solutions for recurrent, but also varying design problems. They were originally introduced in architecture by Alexander et al. [1] and first transferred to the software domain by Beck and Cunningham [2]. Gamma et al. [7] developed a pattern catalog for Software Engineering (SE). Recently, design patterns have encountered high interest in Human-Computer Interaction (HCI), where various pattern collections for different purposes exist, e.g. web design [14], user interfaces [13], groupware applications [11], navigational design [10], or collections of general HCI design patterns [3].

From the SE point of view there are two drawbacks for HCI design patterns that we take into account. Firstly, many HCI design patterns are still merely represented by graphics such as screenshots and a corresponding text passage containing their natural-language description, even though approaches for formalizing them exist [6]. This meets the philosophy to provide patterns understandable by laymen, but constrains their methodical deployment in the software development life cycle. Secondly, there are many synonym patterns in diverse collections, even if the pattern authors use different names for their design patterns and describe them in different ways.

From the HCI point of view common SE approaches neglect to address quality aspects or so-called non-functional software properties [4]. Primarily, they concentrate on describing the functionality of a program, although quality aspects, e.g. usability should

M. Winckler, H. Johnson, and P. Palanque (Eds.): TAMODIA 2007, LNCS 4849, pp. 254–260, 2007.

be built systematically into software from the beginning. As different views of the term *usability* exist [15], our understanding of usability refers to ISO 9241-110:2006 [9].

By means of patterns we start integrating Software and Usability Engineering activities. Design patterns are used for solving problems, but they do not suffice to describe development problems themselves. Therefore, we consider another kind of pattern, which is used for characterizing problems that should be solved, namely the problem frames approach by Jackson [8]. A problem frame is a pattern for structuring a simple problem situation. It classifies the problem without determining *how* to solve it.

In this article, we continue our prior work [16], where we introduced *HCI*Frames, which are patterns especially considering usability problems. In Section 2, we extend and detail our method by extracting usability principles that refer to ISO 9241-110:2006 from given HCI design patterns. These usability principles are incorporated to problem frames, which we introduce in Section 3 by deriving usability concerns for them. In Section 4, a basic problem frame is extended by these usability concerns to obtain an *HCI*Frame. Section 5 concludes our results and gives a prospect of future work.

2 Extracting Usability Principles from HCI Design Patterns

We are interested in a systematic use of HCI design patterns, since these patterns address best practice solutions affecting implicitly the usability of software. Thus, evidence in the early development phases is required for directing a reasonable HCI design patterns deployment. A usability problem has to be specified before deciding on an HCI design pattern for solving it.

Table 1. Classification of design patterns by their underlying principles

Common Principles	Software Engineering design patterns Gamma et al. [7]	Human-Computer Interaction design patterns Tidwell [13]	Schümmer [11]
user's activity	Command	-	Unit of Work
cancel activity	-	Cancelability	-
remember activity	Memento	Command History	Elephant's Brain
create list (of activities)	Iterator	-	-
undo activities	-	Multi-level Undo	-

Smith and Williams note that a pattern is *"a realization of one or more principles"* [12, p. 263], which can be embedded into various (anti-)patterns. *"These principles are applicable during the early phases of software development"* [12, p. 242] and *"help to identify design alternatives"* [12, p. 241]. We examined the problem description sections of several design patterns and deduced their inherent, common principles (Tab. 1, first column) for their classification, accordingly. This classification is still an ongoing job, we present a part of the already obtained results in this article.

For patterns in the same row, we imply that they share the same principle to solve problems, e.g. in the third line, the design patterns "Memento", "Command History", and "Elephant's Brain" are different applications of the same problem-solving principle,

Table 2. Classification of usability principles according to ISO 9241-110:2006

ISO 9241-110:2006 dialogue principles	*Usability Principles* taken from Tab. 1
suitability for the task	*user's activity*
self-descriptiveness	see input hint, input prompt, and progress indicator applied in prior *HCI*Frames [16]
suitability for learning	no match (n.m.)
conformity with user expectations	n.m.
controllability	*cancel activity*
error tolerance	*undo activities*
suitability for individualization	n.m.

which we name "*remember activity*". This classification of design patterns according to their underlying principles is done by analogies, which we see as a powerful even though subjective reasoning technique for pattern application.

To find out, which of the principles in Tab. 1 are of relevance for usability, we have related them to the dialogue principles of ISO 9241-110:2006 [9] given in Tab. 2.

For example, "*user's activity*" of Tab. 1 means that a coherent task can be accomplished by a corresponding user interaction. We relate this principle to the dialogue principle **suitable for the task** in Tab. 2, because both share the need to provide a working implementation of a user task. The "*cancel activity*" principle becomes applicable, when a user interaction shall be stopped immediately. Thus, it supports the dialogue principle **controllability**, which requires that a user should be in the position to control the place and sequence of an interaction. "*Undo activities*" fits the **error tolerance** dialogue principle, which demands that a dialogue should be forgiving. An undo reverses an undesired user interaction, and a preceding software state can be restored. In Tab. 2 "*remember activity*" and "*create list (of activities)*" are unconsidered, because they cannot be related reasonably to the ISO 9241-110:2006 dialogue principles. We still mention them in Tab. 1, because they are necessary to accomplish for instance the "*undo activities*" principle. Investigating these pattern relationships, however, is out of the scope of this work.

For describing usability problems we transfer those principles behind (HCI) design patterns, which are of relevance for usability, into patterns of the SE analysis phase. This yields a strong analysis/design pattern relationship, which can guide developers in selecting among design alternatives that are of importance for solving a specific (usability) development problem. Thereby, we found a reason for the existence of synonymic patterns in diverse collections, it is because they rely on the same basic principles.

3   Problem Description and Decomposition Using Problem Frames

For establishing a continuous pattern-based software development process, we make use of Jackson's problem frames approach [8] for requirements engineering. *Problem frames* are patterns for structuring and classifying simple software development

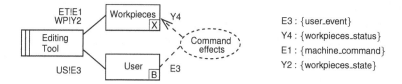

Fig. 1. Problem frame diagram for "Simple Workpieces"

problems. Jackson provides a set of five basic problem frames, which can be extended by combining them or creating variants of them [5], which we do not discuss further.

Each problem frame such as Jackson's "Simple Workpieces" is represented by a *frame diagram* (Fig. 1, cf. [8] for more details) containing different kinds of domains (boxes), interfaces with shared phenomena (labeled lines with related set of operations, actions or events representing domain properties) and a requirements oval.

Problem frames support deriving specifications from requirements. *Specifications* describe the desired machine behavior (interfaces at the box with two vertical bars) and thus are translations of customer requirements into corresponding technical descriptions of software services used by developers. Therefore, the basic *frame concern* of a problem frame must be addressed [8, p. 105ff]. In our method we represent the basic frame concern of "Simple Workpieces" by template statements for its requirement Command effects in (**R_CE**) and its corresponding specification in (**S_CE**) (angle brackets are placeholders for domains and shared phenomena of Fig. 1):

(**R_CE**) : A <user>, who commands the machine <editing tool> to execute <E3_event>, expects to change the <workpieces> state to <Y4_status>.

(**S_CE**) : On behalf of <user> command <E3_event> the machine <editing tool> manipulates the <workpieces> state <Y2_state> by <E1_command> to achieve the desired <workpieces> state <Y4_status>.

In Fig. 2 we instantiate the problem frame "Simple Workpieces" by the example requirement **"A player wants to move Pac-Man to a new location"**. It assigns values to the frame diagram and its basic frame concern stated in (**R1**) and (**S1**):

(**R1**) : A Player, who commands the machine Game to execute move, expects to change the Pac-Man state to new location.

(**S1**) : On behalf of Player command move the machine Game manipulates the Pac-Man state position by turn to achieve the desired Pac-Man state new location.

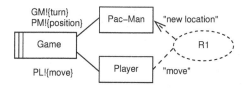

Fig. 2. Instantiated problem frame "Simple Workpieces" used for a Pac-Man Game

By means of problem frames simple problem descriptions can be derived that suffice for specifying the core functionality of a desired software system. However, currently they lack of a systematic account of non-functional properties or quality attributes such as usability. We incorporate our usability principles to problem frames by extending their basic frame concerns where reasonable for guiding usability specifications.

4   *HCI*Frames: Attaching Usability Principles to Problem Frames

By means of usability principles from Section 2 we derive *usability concerns*. They are represented as template requirements and corresponding specifications considering usability needs. *HCI*Frames are created by adding these usability concerns to a problem frame diagram and adapt its domains and shared phenomena correspondingly. By the example of "Simple Workpieces" we incorporate the found usability principles into several usability concerns for developing a new *HCI*Frame for it in Fig. 3.

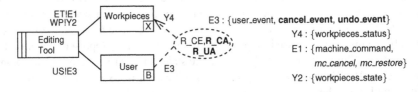

Fig. 3. *HCI*Frame for "Simple Workpieces" (additions in bold face and italic type)

The first usability principle **user's activity** of Tab. 2 is already covered by the shared phenomenon user_event of interface E3. It does not cause any change of the frame diagram itself, e.g. no additional domains have to be introduced. Now (HCI) design patterns that support the principle **user's activity** can be applied for solving a problem specified by "Simple Workpieces", e.g. "Command" and "Unit of Work" in Tab. 1.

In contrast to **user's activity**, a new usability concern for **cancel activity** given by the template requirement (**R_CA**) and its corresponding specification (**S_CA**) is added to "Simple Workpieces" accompanied by a new shared phenomenon at interface E1.

(**R_CA**) : A <user>, who commands the machine <editing tool> to execute <E3_event> for changing the <workpieces> state to <Y4_status> *can stop the execution of this command immediately by issuing command* <**cancel_E3**>.

(**S_CA**) : The <workpieces> state <Y4_status> remains untouched, if a <user> command <E3_event> is in process and canceled by a subsequent command <**cancel_E3**>. The machine <editing tool> ensures if necessary via <E1_cancel> commands that the <workpieces> state <Y2_state> is unchanged.

Comparable to cancel activity a new usability concern has to be created for **undo activities**. Without detailing its corresponding template statements, we add (**R_UA**) to the requirements oval and an additional phenomenon to interface E1, and E3 of the frame diagram for "Simple Workpieces" in Fig. 3 for handling the **undo activities** principle. The resulting *HCI*Frame shows, that if a problem fits the "Simple Workpieces" frame, then specific usability needs such as introduced by the template requirements (**R_CA**), and (**R_UA**) are of relevance and should be considered as well *in addition* to (R_CE). Developers only need to check, if one of these usability concerns is applicable. Because *HCI*Frames and (HCI) design patterns are strongly related to their common usability principles, an implementation of a corresponding solution for these usability problems is supported. Getting back to the prior Pac-Man example, this means that besides move Pac-Man, user interactions for cancel_move and undo_move should be considered for affecting the game's usability.

5   Conclusion and Future Work

By extracting usability principles from HCI design patterns and incorporating them to problem frames, we obtain *HCI*Frames, which are patterns for characterizing usability problems. They allow the exploration of usability needs in early software development, which is a prerequisite for building usability into software applications systematically. By using *HCI*Frames, a developer is guided in the identification, specification and reviewing of usability demands and does not solely depend on personal experience anymore. To determine the efficiency of *HCI*Frame use, more research is needed. Our approach already provides a basis for a continuous pattern-based software development method by explicitly linking patterns of software analysis to corresponding patterns of software design via common usability principles.

Motivated by the findings presented here, we are working on additional *HCI*Frames and their proper implementation by means of corresponding (HCI) design patterns. Furthermore, we are interested in investigating interactions of usability requirements with other quality aspects such as security, safety or performance. How possible conflicts of these can be resolved by our method, is future research, as well.

References

[1] Alexander, C., Ishikawa, S., Silverstein, M., Jacobson, M., Fiksdahl-King, I., Angel, S.: A Pattern Language. Oxford University Press, New York (1977)
[2] Beck, K., Cunningham, W.: Using Pattern Languages for Object-Oriented Programs. OOPSLA- 1987 Workshop on the Specification and Design for OO-Programming (1987)
[3] Borchers, J.: A Pattern Approach to Interaction Design. John Wiley & Sons, USA (2001)
[4] Chung, L., Nixon, B.A., Yu, E., Mylopoulus, J.: Non-Functional Requirements in Software Engineering. Kluwer Academic Publishers, Boston, USA (2000)
[5] Côté, I., Hatebur, D., Heisel, M., Schmidt, H., Wentzlaff, I.: A Systematic Account of Problem Frames. In: EuroPLoP 2007, Universitätsverlag Konstanz (to appear, 2008)
[6] Folmer, E., van Welie, M., Bosch, J.: Bridging Patterns: An Approach to Bridge Gaps Between HCI and SE. Journal of Information and Software Technology 48(2) (2006)
[7] Gamma, E., Helm, R., Johnson, R., Vlissides, J.: Design Patterns – Elements of Reusable Object-Oriented Software. Addison Wesley, Boston, USA (1995)
[8] Jackson, M.: Problem Frames – Analysing and Structuring Software Development Problems. Addison-Wesley, Reading (2001)
[9] ISO 9241-110:2006. Ergonomics of Human-System Interaction – Part 110: Dialogue Principles. International Organisation for Standardization (2006)

[10] Rossi, G., Schwabe, D., Lyardet, F.: User Interface Patterns for Hypermedia Applications. In: Proc. of the Working Conference on AVI, ACM Press, New York (2000)

[11] Schümmer, T.: A Pattern Approach for End-User Centered Groupware Development. PhD thesis, FernUniversität in Hagen (2005)

[12] Smith, C.U., Williams, L.G.: Performance Solutions: A Practical Guide to Creating Responsive, Scalable Software. Addison-Wesley Professional, Reading (2001)

[13] Tidwell, J.: Designing Interfaces, Sebastopol, USA. O'Reilly Media (2005)

[14] van Duyne, D.K., Landay, J., Hong, J.: The Design of Sites - Patterns for Creating Winning Websites. Prentice-Hall, Englewood Cliffs (2002)

[15] van Welie, M., van der Veer, G.C., Eliens, A.: Breaking down Usability. In: Proceedings of Interact 1999, Edinburgh, Scotland (1999)

[16] Wentzlaff, I., Specker, M.: Pattern-based Development of User-Friendly Web Applications. In: Workshop Proceedings of the 6th ICWE, ACM Press, New York (2006)

From Task Model to Wearable Computer Configuration

Bertrand David, Olivier Champalle, Guillaume Masserey, and René Chalon

LIESP, Ecole Centrale de Lyon, 69134 Ecully, France
{Bertrand.David, Olivier.Champalle, Guillaume.Masserey,
Rene.Chalon}@ec-lyon.fr

Abstract. This article describes a method for choosing of interaction peripherals for wearable computer in Mobile and Augmented Reality context. This method is based on a transformational process starting by user tasks modeling and their decomposition on user, machine and interaction tasks. Interaction tasks are expressed by interaction atoms (device independent) which are realized by interaction techniques related to interaction devices. A referential of interaction devices helps designers in choosing devices in relation with tasks to be supported and contextual requirements (functional and non-functional). A well organized selection process based on several devices/criteria matrixes allows explicit comparison of configurations in regard with usability criteria.

Keywords: task model, interaction tasks, interaction atoms, interaction techniques, wearable computer peripherals, configuration process.

1 Introduction

The engineering of mixed [1] and mobile [2] systems is not an easy activity, because it requires mastering interaction devices and technologies for wearable computer to satisfy application requirements. Our objective was to elaborate a process organizing the study and the selection of wearable computer and associated devices in adequacy with the tasks allocated to the actor.

The diversity of the interaction devices used with a PDA or a Tablet PC, such as HMD (head-mounted display) for augmented reality, datagloves, RFID readers and so on, is very important. These devices are more or less specialized and adapted or adaptable to tasks to carry out. Their great number and their specialization contribute to make this choice difficult. An unsuited choice can compromise effective and ergonomically valid tasks achievement. Moreover the tasks independence in relation to the contexts and the devices is known as a very important constraint for user interface plasticity [3]. How to determine and compose logically interaction devices most adapted to the needs expressed by application tasks according to working contexts and in the same time to maintain this independence as long as possible, is the question which we try to answer. Our study aims to propose a process to determine in a constructive way the devices most adapted to the application tasks in adequacy with different contexts of use while minimizing the number of them.

Our process is organized in two major stages, in the first stage we acts to identify and model the application tasks that the actor (user) will have to carry out, then we

M. Winckler, H. Johnson, and P. Palanque (Eds.): TAMODIA 2007, LNCS 4849, pp. 261–266, 2007.
© Springer-Verlag Berlin Heidelberg 2007

decompose these tasks to discover interaction tasks which put in interaction the actor and the augmented reality based information processing system, and finally to identify interaction atoms concerned. The second stage of our process provides to the designer a reference model of interaction devices organized to facilitate the choice according to an approach of Design Rationale [4]. The choice of devices is based on a logical reasoning and rational QoC taking into account various criteria [5]. This process proposes an iterative approach to analyze progressively the tasks to be carried out, with the satisfaction of main criteria "interaction continuity in and between the tasks", to reduce of the number of devices in respect of working contexts.

2   First Stage of the Process: Multilayer Modeling

Identification of tasks in charge of the actor using wearable computer constitutes the starting point of our process. Task modeling is a very active research field, with different formalisms and associated tools as CTT with CTTE [6]. Both, after having considered high level tasks, very abstract, gradually transform them into more precise tasks: user tasks, known as cognitive tasks, machine tasks, known as calculation and interaction tasks, which express the exchanges between the actor and the system. These interaction tasks are directly concerned by the choice of interaction devices to be used as support for man-machine interaction.

An **application task** results from the requirement analysis done and expressed by the future users. These tasks are the tasks which the users want to achieve. They can be in large number. The concept of **interaction task** finds naturally and commonly its place in all the models of tasks and in particular those quoted above [6]. Historically it is in the article of J.D. Foley et al. [7] where they are defined and studied in a comprehensive way. Foley determined 6 different: Selection, Position, Orientation, Path, Quantity and Text input. Obsolete for some, we think that they constitute an interesting starting point for at least illustrating the principle of the interaction tasks, because they are interaction oriented and generic. They can not cover all the interaction tasks, but they constitute a good base of it. Each one corresponds to "a sequence of interaction, identified, named and distinguishable in the decomposition of an application task and what is important, generic (semantically neutral) and independent of the context and devices". These tasks constitute building blocks able to participate, according to the point of view, either in the construction or decomposition of application tasks. They are user-based and are the units of action which the user can apprehend. Next step is the decomposition of interaction tasks using **interaction techniques.** Several definitions have been proposed considering them either as peripherals dependent or independent. In this way J. Foley associated to his generic tasks precise interaction techniques directly related to interactions devices. Another historical way, which is concerned by portability, i.e. independence between interaction devices (mainly graphical) and applications using them was in GKS (concepts of logical inputs and outputs), PHIGS and OSF/Motif (concept of logical input devices). This elementary level seems to exist, even if the four key concepts of exchange between the user and the application (via devices) such as: pick, choice, locate and valuate slightly evolved: for example, [8] added two primitives related to cooperation (sender and receiver actions).

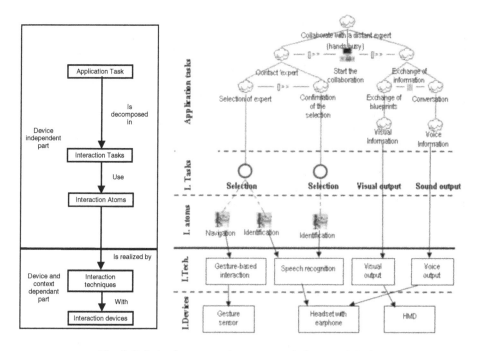

Fig. 1. Relation between tasks, atoms, techniques and devices

We call **interaction devices** all physical devices, either traditional (not-carried), like the alphanumeric keyboards, the various types of mouse or joystick, or carried (wearable) devices like glasses integrating opaque screen, "see-through" HMD, dataglove for gestural interaction, and so on. Our process is concerned by the decomposition of application task into a series of interaction and calculation tasks in order to determine the interaction devices most appropriate to the interaction. We thus take into account all kinds of physical devices, existing or ad hoc, wearable or not, ubiquitous or non-ubiquitous. The choice of devices is done first for each interaction task separately but so considered with the whole of the interaction tasks to which it belongs. To evaluate the capacity of a device to fit interaction task requirements, in relation with the diversity of possible interaction tasks, an intermediary level between interaction tasks (device independent), interaction techniques (device dependent) and devices themselves, we propose to use a new intermediate level, needed for portability reasons in relation to plasticity requirements. We call them "**interaction atoms**", which are for us device-independent smallest elements (thus atoms) of exchange between the application and interaction devices. We identified four different atoms that we define: "**Navigation atom**" to reach the entity to be selected; "**Identification atom**" inspired by [9] in charge of entity selection; "**Location atom**" to collect area location; and "**Value atom**" used to collect alphanumeric values known only by the user himself.

To emphasize the relationship between interaction atoms, techniques and devices, we present a scenario issued from HMTD project [10], which aim is to organize the assistance to maintenance in an industrial situation. In this scenario, a technician, in competence failure, would collaborate remotely with an expert. This last one is able to guide the technician by graphic, oral or textual indications. The context of intervention is the following: the technician is working in mobility in a noisy environment and would collaborate remotely without the use of his two hands occupied to fix the machine. In the diagram of Figure 1 we summarize our approach. In the tree (on the right part), we clearly let appear the various layers of Figure 1a and the context and the devices independent and dependent parts. The connection between these two parts takes place through interaction atoms "Navigation" and "Identification" and interaction techniques "Voice text input" and "gestural interaction", technique integrating the gestural modality. The input interaction devices which we are proposing are appropriate in the context of the application task, i.e. gestural sensors (based on dataglove technology) distributed on the body, in order to compensate impossibility for the actor to use his two hands, and a microphone allowing vocal conversation.

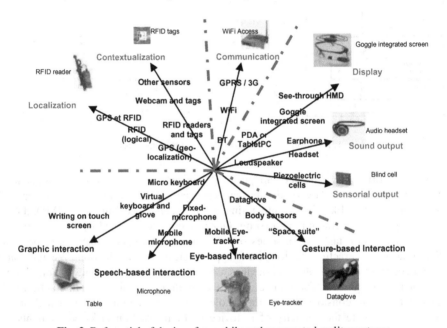

Fig. 2. Referential of devices for mobile and augmented reality systems

3 Second Stage of the Process: Choice of Devices

Our **device referential** was elaborated to integrate all the devices potentially being able to be selected during the configuration of the wearable computer for the activities of a particular actor. This referential is organized in axes (figure 2), which can be used or not in the configuration to build. If an axis is not used, it takes value 0. More the device is located towards the end of the axis more powerful it is. For example for the axis Display, the various devices are located according to the criterion of gaze continuity to catch information. This referential is appropriated for the design of mobile and AR systems. Its organisation is based on 4 groups. Three groups propose input, output and information exchange devices. Last one is devoted to system communication.

The principle of devices allocation is the following: To assign a device to an interaction task, it is necessary to know which interaction atoms and techniques it is able to carry out. In our process that means to evaluate:

1. **Device adequacy** with interaction task in relation with the criteria such as the continuity of the interaction or the minimization of the number of devices.
2. **Device capacity** to realization the task in respect with environmental no-functional (magnetic fields. temperature...) or user-related (0, 1 or 2 free hands, special working conditions) requirements.
3. **Device performance** related the interaction task and to working situations.

A multicriteria matrix is defined in the following manner; the criteria are on the columns (C1, C2... CN), the devices are on the lines. The last column contains the score of the device. The score is the total value of the device; its value is defined by a formula established by the designer and used to calculate the value of the scores of each device of the same matrix. The simplest formula being the sum of the values of the device in each criterion, other formulas such as the sum of the value of the weighted criteria can prove to be relevant. The last line contains one or more values characteristic for each one of the criteria and the score. It can be the average value of the criterion or the score, or the value MAM (Minimum/Average/Maximum) which makes possible to compare deeply different devices.

I.T.	Device		Mobility	Efficiency	User satisfaction	SCORE
SCROLL	Mobile	Eye-tracker	2	4	2	8
	Mobile	microphone	5	2	2	9
	Average		3,5	3	2	8,5
CHOOSE AN ITEM	Mobile	Eye-tracker	2	5	3	10
	Mobile	microphone	5	2	2	9
	Average		3,5	3,5	2,5	9,5
CONFIRM	Mobile	Eye-tracker	2	3	2	7
	Mobile	microphone	5	4	4	13
	Average		3,5	3,5	3	10

Fig. 3. Matrixes device/criteria for three interaction techniques

The assignment of notes to each criterion and to each device must be done with care, most objectively possible and can be carried out only by field experts with appropriate knowledge of mobile and AR systems in relation with usability appreciation. Once all elements collected and modelled selection process can start. It is based on in-depth inspection of application tasks to which interaction tasks then devices are assigned according to a compromise tending to maximize the performance, within the meaning of the values of the device in each criterion. It is also necessary to take into account all the interaction techniques used by the task in order to make a good choice of device in relation with the devices which already were selected to carry out other task and sub-task to be able to minimize the number of devices, the cost of them, their weight and to maximize the continuity of the interaction and any other criterion relating to the overall appreciation of the result. A tool supporting the process manipulates different criteria and their values, calculating the score progressively in relation with options chosen.

We present in figure 3, different matrixes device/criteria comparing the use of two devices (mobile eye-tracker and mobile microphone) for three interaction techniques (scroll, choose an item and confirm). We can observe that the wearable microphone appears as the most appropriate device in relation with our needs.

4 Conclusion

In this paper, we described a process organizing the choice of devices for wearable computer in the context of mobility and augmented reality. We described the various elements which it requires and gave an outline of its effectiveness and its reproducibility on a concrete example. This process wants to be generic and applicable to a large set of existing interaction devices and to devices newly introduced or created specifically mainly in the context of augmented reality and mobility. The transformational process presented can be improved by at least two levels of patterns, firstly between interaction tasks and interaction atoms and secondly related to interactions techniques depending on interaction devices. Both are important, for UI plasticity, to remain as long as possible independent of interaction device is required. For augmented reality, association with existing devices or design of new augmented real objects is another important challenge which was not completely tackled in this paper.

References

1. Wellner, P., Mackay, W., Gold, R.: Computer Augmented Environments: Back to the Real World. Communications of the ACM 36(7), 24–27 (1993)
2. Plouznikoff, N., Robert, J.-M.: Caractéristiques, enjeux et défis de l'informatique portée. In: Actes du congrès IHM 2004, pp. 125–132 (2004)
3. Thevenin, D.: Adaptation en Interaction Homme-Machine: Le cas de la plasticité. Thèse en informatique, Université Joseph Fourrier, Grenoble, p. 212 (2001)
4. Moran, T.P., Carroll, J.M.: Design Rationale: Concepts, Techniques, and Use. Lawrence Erlbaum Associates Publishers, Mahwah (1996)
5. Lingrand, D., de Morais, W.O., Tigli, J.Y.: Ordinateur porté: dispositifs d'entrée-sortie. In: Actes du congrès IHM 2005, pp. 219–222 (2005)
6. Paterno, F.: Model-Based Design and Evaluation of Interactive Applications. Applied Computing Series. Springer, Heidelberg (2000)
7. Foley, J.D., Wallace, V.L., Chan, P.: The human factors of computer graphics interaction techniques. IEEE Computer Graphic Applications 4(11), 13–48 (1984)
8. Yeh, R.B., Brant, J., Boli, J., Klemmer, S.R.: Large, Paper-Based Interfaces for Visual Context and Collaboration. In: Dourish, P., Friday, A. (eds.) UbiComp 2006. LNCS, vol. 4206, Springer, Heidelberg (2006)
9. Jacob, R.J.K., Leggett, J.J., Myers, B.A., Pausch, R.: Interaction Styles and Input/Output Devices. Behaviour and Information Technology 12(2), 69–79 (1993)
10. Champalle, O., David, B., Chalon, R., Masserey, G.: Ordinateur porté support de réalité augmentée pour des activités de maintenance et de dépannage. In: UbiMob (2006)

Generating Interactive Applications from Task Models: A Hard Challenge

Sybille Caffiau[1,2], Patrick Girard[1], Dominique Scapin[2], and Laurent Guittet[1]

[1] LISI, Téléport 2-
1 avenue Clément Ader,
86961 Futuroscope Cedex, France
{caffiaus, girard, guittet}@ensma.fr
[2] INRIA, Domaine de Voluceau -Rocquencourt- B.P.105,
78153 Le Chesnay, France
{Dominique.Scapin}@inria.fr

Abstract. Since early ergonomics, notations have been created focusing on the activities, jobs and task descriptions. However, the development of a wide variety of devices led to the generation of different interfaces from the same description of the tasks. The generation of complete current interfaces needs different types of information, some of which are not represented in usual task models. The goal of this paper is to present information that seems to be lacking in the task models.

Keywords: Task models, generation.

1 Introduction

Since early ergonomics, activities, jobs and task descriptions have been the center of any ergonomic diagnosis for assessment, evaluation and eventually for design and redesign. Lots of efforts were dedicated to data gathering, such as interviewing methods, and to identify issues with cognitive tasks (e.g. in air traffic control, nuclear power plants, etc.). Models for description, namely task models, have been then published and used [1, 2]. Tools supporting these models were later on developed, often not usually formal enough to allow full simulation and reuse of data.

Benefits from task-based modeling are nowadays largely reported in research [3]. Validation appears as the first aim of task-based approaches. In order to facilitate validation, some approaches, the model-based systems (MBS) [4], were developed to product user interfaces (UI) from models (of whom one is task models). More, the development of numerous devices and platforms requires to product UI capable of adapting to the context of use [5]. In order to design these kind of UIs, one strategy is to derive different UIs for several platforms from the same task model containing common information. This approach has been followed by ARTStudio [6], TERESA [7] and Dygimes framework [8]. After several steps, they produce final UIs adapted for a particular platform.

All these approaches are based on the generation of (all or a part of) UIs. However, during the different steps of generations, somme information are added (by users or

M. Winckler, H. Johnson, and P. Palanque (Eds.): TAMODIA 2007, LNCS 4849, pp. 267–272, 2007.

tools). Thus, the initial task model is modified. Then, validation according initial task models becomes complicated.

This paper is based on both a literature survey and case studies (on an email system, on a medical system). Exploring these case studies from the task model data highlights four challenges imposing to complete task models: interface presentation, definition of task to dialogue model transformations, connecting tasks with errors and undo patterns, and finally support rich forms of interaction (post-WIMP). In this paper, we expose these challenges respectively in section 2, 3, 4 and 5.

2   Tasks and Interface Presentation

Task models does not naturally contain elements of interface presentation. However, presentation has to provide mandatory elements to allow users to perform the tasks specified in task models. This consistency between task model and presentation may be exploited to verify that presentation allow to perform the feasible tasks (according to the scheduling).

Presentation contains interactive objects (widgets) that users need to carry out their tasks, applying some recommendations [9] (for example, to complete fields in a form, the user may use a customary order). A way to arrange widgets is to lay them according to the order of corresponding tasks as defined in the task tree (TERESA behaves that way). This approach uses semantics of order in the task model description. These semantics are useful for the presentation, completing the operators semantic. Thus, tasks linked by the "concurrent" operator should be performed concurrently, but the usual order is the order of description.

Furthermore, application presentation has to adapt to the platforms taking into account their space constraints. However, deducting the space constraints from the task model is impossible. Therefore studied approaches either respect the definition of the position of every element in the windows (as an example ARTStudio) or place the widgets according to screen size constraints (as an example Dygimes). Taking into account space constraints may impose addition of actions and thus modify task model. For example, consulting a menu on a computer necessitates less actions than on a phone.

At last, one of the functions of the presentation is to present the required information in order to execute a task for the user. However, existing approaches do not integrate this functionality. Cognitive tasks are usually added before interactive tasks, in order for the user to define an action strategy. Frequently, the execution of these cognitive tasks requires data to be displayed. For example, one needs to access a list content to pick a name from it. Such requirements could be fulfilled using objects, but, in our knowledge, no researcher's work has yet followed this trend of researches.

3   Tasks and Dialogue Control

In most architectural models for HCI, the dialogue controller plays a central role, split in two responsibilities. First, it must associate user actions and functional core procedures and functions. Second, it must control the dialogue, e.g. the exchange between the user and the application. That last point stands for ordering possible user actions depending on functional core and interface states, which is closely related to temporal control.

Temporal Control. Dialogue and task model seems to be very closed as shown by simulation tools of some task model editors (such as ConcurTaskTrees Environment [3] (CTTE[1]) or K-MADe[2] [10]). These task model editors supply designers to select from a set of enabled tasks which they want to evaluate (to create scenarios). More, an evaluation of the sets of feasible actions has to be performed on the dialogue control of interactive applications. The evaluation of enabled task sets [3] and feasible actions intuitively appears to share close similarities, and are even sometimes considered as identical [8, 7].

Nevertheless, is it true that these two sets can be considered as identical? Due to the difference between the points of view concerning the application that these two sets represent, some differences between the feasible actions and the enabled tasks sets exist. For example, task models present tasks entirely performed by user in the set of feasible tasks whereas they may not correspond to actions. Thus, whilst task model can express that a task can be performed only when a user task was carried out (using enabled operator in CTT or sequential operator in K-MAD), it is impossible to translate this relation in actions.

Furthermore, passing from a set of enabled tasks to another is performed through the execution of specific tasks (amongst a set of enabled tasks), such as when a user ought to enter a text before performing another task. In that example, only the user knows when the text is completed, the interface knows the end of the execution of the task when the user executes the following task. Thus, the second task can be performed as soon as and only when the first task begins. In order to generate interface from task models, detecting when the execution of these specific task ends has to be done. How can this be automatically done?

Link between Tasks and Functional Core. Interfaces need to be linked with the functional core in order to enable functions and procedures to be performed. Through this link, the various available actions are translated according to previously executed actions. Some information concerning the linked tasks is needed for the translation process, and several variables are manipulated.

Task model links are used to represent task decompositions as well as temporal organization between tasks. In task models, links can be expressed between sister tasks or between a mother task and its daughters. However, task executions may be linked through other relationships. For example, when the execution of a task can interrupt a set of others, they are linked together even if they are neither sisters nor mother and daughter. Representing the relations between tasks in a task model is sometimes challenging whereas it is necessary to identify and exploit all relations to design the dialogue. A first approach lies in the use of the deactivation operator. However, if the use of this operator allows to represent some conditions concerning the execution of the tasks, it does not answer the deletion issue. The temporal operators are not satisfactory for a precise control, but K-MAD [11] proposes the use of objects and conditions

---

[1] http://giove.cnuce.cnr.it/ctte.html
[2] http://www-rocq.inria.fr/merlin/kmade/ http://kmade.sourceforge.net/download.php

to improve the description. The semantics of these objects and conditions allows to represent some relation between tasks (the use of the same objects) but not all (deletion). More, task models present the user's viewpoint, thus the defined objects are the ones manipulated by user (corresponding to the state-of-the-world objects) and not the ones only required by the system (ex: boolean). How to deduct these non real-world objects from task models while they are not manipulated by the user?

4 The Human Factor

A great particularity of users is that... they often make errors, mistakes, and also, change their mind. Task models are not a good support to handle user errors, and express ways to correct them. Even if they can be used efficiently to explain errors, we will see in this section that they are not the best way to express error correction.

Whereas task models usually describe user activities without errors (the intention of the user), interface need to be designed for (the task execution). Including errors in the model leads to very hard representations. In order to take into account invalid data entries, tasks are split into two tasks, one to treat the entry of a valid data and another to the entry of invalid entries. However, the task models do not explain how to choose between the execution of these tasks although this information is necessary in order to perform error protection [9]. How should we complete task trees to, at the same time, allow user error anticipation and keep model readability?

The user may change his/her goal while using the application. Then, the interface should allow to undo a user action, as well as to go back to some previous state. However, task models do not take very well into account "undo" tasks. One can think of adding an "undo" task to each user action. But this design raises two questions:

(1) Can every task be undone? For example, when the user sends an email (clicking on a button "send"), the system realizes the associated action. This is an action you cannot undo, as it is impossible to have an email back once sent.

(2) Does a same "undo" task allow several user actions? For example, is undoing a writing task undoing all that was writing or only undoing the last word?

5 Tasks and Interaction

Task models are not designed to indicate what interaction is used to perform tasks. However, to make a complete interface, it is necessary to know what interaction is used. In order to proceed with generation from task models information are added. Some approaches such as *Dygimes Framework* [8], associate atomic tasks with the widget that allows its execution. Interaction with this type of approach is only composed of possible interactions with widgets. Furthermore, it assesses a bijective link between atomic tasks and widgets, which is very reducing for interaction (tasks may be executed differently according to the chosen interaction instruments).

Completing or modifying task models becomes necessary due to the fact that an atomic task may be performed by a succession of interactive actions (using, for example, *drag and drop*), and that knowing where the action is done (on a file, in the message field...) may be important. Adding this information in the task models signifies inserting data that do not belong to the abstraction level of task models.

Today, more and more applications use new interaction techniques, generally grouped under the name "post-WIMP", in order to enhance direct manipulation principles [12]. Following these principles leads to the fact that user actions and system responses are very close and to the deletion of intermediaries such as dialogue boxes [13]. The order of the task execution may be modified according to the chosen interaction or instruments. Thus, some tasks may be deleted or added.

Even if all interactions for a given task could be represented in task models, how can we indicate when a task may be performed by two different interaction techniques? In *SUIDT* [14], a concrete task is created for each interaction. For example, if a task can be performed either clicking a button or shortcutting ("Ctrl+S"), then the task is refined in two concrete tasks linked by the alternative operator. This design increases the number of concrete tasks. Furthermore, as previously stated, the interaction chosen may modify or delete completely a task. Then, modifications of the task model may be made at a higher level and is not limited to adding concrete tasks.

Moreover, the scheduling of tasks is very close to the dialogue of the application. However, adding the interaction may modify the dialogue itself. For example, moving or deleting a file are completely different tasks from the point of view of the task model. Nevertheless, with *Drag and Drop*, their beginning phases are merged. The user starts by clicking on the file, and drags it. At this stage, it is not possible to know what is his/her goal, moving or deleting. The goal appears when the document is dropped: at another place in the document for moving, out of the window for deleting. The equivalence between the task model and the dialogue model is broken.

6   Conclusion and Perspectives

Our study aimed to find challenges to generate interactive applications from task models. We have identified four different ones partially filled by generation approaches. Each of them reveal different ways for future work.

How to rely presentation to task models will be our first challenge. Particularly, we will study the use of the cognitive aspects of activity in order to check the correspondence between the user needs and the presentation.

Concerning the management of user errors, we established that task models can participate to prevent errors, but are not well adapted to correct them. Connecting task models to errors and "undo" patterns is, in our opinion, a promising research trend that will encompass our second challenge.

The dialogue control seems to be very close to task models, as shown in the simulations of task model editors and in [15]. Nonetheless, our study shown that it is not so easy. Complex task models cannot be completely derived towards dialogue models. Transformations must be defined. Being able to keep links during this transformation is our third challenge. Even if generating full dialogue control from task models is impossible, this link requires to be exploited. We aim at using task models to help the design of the dialogue and to validate it. Then, we will study how to establish the communication between these two models using, for example the MDE (Model-Driven Engineering) approaches[3] as Metamodels.

At last, we conclude with the study of rich models of interaction that evolve into post-WIMP interfaces, opening new ways for transformations between models.

References

1. Balbo, S., Ozkan, N., Paris, C.: Choosing the right task-modeling notation: A taxonomy. In: Diaper, D., Stanton, N.A. (eds.) The handbook of task analysis for human-computer interaction, pp. 445–466. Lawrence Erlbaum Associates, Mahwah (2004)

2. Limbourg, Q., Vanderdonckt, J.: Comparing task models for user interface design. In: Diaper, D., Stanton, N.A. (eds.) The handbook of task analysis for humain-computer interaction, pp. 135–154. Lawrence Erlbaum Associates, Mahwah (2004)

3. Paternó, F.: Model-based design and evaluation of interactive applications. Springer, Heidelberg (2001)

4. da Silva, P.P.: User interface declarative models and development environments: A survey. In: 7th Eurographics workshop on Design, Specification and Verification of Interactive Systems DSVIS 2000, pp. 207–226. Springer, Heidelberg (2000)

5. Calvary, G., Coutaz, J., Thevenin, D., Limbourg, Q., Souchon, N., Bouillon, L., Florins, M., Vanderdonckt, J.: Platicity of user interfaces: A revised reference framework, Tamodia. Bucarest, pp. 127–134 (2002)

6. Thévenin, D.: Adaptation en interaction homme-machine: Le cas de la plasticité. Thesis. Université Joseph Fourier. p. 213 (2001)

7. Mori, G., Paternó, F., Santoro, S.: Tool support for designing nomadic applications. In: Intelligent User Interfaces (IUI 2003), pp. 141–148 (2003)

8. Luyten, K.: Dynamic user interface generation for mobile and embedded systems with model-based user interface development. Thesis. School of Information Technology, University Limburg, Diepenbeek, Belgium, p. 194 (2004)

9. Bastien, C., Scapin, D.: Ergonomic criteria for the evaluation of human-computer interfaces. Technical report, INRIA (1993)

10. Baron, M., Lucquiaud, V., Autard, D., Scapin, D.: K- made: Un environnement pour le noyau du modéle de description de láctivité. In: IHM 2006, pp. 287–288. ACM Publishers, New York (2006)

11. Lucquiaud, V. (ed.): Proposition dún noyau et dúne structure pour les modéles de tâches orientés utilisateurs. 17th French-speaking conference on Human-computer interaction, pp. 83–90 (2005)

12. Shneiderman, B.: Direct manipulation: A step beyond programming languages. IEEE Computer 16(8), 57–69 (1983)

13. Beaudouin-Lafon, M.: Instrumental interaction: An interaction model for designing post-wimp user interfaces. In: CHI, The Hague, Netherlands. pp. 446-453 (2000)

14. Baron, M., Girard, P.: Suidt: A task model based gui-builder. TAMODIA: Task MOdels and DIAgrams for user interface design. Inforec Printing House, 64–71 (2002)

15. Navarre, D., Palanque, P., Paterno, F., Santoro, C., Bastide, R.: A tool suite for integrating task and system models through scenarios. In: Johnson, C. (ed.) Interactive systems design, specification, and verification (dsv-is 2001), pp. 88–113. Springer, Heidelberg (2001)

---

[3] http://planetmde.org

Investigating the Role of a Model-Based Boundary Object in Facilitating the Communication Between Interaction Designers and Software Engineers

Maíra Greco de Paula and Simone Diniz Junqueira Barbosa

SERG, Departamento de Informática, PUC-Rio
R. Marquês de São Vicente, 225
Gávea, Rio de Janeiro, RJ, Brasil, 22451-900
{mgreco, simone}@inf.puc-rio.br

Abstract. Interaction designers and software engineers design interactive systems under different yet complementary perspectives. It is necessary, however, to build bridges between the two areas, so that both professionals may contribute with their own expertise to the quality of the final product. One way to foster this communication is by means of shared representations. This paper presents a qualitative study that investigated the use of a set of HCI design representations as a boundary object to convey to software engineers the interaction design solution in the form of a blueprint of the application's apparent behavior.

Keywords: communication between HCI professionals and software engineers; boundary objects; interaction modeling.

1 Introduction

Interactive systems development processes involve professionals from various disciplinary backgrounds, each one with a different focus and purpose. Among these disciplines, we may cite human-computer interaction (HCI) and software engineering in general. HCI focuses, generally, on understanding the characteristics, needs, wants, and values of the system's users, their usage context, the specific goals and tasks the users need or want to achieve with the system, why and how, in order to design the user–system interaction and prototype the system's user interface, constantly evaluating with users the produced artifacts (Preece et al. 1994). And software engineering has as its main goal the specification, implementation, and testing of the interactive system's architecture and functionalities (Pressman 2005).

The work of each professional influences and constrains one another, and all share a common goal: in the end, an interactive system must be built that addresses the needs of the applications' users and stakeholders. To achieve this goal, it is paramount that these professionals communicate with each other to create a shared understanding and consensus about the problems to be addressed and what must be ultimately built, avoiding that each professional carries on with his work based on different hypotheses and, moreover, avoiding duplicate work. This paper explores the role of an interaction model, together with some detailed information about it, in mediating the communication between HCI professionals and software engineers. It assumes that HCI design precedes the (functional) software design, a decision which also needed to be evaluated among software engineers (in particular, software designers).

M. Winckler, H. Johnson, and P. Palanque (Eds.): TAMODIA 2007, LNCS 4849, pp. 273–278, 2007.
© Springer-Verlag Berlin Heidelberg 2007

This paper is organized as follows: section 2 briefly presents the semiotic engineering theory of HCI, section 3 presents the model-based communicative tool proposed to enhance the communication between HCI professionals and software engineers, section 4 presents a case study and section 5 concludes the paper.

2 Theoretical Motivation: Semiotic Engineering

Semiotic engineering is a theory of HCI that describes and explains the user–system interaction as a communication process between people (software designers and producers, stakeholders and users) through software (de Souza 2005). This communicative phenomenon occurs because interactive artifacts are intellectually built according to the decision-making processes of designers, and are communicated by them to users through signs[1] at the user interface that must be interpreted, learned, used and adapted to various contexts. Thus, this theory aims to support the designers' production of this discourse, to present the computational resources to users. Through the designer–to–user discourse, the HCI designer must support users by communicating to them: the range of goals they may achieve with the system, the various paths to achieve these goals, the user interface signs that users may use or manipulate in an interaction path to achieve a goal; and the user interface signs that tell users the answers the system gives during the interaction (de Souza 2005, p.111). The designer must make it explicit for users the design logic underlying what is being presented, so that they may produce an interpretation of the discourse that is compatible with what the designer defined. To achieve this, the designer puts in the user interface his "representative" – the designer's deputy –, and it is with this deputy that the user will interact while using the interactive system.

As mentioned in the introduction, there are multiple professionals involved in the development process. Ultimately, software engineers are also involved in building this interactive discourse, because they are responsible for specifying the software's functionalities and implementing the entire software. In building the software, however, the software engineer should not make decisions that are incompatible or that negatively affect the discourse as defined by the HCI designers, because this will have an impact on the user interaction with the system, and ultimately on its perceived quality.

In order for the application to be compatible with the interaction design, it is important that the software engineer get to know and understand the user–system interaction design as early as possible. For the interaction design to be adequately conveyed to software engineers, this paper proposes to use a set of representations that represent the user–system communication.

3 Supporting the Communication Between Interaction Designers and Software Engineers

Our goal is to increase the understanding and support the communication between HCI professionals and software engineers about the interaction design. The set of representations used in this communication make up a "communicative tool" composed of the following components (Fig. 1): the presentation of knowledge about the

---

[1] A sign is "anything that stands for something for someone" (Peirce, 1931-1958).

domain, its users, the tasks they need to achieve and the context of use (part 1); a language to design the user–system interaction (part 2); elements to support the explanation of the design solution (part 3); and correspondences with software design representations (part 4). Part 1 is a subset of the artifacts and knowledge produced by the requirements elicitation activity, and due to space constraints will not be described here. Likewise, this paper will also omit the description of part 4, because it only consists of UML skeletons that aim to save software designers some time in their initial representations.

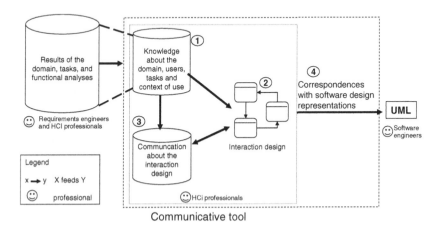

Fig. 1. Components of the communicative tool

3.1 Interaction Design

To communicate the interaction design to software engineers, we have decided to use MoLIC, the Modeling Language for Interaction as Conversation (Barbosa & Paula 2003, Silva, 2005). MoLIC is grounded in the semiotic engineering, and it has been conceived to support the HCI designers in representing all possible conversations that may take place between the user and the designer's deputy during the usage of the interactive system. MoLIC is currently composed of four artifacts: a goals diagram, a conceptual sign schema, and an interaction diagram complemented by a textual specification. The goals diagram indicates what users may do with the application. The sign conceptual schema defines and organizes the concepts involved in the system, especially those that emerge at the user interface. The interaction diagram represents how the goals may be achieved during interaction, and the textual specification further details the content of the interaction diagram by detailing the content of the signs, as well as restrictions on their expression.

When interaction is viewed as conversation, an interaction model should represent the whole range of communicative exchanges that may take place between users and the designer's deputy. In these conversations, designers establish *when* users can "talk about" the domain concepts and other application signs. The designer should clearly convey to users *when* they can talk about *what*, and what kinds of *response* to expect from the designer's deputy. Fig. 2 presents a diagrammatic representation of a partial interaction model for a "search documents" goal in an intranet. Scenes represent a moment in the interaction where the user may take his turn to participate in the conversation, whereas system processes represent the designer's deputy's turn. The arrows represent the transition utterances where either user (u:) or designer's deputy (d:) gives turn to the other interlocutor to proceed with the conversation.

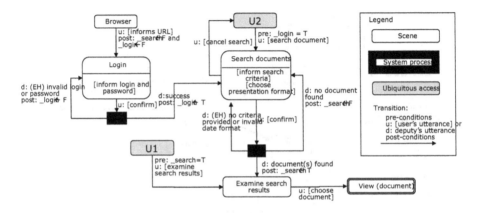

Fig. 2. Sample abbreviated interaction diagram

3.2 Communication About the Interaction Design

Since the goals of this work are the communication and negotiation of HCI design decisions, it is necessary to facilitate the understanding of the HCI design by software engineers. To do this, it is essential to make explicit the HCI design logic that under-lies the solution represented in the interaction model. Therefore, we have decided to create a component that acts like a communication layer on top of this model. This layer makes use of questions that either the interaction designer or the software engineer may pose about MoLIC elements, in order to make explicit the HCI designer-to-user communication represented in MoLIC. The questions are the following[2]: What's this? What's this for? Why must/can this be done? How can/must the user do this? Is it possible to undo this? How? Who can do this? On what/whom does this depend? Is there another way of doing this? Who/What is affected by this?. The answers to these questions should be elaborated taking into account what software engineers' will need to know about the interaction and usability goals to make appropriate software design decisions or to negotiate with HCI designers about the interaction design solution and the constraints it has imposed on their work.

---

[2] These questions were inspired in the works of communicability evaluation (Prates et al. 2000) and help systems design (Silveira 2002).

4   Case Study

To evaluate this work, a qualitative case study was planned, conducted and analyzed (Yin, 2003, p.15), with an overall goal to obtain evidence about the usefulness and ease of use of the communicative tool to support the communication of the HCI design solution between HCI designers and software engineers. The case study involved the participation of three software engineers with practical experience in software development using UML and comprised the following steps: [1] responding a survey about the participants' knowledge of HCI; [2] attending a seminar about the communicative tool; [3] a hands-on session where the software engineer should make use of the communicative tool to specify the software functionalities in UML; and [4] an interview to capture data about the participant's understanding of the produced documentation and its perceived usefulness. The summary of results is presented according to the category of analysis.

The role of HCI professionals in the software development process: All participants recognized the importance of having a professional in the software development team whose responsibility is to think about the user–system interaction and the system's usability. However, participant 2 believes that the HCI professional must define only the presentation of the user interface, to facilitate the user–system interaction, and not the interaction semantics. **The understanding of the HCI design solution represented in the tool:** All of the three participants understood the HCI design. **Usefulness of each one of the tool's components:** All of the three participants understood the purposes of each tool component, as well as MoLIC's semantics and notation. However, there were divergences in the opinions regarding the usefulness of each component. For participant 1, the part about the knowledge about the domain, users, tasks etc. and the communication about the HCI design (parts 1 and 3 of the tool) will only be useful when the application domain is more complex. For participant 2, MoLIC's goals diagram is unnecessary, and the description of the domain concepts (part 1 of the tool) and the description of MoLIC signs are redundant. All three participants agree that the communicative tool as a whole is useful for their work as software engineers. **Information, knowledge or decisions that were necessary but weren't represented in the tool:** Participant 2 stressed that, together with the tool, he needs the requirements specification document. Participant 3 said that he needed information regarding project management. **Usefulness and adequacy of the correspondences with UML (part 4):** All participants found the definition of the correspondences with UML useful, although they didn't use all of them. **Comparison with the usage of different artifacts used to represent HCI concerns:** Participant 1 said he prefers to work with the communicative tool than with a list of requirements and UML diagrams. Participant 2 said he prefers to work directly with UML, instead of the tool. Participant 3, in its turn, said he needs to develop a pilot project with the tool in order to decide whether to adopt the tool. All three participants agreed that screenshots or user interface sketches do not substitute the role of the communicative tool in the development process. **The order of the activities - first the HCI design solution modeling and only later the software specification:** All three participants agreed with the order of the modeling used in the case study. **Adoption of the communicative tool in practice:** Participant 1 agrees with the adoption of the tool. Participants 2 and 3 agreed that a pilot project must be conducted to measure the cost/benefit ratio of such an adoption.

5   Concluding Remarks

As seen in the case study results, the tool was overall well accepted by software engineers. All three participants agreed that it is useful and that it facilitates the work of specifying the internal software functionalities. Moreover, the tool's components were understood an used easily and quickly. From this small case study, we may state that the communicative tool has served as a boundary object between the areas of HCI and software engineering. Boundary Objects are objects that support the intersection between different social world and provide information for each world (Star and Griesemer 1989). The MoLIC language and the communication about it, in the context of this work, has the goal of representing all the information about the HCI design solution that both HCI professionals and software engineers need to carry on with their work. As for future work, we need to conduct more specific case studies to explore in depth some of the considerations made by the participants, and to evaluate whether and how the tool should be revised.

Acknowledgements. The authors would like to thank CNPq for the financial support to this work.

References

1. Barbosa, S.D.J., Paula, M.G.: Designing and Evaluating Interaction as Conversation: a Modeling Language based on Semiotic Engineering. In: Proceedings of the 10th International Workshop on Design, Specification, and Verification, Portugal (2003)
2. de Souza, C.: The Semiotic Engineering of Human-Computer Interaction. The MIT Press, Cambridge (2005)
3. Peirce, C.S.: Collected Papers, pp. 1931–1958. Harvard University Press, Cambridge, MA
4. Prates, R.O., de Souza, C.S., Barbosa, S.D.J.: A Method for Evaluating the Communicability of User Interfaces. ACM Interactions, 31–38 (2000)
5. Preece, J., Rogers, Y., Sharp, E., Benyon, D., Holland, S., Carey, T.: Human-Computer Interaction. Addison-Wesley, Reading (1994)
6. Pressman, R.S.: Software Engineering: A Practitioner's Approach. McGraw-Hill Professional, New York (2005)
7. Silva, B.S.: MoLIC Segunda Edição: Revisão de uma linguagem para modelagem da interação humano-computador. Dissertação de Mestrado, PUC-Rio, Brasil (2005)
8. Silveira, M.S.: Metacomunicação Designer-Usuário na Interação Humano-Computador. Tese de Doutorado, PUC-Rio, Brasil (2002)
9. Star, S.L., Griesemer, J.R.: Institutional Ecology, Translations and Boundary Objects: Amateurs and Professionals in Berkeley's Museum of Vertebrate Zoology. Social Studies of Science 19(3), 387–420 (1989)
10. Yin, R.K.: Case Study Research: Design and Methods. SAGE Publications, Thousand Oaks (2003)

Looking for Unexpected Consequences of Interface Design Decisions: The MeMo Workbench

Anthony Jameson[1], Angela Mahr[1], Michael Kruppa[1],
Andreas Rieger[2], and Robert Schleicher[3,*]

[1] German Research Center for Artificial Intelligence
[2] Technische Universität Berlin — DAI-Labor
[3] Deutsche Telekom AG Laboratories

Abstract. This paper discusses and illustrates work in progress on the MEMO workbench for early model-based usability evaluation of interface designs. Characteristic features of the workbench include (a) the prediction of errors via rules that refer to user attributes; and (b) the automatic generation of methods for performing specific tasks and for recovering from errors.

1 Introduction and Example

This short paper discusses work in progress in the project MEMO, which is an effort at T-Labs, a research division of Deutsche Telekom, to introduce task modeling into the design and development process for interactive systems. The MEMO workbench ([1]) is intended to enable the evaluation of the usability of new designs in an early phase of the design process.

Before discussing the salient features of the MEMO workbench on a general level, we will introduce a simple example that will make the subsequent discussion easier to follow. Our minimal example system is inspired by a part of a web site that allows a user to determine, for a given telephone rate package, how much it costs to make a phone call to a particular foreign country. The example system as modeled in MEMO offers information only on the 5 countries shown in the top screen shot of Figure 1. Together with the screens labeled "2" and "3", this screen illustrates the correct method for finding the rate for a call to the United States of America: The user clicks on the radio button for that country and then clicks on the "Next" button, which takes her to a screen showing the desired rate. The two lower right-hand screens ("4" and "5") show the analogous sequence when the country clicked on is the United Arab Emirates.

One topic of interest for MEMO is the prediction of possible errors and their consequences. Even with the simple first task, the user could commit a *description error* ([2]), clicking on the first country in the list whose name starts with "United". This error takes her to State 4, which is off the correct path for her task. At this point she might notice that the wrong country has been selected, in which case she can easily get back onto the correct path by clicking on "United States of America". But if she instead proceeds to click on "Next", she will end up looking at an incorrect rate (State 5).

---

* The research described in this paper is being conducted in the context of the project MEMO, which is funded by Deutsche Telekom AG Laboratories.

M. Winckler, H. Johnson, and P. Palanque (Eds.): TAMODIA 2007, LNCS 4849, pp. 279–286, 2007.

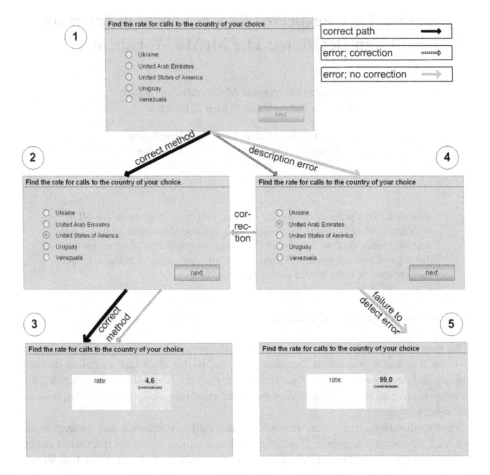

Fig. 1. Screen shots illustrating the possible system states that can be reached in the simple example used in this paper as well as the possible paths through these states during the performance of the task of finding the rate for phone calls to the United States of America

2   Goals of MeMo and Relationship to Previous Work

In this simple example, the overall purpose of the MEMO workbench is to allow the interface designer to predict how often each of the paths shown in Figure 1 will be taken by users who are performing the task of finding the rate for the United States—different predictions being made for each combination of user attributes such as visual acuity and the amount of attention devoted to the task.

More generally, MEMO is intended to allow the interface designer to compare a number of alternative designs for a given interface in terms of the likely behavior of users on a specified set of tasks given different combinations of attributes.

We can locate MEMO in the space of existing approaches to model-based evaluation by mentioning some important sources of inspiration. A number of aspects of the MEMO workbench were inspired by CogTool (see, e.g., [3]). Both CogTool and

MEMO enable an interface designer to (a) construct a medium-fidelity prototype of each of several variants of a to-be-designed system; (b) specify how users are likely to interact with each variant of the system while performing specified tasks; and (c) run simulations to predict certain aspects of the users' performance on these tasks (e.g., execution time).

Instead of aiming to match COGTOOL's sophisticated prediction of execution times, MEMO aims at a more explicit and automated prediction of error-related behavior: Errors are generated during simulations by rules that aim to capture known types of error. In this way, MEMO builds both on well-known taxonomies and analyses of human error (e.g., [2]; [4]) and on recent efforts to use these concepts to predict errors in the context of model-based evaluation (see, e.g., [5]; [6]; [7]; [8]). Relative to most such approaches, MEMO tries to automate the prediction of errors to a greater extent, as opposed to relying on human judgment for the specification of likely errors. It is clear that there are limits to such automation, but it seems worthwhile to explore these limits.

In a similar vein, another salient feature of MEMO is the use of automatically computed methods for performing particular tasks—and recovering from errors—as an alternative (or complement) to methods that are explicitly specified by an analyst.

For the realization of the vision sketched so far, a number of questions need to be dealt with. In the following sections, we discuss the approach to each question that is being taken with MEMO.

3   What User Attributes Should Be Distinguished?

Even if an interface design is generally successful, it may be problematic for users who have particular (combinations of) attributes (e.g., low visual acuity combined with a limited knowledge of English). Especially problems that are likely to arise only given a combination of two or more attributes may be hard to discover without a systematic, exhaustive search through the space of combinations. In MEMO workbench, various aspects of the simulation of users can be made to depend on such attributes, which can include: perceptual and motor capabilities (e.g., visual acuity); relevant prior knowledge and experience (e.g., amount of experience with systems like the one under consideration); and temporally variable factors (e.g., the amount of attention that the user is devoting to the performance of the task).

4   How Is the System Design to Be Specified?

For reasons that will become clear below, in MEMO each system is modeled with a state diagram, as in COGTOOL ([3]). Figure 2 illustrates how a designer can model a system in terms of (a) drawings of individual screens, each of which contains one or more widgets; and (b) transitions between screens that are made when certain actions are performed with the widgets. As is well known, this type of modeling works much better for some types of system than for others.

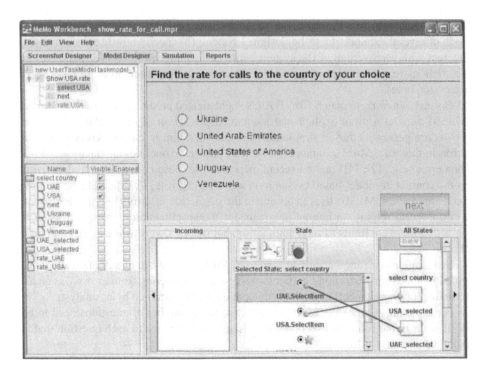

Fig. 2. Screen shot of the MEMO workbench's interface for specifying a system variant along with ideal methods for the performance of tasks with that system variant

5   How Are the Tasks and Ideal Methods to Be Specified?

It is assumed that the designer wants to simulate users' performance on a number of tasks for a number of system variants. A typical approach in model-based evaluation is to specify somehow a correct or "ideal" method of performing each task for each variant and then perhaps to characterize various deviations from this method (see, e.g., [8]).

One way of specifying an ideal method for a task (realized, for example, in COG-TOOL) is to demonstrate a relevant sequence of steps by operating the relevant widgets in the system model; and the simple method that can be seen in the upper left-hand window of Figure 2 was in fact defined in this way. This approach can become tedious or even impractical, however, when a large number of tasks and (similar) system variants are considered.

An alternative approach that we are currently pursuing is available if each task can be specified in terms of an initial state and a goal state (e.g., States 1 and 3 in Figure 1). In this case, the problem of finding an ideal method for the task can be seen as the problem of finding a good route from the initial state to the goal state within the state diagram, where the goodness of a route depends on properties such as the number of steps or the predicted total execution time. To be sure, a method automatically derived in this way may not be realistic for all users. For example, the quickest way to accomplish a particular task in a complex commercial website may be to go to the site map and click on one of the hundreds of links found there—a method unlikely to be applied by most users. We therefore expect that the automatic generation of methods will have to be subjected to some constraints, both general ones and constraints for users with particular attributes (e.g., the constraint that keyboard shortcuts are not employed by users who lack previous familiarity with the system in question).

In this way, the generation of an appropriate method for a given task is analogous to the problem of finding a route with a navigation system from a starting point to a destination; and the imposition of constraints on the nature of the methods is analogous to the use of constraints such as "no highways".

6   How Should the Basic Simulation Process Work?

As was mentioned above, the basic goal of MEMO is to predict what will happen when a user with certain attributes performs a certain task with a particular variant of the system. For the moment, we assume for the sake of exposition that the simulated user always performs the task according to the ideal method that has been derived for users with the attributes in question; the simulation of errors will be discussed below.

For a given system variant, the generation of simulation runs proceeds as follows:

1. The designer specifies a set of *user groups* for which the simulation is to be carried out, each user group being defined in terms of a combination of values for particular attributes.

2. The designer lists the tasks for which the simulation is to be carried out.

3. The designer specifies a certain number of simulation runs for each user group and each task.

4. In each simulation run, the system generates a trace by assuming that the simulated user applies the ideal method for the user group in question.

5. Once all of the simulation runs have been completed, the system generates a report on the results for each user group and task. In the case considered so far, where no errors are simulated, this report reflects aspects of performance such as the time required by each user group to perform the task and the frequencies with which particular types of operation (e.g., clicking on icons) are performed.

In the case of our simple example, the error-free simulations simply reflect the fact that, for all user groups, each of the possible tasks is performed straightforwardly with two mouse clicks. With realistically complex systems and tasks, however, this simulation approach can yield some interesting results. For example, it may turn out that the ideal method for a particular task involves an unacceptably large number of operations (of a certain type) for at least one user group (e.g., a group that is assumed always to use menus rather than keyboard shortcuts).

7   How Should the Workbench Predict Errors?

One way of modeling behavior that involves errors (used, e.g., in COGTOOL) is to treat a method that contains an error simply as one possible method for performing the task. The remarks made above about the limitations of the manual specification of correct methods apply to an even greater extent here: Once errors are considered, the number of possible methods for performing a task becomes very large, especially since errors can occur in combination.

The approach currently being explored in MEMO is to use a set of general error generation rules to produce incorrect behavior at various points during a simulation: The general procedure for simulating the performance of a given task is to assume that the user will perform the correct next step unless an error generation rule applies to the situation, in which case an error is generated with a probability specified by the rule. In our introductory example, the following rule will generate a description error in some of the simulation runs:

- If the correct action is to select the item I with the label L,
- and there is another item I' whose label begins with the same word as L,
- then the user will select I' with a probability of p_1 if the user's attention to the task is low and p_2 if it is high.

Even this highly simplified rule captures the important fact that this error can occur and that it is more likely under certain conditions than under others. The introduction of error generation rules affects the generation of simulation runs as follows:

Whenever the simulated user enters a given state, the workbench checks whether there is an error generation rule that applies in that state (taking into account the next action specified by the ideal method currently being applied by the simulated user). If so, with a probability specified by that rule, the incorrect action prescribed by the rule is simulated, and the system enters a state that is not on the ideal path for the task in question.

We still need to deal with the question of the extent to which errors are detected and recovered from and the consequences that they have.

8   How Should the Workbench Predict Error Recovery?

For the sake of exposition, we assume for the moment that the user will do the right thing as soon as an error has occurred: recognize the error and recover from it in the most straightforward possible way.

When an error step is predicted during a simulation run, the MEMO workbench in effect views the user as being confronted with a new task which in general overlaps partly with the original task: The user's task is now to recover from the error and then proceed towards the original goal state. More concretely, the workbench computes on the fly an appropriate method for getting to the goal state starting from the state that resulted from the error; in doing so, the workbench uses the same algorithm that is used for generating ideal methods in the first place.

In our simple example, the workbench's reporting would reveal that, in the simulation runs that contained a description error, the user would quickly recover simply by clicking on the correct country.

If the workbench operated in exactly this way, it would of course yield overly optimistic predictions, assuming optimal error recovery behavior in all cases. Still, the reporting would contain some useful information. For example, a comparison between the simulation runs that contained errors and those that did not might reveal that all of the predictable errors can be straightforwardly recovered from as long as they are detected immediately—or at the other extreme, it might reveal cases in which no recovery at all was possible. Still, it should also be possible to simulate cases in which the user does not detect an error.

9   How Should the Workbench Simulate Failed Error Detection?

On the whole, the question of when users will recognize that they have made an error is a complex one (see, e.g., [5]). MEMO's current approach to error detection is applicable in cases where detection of an error by the user is in principle so straightforward that failure to detect the error can be viewed as an error in itself.

As an illustration, consider our simple example: Once a user has mistakenly clicked on "United Arab Emirates", the screen shows a filled radio button next to the unintended country; so if the user quickly checks the result of her action before clicking on "Next", she will see the need to do exactly what the MEMO workbench predicts according to the principles described in the previous section: Click on the radio button next to "United States of America" and then proceed.

The user can fail to notice her error if she doesn't bother to check but just proceeds to click on "Next". This pattern of omitting a verification step can be modeled roughly with a rule such as the following:

- If on the current screen item I' is marked has having been selected
- and the item that really ought to be selected is some other item I
- and there is a button B that the user can click on to proceed to the next screen
- then the user will (incorrectly) click on B with probability p_1 if the user's attention to the task is high and p_2 if it is low.

Like the first error-generation rule introduced above, this one is hard to formulate in such a way that (a) it applies with some generality and (b) the probabilities p_1 and p_2 are empirically reasonably accurate. Still, even a rough formulation can lead in our example to the useful prediction that some users—especially those with low attention to the task—will end up in an incorrect final state (i.e., looking at an incorrect rate)—provided that they clicked on the wrong country in the first place. Given that the first error was likewise more probable given low attention to the task, the MEMO workbench will predict a nonnegligible frequency of ending up in the wrong state only for users who show low attention to the task.

Note that, in a different but analogous setting, the first error might be likely given user attribute A (e.g., poor knowledge of English) while the second one was associated with some completely different attribute (e.g., poor visual acuity). In this case, the workbench would predict a nonnegligible frequency of ending up in the wrong state only for users who have *both* of the problematic attributes—thereby uncovering an undesirable outcome that would be hard to detect without systematic search through a large number of attribute combinations and simulation runs.

In sum, this approach to the modeling of (the lack of) error detection is applicable only in cases where errors are basically easy to detect. But it does help call attention to the subset of these cases in which an error is committed and not detected, so that the implications of these cases can be contemplated by the designer.

10   Conclusions and Current Work

Some of the characteristic features of the MEMO approach appear to work quite naturally for some types of system, task, and error and less well for others: the representation of a system with a state diagram; the automatic derivation of ideal methods for performing tasks; the rule-based prediction of errors and error detection; and the dependence of predicted behavior on user attributes. We have argued that, where applicable, these features of MEMO make possible some useful types of simulation and analysis that go beyond what is possible with user testing, inspection-based evaluation, and other types of model-based evaluation. The special promise of these features lies in the ability of the MEMO workbench to search systematically through a large space of possibilities that is defined by different system variants, different tasks, different user attributes, and the nondeterministic occurrence of errors. The simulations generated in this way can hardly be as accurate as those yielded by more focused, hand-crafted simulation models, but they may have a greater ability to uncover potential problems that arise only in certain specific situations.

References

1. Möller, S., Englert, R., Engelbrecht, K., Hafner, V., Jameson, A., Oulasvirta, A., Raake, A., Reithinger, N.: MeMo: Towards automatic usability evaluation of spoken dialogue services by user error simulations. In: Proceedings of INTERSPEECH 2006. the Ninth International Conference on Spoken Language Processing, Pittsburgh, PA (2006)
2. Norman, D.A.: Design rules based on analyses of human error. Communications of the ACM 26, 254–258 (1983)
3. John, B.E., Salvucci, D.: Multipurpose prototypes for assessing user interfaces in pervasive computing systems. pervasive computing 4(4), 27–34 (2005)
4. Reason, J.: Human Error. Cambridge University Press, Cambridge, New York (1990)
5. Wood, S.D., Kieras, D.E.: Modeling human error for experimentation, training, and error-tolerant design. In: Proceedings of the Interservice/Industry Training, Simulation and Education Conference, Orlando, FL (2002)
6. Paternò, F., Santoro, C.: Preventing user errors by systematic analysis of deviations from the system task model. International Journal of Human-Computer Studies 56(2), 225–245 (2002)
7. Baber, C., Stanton, N.A.: Task analysis for error identification. In: Diaper, D., Stanton, N. (eds.) The Handbook of Task Analysis for Human-Computer Interaction, pp. 367–379. Erlbaum, Mahwah, NJ (2004)
8. Bastide, R., Basnyat, S.: Error patterns: Systematic investigation of deviations in task models. In: Coninx, K., Luyten, K., Schneider, K.A. (eds.) Task Models and Diagrams for User Interface Design, pp. 109–121. Springer, Berlin (2006)

Task Modelling for Collaborative Systems

Víctor M.R. Penichet, María Lozano, José A. Gallud, and R. Tesoriero

Computer Science Research Institute (I3A)-University of Castilla- La Mancha,
Av. España s/n, 02007 Albacete, Spain
{victor.penichet, maria.lozano, jose.gallud,
ricardo.tesoriero}@uclm.es

Abstract. The development of Collaborative Systems implies taking into account not only a greater number of users but also the interactions among them to accomplish complex tasks. Besides, the nature of these tasks is different from traditional tasks considered in mono-user systems. Theses differences justify the need to tackle the task modelling for collaborative systems in a different way than traditionally, considering the special features that this kind of systems have. In this paper we propose a conceptual model to describe tasks and group tasks for multi-user systems in order to make a precise characterization. This characterization is applied to a simple example to show its applicability.

Keywords: Tasks, task modeling, Group, Conceptual Model, Computer-Supported Cooperative Work.

1 Introduction

Web development has experienced a spectacular change in the last years mainly motivated by the improvements in technology, infrastructures and the way of developing software applications more focused on the users' needs.

The user interacts with the system performing tasks. This is one of the typical topics concerning HCI. However, the user also interacts with other users through the system performing cooperative tasks. And that is the typical topic concerning CSCW (Computer-Supported Cooperative Work).

In this paper we propose a conceptual model to describe the tasks that should be performed to achieve the application goals. To get this, we have based on the concepts proposed by relevant authors in the area of task analysis and collaborative environments, in such a way that every task, identified and described by means of a task analysis process, has into account the traditional and most relevant tasks characterizations.

A good characterization of the tasks makes possible the development of the application with a high quality level.

The rest of the paper is organized as follows: In the next section, some related works are analyzed. Section 3 introduces the conceptual model we propose and describes the way in which group tasks are characterized. Section 5 describes an example of application with the proposed concepts. Finally, section 6 contains some conclusions and final remarks concerning this work.

M. Winckler, H. Johnson, and P. Palanque (Eds.): TAMODIA 2007, LNCS 4849, pp. 287–292, 2007.
© Springer-Verlag Berlin Heidelberg 2007

2   Related Work

As commented before, current software combines collaboration among users to perform tasks and the use of the Web as an infrastructure.

Therefore, the specification of systems has to take into account some special characteristics regarding such systems.

Some mechanisms, as described in [6] [7] [10], provides a way to represent the organization of the tasks performed in a system in order to provide the designer with a clearer information about what does who, in what way something has to be carried out, etc. Some other works characterize groupware systems and the way the users interact each other [1] [2] [3] [4] [5]. The conceptual model we propose in this paper describes the tasks which are necessary to perform in the system to inform the designers about the nature of such tasks.

In [1], a conceptual model is proposed to characterize groupware systems. This model describes objects and operations on such objects, dynamic aspects, and the interface between the system and the users and amongst users. This characterization describes a groupware system from its users' point of view.

Our approach is centred on the description of the tasks that take place in a groupware system, also taking into account the task features found in the aforementioned mechanisms to analyze tasks [6] [7] [10].

Other approaches, as the ones used to classify CSCW tools, could be used to characterize the tasks the users must perform as a group to achieve a common objective. Typical CSCW features, as described in [8] or time-space features as proposed in [5], are not enough to described group tasks. However, the combined use of all these features together with features from the task analysis [6] provides a rich way to describe the tasks in a system. Such information helps the designers to achieve better quality systems.

This paper presents a conceptual model to describe tasks in general and group tasks in particular, and an example where it is applied. It is based on all these features that have been considered fundamental throughout the years.

3   A Task Conceptual Model Considering Group Tasks

When modelling the tasks a user has to perform, it is known that it is necessary to consider many other concepts such as the objectives of the tasks, the roles, the own user, the context, etc. Nevertheless, by means of the model presented in this paper, we specially try to characterize tasks. That is the reason why we will focus on it. Figure 1 shows the conceptual model we use to relate the different concepts we identify as fundamental regarding tasks when representing human-computer and human-computer-human interactions within a CSCW system. This model is connected to some other models to characterize concepts related to context, awareness, roles, groups, users, and so on. As we mentioned before, the objective of this work is task characterization, thus, these other concepts are not shown here, in spite of being taken into account when modelling CSCW systems.

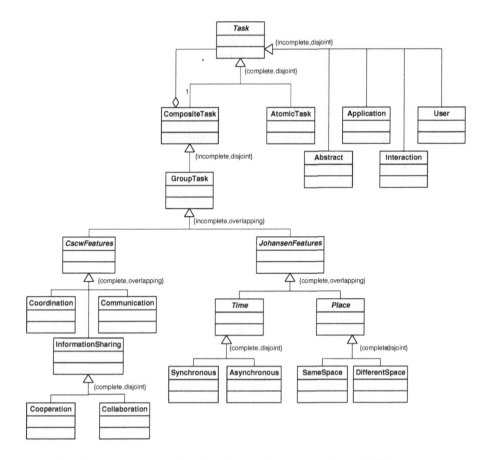

Fig. 1. A conceptual model to describe and characterize tasks in CSCW systems

As has been traditionally considered, we also take into account that some tasks – composite tasks– are decomposed into other more specific tasks, and these ones in other more specific, and so forth. Finally, there are *atomic tasks* which cannot be divided into other tasks. Atomic tasks are the smallest granularity level.

Paternò has established a classification of tasks based on the allocation of their performance, and has classified them into application, user, interaction or abstract tasks [6]. This classification is widely accepted as has shown to be good for modelling tasks and provides a way of clearly identifying different tasks to be performed in the system to reach an objective. Thus, it has been taken into account in the definition of the proposed conceptual model.

A special group of tasks has been traditionally called cooperative tasks. However, in this characterization, we have preferred to call them *group tasks* over the other term, inasmuch as it refers to CSCW tasks [3], whose bases are *coordination, communication* and *information sharing* [8].

Typical concepts around CSCW provide a way to characterize tasks depending on their orientation to the coordination, to the communication [111], to the cooperation or to the collaboration [4] [8] [9].

Additionally, a group task could be characterized depending on its time-space features. Johansen [5] established a time-space matrix which clarifies these concepts and which describes how a task could be performed in the same place or in different places, as well as in a synchronous (real-time) or asynchronous way.

4 Example of Application

An easy example is explained in this section to show all these concepts in practice. The example is about a typical shared whiteboard. Some sub-problems are explicitly obviated to focus the problem on the co-participation of the users within the application: how different users draw a design together.

CTT graphical notation has been used in the example to describe the organization of the tasks, as can be appreciated in the following figures.

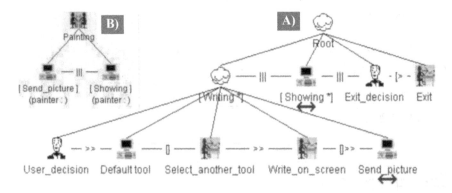

Fig. 2. a) Organization of roles tasks using CTT. b) Decomposition of the composite task 'Painting'. This task is characterized as a *composite group task oriented to the synchronous cooperation within different places.*

4.1 Description of the Application

It is no worth describing the shared whiteboard application because it is well-known. Basically, this system allows the user to draw on the screen, to show what a user and the rest of them are drawing, and to go out of the system. Every task could be performed without taken into account the others, that is, whatever task could be perform in every moment. They are tasks that could be performed concurrently, but the last one finishes the session. That is represented by the second level tasks on Figure 2a. These tasks are characterized in the following sections according to the conceptual model we have presented.

4.2 Group Task Characterization

Because of the lack of space we will focus on group task characterization. The users of the system need to participate all together. They need to cooperate to achieve a common design. The task representing several users with the role 'painter' is 'Painting'. This task is also a *composite* task divided into two tasks (see Figure 2b):

'Send_picture' and 'Showing'. These two tasks are performed depending on the tasks a user playing the role 'painter' performs.

The composite task called 'Painting' is composed by two tasks which could be performed by different users playing the role 'painter'. Actually, such tasks would be performed by users' application because they are application tasks. That is a normal situation in order to achieve a common design by using a shared whiteboard.

Therefore, the 'Painting' task is also a *group* task. This *composite* and *group* task is performed in real-time, that is, every user can see on the screen whatever another user draws immediately. The design is done by a group of users in a *synchronous* way, according to Johansen's features.

Commonly, the users of this shared whiteboard will achieve a common design with independence of the place they are and they will make use of the Internet as a way of cooperation among them. According to Johansen's spatial features, it is a task oriented to *different places*.

In spite of the fact that the users are somehow coordinated to generate a common design, it is not a coordination task. Something similar happens with the communication. The 'Painting' task is a *cooperative* task because different users cooperate among them to draw a common design, therefore the 'Painting' task is characterized as a *composite group task oriented to the synchronous cooperation within different places*.

5   Conclusions

This work briefly presents a conceptual model to describe the tasks involved in collaborative systems. This conceptual model has been built taken into account some traditional and widely accepted concepts and classifications in the CSCW and Task Analysis fields.

The proposed conceptual model allows the complete specification of all kind of tasks that might be involved in collaborative environments, in which the participation of several users making use of the network infrastructure is frequent. This proposal helps designers of collaborative systems by providing them with the most complete and structured information regarding tasks according to the traditional foundations.

Even more, this conceptual model is an open system that could allow new ways of characterizing tasks. It also could allow the introduction of new features identified upon the group tasks to provide an accurate definition.

The proposed characterizations of tasks has been applied to a simple example of a shared whiteboard to show its applicability and how this conceptual model can help designers in the identification and characterization of complex tasks usually involved in multi-user systems.

As a result, we can conclude that the correct and complete specification of all the tasks to be performed in collaborative systems provides designers with a very useful source of information to make possible the development of this kind of applications with a high quality level.

Acknowledgements

We would like to acknowledge the CICYT TIN2004-08000-C03-01 and the Junta de Comunidades de Castilla-La Mancha PCC-05-005-1 and PAI06-0093-8836 projects for funding this work.

References

1. Ellis, C., Wainer, J.: A Conceptual Model of Groupware. In: Proceeding of CSCW 1994, pp. 79–88. ACM Press, New York (1994)
2. Greenberg, S.: The 1988 conference on computer-supported cooperative work: Trip report. ACM SIGCHI Bulletin 21(1), 49–55 (1989)
3. Greif, I.: Computer-Supported Cooperative Work: A Book of Readings. Morgan Kaufmann, San Mateo CA (1988)
4. Grudin, J.: Computer-Supported Cooperative Work: History and Focus. Computer 27(5), 19–26 (1994)
5. Johansen, R.: Groupware: Computer support for business teams. The Free Press, New York (1988)
6. Paterno´, F.: Model-based Design and Evaluation of Interactive Applications. In: Paternó, F. (ed.) Model-based Design and Evaluation of Interactive Applications, Springer, Heidelberg (1999)
7. Pinelle, D., Gutwin, C., Greenberg, S.: Task analysis for groupware usability evaluation: Modeling shared-workspace tasks with the mechanics of collaboration. ACM Transactions on Computer-Human Interaction (TOCHI) 10(4), 281–311 (2003)
8. Poltrock, S., Grudin, J.: CSCW, groupware and workflow: experiences, state of art, and future trends. In: CHI 1999 Extended Abstracts on Human Factors in Computing Systems, pp. 120–121. ACM Press, New York (1999)
9. Poltrock, S., Grudin, J.: Computer Supported Cooperative Work and Groupware (CSCW). In: Costabile, M.F., Paternó, F. (eds.) INTERACT 2005. LNCS, vol. 3585, Springer, Heidelberg (2005)
10. Van der Veer, G.C., Van Welie, M.: Task based groupware design: Putting theory into practice. In: Proceedings of the 2000 Symposium on Designing Interactive Systems, pp. 326–337. ACM Press, New York (2000)
11. Wikimedia Foundation, Inc, http://www.wikipedia.org

RenderXML – A Multi-platform Software Development Tool

Francisco M. Trindade and Marcelo S. Pimenta

Federal University of Rio Grande do Sul - Institute of Informatics
Av. Bento Gonçalves, 9500 - Bloco IV
Porto Alegre, RS – Brazil
{fmtrindade, mpimenta}@inf.ufrgs.br

Abstract. As the technology evolves, the existence of different computational devices has made ad-hoc software development no longer acceptable in the development of multi-platform software applications. This article presents RenderXML, a software tool developed to facilitate the creation of multi-platform applications. RenderXML acts as a renderer, mapping concrete UI's described in UsiXML to multiple platforms, and also as a connector, linking the rendered UI to application logic code developed possibly in multiple programming languages.

Keywords: Multi-platform, UsiXML, Rendering, User Interface.

1 Introduction

Computer software development has nowadays as an important requirement the possibility of execution in more than one platform, either through desktop computer, handhelds or mobile phones. To address this demand, *ad-hoc* software development is no longer acceptable in terms of the cost and time required for software construction and maintenance. In this way, many research projects are being developed in order to allow the creation of software applications that can be executed in multiple use contexts, with minimal alteration of its algorithm.

One of the proposed solutions is the development user interfaces (UI) with plasticity, capable of adapting themselves to different use contexts. In order to obtain plasticity, High-level UI Descriptions (HLUID) are commonly used, enabling the definition of UI's in a platform independent form. Among the available HLUID's, UsiXML [8] is based on the *Cameleon reference framework* [4], allowing the description of UIs for multiple use contexts.

This paper presents RenderXML, a software tool developed to facilitate the creation of multi-platform applications. RenderXML acts as a renderer, mapping concrete UI's described in UsiXML to multiple platforms, and also as a connector, linking the rendered UI to application logic code developed possibly in multiple programming languages. Thus, RenderXML is intended to support not only the development of new (multi-platform) applications but also the migration of legacy applications to a multi-platform environment.

The main goal of this application is to help the UI developer, acting in the UI engineering process. As explained later in this paper, the tool doesn't have the objective of helping in the UI definition.

M. Winckler, H. Johnson, and P. Palanque (Eds.): TAMODIA 2007, LNCS 4849, pp. 293–298, 2007.

The paper is structured as follows: firstly, we describe some related work and the main concepts of RenderXML, discussing its features and benefits, and how to use it. An actual multi-platform application example illustrates the process of multi-platform UI rendering and multilanguage application logic connection. Some concluding remarks and future work are presented in the final section.

2   Related Work

The accomplishment of multi-platform UIs is also the goal of some related works in the literature, which can be classified in two categories: a) tools working with UsiXML UI descriptions and b) UI rendering tools, for UsiXML or other UI models.

Among the projects which use UsiXML, SketchiXML [5] can generate a UsiXML Concrete UI (CUI) and also a UIML UI specification, receiving as input hand sketched UI descriptions, having as main objective the creation of evolutionary UI prototypes. Working with another kind of input, GrafiXML [7] is a visual designer which allows the creation of CUI specifications, based on the visual positioning of UI components by the developer.

In the category of UI rendering tools, QTKiXML [6] can map UsiXML description to the Tcl-Tk language. FlashiXML [3] can also map UsiXML descriptions, but to UI's described in vectorial mode, being interpreted by Flash or SVG plug-ins. InterpiXML [11] performs the mapping of UsiXML CUI descriptions using *Java Swing* UI components.

Using another UI models, Uiml.NET [9] and TIDE [2] map UIs specified in UIML [1] to the .Net and Java platform respectively. TERESA (Transformation Environment for InteRactivE System representations) [10] uses the TERESAXML language to perform forward engineering design and development of multi-platform applications.

3   RenderXML

In order to create multi-platform UIs based on the *Cameleon Reference Framework*, the lifecycle shown in Figure 1 must be followed. This lifecycle is based on a generic task-model, which envisions all the tasks to be performed by the interactive system, and is mapped to a final UI for a specific device through multiple reification steps.

In practice, to obtain a final UI following the mapping steps presented in Figure 3, a generic task model (Task Model) has to be created, which is specified to a task model of a specific kind of device (Task Model Desktop). From the specific task model, the UI is further specified to an abstract UI (Abstract UI Desktop), which is dependent on the kind of interaction being used, and then to a concrete UI (Concrete UI Desktop), which depends on the target platform of the application. Finally, the concrete UI can be mapped to a final UI to be executed in a device (Desktop computer).All these steps can be performed supported by tools, which perform an automatic or semi-automatic mapping from one level to another.

RenderXML is a rendering tool projected to work in the last level of this transformation process, mapping concrete UIs described in UsiXML to final UIs for a specific device. In addition, RenderXML offers to the user another level of independence,

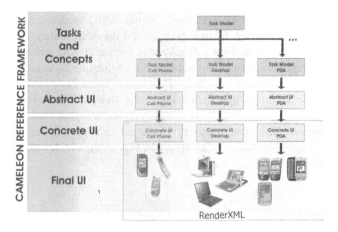

Fig. 1. Multi-platform UI development process

allowing the connection of the rendered UI to application logics developed in different programming languages.

We should clarify here that RenderXML is a rendering tool, and not a design tool. Thus, RenderXML does not detect or solve usability problems of the specified UI. As shown in Figure 3, this kind of problems should be solved in earlier phases of the UI mapping process, in a manual or automatic way, with the utilization of other UsiXML.

With these features, RenderXML is an useful tool in the prototyping and development process of multi-platform applications. Since UsiXML allows the specification of all needed features of an UI, it can be used in the development of final UIs. In this particular situation, it is very important the possibility of developing UIs to multiple platforms using only one design language, setting the UI developer free from the need of mastering many different technologies. Using RenderXML the UI developer needs to know only UsiXML. In addition, the possibility of multi-language application logic connection allows applications developed in different programming languages to have their UI created with UsiXML.

It should be clarified here that RenderXML is a rendering tool, and not a UI design tool. In fact, RenderXML is not supposed to guide the designer's choice among design alternatives. Clearly, RenderXML does not check the designer's decisions and does not evaluate or identifies (actual or potential) UI usability aspects. As shown in Figure 3, this kind of problems should be solved in earlier phases of the UI mapping process, in a manual or automatic way, with the utilization of other UsiXML based tools.

In order to be used in these situations, RenderXML is specified as described in the next sections.

3.1 Architecture Overview

The proposed architecture is shown in Figure 2. In this representation, dotted lines describe the UI rendering process, and normal lines the logic application connection.

In order to perform the UI rendering, RenderXML receives as input a CUI UsiXML description (*UsiXML UI* in Figure 2), and forwards it after validation to the target platform renderer (*Platform 1 Renderer* in Figure 2). The renderer is responsible for the UI components instantiation, being the application logic method calls redirected to the UsiXML kernel (*Translation Process* in Figure 2).

To connect the UI to its application logic, the RenderXML kernel (*Translation Process* in Figure 2) receives methods invocations and translates them to a language independent format. This description is forwarded to a plug-in for the target programming language (*Language 1 Connector* in Figure 2), which calls the method in the application logic being executed.

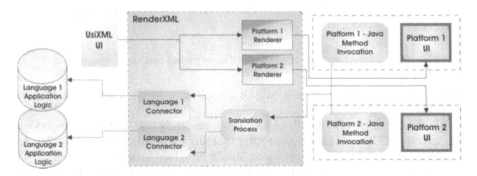

Fig. 2. RenderXML architecture

4   Using RenderXML: A Multi-platform Calculator

To evaluate the first implementation of RenderXML and the idiosyncrasies of the process of multi-platform development, an example application was implemented: a multi-platform calculator. The main goal was the UI rendering in three different platforms, *Java Swing* and *Microsoft Windows Forms* for a desktop version of the application, and *Java Swing* also for its mobile version, using the J2ME *Connected Device Configuration* (CDC). In addition, all UI's should be able to connect to two different application logics, in Java and C#.

```
<cuiModel id="5-cui_20" name="5-cui">
    <window id="window_1" name="window_1"
        width="192" height="200">
        <flowBox id="flow_box_2" name="flow_box_2" alignment="left">
            <inputText id="input_1"
                name="input_1" isVisible="true"
                isEnabled="true" textColor="#000000"
                maxLength="50" numberOfColumns="15" isEditable="true"/>
            <button id="button_1"
                content="/uiModel/resourceModel/cioRef[@cioId='button_1']/resource/@content"
                name="button_1" isVisible="true"
                isEnabled="true" textColor="#000000"/>
                ...
        </flowBox>
    </window>
</cuiModel>
```

Fig. 3. Calculator UsiXML description

To this, a UsiXML CUI description of the calculator UI was created. In Figure 3 a part of this description can be seen. In this description there is a window (*window* element), which uses a flowbox layout manager (*flowbox* element), and is composed by a display (*inputText* element) and buttons (*button* element).

To maintain programming language independence, the CUI UI description directs its methods invocations to RenderXML, informing its name and parameters. This definition is translated to the application logic programming language being executed, and the method is invoked.

In this way, an UI for the three different platforms can be created, and it can be tested with logic application developed in three different programming languages. Having as example Figure 4, 6 different UI-application logic combinations could be created (A,1; B,1; A,2; B,2; A,3; B,3). In this case, the mobile version of the UI could be connected to a C# source code only if the device used to display the UI could execute C# applications.

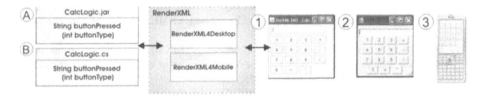

Fig. 4. Example application

5   Conclusion and Future Work

This paper described a practical approach to the prototyping and development of multi-platform applications, and presented the first version of RenderXML, which acts as a UI renderer in multiple platforms, and also allows the UI connection to application logic developed in multiple programming languages. RenderXML stimulates the utilization of HLUID's (like UsiXML) in the development of multi-platform applications, as much in the development of new applications, as in the migration of legacy applications to a multi-platform environment.

Future work consists in the evolution of RenderXML, allowing the creation of UI's to other (conventional or not) devices and platforms, in addition to multimodal UI's. Examples of devices/platforms we intend to investigate are mobile phones, smartphones, PDA's, web-based interfaces and desktop interfaces.

The final objective is to allow the creation of UsiXML-based user interfaces for a great number of platforms and devices, and also expand the number of supported programming languages. In particular, our work aims to provide a tool which can be used in actual user interface developing in such diversity of contexts of use.

Acknowledgments. This research is partially funded by CNPq (LIFAPOR/CNPq-Grices Project).

References

1. Abrams, M., Phanouriou, C., Batongbacal, A.L., Williams, S.M., Shuster, J.E.: UIML: An Appliance-IndependentXML User Interface Language. In: Proceedings of the 8th International WWW Conference, Toronto, Canada, pp. 11–16. Elsevier Science Publishers, Amsterdam (1999)
2. Ali, M.F., Pérez-Quiñones, M.A., Abrams, M., e Shell, E.: Building Multi-Platform User Interfaces With UIML. In: Proceedings of 2002 International Workshop of Computer-Aided Design of User Interfaces: CADUI 2002, Valenciennes, France (2002)
3. Berghe, Y.: Etude et implémentation dún générateur dínterfaces vectorielles á partir dún langage de description dínterfaces utilisateur, M.Sc. thesis, Université catholique de Louvain, Louvain-la-Neuve, Belgium (September 2004)
4. Calvary, G., Coutaz, J., Thevenin, D., Limbourg, Q., Bouillon, L., Vanderdonckt, J.A: A Unifying Reference Framework for Multi-Target User Interfaces. Interacting with Computers 15(3), 289–308 (2003)
5. Coyette, A., Faulkner, S., Kolp, M., Limbourg, Q.: SketchiXML: Towards a Multi-Agent Design Tool for Sketching User Interfaces Based on UsiXML. In: Proc. of Tamodia 2004 (2004)
6. Denis, V.: Un pas vers le poste de travail unique: QTKiXML, un interpréteur dínterface utilisateur á partir de sa description, M.Sc. thesis, Université catholique de Louvain, Louvain-la-Neuve, Belgium (September 2005)
7. Lepreux, S., Vanderdonckt, J., Michotte, B.: Visual Design of User Interfaces by (De)composition. In: Doherty, G., Blandford, A. (eds.) DSVIS 2006. LNCS, vol. 4323, pp. 157–170. Springer, Heidelberg (2007)
8. Limbourg, Q., Vanderdonckt, J., Michotte, B., Bouillon, L., Florins, M., Trevisan, D., UsiXML, A.: User Interface Description Language for Context-Sensitive User Interfaces. In: Proc. of the AVI 2004 Workshop Developing User Interfaces with XML: Advances on User Interface Description Languages UIXML 2004. EDM-Luc, Gallipoli, pp. 55–62 (May 25, 2004)
9. Luyten, K., Thys, K., Vermeulen, J., e Coninx, K.: A Generic Approach for Multi-Device User Interface Rendering with UIML. In: 6th International Conference on Computer-Aided Design of User Interfaces (CADUI 2006), Bucareste, Romênia (2006)
10. Mori, G., Paternó, F., Santoro, C.: Tool Support for Designing nomadic Applications. In: Em Proc. of 7th ACM Int.Conf. on Intelligent User Interfaces, pp. 141–148. ACM Press, New York (2003)
11. Ocal, K.: Etude et développement dún interpréteur UsiXML en Java Swing, Haute Ecole Rennequin, Liége (2004)

Author Index

Lecture Notes in Computer Science

Sublibrary 2: Programming and Software Engineering

For information about Vols. 1– 4204
please contact your bookseller or Springer